Thomas Drew and the Making of Victorian Belfast

Irish Studies
Kathleen Costello-Sullivan, *Series Editor*

Select Titles in Irish Studies

Broken Irelands: Literary Form in Post-Crash Irish Fiction
   Mary M. McGlynn

Finders: Justice, Faith, and Identity in Irish Crime Fiction
   Anjili Babbar

The Irish Revival: A Complex Vision
   Joseph Valente and Marjorie Howes, eds.

The Last Bohemian: Brian Desmond Hurst, Irish Film, British Cinema
   Lance Pettitt

*Modernity, Community, and Place
in Brian Friel's Drama*, Second Edition
   Richard Rankin Russell

Poetry, Politics, and the Law in Modern Ireland
   Adam Hanna

*Stepping through Origins: Nature, Home,
and Landscape in Irish Literature*
   Jefferson Holdridge

Unaccompanied Traveler: The Writings of Kathleen M. Murphy
   Patrick Bixby, ed.

For a full list of titles in this series,
visit https://press.syr.edu/supressbook-series/irish-studies/.

Thomas Drew
and the Making of Victorian Belfast

Sean Farrell

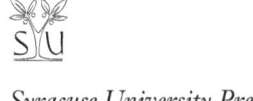

Syracuse University Press

The epigraph on p. v is from Gyanendra Pandey, *The Construction of Communalism in Colonial North India* (Delhi: Oxford Univ. Press, 1990). Reproduced with permission of Oxford University Press India © Oxford University Press 1990.

Copyright © 2023 by Syracuse University Press
Syracuse, New York 13244-5290

All Rights Reserved

First Edition 2023

23 24 25 26 27 28   6 5 4 3 2 1

∞ The paper used in this publication meets the minimum requirements of the American National Standard for Information Sciences—Permanence of Paper for Printed Library Materials, ANSI Z39.48-1992.

For a listing of books published and distributed by Syracuse University Press, visit https://press.syr.edu.

ISBN: 978-0-8156-3821-6 (hardcover)
          978-0-8156-3814-8 (paperback)
          978-0-8156-5696-8 (e-book)

Library of Congress Cataloging-in-Publication Data

Names: Farrell, Sean, 1966– author.
Title: Thomas Drew and the making of Victorian Belfast / Sean Farrell.
Description: Syracuse, New York : Syracuse University Press, 2023. |
    Series: Irish studies | Includes bibliographical references and index.
Identifiers: LCCN 2023019383 (print) | LCCN 2023019384 (ebook) |
    ISBN 9780815638148 (paperback) | ISBN 9780815638216 (hardcover) |
    ISBN 9780815656968 (ebook)
Subjects: LCSH: Drew, Thomas, 1800–1870. | Church of Ireland—Clergy—
    Biography. | Church of Ireland—History—19th century. | Anti-Catholicism—
    Northern Ireland—Belfast. | Middle class—Northern Ireland—Belfast. |
    Religion and politics—Northern Ireland—Belfast. | Belfast (Northern Ireland)—
    Religion—19th century. | Belfast (Northern Ireland)—History—19th century.
Classification: LCC BX5595.D69 F37 2023 (print) | LCC BX5595.D69 (ebook) |
    DDC 283/.4167092—dc23/eng/20230627
LC record available at https://lccn.loc.gov/2023019383
LC ebook record available at https://lccn.loc.gov/2023019384

Manufactured in the United States of America

What I would emphasize, however, is that the use of the term "communalism" remains an heuristic device; that both the term and the politics and attitudes that it seeks to encapsulate have a history which can be charted; and that the boundaries separating these attitudes and politics from others existing at the same time are not as clear as has generally been supposed.

—Gyanendra Pandey, *The Construction of Communalism in Colonial North India*, viii.

Contents

List of Illustrations and Tables *ix*

Acknowledgments *xi*

Map of Belfast, 1861 *xv*

Portrait of Thomas Drew, 1852 *xvii*

Introduction: Historicizing Sectarianism *1*

1. Thomas Drew and the Making of Christ Church *22*
2. Speaking with a Clear Voice: Everyday and Political Sermons *86*
3. Evangelical Protestantism in Action: The Mant Controversy, 1842–1843 *117*
4. A Trustee of the Poor? Thomas Drew and the Hungry Forties *148*
5. Belfast's Populist Political Parson: Thomas Drew and Anti-Catholic Politics *199*
6. Thomas Drew and the Belfast Riots of 1857 *243*
7. A Clerical Watchman: Life after Belfast, 1859–1870 *269*

Conclusion: Thomas Drew and the Making of Victorian Belfast *297*

Bibliography *307*

Index *343*

Illustrations and Tables

MAPS

1. Belfast, 1861   *xv*
2. Belfast, 1833   *25*
3. Christ Church neighborhood, 1833   *27*
4. Primary sites of 1857 riots   *246*

ILLUSTRATIONS

1. Thomas Drew, 1852   *xvii*
2. Christ Church, 1837   *37*
3. Thomas Drew, 1839   *41*
4. Bishop Richard Mant   *119*
5. William McIlwaine   *126*
6. Barefoot girl, York Street Mill, 1842   *167*
7. Thomas Drew, circa 1850   *203*
8. Architectural plans, Loughinisland Parish Church   *276*
9. Attack on St. Malachy's Church, Belfast riots, 1864   *282*

TABLES

1. Religious denominations and population in Belfast, 1831–1861   *28*
2. Occupations listed in the Christ Church Census, 1852   *78*

Acknowledgments

One of the primary conceits of the historical profession is the idea that books are solitary enterprises. This is especially true with a project that has taken this long to complete. The idea for this book first came to me about fifteen years ago in the Linen Hall Library in Belfast, one of my favorite places in the world. Since that time, colleagues, family members, friends, and students have helped me bring this book to fruition. What follows is my wholly inadequate and doubtless selective effort to say thanks.

Thomas Drew and the Making of Victorian Belfast is based on my analysis of a wide array of nineteenth-century sources held in archives and libraries in Ireland and the United Kingdom. Like all historians, I am dependent on the people who curate, protect, and provide access to these materials. I would like to thank the archivists, librarians, and volunteers at the following institutions, without whose expertise and thoughtful help I could not have written this book: the British Library, the Down and Connor Diocesan Archives, the Linen Hall Library, Loughinisland Parish Church, the Museum of Orange Heritage, the National Archives of Ireland, the National Library of Ireland, the Public Record Office of Northern Ireland, Queen's University Belfast, the Representative Church Body Library, St. Aidan's Church, St. George's Church, Trinity College Dublin, and Union Theological College. I am truly grateful.

The ongoing COVID-19 pandemic has provided a powerful reminder of how fortunate I am to work at Northern Illinois University, where colleagues and students have provided both inspiration and a strong sense of community. E. Taylor Atkins, Andy Bruno, Aaron

Fogleman, Valerie Garver, Anne Hanley, Beatrix Hoffman, Emma Kuby, Brian Sandberg, Jim Schmidt, and Andrea Smalley have all read and/or talked through parts of this manuscript. While they bear no responsibility for any of its errors, the book is much better for their feedback. NIU provided critical research support through Research and Artistry grants and its sabbatical program, which provided much needed funds and time that allowed me to spend three to four weeks in Belfast and Dublin most summers. A host of undergraduate and graduate students have played critical roles at various stages of this project, but my former and current doctoral students Mathieu Billings, Ian Burns, the late David Downs, J. Hollis Harris, Kevin Luginbill, and Journey Steward deserve particular mention for both their insight and suffering.

Much of the material is this book has been presented at academic conferences in Canada, Ireland, and the United States, a form of cultural and intellectual community very much under threat. I am very fortunate to have spent my professional life in the American Conference for Irish Studies, an organization that provides a mixture of intellectual exchange and social fellowship like no other that I have ever encountered. Colin Barr, Guy Beiner, Jill Bender, Kate Costello-Sullivan, Michael de Nie, Jim Donnelly, Jason Knirck, Jose Lanters, Cian McMahon, Tim McMahon, Tim O'Neil, Jim Rogers, Ken Shonk, Paul Townend, Mary Trotter, and Nick Wolf all have endured far too many conversations and presentations about various aspects of Thomas Drew's career and/or nineteenth-century Belfast for one lifetime. I thank them for their endurance and for sharing their insights whenever they could get in a word. In Canada, Danine Farquharson, William Jenkins, David Wilson, and Julia Wright have provided friendship and support through years of meetings of the Canadian Association for Irish Studies.

I have now been going to Ireland on research trips since I first arrived at the doorstep of the Institute of Irish Studies at Queen's University Belfast in the fall of 1993, a testament to my continuing fascination with nineteenth-century Ireland as well as the power of routine and a lack of imagination. My northern forays have been much more congenial and productive because of the kindness and knowledge of Dominic Bryan, Marie Coleman, Peter Gray, Janice Holmes, Eamon Hughes, Liam Kennedy, Caroline Magennis, Olwen Purdue, and Brian Walker, amongst many others in Belfast. Before the world masked up, Ida Milne drove north to the rescue, providing her characteristic warmth and wit on a memorable drive back to Dublin Airport in March 2019. In Dublin, Gillian O'Brien has never been much help with trains, but has been a constant source of friendship and support. Ray Gillespie, Mary Hatfield, Caroline Burke McGee, Ida Milne, Ciaran O'Neill, and Stephanie Rains always have been willing to interrupt their own busy lives to have a cup of tea, a glass of wine, or a bite of food, which is much appreciated. A Summer Stipend from the National Endowment for the Humanities provided critical research support, and a fellowship from the Irish American Cultural Institute and the Centre for Irish Studies at the University of Galway allowed me to complete a significant part of this book in Galway. My particular thanks to Louis de Paor, Méabh Ni Fhuartháin, Nessa Cronin, Leo Keohane, and Samantha Williams for their hospitality and support at Irish Studies in Galway. In the History Department, Sarah-Anne Buckley and John Cunningham made sure I was well looked after while I was at the University of Galway. It was a wonderful opportunity to get a chance to think and write about the north of Ireland, while getting to learn a little bit about living in the west.

I am fortunate that this book found a home at Syracuse University Press, where a number of dedicated and talented people deserve thanks for their hard work. Kathleen Costello Sullivan provided constant and thoughtful support for the project, while Deb Manion answered thousands of queries, adroitly helping me to jump through bureaucratic hoops and move the project into the production process. Finally, Jessica LeTourneur Bax strengthened the book with her detailed and professional copyediting, no easy task when dealing with a cantankerous author set in his ways.

Family support has enabled me to complete this project. Donald and Eleanor Farrell were the best parents one could ask for, models for my own parental efforts and professional career. I am so sorry that my father passed away in August 2022 before he could see this book come to light. Time has only made it more clear how fortunate I was to find Leila Porter, whose own brilliance and much-tried patience have made this book possible. Our twelve year-old son, Liam Farrell, has not helped at all with the book, but has served as an insistent and timely reminder that there is a life that needs to be lived away from the computer or archive. Long may it be so.

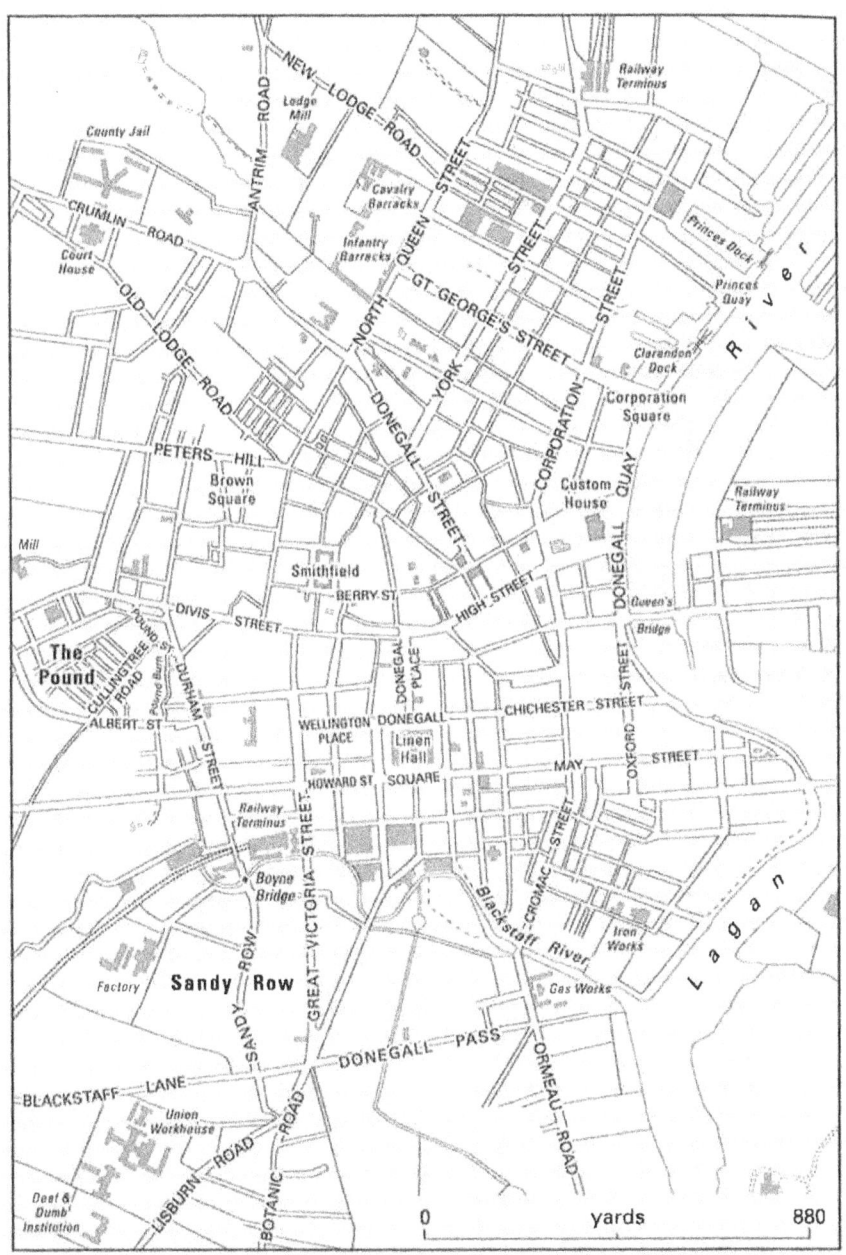

Map 1. Belfast, 1861. Source: Doyle, *Fighting like the Devil for the Sake of God*, xiv. Courtesy of Mark Doyle and Manchester Univ. Press.

1. Thomas Drew. Source: Artist unknown, 1852. © National Museums Northern Ireland Collection, BELUM U2342_PCF. Courtesy of the Ulster Museum.

Thomas Drew and the Making of Victorian Belfast

Introduction
Historicizing Sectarianism

There could be no doubt. The Reverend Thomas Drew was, in the eyes of the *Dublin Evening Post*, the "very incarnation of political and sectarian fury, and whom no one will deny to be the man most odious in all Ulster." A few days earlier, the newspaper had described Drew's vitriolic anti-Catholicism as a kind of fitful insanity: "There is a rancor and a rage in this gentleman's printed denunciation of the Catholic religion which makes it impossible for him to be at once sincere and sane . . . when he so speaks or writes *one gets* the idea of rabid seizure, or of polemical delirium tremens."[1] Four years later, in October 1870, the Reverend Robert Hannay sketched a very different picture of the Church of Ireland minister at a special funeral service held for Drew at his former church in Belfast. Drew, he made clear, had been a dedicated clergyman whose tireless work made it easier for those who followed in his footsteps. Even Drew's numerous political opponents—Hannay argued that he had no personal enemies—had to admit "he was straightforward, manly, and honourable in all that he did." The vicar concluded his sermon by arguing that "there was no minister in the country who was ever loved so much," celebrating Drew's sympathy for the poor and the suffering as well as his commitment to Conservative and Protestant politics.[2] These two portraits,

---

1. *Dublin Evening Post*, September 15, 1866, September 19, 1866; emphasis mine.
2. *Belfast News-Letter*, October 25, 1870. Robert Hannay was one of Drew's successors at Christ Church, and went on to a very successful career in the Church

written and performed in radically different genres and settings, nevertheless capture the seemingly contradictory dynamics of the controversial Belfast minister's public career.

Thomas Drew was a man who generated intense feelings. For many of his British and Irish contemporaries, Drew was the epitome of Orange fanaticism, a ranting clergyman whose confrontational performances helped to create the sectarian antagonism and violence that plagued Victorian Belfast. In stark contrast, thousands of Orangemen and their allies saw him as an active and loyal champion of Protestant interests that they believed were too often ignored by British and Irish politicians obsessed with appeasing the Catholic majority in Ireland. Most of Drew's congregants knew him as a compassionate and dedicated pastor, devoted to providing religious education and social support for Protestant working-class families. Drew was a significant touchstone for a number of overlapping communities in Victorian Belfast, and these were critical and formative years for the northern town. Between 1830 and 1870, Belfast became Ireland's second largest city, unmatched in commercial vitality and industrial production, featuring a rich and dynamic civic culture embodied by the impressive Custom House (1857) and Ulster Hall (an all-purpose venue opened in 1862). Viewed from this perspective, Belfast's mid-nineteenth-century experience echoed that of other provincial, manufacturing cities in Victorian Britain. Other aspects of Belfast's development were more distinctive, most notably the city's often claustrophobic politics and too frequent bouts of sectarian conflict. Belfast's modern tradition of communal violence emerged in these years amidst the toxic intimacies of the fast-growing city.[3] Thomas Drew was one of the people who helped make that world.

---

of Ireland, becoming vicar of Belfast. He was the father of the famous Irish writer James Owen Hannay, who wrote under the pseudonym George A. Birmingham. For Hannay's recollections of an encounter with an elderly but indomitable Drew, see Birmingham, *Pleasant Places*, 3–4.

3. Doyle, *Fighting like the Devil for the Sake of God*; Farrell, *Rituals and Riots*; Hirst, *Religion, Politics and Violence in 19th Century Belfast*. Sectarian conflict was not

Belfast is often associated with Catholic-Protestant division, a kind of global watchword for the seemingly enduring power of religious conflict. As a half century of scholarship has made clear, the trauma and violence of the Troubles in Northern Ireland (1966–98) strengthened sectarian interpretations of the Irish past, narratives built upon often unexamined assumptions of Catholic-Protestant antagonism.[4] Recent scholarship on the history of Victorian Belfast has moved decisively away from this two-nations framework, focusing instead on many of the elements the northern capital had in common with other provincial cities in Victorian Britain: industrial and urban growth, dramatic changes in the built environment, the creation and evolution of its philanthropic institutions, and the range and vitality of its civic, intellectual, and political culture. This new history of Belfast has dramatically improved our understanding of the northern capital's nineteenth-century experience.[5] And yet the problem of sectarianism remains, for Belfast's nineteenth-century growth coincided with increasingly public Catholic-Protestant antagonism, expressed most forcefully in large-scale communal riots in 1857, 1864, 1872, and 1886. By 1900 Belfast was as well-known for battles between the "Sepoys of Sandy Row and The Pound" as it was for the textiles and ships made in the city's factories and yards. One of the challenges for the historian of nineteenth-century Belfast, then, is to historicize sectarianism; to

---

new to Belfast. There is, however, something qualitatively different in the routinized, larger-scale, and more expressly political clashes that occurred from the 1830s onward. For earlier instances of nineteenth-century sectarian conflict, see Hirst, *Religion, Politics and Violence in 19th Century Belfast*, 19–34, and Wright, *Crime and Punishment in Nineteenth-Century Belfast*, 18–24.

4. On the relationship between the Troubles and Irish historiography, see McBride, "Shadow of the Gunmen," 686–710. See also Regan, "Irish Public Histories as an Historiographical Problem," 265–92.

5. The best introduction to the new history of Belfast is Connolly, *Belfast 400*. For more specialized studies, see Bew, *Glory of Being Britons*; Connolly, Bryan, and Nagle, *Civic Identity and Public Space*; Holmes, *Shaping of Ulster Presbyterian Belief and Practice*; Hughes, *Scots in Victorian and Edwardian Belfast*; Johnson, *Middle-Class Life in Victorian Belfast*; Purdue, *Belfast*; Wright, *"Natural Leaders" and Their World*.

show how its seemingly simplistic binary politics coexisted and overlapped with other cultural, political, and socioeconomic forces in the most dynamic city in mid- to late nineteenth-century Ireland. This book is designed to do just that.

Thomas Drew and the Making of Victorian Belfast examines Drew's public career to chart both the formation of the Christ Church community and the complex histories of anti-Catholicism in Belfast. It is not a traditional biography as much as a microhistory that uses Drew to explore the development of the mid-nineteenth-century town.[6] Victorian Belfast recently has been described as a city made by outsiders, a generation of hardworking middle-class elites who shepherded the burgeoning urban community through an era of dramatic and tumultuous growth.[7] Belfast's middle-class leaders had a great deal in common with their British counterparts, who wielded liberal notions of urban improvement, philanthropy, progress, and respectability to remake industrial cities across the British mainland. In his celebrated study of the middle class in Victorian England, Simon Gunn argues that the figure of the clergyman often stood at the center of these civic cultures, a spiritual director and/or coordinator of increasingly large urban congregations with expansive networks of prayer stations, schools, and other institutions clustered around church and chapel.[8]

Drew was one of these clerical elites, a Limerick-born preacher who arrived in Belfast at the age of thirty-two and built the early Victorian town's largest Church of Ireland congregation. He was an ambitious and active minister who worked hard to bring evangelical religion and conservative social respectability to Protestant working-class communities. Drew was hardly alone in this project, working alongside Presbyterian ministers such as Henry Cooke, John Edgar, and James Morgan, as well as his redoubtable Anglican ally and friend William McIlwaine. But unlike most of his cohort of civic leaders in

---

6. For the introduction to a model study that takes this type of approach (albeit on a much larger stage), see Sunderland, *Baron's Cloak*, 1–11.
7. Johnson, *Middle-Class Life in Victorian Belfast*, 19–22.
8. Gunn, *Public Culture of the Victorian Middle Class*, 107.

Belfast, Drew was also a sectarian rabble-rouser, a man whose confrontational public lectures and performances strengthened lines of communal division. The Christ Church minister was one of the most prominent middle-class leaders of the Orange Order in Belfast, a position he used to foster and legitimize confessional identities and sectarian violence in the growing city. The significant roles that Drew played in the making of modern Belfast stemmed from his ability to straddle these two overlapping worlds. In many ways, Drew's hybrid appeal embodied some of the primary contradictions of Victorian Belfast; he was a conservative middle-class leader whose populist anti-Catholicism helped to prevent the development of any type of broadly shared civic consensus. This mix was also essential to his success, since the congregation's educational, evangelical, and philanthropic initiatives allowed Drew to maintain ties to the leaders of a Belfast civic establishment often uncomfortable with the bombastic public sectarianism that delighted his largely working-class Orange supporters. In this last sense, he can be seen as part of a generational cohort of Irish public figures who were increasingly sensitive to what Maura Cronin has called the "reciprocal nature of popular leadership."[9]

Drew was one of Belfast's first populist political pastors, one of the men who created the template of the partisan Protestant minister that has played such an outsized role in modern Ulster history. The links between politics and religion at Christ Church, however, were anything but simple. As Robert Hannay's funeral sermon makes clear, there was much more to Drew's appeal than his anti-Catholic rhetoric and aggressive Orange and Conservative politics. From the first days of his ministry, Drew effectively placed the church at the heart of fast-developing west Belfast. To be sure, Christ Church was a center of Orange activism, but Drew's energetic pastoral style and ambitious philanthropic, religious, and social initiatives also brought people into the congregation. Christ Church's extensive network of day and

9. See Cronin, "Popular Politics, 1815–1845," 134.

Sunday schools was particularly important in this regard. This book makes clear that Drew's multifaceted appeal was the key to his success, which depended on the support of a wide array of people with different beliefs and interests.

Thomas Drew was born in 1800 to a prominent Church of Ireland family in Limerick, Ireland. After graduating from Trinity College Dublin in 1826, he served as a curate in a North Antrim parish before becoming the first minister of Christ Church, a new Anglican church opened in 1833 to cater to a largely working-class district in the rapidly expanding town. Known for his fierce anti-Catholic polemics, populist conservative politics, and pragmatic evangelical faith, Drew quickly built one of the largest Anglican congregations on the island, largely working class, but with a small but significant cohort of wealthier members. He was an active and energetic minister; one of the Church of Ireland's leading advocates for church construction and religious education in Belfast and its hinterland.

It was Drew's anti-Catholicism, however, that dominated his public persona. His militant Protestant politics and unrestrained speaking style made him one of the Orange Order's most prominent public faces. This was particularly true in the 1850s, when Drew's fiery speeches at the monthly meetings of the Christ Church Protestant Association and involvement in the Belfast riots of 1857 were widely reported in British and Irish newspapers. A lifelong Orangeman, Drew had strong ties to thousands of loyal supporters in various citadels of conservative Protestantism in Ulster, connections that led one contemporary to describe him as "the unmitred Bishop of Belfast."[10] His ceaseless energy and confrontational style made him an effective catalyst of congregational and popular support. The verbal violence of his well-publicized political sermons helped to create sectarian confrontations that confirmed and legitimized the anti-Catholic prejudices of many of his supporters and strengthened communal lines of division in Victorian Belfast.

---

10. *Downshire Protestant*, April 25, 1859.

Drew's influence with his conservative evangelical and Orange base, however, came at a significant political cost. His rhetorical extremism and sensationalism meant that Drew largely was ineffective outside of the supportive space of the Orange lodge or Protestant meeting. For all of Drew's reputation as a Protestant champion, it is vital to remember that nearly every one of his national political campaigns ended in failure (he was much more successful in local politics). British and Irish Catholics retained their political rights and the British government continued to provide financial support for the Catholic seminary at Maynooth; nondenominational and voluntary religious education was maintained in the national schools, and the Church of Ireland lost its privileged position as an established church in 1869. If Drew's anti-Catholicism helped him mobilize and maintain a core constituency of conservative British and Irish Protestant support, it also placed severe constraints on his influence outside those circles. Drew's political career thus mirrored those of other militant Protestant politicians and preachers in modern Britain, Ireland, and across the British Empire. From Henry Cooke to Ian Paisley, Belfast's political ministers have had limited success outside of the province; Drew was no exception to that rule.[11]

Drew's career is also a good illustration of the hybrid politics that made anti-Catholicism such a powerful and constitutive force in modern British and Irish life. The complex operation of anti-Catholic politics has been widely noted for Victorian England, but there are relatively few such studies for nineteenth-century Ireland.[12] To the

---

11. Downer, "William Murphy and Orangeism in Mid-Victorian England," 26–29; Doyle, "Martyrs of Liberty," 149–64; MacRaild, "Transnationalising 'Anti-Popery,'" 224–43; Miller, "Demise of the Confessional State in Ireland," 109–24. For a classic study of English anti-Catholic politics, see Arnestein, *Protestant Versus Catholic in Mid-Victorian England*.

12. For a useful survey of Northern Ireland, see Brewer and Higgins, *Anti-Catholicism in Northern Ireland*, 1. For a more recent and detailed discussion of a key early Victorian figure, see Wright, "'Perverted Graduates of Oxford,'" 127–48. The scholarship on Victorian England is far too extensive to list here. The following

extent that Drew appears in Irish histories, it tends to be as a sectarian blowhard and political gadfly.[13] This is patently true on one level, but Drew was a more complex figure than the seeming continuity and volume of his rhetoric might imply. One of this study's fundamental assumptions is that Drew's religious faith, pastoral style, and paternalist advocacy for working-class men, women, and children mattered; that it is only when we consider how these combined with his controversial anti-Catholic performances and Orange activism that we can come to terms with the successful formation of the Christ Church community and the broader development of anti-Catholic politics in Belfast. Drew's career illustrates the shifting complexity of this landscape. Throughout the 1830s, 1840s, and 1850s, his hyperbolic and confrontational anti-Catholicism fused with a lively, often contradictory, and always shifting balance of conservative paternalism and simple evangelical faith to make him a stout champion and prophet of an aggressive and fundamentally defensive Protestant polity. Drew was one of the first of modern Ulster's populist political ministers, clergymen whose fearful syntheses of anti-Catholic rhetoric, evangelical religion, and independent conservatism attracted and maintained support from sizeable communities of Belfast Protestants.

Drew's polarizing career has important implications for the history of sectarianism in modern Ireland. Anti-Catholicism is a primary tap root for modern Irish sectarianism, but the two should not be conflated. Sectarianism has a relational dimension to it, and cannot defined simply as the actions, attitudes, and practices informed by negative beliefs about Catholics. Recent scholarship has also made

---

works have been particularly influential on my thinking: MacRaild, *Faith, Fraternity and Fighting*; Pax, *Popular Anti-Catholicism in Victorian England*; Wolffe, *Protestant Crusade in Great Britain*.

13. For a sample of such approaches, see Boyd, *Holy War in Belfast*, 10–34; Doyle, *Fighting like the Devil for the Sake of God*, 16–17, 26–27, 84–85; Farrell, *Rituals and Riots*, 143–47; Hirst, *Religion, Politics and Violence in 19th Century Belfast*, 44–47. A recent survey of Belfast history briefly mentions Drew's energetic pastoral work alongside his confrontational anti-Catholicism. See Connolly, *Belfast 400*, 247.

clear that sectarian divisions must also be seen as fluid and dynamic, neither universal nor continuous.[14] If the confrontational tone and volume of Drew's anti-Catholic rhetoric was extreme, there was nothing particularly novel about his ideas, which largely echoed the central tenets of nineteenth-century British and Irish anti-Catholicism; that Roman Catholicism was superstitious in belief, idolatrous and inhumane in practice, and dangerous in its politics.[15] It was time and place that made Drew's career significant. John Wolffe has argued that there is "nothing inevitable about the translation of Protestant-Catholic difference into Protestant-Catholic conflict."[16] Drew's anti-Catholicism was translated into sectarian action because his performances were staged near communal flashpoints at particularly fraught moments in an increasingly divided city. If Drew helped to make Victorian Belfast, it was the town's contentious and formative landscape that created opportunities for him.

Commentators have written extensively about sectarianism since the mid-seventeenth century, a historiography often shaped by periodic crises in British and Irish politics. Since the late nineteenth century, many of these works have featured a two-nations framework, a sectarian compass that emphasized the timeless and intractable nature of conflict between Irish Catholics and British and/or Irish Protestants. Few modern writers have articulated this idea as clearly as Thomas MacKnight, the late nineteenth-century editor of the *Northern Whig*, a Belfast newspaper typically associated with Ulster liberalism. Writing in an era dominated by confrontations over Irish Home Rule, MacKnight's explanation for continuing political contention in Ireland was a simple one: "The plain, the undeniable truth is that

---

14. Brewer and Higgins, *Anti-Catholicism in Northern Ireland*, 2–5; Cronin, "Popular Politics, 1815–1845," 140–44. For other influential definitions and treatments of sectarianism, see Liechty and Clegg, *Moving beyond Sectarianism*, 9–14, 102–83; Wright, *Northern Ireland*, 11. In a recent essay, Ian McBride laments the absence of work on anti-Protestantism. See McBride, "Religion," 294.

15. Norman, *Anti-Catholicism in Victorian England*, 13–22.

16. Wolffe, "Exploring the History of Catholic-Protestant Conflict," 1–21.

there are two antagonistic populations, two different nations on Irish soil. . . . There is no community of feeling, and therefore can be no common citizenship between the two sections of the Irish people."[17] MacKnight's argument rested on an assumption that sectarian division in the north of Ireland was national and natural. Both the power and limitations of this two-nations framework can be seen in work that emerged during the Irish Troubles nearly a hundred years later. Within this powerful historiographical tradition, religious nationalism was what mattered; conflicting visions of faith, history, and nation arrayed in dramatic opposition.[18]

Recent historical scholarship on religion and politics in nineteenth-century Ulster has eschewed the two-nations model, instead emphasizing the importance of context and contingency in more subtle analyses of the ways that communal divisions operated in complex northern communities. In general, historians have stressed both the multiple variables at play in Catholic-Protestant conflict, and the ways that sectarian binaries often obscure and erase the shifting complexities of relationships between Anglicans, Catholics, Presbyterians, and other communities of faith.[19] As Kyla Madden puts it: "Sectarian awareness was ever present in Ulster's mixed communities; it was part of the atmosphere and had a constant regulatory effect. . . . But the

---

17. MacKnight, *Ulster as It Is*, 380–81.

18. For variations on this theme, see Baker, "Orange and Green," 787–815; Boyd, *Holy War in Belfast*; Budge and O'Leary, *Approach to Crisis*; Stewart, *Narrow Ground*; Tanner, *Ireland's Holy Wars*.

19. The literature touching on sectarianism in the long nineteenth century is far too large to summarize here, but key texts include Blackstock, *Loyalism in Ireland*; Connolly, *Religion, Law and Power*, 263–313; Cullen, *Emergence of Modern Ireland*; Cullen, "Late Eighteenth-Century Politicisation in Ireland"; Donnelly Jr., *Captain Rock*, 119–49; Doyle, *Fighting like the Devil for the Sake of God*; Elliott, *Catholics of Ulster*; Farrell, *Rituals and Riots*; Hirst, *Religion, Politics and Violence in 19th Century Belfast*; McBride, *Siege of Derry in Ulster Protestant Mythology*; Madden, *Forkhill Protestants and Forkhill Catholics*; Miller, "Armagh Troubles," Clark and Donnelly, *Irish Peasants*, 155–91; Miller, *Peep O'Day Boys and Defenders*; Smyth, *Men of No Property*; Whelan, *Bible War in Ireland*; and Whelan, "Politicisation in County Wexford," 156–78.

sectarian impulse was not the only impulse regulating social behavior. For a majority of the people most of the time, differences of religion between neighbors did not interfere with how one led one's life."[20] Even when conflict was expressed in religious terms, political divisions often prefigured religious ones as often as not.[21] The very term *sectarian* can thus have a distorting effect on history, compressing the diversity of the northern experience into the tyranny of a Catholic-Protestant lens.[22]

What these works make clear is the necessity of treating sectarianism as a complex historical subject. Too often it is still assumed to be a "bad thing," simple and static, a variable that does not require explanation beyond the intellectual shorthand of categorization or labeling. Historicizing sectarianism requires close attention to time and place as well as a heightened sensitivity to the ways that complex motivations and events are reworked into reductionist narrative explanations. The reduced scale of this book— the examination of a single minister's public career—is designed in part to overcome these challenges.[23] This is not simply an Irish issue, as the vast historiography on communalism in South Asia makes clear.[24] But sectarianism was a potent force in nineteenth-century Irish life, reflecting a very real history of power relations rooted in English conquest and the use of

20. Madden, *Forkhill Protestants and Forkhill Catholics*, 7.
21. McBride, "Religion," 299.
22. Wright, "Reconciling the Histories," 98; Ford, "Living Together, Living Apart," 1–23.
23. Kyla Madden's examination of early nineteenth-century Forkhill is a model study; see Madden, *Forkhill Protestants and Forkhill Catholics*. For two classic "local" studies within modern Irish historiography, see Donnelly Jr., *Land and People of Nineteenth-Century Cork*; Fitzpatrick, *Politics and Irish Life*.
24. For an introduction to key issues, see Pandey, *Construction of Communalism in Colonial North India*; Datta, *Carving Blocs*; Das, *Communal Riots in Bengal*; Gould, *Religion and Conflict in Modern South Asia*. For the dialogue between nineteenth-century sectarian violence in Ireland and communal violence in India, see Doyle, *Communal Violence in the British Empire*, and Farrell, "Challenging the Consensus of Complex Avoidance," 1023–35.

religious markers of identity to define political, economic, and cultural power on the island of Ireland. Sectarianism also must be seen a kind of language informed by communal memories and histories that often served as a way of articulating grievances generated by a host of other factors—work, access to land, relationships with authority, to name but a few. Attacks that were not necessarily sectarian in motivation could be experienced as such.[25]

Sectarianism has also been a convenient label designed to whitewash alternative explanations for historical events and, more nefariously, to serve various political interests. For example, Guy Beiner has shown how the local experience and remembrance of the Rebellion of 1798 in Ulster continually challenged the sectarian narratives that came to dominate nineteenth-century historiography. As the nineteenth century progressed, an increasingly conservative and unionist establishment worked to suppress more complex and liberal stories of the "Turn Out" in 1798.[26] Drew was an enthusiastic participant in efforts to keep sectarian difference at the center of public debate. His 1859 book *Protestant Anniversaries*, a short primer designed to celebrate Protestant heroes and martyrs of the past, contains twenty-seven references to the Rebellion of 1798, featuring the murders of loyal men and the alleged massacres of Protestants at Prosperous in County Kildare, and Scullabogue in County Wexford.[27] The Williamite War and other events of the late seventeenth century were even more important public markers for Drew. Drew's most famous sermon, his July 1857 lecture to Belfast Orangemen at Christ Church, ended with an extended celebration of the Protestant heroes who had saved England and Ireland from Roman Catholicism in 1690–91: "Gallant William, and world-famed Schomberg, and fearless George

---

25. Lewis and McDaid, "Bosnia on the Border?," 635–55. For a balanced assessment of controversies around the role that sectarianism played in republican violence in County Cork, see Bielenberg, Donnelly Jr., and Borgonovo, "'Something of the Nature of a Massacre,'" 7–59.

26. Beiner, *Forgetful Remembrance*.

27. Drew, *Protestant Anniversaries*.

Walker."[28] At public sermons and political meetings throughout his career, Drew wielded pointed interpretations of the Irish past to attack Catholics, liberals, and nationalists and strengthen the conservative and Protestant interest.

All of these factors underline the importance of paying close attention to the histories involved in the construction of sectarianism. The seemingly enduring power of communal lines of division in modern Ulster ultimately is rooted in the fact that sectarianism can accommodate seemingly contradictory forces in appealingly powerful, simple, and useful narratives. Drew helped to maintain the vitality of that language, both through his confrontational anti-Catholic performances and the everyday success of his ministry at Christ Church. As Belfast's leading Orange cleric, he came to embody the idea that the northern capital was irrevocably divided and fundamentally irrational.

Thomas Drew's Christ Church was crucial to the making of Victorian Belfast. Opened in 1833 to cater to the town's growing plebeian population, Christ Church quickly grew to become one of the largest and most important Church of Ireland congregations on the island. While the congregation retained a working-class majority throughout Drew's tenure, it also featured a sizeable number of middle-class and professional members, a diversity that reflected both the spatial and social intimacy of early Victorian Belfast and the appeal of the dynamic, evangelical conservatism of its minister. Historians have noted the cross-class nature of Christ Church's congregation,[29] but none have explored the church's role in these formative years in any detail. This is a significant problem, for Drew's Christ Church acted as the first site of substantial cross-class contact for many of the city's working-class Anglicans and it seems clear that the history of Christ Church lies at the heart of the development of nineteenth-century Belfast religious and political conservatism. Drew's activist church was especially critical in the formative 1830s and early 1840s, when

---

28. *Downshire Protestant,* July 17, 1857.
29. Hempton and Hill, *Evangelical Protestantism in Ulster Society,* 105, 109.

both the town's public infrastructure and the Orange Order were relatively weak.

Both the church and its most famous minister left a rich imprint on the historical record. Christ Church's baptismal and marriage records remain intact, and a detailed 1852 religious census of Christ Church District allows us to reconstruct the social profile of a large proportion of the congregation. Moreover, in 1858, the Reverend Abraham Dawson, Drew's curate at the time, completed a history of the church titled "The Annals of Christ Church, Belfast," an unpublished account that charts the church's official self-narrative of its early years.[30] While Drew did not leave an extensive collection of private papers, we have a number of his letters with Belfast and Ulster contemporaries, and his remarkable energy and determination to remain in the spotlight means that the public record is littered with his sermons, speeches, and publications. Further, the Belfast District minute books of the Orange Order allow us to examine important parts of Drew's Orange career, at least for the critical decade of the 1850s. There is no shortage of source material to chart Drew's key role in the making of Victorian Belfast.

Chapter 1 opens with a brief profile of Belfast in the 1820s and early 1830s, a period marked by demographic growth and wrenching economic change, as wages in the textile industry plummeted amidst the gradual shift from household to factory production and the influx of men and women in search of jobs in the expanding town. Urban growth created widespread anxiety and a powerful sense of purpose for Belfast's ministers, who responded with a host of social and spiritual initiatives to save lives and souls by bringing working-class people into their churches. The importance of these projects was only reinforced

---

30. Baptism Registers for Christ Church, Belfast, 1835–52, Public Record Office of Northern Ireland (hereafter PRONI), MIC/583/23/3; Christ Church Census, 1852, PRONI, CR1/13D/1-2; Dawson, "Annals of Christ Church, Belfast," PRONI, T.2159/1. My thanks to Brian Walker and the late Reverend Niall Bayly for letting me consult the actual manuscript. A transcript of the unpublished manuscript can be found at the Public Record Office of Northern Ireland, T.2159/1.

in the minds of evangelical Protestants by the rise of a more assertive Irish Catholic politics, personified on a national level by Daniel O'Connell and the Catholic Association's successful crusade for Catholic emancipation. It was the combination of three factors—Belfast's chaotic and rapid growth, the increasing influence of evangelicalism within the Church of Ireland, and the emergence of an organized and powerful Irish Catholic and nationalist politics—that created fertile ground for Drew's public career.

Fearful of the fast-growing working-class population in a town that only had two Anglican churches, Belfast religious and political elites initiated the push for the construction of a new church in the late 1820s. Christ Church opened in the summer of 1833, located behind the Royal Belfast Academical Institution on the southwest edge of town and designed to accommodate its growing proletarian population. Drew threw himself into his ministerial work with the energy that would disrupt northern politics for the better part of three decades, creating an array of outreach projects that brought both organized religion and social support into the heart of fast-developing west Belfast. Drew's anti-Catholicism and Orange politics were clear from the beginning. He actively opposed Catholic emancipation in the late 1820s and his frenetic outreach efforts were shaped by his antipathy to Roman Catholicism as well as his ambitions for a successful clerical career.

Drew's hard work certainly paid off. By 1838, Christ Church was one of the largest Anglican congregations in Ireland, with four hundred regular congregants and approximately one thousand boys and girls in a network of Sunday schools that stretched across urban, suburban, and rural areas to the south and west of town. In chapter 1, I argue that Drew's pastoral activism, his social outreach programs, and particularly the creation of the church's network of Sunday and day schools, were central to his mission at Christ Church, catering to an Anglican working-class population making the difficult social transition into life in a rapidly industrializing town. At the same time, it is clear that Christ Church immediately became a controversial site of Orange activity, marked publicly by Drew's decision to give a special

12th of July sermon to Belfast Orangemen in 1835. By the early 1840s, Christ Church lay at the center of life in Protestant west Belfast, bringing working-class men and women into nascent social networks with middle- and upper-class congregants and providing a sense of community in an era of turbulent economic change. By detailing the ways that Drew's Orange politics and pragmatic evangelical initiatives helped to forge the Christ Church community in these early years, chapter 1 highlights the hybrid nature of Drew's appeal in early Victorian Belfast.

In their thoughtful survey of the history of evangelical religion in modern Ulster, David Hempton and Myrtle Hill show how many of Belfast's leading evangelical ministers used a range of strategies to strengthen ties to their new urban constituencies, drawing special attention to Drew's efforts to make Christ Church a vital center for religious fellowship and material aid. In a speculative aside, they suggest that the anti-Catholicism at the heart of a particular kind of evangelical Protestantism helped ministers gain "a real foothold in working-class culture."[31] This raises interesting and important questions about evangelical Protestantism and the making of early Victorian Belfast. Historians have focused on Drew as an essentially political actor, as an Orange minister, an anti-Catholic polemicist, and one of Belfast's famous political pastors. In chapters 2 and 3, I start from a somewhat different premise, arguing that Drew's theological beliefs and preaching style were a significant part of his success. Chapter 2 is based on a close examination of nearly forty political and religious sermons published over the course of his ministry at Christ Church. It opens by sketching the central tenets of Drew's conservative evangelical Protestantism and the simple measured optimism of his sermons, lectures that differ radically in tone and content from his better-known political anti-Catholic diatribes. The central message of Drew's everyday sermons detailed the religious and social reformation of Protestant working-class families, a simple social gospel designed

---

31. Hempton and Hill, *Evangelical Protestantism in Ulster Society*, 111–12, 123.

to bring spiritual hope and ordered civility to a potentially turbulent environment in a rapidly growing town. In many ways, these sermons echo the messages and tone of Hannah More's famous repository tracts, designed to promote Christian virtue, respectability, and social stability in a volatile age. These more conventional evangelical sermons dominate Drew's early published work, reflecting his focus on efforts to establish and build the Christ Church community in the late 1830s and early 1840s. If Drew's Orange politics defined his public persona, it was the social conservativism and evangelical gospel of his everyday sermons that dominated his parishioners' experience at Christ Church.

Both Belfast and Irish politics changed dramatically in ensuing decades, and the political and sectarian dimensions of Drew's ministry are particularly evident in his Orange sermons of the 1850s, occasional sermons that were tied to the holy days of the Orange ritual calendar. These widely publicized lectures were rooted in a deeply pessimistic reading of a contemporary world dominated by binary religious struggle between Catholics and Protestants. For all their global pretensions, however, Drew's sermons were firmly focused on Belfast and Ireland. After 1848, Drew consistently called for the revival of a forceful Protestant masculinity to restore Irish Protestant hegemony in the face of the British government's dangerous appeasement of the Catholic threat. It was reports of these confrontational speeches, given in both churches and public squares across Ulster, that made Drew such a notorious figure in the Irish Catholic imagination.

Drew's Orange sermons were certainly crucial in establishing his reputation as a Protestant champion and anti-Catholic bigot. Religious lines of division in Victorian Ulster, however, were rarely that simple. Both inter- and intradenominational clashes often were nearly as fierce as sectarian rivalries, as Drew and his allies used their anti-Catholic credentials against Protestant rivals in public clashes over a range of political and religious issues. Chapter 3 examines these dynamics through a detailed examination of the so-called Mant controversy of late 1842 and 1843, an episode that shows how Drew and other populist evangelical clergymen mobilized lay communities around religious issues. The ostensible reason for the clash was the Down and Connor and Dromore Church Architecture Society, a seemingly arcane church association devoted to studying aspects of Anglican church architecture past and present. Richard Mant, the High Church bishop of Down and Connor, was an active participant and supporter of the fledging organization, putting him into direct conflict with an emergent alliance of low-church evangelical ministers and their supporters, all offended by the "Popish novelty" of this academically minded association.

The Mant controversy also highlights the rise of evangelicalism within the Church of Ireland in Belfast, the complex struggle between evangelicals and high churchmen within the Anglican Church, and the increasing importance of lay voices in these clashes. Recent studies have shown that Anglican churches across the United Kingdom were more effective in their appeals to proletarian communities than British historical scholarship traditionally allowed; Christ Church's growth in the late 1830s and 1840s is further testament to this work. Religion mattered to many working-class Victorian men and women and churches lay at the center of many fast-developing urban communities, but in divided Belfast and the surrounding region, anti-Catholicism simplified the task of forging these ties, providing both a familiar language and common foe for often relatively diverse social groupings. The chapter's examination of the Mant controversy and its surrounding milieu thus makes it clear that churches could act as crucial sites of popular mobilization, strengthening some of the cross-class ties that characterized popular Protestant politics in Victorian Belfast.

Drew was known as one of Belfast's foremost advocates for the Protestant working class. A firm conservative in his politics, Drew was nevertheless an opportunist by inclination and his working-class advocacy often featured a muscular if inconsistent critique of the excesses of industrial capitalism and liberal political economy—a clerical predecessor to the populist "Orange democracy" of William Johnston of Ballykilbeg. While Drew's advocacy often was as rhetorical as it was real, his reputation as a champion of the Protestant working class was an essential part of his persona. Chapter 4 begins with an overview of Drew's defensive paternalism, sketching out the basic tenets of his beliefs as well as his active participation in Belfast's increasingly dynamic associational culture. The sheer breadth of Drew's civic engagement reflects the hybridity of anti-Catholicism, which shaped Drew's active involvement in societies dedicated to antislavery, church construction, domestic and overseas missionary work, poor relief, and religious education.

The economic vicissitudes of the 1840s created a difficult environment for a conservative evangelical populist, and chapter 4 concludes with a close examination of the ways that Drew negotiated two of the decade's most challenging social crises: the suffering of the Ballymacarrett weavers in the depression of 1842–43 and the horrific tragedy of the Great Irish Famine. Drew's response to the plight of the weavers highlights the nature and the limits of his Protestant populism. For all of his paternalist rhetoric, when push came to shove, Drew consistently lined up with conservative landlords and businessmen throughout his career. Distressed weavers asking for assisted emigration to North America were to be treated generously and humanely, of course, but they were not to receive aid from ratepayers. Drew's paternalism was not completely hollow, however, as evidenced by his work as secretary for the Belfast General Relief Fund in 1847. Laboring assiduously to raise funds for relief across Ireland, Drew's work with the fund also highlights some of the ways the Great Famine sharpened notions of regional and religious difference across Belfast and the north.

The standard narrative of the 1850s in Belfast is dominated by deepening sectarian conflict. There are good reasons for this focus. The aftermath of the 1848 rebellion sharpened political tensions across the island and province, fractures that were only accentuated by continuing controversy over the Maynooth Grant, the controversialist public sermons of evangelical ministers, Anglican in-migration into the city, the dramatic growth of the Orange Order in Belfast, and the horrific sectarian riots of the summer of 1857. Not surprisingly, Drew and Christ Church were at the center of nearly all of these developments. In 1854, Drew formed the Christ Church Protestant

Association to give voice to his brand of conservative populist Protestant politics, and while he did not join many of his colleagues in the street preaching that triggered so much public contention in the summer of 1857, his anti-Catholic sermons and his reputation for such harangues played critical roles in creating a deeper sense of Catholic/Protestant division in the city.

And yet, for all the signs of sharpening conflict, the binary logics of sectarian division were never all-consuming. Focusing on the Christ Church Protestant Association, the Orange Order, and the Belfast Riots of 1857, chapters 5 and 6 examine both the power and limits of anti-Catholic politics in Victorian Belfast, showing how Drew's combative style and trenchant sectarianism had a kind of Janus-faced impact in Belfast, mobilizing significant but ultimately limited Protestant and Orange constituencies and dramatically sharpening communal lines in the city while alienating important elements of a Protestant and British establishment unwilling to support a figure whose rhetorical extremism had such a destabilizing impact on communal relations. In doing so, I insist that sectarianism must be understood as a complex historical subject, a protean language capable of coexisting with seemingly contradictory cultural, political, and social forces. As Alan Ford has argued in an important essay on sectarianism in early modern Ireland, it is people's ability to live both together and apart (often simultaneously) that makes sectarianism such a fascinating but difficult subject.[32]

Chapter 7 provides a brief consideration of Drew's life and legacy after he left Christ Church in January 1859. In that month, he started a new position as the rector of Loughinisland Parish Church in south County Down. He died a little more than a decade later, in 1870. In many ways, Drew's departure from Belfast marked the end of this formative era in the city's nineteenth-century history (a marker reinforced on a broader scale by the 1859 evangelical revival). While particular issues and meanings changed, the basic template of

---

32. Ford, "Living Together, Living Apart," 1–23.

Drew's success—an adaptive combination of conservative and Orange politics, combative anti-Catholicism, evangelical Protestantism, and populist advocacy for the Protestant working class—has proven to be a potent force throughout Belfast's modern history. The remarkable careers of Drew's Presbyterian contemporary, Henry Cooke, as well as late nineteenth- and twentieth-century figures like Richard Rutledge Kane, William Nicholson, and Ian Paisley, are testament to the powerful fusion of political, religious, and social forces involved in Drew's largely successful and divisive crusade to build the house of God in Belfast.

1

Thomas Drew and the Making of Christ Church

When Thomas Drew arrived at Christ Church in 1833, he came to a town that was well on its way to becoming a city.[1] Early Victorian Belfast was the most dynamic urban center in Ireland and one of the fastest growing towns in the British Isles. Drawn primarily from surrounding Ulster counties, newcomers crowded into Belfast's central slums as well as the fast-developing neighborhoods and industrial suburbs on the edges of the town core.[2] This was hardly an ideal environment for an ambitious minister trying to build a substantial congregation. And this was exactly what Drew was selected to do at Christ Church, a new church designed to cater to the Protestant working-class families living in and around the expanding textile zone west and southwest of the town center. An energetic pastor and Orange firebrand, Drew was seemingly well suited for his new surroundings. This would be vital. From the outset, it was clear that Drew's ability to bring people into the fold, to create a community at Christ Church, would define the success or the failure of his ministry.

After a brief contextual account of the church's origins in late Georgian Belfast, this chapter focuses on Drew's efforts to create a Protestant community at Christ Church in the 1830s. The results were easy to see.

---

1. While Belfast was not officially labeled a city until 1888, I use the term *city* to describe Belfast after 1850 to denote its rapidly changing nature and scale.

2. According to the 1841 census, 85 percent of the Belfast population was born in Antrim, Down, or Belfast. For a good discussion of the issue, see Hirst, *Religion, Politics and Violence in 19th Century Belfast*, 15.

By the end of the decade, Christ Church was the largest Church of Ireland congregation in Belfast, featuring a largely working-class membership that lived between the Shankill Road and Sandy Row, neighborhoods that would become synonymous with the Orange Order and hardline Protestant politics. But the making of Christ Church was not simply a matter of Orange politics. Drew's frenetic work in church extension and religious education were also integral to community formation, helping to make the church a crucial site for a socially diverse congregation living in a rapidly changing environment. It was the mixture that was the key to Drew's success, not least in maintaining relationships with his conservative and respectable middle-class allies. While many of Belfast's civic leaders were uncomfortable with Drew's confrontational anti-Catholic performances, other aspects of his crusade to build the house of God in Belfast dovetailed perfectly with their own agendas of conservative urban growth and social stability. In an important essay, Sean Connolly has highlighted the contradictions at the heart of Victorian Belfast's civic culture, arguing that the northern capital should be seen as both a representative if extreme example of the nineteenth-century British city and an exceptional Irish variant where genuine urban achievements were largely undermined by a system of politics that was narrow, defensive, and sectarian.[3] Drew's efforts at Christ Church embodied these contradictions. He helped to bring his largely plebeian congregation more firmly within the orbit of the developing urban community. He did so, however, in a way that greatly sharpened communal division, strengthening fractures that inhibited the political development of Victorian Belfast.

EARLY VICTORIAN BELFAST: THE MAKING OF A CITY

Victorian Belfast was a rapidly changing place; a shock city created by rapid economic transformation and population growth.[4] Migrants

---

3. Connolly, "Belfast: The Rise and Fall of a Civic Culture," 48.

4. *Shock City* is a term coined by Asa Briggs to describe rapidly emergent industrial cities like Manchester, Chicago, and Melbourne; see Briggs, *Victorian Cities*. For a more recent treatment, see Platt, *Shock Cities*.

from across the province pushed the population from roughly 18,000 in 1791 to 120,000 in 1861, drawn to Belfast by the growth of textile production and, from the early 1840s, jobs in harbor construction and other maritime industries.[5] This made Belfast one of the fastest growing cities in the British Isles, a factor that underlay the town's transformation into Ireland's leading industrial center and second-largest city. Early Victorian Belfast's steep growth trajectory presents historians with real challenges, necessitating careful attention to the peculiar and fast-changing dynamics of place and time. Belfast was a very different place when Drew arrived in late 1832 than it was when he departed in 1859.

The rapid pace of population growth and spatial change is best tracked by looking at contemporary maps. The 1833 Ordnance Survey map of Belfast shows a relatively compact town nestled against the confluence of the River Lagan and Belfast Lough. The vast majority of Belfast's inhabitants lived north and east of a line drawn from the town's commercial center on High Street west to the working-class neighborhoods built up around Mill Street and the lower Falls Road. Cotton and linen factories dotted Belfast's western edge, industrial sites that would soon help to extend the town inland from its original urban core.

Belfast's remarkable mid-nineteenth-century growth was enabled by changes in property ownership. The Donegall (Chichester) family had presided over the town's development since the early seventeenth century, owning much of the very land upon which Belfast was built. The relationship between the Donegalls and the town began to shift in the 1820s, as George Augustus Chichester (1769–1844), the notoriously profligate second Marquess of Donegall, was forced to lease land to Belfast's leading merchants to remain financially solvent. Lord Donegall died in 1844, and the family sold nearly all of its considerable Belfast holdings in the late 1840s and 1850s to pay off further

---

5. Gillespie and Royle, *Irish Historic Towns Atlas No. 12*, 10 (contemporary estimate for 1791); Vaughan and Fitzpatrick, *Irish Historical Statistics*, 36–37.

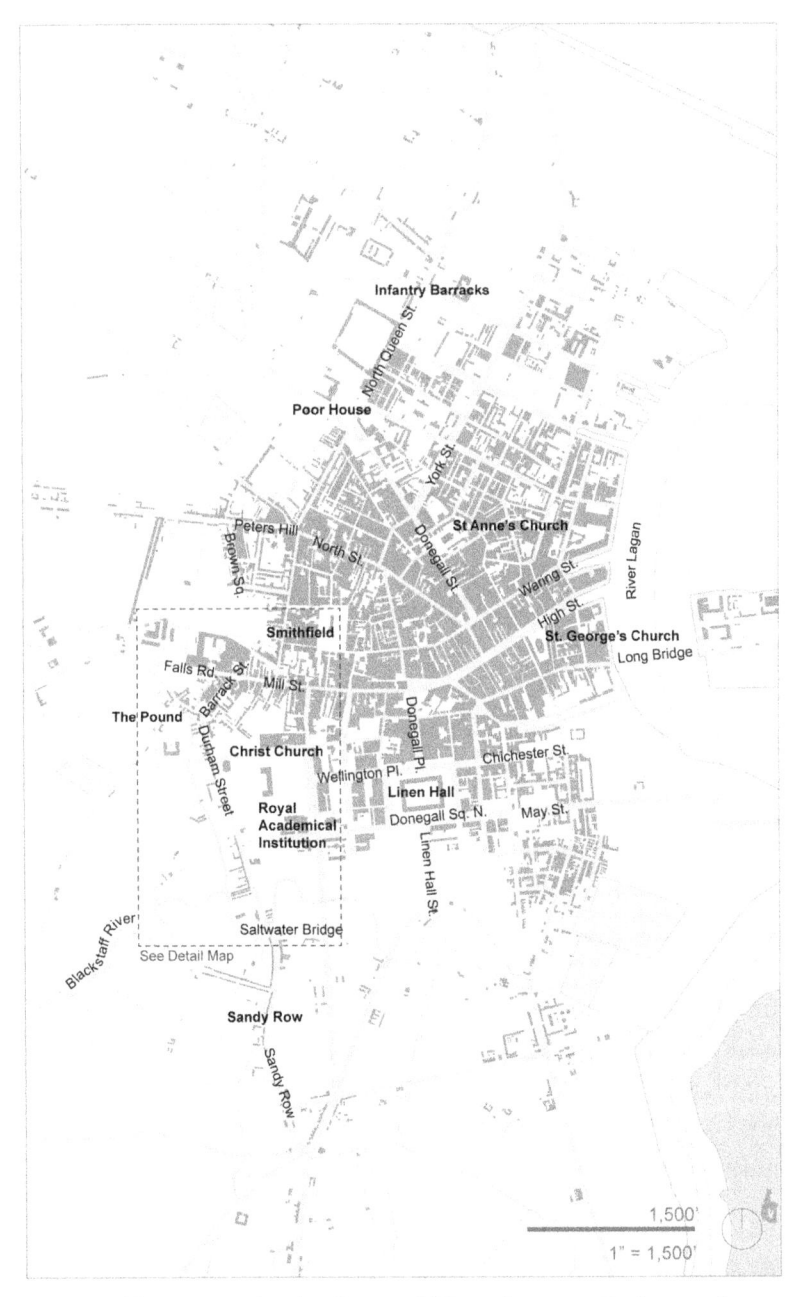

Map 2. Belfast, 1833. Map by Conor O'Shea. Sources: Ordnance Survey Northern Ireland First Edition (1832–46), "PRONI Historical Maps Viewer," https://www.nidirect.gov.uk/services/search-proni-historical-maps-viewer; Gillespie and Royle, *Irish Historic Towns Atlas No. 12*.

debt.[6] The Donegall estate sale freed up a long constrained urban land market that quickly attracted property developers, speculators, and builders, who took advantage of open green-field sites on the town's periphery to build the locally sourced redbrick and slate-roofed houses that dominated Victorian Belfast's working-class neighborhoods.[7] Belfast's growth rate was so dramatic that the town council was forced to expand its municipal boundaries in 1853. The relatively open spaces of the town's western edge can be seen by a closer examination of the 1833 Ordnance Survey map, which highlights Christ Church's early suburban setting. This changed dramatically by the late 1850s and 1860s, when the church was increasingly surrounded by fast-growing neighborhoods of working-class families brought by train to the nearby railway station, completed in 1848.

But it was not simply a matter of numbers. Belfast's demographic growth had a transformative impact on the town's religious geography and politics. At the turn of the century, its population was modest in size, comparatively prosperous, and largely Presbyterian. The town's religious landscape was much more diverse by the 1830s.

The most dramatic change was the surging growth of the Catholic population in Belfast. At the turn of the century, Catholics constituted roughly 10 percent of the town's population. By 1834, one third of Belfast's population was Catholic and this remained true when the census was taken in 1861, when the city population had grown to 120,000. While the Catholic proportion of the population declined after 1861 (it was 24 percent in 1901), contemporaries had little way of knowing that, and public awareness of the town's Catholic population growth was a vital (and often hypersensitive) backdrop for mid-Victorian Belfast politics. The complexity of the northern capital's Protestant demographics is belied by the seeming stability

---

6. Maguire, "Lord Donegall and the Sale of Belfast," 570–84. See also Maguire, *Living like a Lord*.

7. Cullen, "Provision of Working and Lower-Middle Class Housing," 238–41; Royle, "Socio-Spatial Structure of Belfast in 1837," 1–9; Gillespie and Royle, *Irish Historic Towns Atlas No. 12*, 1–2.

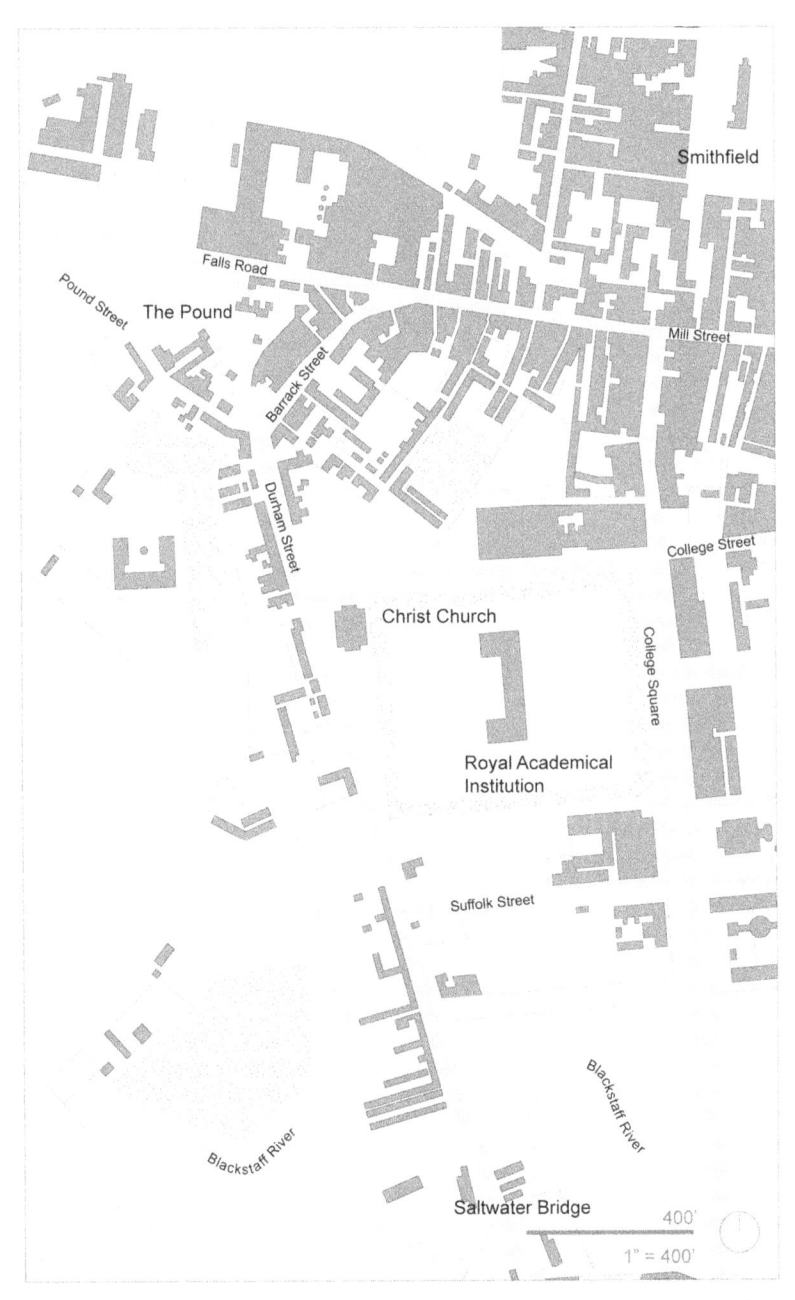

Map 3. Christ Church neighborhood, 1833. Map by Conor O'Shea. Sources: Ordnance Survey Northern Ireland First Edition (1832–46), "PRONI Historical Maps Viewer," https://www.nidirect.gov.uk/services/search-proni-historical-maps-viewer; Gillespie and Royle, *Irish Historic Towns Atlas No. 12*.

TABLE 1

RELIGIOUS DENOMINATIONS AND POPULATION
IN BELFAST, 1831–1861

	Church of Ireland (%)	Presbyterian (%)	Catholic (%)
1808			16
1831	27	39	33
1861	25	35	34

Sources: Connolly, *Belfast 400*, 246; 1808 data from contemporary estimates in Budge and O'Leary, *Approach to Crisis*, 32; 1831 data calculated retrospectively from census enumerator's lists for *First Report of the Commissioners of Public Instruction, Ireland*, HC 1835 (45), xxxiii, 2162; 1861 data from Vaughan and Fitzpatrick, *Irish Historical Statistics*, 58.

in table 1, where the percentages mask a Belfast Protestant population that was becoming more diverse, evangelical, and much larger in size. Although Presbyterians remained the largest single denomination, the Church of Ireland population increased in the 1840s and 1850s, bringing a more conservative element to Belfast's Protestant working-class politics. Whatever their religious identity, many of the poorer immigrants settled in the town's central slums and adjacent neighborhoods, crowding into dilapidated housing stock that was only upgraded after 1850.

While a close examination of census data and various investigative reports show a modest degree of mixed religious settlement in the mill districts of west Belfast, the basic foundations for the area's communal neighborhoods largely had been established by the late 1820s and 1830s. New Catholic migrants generally moved into terraced row houses west of the town center, neighborhoods bordering on Smithfield, an area within easy walking distance of both St. Mary's Church and St. Patrick's Church. The heart of Catholic west Belfast was the Pound, named after the old cattle pound, a district bordered by Divis Street and the lower Falls Road to the north, Barrack Street and Durham Street to the east, and Albert Street to the south. New Anglican families coming to the area largely settled in and around Brown Square, Durham Street, and the new industrial suburb of Sandy Row.

Christ Church was founded to capture unchurched Protestants living in these neighborhoods. These settlement patterns had a lasting impact. As Raymond Gillespie and Stephen Royle have shown in the Royal Irish Academy's indispensable town atlas, the basic religious geography of west Belfast has proven to be remarkably resilient.[8]

These settlement patterns also had a dramatic impact on Belfast politics, where the stakes were heightened dramatically by the successful campaign for Catholic emancipation in the late 1820s and the passage of the Reform Act of 1832, which moved the town's previously closed parliamentary elections into an increasingly fractious public arena. After 1832, Whigs and Tories fought over Belfast's two parliamentary seats in every election, contests that were sharpened dramatically by the rise of a new, more public, Catholic politics. By the mid-1830s, the combination of rising political contention and the close proximity of the town's ethnic neighborhoods generated increased levels of political violence in west Belfast.[9] One of the town's first fatal sectarian riots occurred on the very doorstep of Christ Church on July 12, 1835, when activists from Sandy Row and the Pound placed orange and green markers near the boundaries of the two neighborhoods. The situation quickly devolved into a stone-throwing melee. Magistrates called out the army to contain the violence. Soldiers fired into a Protestant crowd, killing four people. The *Northern Whig* placed part of the blame on Drew, who, it claimed, had "suitably entertained" the Sandy Row Orangemen in his church that day. Drew's efforts were,

---

8. Gillespie and Royle, *Irish Historic Towns Atlas No. 12*, 8. This discussion is also informed by the research of Brian Gurrin, Liam Kennedy, and Kerby A. Miller, who kindly provided preliminary estimates of their major study of religious demography in modern Ulster. For an excellent overview, see Miller, Kennedy, and Gurrin, "Great Famine and Religious Demography in Mid-Nineteenth-Century Ulster," 426–34.

9. In a recent survey, Stephen Royle highlights the ways that segregation both limited and reinforced sectarian strife, reducing potentially difficult interaction but reinforcing the perpetuation of communal myths. See Royle, "Workshop of the Empire," 219. For a nuanced analysis of the shifting uses of public space, see Bryan, Connolly, and Nagle, *Civic Identity and Public Space*, 74–78.

the paper argued, part of a broader campaign to make the Church of Ireland more popular in Belfast.[10] From the outset of his ministry, Drew and Christ Church were associated with religious division and party violence.

The town that the migrants helped to make was a one of dramatic contrasts. Contemporary accounts often celebrated Belfast as a center of progress, an urban beachhead of "English civility in Ireland."[11] There certainly were clear signs of the town's civic pride, industrial growth, and relative prosperity—the dramatic increase in textile factories; the expansion of urban infrastructure, including its gaslit streets (1823); harbor projects; and the growth of an impressive network of largely private philanthropic institutions, associations peopled by what was eventually Ireland's largest urban middle class. According to Jonathan Jeffrey Wright, Belfast featured at least twenty-five active charitable and evangelical groups in 1832, organizations that ranged from the Association for Discountenancing Vice and Promoting the Knowledge and Practice of the Christian Religion to the Ulster Female Penitentiary.[12] If the Scottish travel writer Henry Inglis was critical of the aesthetic quality of the buildings that had been built in the fifteen years before 1834 (fully one third of Belfast in his estimation),[13] he was nonetheless impressed by Belfast and its people. He was not alone. Writing in their famous Irish travel guide (1840), Samuel and Anna Hall concurred: "As we drew near to Ireland's only manufacturing town, its peculiar character became apparent. It was something new to perceive rising above the houses numerous tall and thin chimneys which are indications of industry, occupation, commerce, and

---

10. *Northern Whig*, July 13, 1835; *Belfast Commercial Chronicle*, July 13, 1835; Barrow, *Tour around Ireland*, 33–35.

11. Inglis, *Ireland in 1834*; Heaney, *Scottish Whig in Ireland*; Scott, *Hall's Ireland*; Thackeray, *Irish Sketch Book*.

12. For a complete listing, see Wright, *"Natural Leaders" and Their World*, 245–46.

13. Inglis, *Ireland in 1834*, 251–52.

prosperity, with the volumes of smoke that issued from them giving unquestionable tokens of full of employment."[14] Although many of the town's working-class families doubtless would have questioned this rather sunny assessment of civic and economic progress, Belfast stood apart as Ireland's only significant industrial center, a seemingly British city in the making.

There were other sides to the Belfast story. Late nineteenth-century Belfast may have had the best housing stock in Ireland, but this, like so much else, was a relatively recent development, a product of its post-1850 growth. Prior to Lord Donegall's land sale, the town's working-class housing was at least as bad as Dublin's notorious tenements. Most working-class homes in both Sandy Row and the Pound were given second- and third-class ratings in the 1837 town valuation. As Catherine Hirst has noted, if anything, the homes in Protestant Sandy Row were worse than those in the largely Catholic Pound. Tea Lane, featuring terraced row houses built in the 1820s for workers in local textile mills and brickyards, had thirty-eight homes that were classified as too poor to be rated.[15] These neighborhoods were located in the heartland of the Christ Church congregation. According to the church's 1852 census, 138 men, women, and children lived on Tea Lane, most claiming to be regular in their church attendance.[16] Conditions were made all the worse by the regular flooding of the Blackstaff River, which crossed the district running under Durham Street at Saltwater Bridge south of Christ Church. By the early Victorian

---

14. Scott, *Hall's Ireland*, 342.

15. 1837 valuation, PRONI, val. 1B/79; Cullen, "Provision of Working and Lower-Middle Class Housing," 238–41; Hirst, *Religion, Politics, and Violence in 19th Century Belfast*, 17; Royle, "Socio-Spatial Structure," 2–8. For contemporary observations see Batt, "Belfast Sixty Years Ago; reports of the Belfast Town Mission, 1828, 1830, 1833–38, Gamble Library, Union Theological College; *Third Report of the Commissioners for Inquiring into the Condition of the Poorer Classes in Ireland*, 1–23; O'Hanlon, *Walks among the Poor of Belfast*, 38; Malcolm, *Sanitary State of Belfast*, 4–5.

16. Christ Church Census, 1852, PRONI, CR1/13D/1.

period, the river was already an environmental disaster, made into a "foul and open torturous stream" by effluvia from the growing number of factories and houses that lined its banks. The combination of low-lying geography, industrial waste, and poverty created a hazardous zone for endemic disease, emblemized by deadly cholera outbreaks in Belfast in 1832, 1848–49, and 1853.[17]

The reports of the Belfast Town Mission's scripture readers in the 1830s paint a similar picture of a manufacturing town in transition, with families struggling with alcoholism, poverty, and disease, all made worse in missionary minds by widespread ignorance of the Bible. The reports also provide glimpses of a range of working-class responses to evangelical efforts that belie simple top-down narratives of spiritual reformation. In 1828 one man complained that Belfast had far too much religion already and would not let the scripture reader read from the Bible. More characteristically, the reports took a melodramatic turn, featuring narratives of regretful rejection or initially skeptical men and women whose lives were changed by their acceptance of biblical truth. According to these stories, the spread of vital religion offered the only hope for the Belfast poor.[18]

It was this sharply drawn landscape of urban sin and suffering that gave Belfast evangelicals such a powerful sense of anxiety and purpose. Abraham Dawson, curate at Christ Church in the 1850s, wrote that the area had been infamous for its "drunken rows and unseemly brawling" while the Reverend James Morgan, minister of nearby Fisherwick Presbyterian Church, labeled the state of society in Belfast "awful" after detailing a dramatic scene in which he witnessed two women fighting, one man vomiting whiskey, and a boy crying after

17. For the cholera outbreaks in Belfast in 1832 and 1848–49, see the 1833 *Report of the Belfast Town Mission*; Roney, *Irish Rebel and California Labor Leader*, 23–25; and Morgan's memoir, *Recollections of My Life and Times*, 168–71. See also Farrell, "Asiatic Cholera and the Development of Public Health in Belfast."

18. *Report of the Belfast Town Mission*, 1828, 1830, 1833–38. My thanks to Robyn Atcheson for bringing this material to my attention. See also Morgan, *Recollections of My Life and Times*, 36–37.

being struck by a stone.[19] Matters improved dramatically after 1860, and social conditions were certainly better outside of the town's central slums. Writing in 1853, the Reverend William O'Hanlon reported that despite generally poor housing conditions and a fearsome reputation for violence, Sandy Row was a much healthier place to live than many of Belfast's other working-class districts, with residents benefiting from greater access to light, air, and space in the new suburban setting. Belfast's newfound prosperity clearly did not reach most of its inhabitants; at mid-century, life expectancy for Belfast millworkers, for example, was forty-five years.[20]

With people crowded into low-quality housing and often working for low wages in unregulated textile mills, early nineteenth-century industrial towns and cities were tinderboxes of potential unrest. The early 1830s and 1840s saw a dramatic rise in sociopolitical conflict across the United Kingdom, and Belfast was no exception. The reorganization of textile work around Belfast's newly created mills hit handloom weavers and their families with particular force.[21] In 1835 an estimated ten thousand cotton weavers lived in and around Belfast on wages that ranged between three shillings and six pence to eight shillings per week.[22] After decades of falling wages, the town's handloom weavers were in steep decline in these years, replaced and supplemented by men and women from Ulster's rapidly deindustrializing rural districts who traveled to the northern capital to find work in the

---

19. Dawson, "Annals of Christ Church, Belfast," PRONI, T.2159/1, 10; Morgan, *Recollections of My Life and Times*, 301–2.

20. Sawyer, *"We Are But Women,"* 34; Jones, *Social Geography of Belfast*, 213; Kinealy and Mac Atasney, *Hidden Famine*; Sibbett, *For Christ and Crown*. For a worm's-eye view of cholera's impact in Belfast in this era, see the 1833 *Report of the Belfast Town Mission*, and Morgan, *Recollections of My Life and Times*, 168–71.

21. For Belfast, see the testimonies of John Boyd and Alexander Moncrieffe, *Select Committee on Hand-Loom Weavers' Petitions*, 83–123.

22. Testimony of John Boyd, *Select Committee on Hand-Loom Weavers' Petitions*, 86; O'Connor, *Labour History of Ireland*, 16; Patterson, "Industrial Labour and the Labour Movement," 158–83.

textile mills of Belfast and its industrial suburbs. For many working families, things would only begin to improve in the 1850s.

The chronic instability and economic difficulties of the period can be seen in a number of contemporary sources. One of the most interesting is the diary of James MacAdam, a merchant who, with his more famous brother Robert, opened the Soho Iron Foundry on Townsend Street in 1836, located on the very boundaries of Christ Church District.[23] While the foundry eventually was successful, MacAdam's diary details the regular firing, rehiring, and firing of employees, anxiety about slumping sales, and a vivid description of an influenza outbreak that wracked the city in 1837.[24] The shock of immersion in this new industrial environment can also be seen in the poetry of Aodh Mac Domhnaill, who moved from north Meath in 1842 to work in the foundry. This alien space is richly described in his narrative poem, "Peter Galligan's Welcome" (Fáilte Pheadair Ui Ghealacáin):

> I was brought into a fairy fort that left me frightened and overwhelmed;
> There were great numbers of the fairy host there worshipping demons,
> Their skin was like coal and their faces black as shoes; . . .
> It was thought the wheel of every spinning wheel in the province
> Was racing there at brake-neck speed
> When I saw that awful and monstrous vision,
> I was left with no power in my limbs nor interest in women.[25]

Finally, Jonathan Jeffrey Wright's recent reconstruction of the life of the infamous John Linn, convicted of killing his father in 1833, underlines the narrow margins and vulnerability of working-class life

---

23. See Hughes, *Robert Shipboy MacAdam*.

24. Diary of James MacAdam (1836–42), PRONI, D.2930/7/4–5. For solid accounts of the social history and geography of Belfast in this era, see Kinealy and Mac Atasney, *Hidden Famine*, 14–17; Jones, *Social Geography of Belfast*.

25. Quoted in de Brun, "Expressing the Nineteenth Century in Irish," 87. For the poem in the original Irish, see Mac Domhnaill, *Dánta*, 84–87.

in pre-Famine Belfast. Born into a relatively successful and "respectable" plebeian household in Smithfield (his father was a wheelwright), Linn's dissolute habits and eventual incarceration had a catastrophic impact on his family; three of his daughters were admitted to the Poor House run by the Belfast Charitable Society. Two of the girls died shortly thereafter.[26] For all its commercial vitality and civic pride, Belfast's rapid demographic growth and the endemic poverty and chronic unemployment created by an economy in transition made for a challenging environment for working-class people and middle-class reformers alike.

Christ Church was one of nearly fifty churches and meeting houses built in Belfast between 1830 and 1860. The public proliferation of religion in Belfast struck visitors like the famed English writer William Makepeace Thackeray, who noted the number of houses of worship in Belfast with both wonder and anxiety in the early 1840s.[27] While popular demand and growing denominational competition were critical factors in the construction of this new religious landscape, the remarkable churching of early to mid-Victorian Belfast was a critical part of a broader middle-class effort to foster civility and social stability in this new and fast-developing urban environment. These same dynamics, however, strengthened sectarian antagonism in the working-class districts of early Victorian Belfast. And this notion is essential for the argument here, for it was in this hot house atmosphere that confessional allegiances were turned into increasingly contentious and often antagonistic political identities. Drew's Christ Church was instrumental to this process. And it is to that story that we now turn.

BUILDING CHRIST CHURCH

In 1830 Richard Mant, the Church of Ireland bishop of Down and Connor, approached the church's Board of First Fruits with a proposal to build a new church with seating for 1,500. Fully two thirds of these

26. Wright, *Crime and Punishment in Nineteenth-Century Belfast*, 26–28, 53–54.
27. Thackeray, *Irish Sketch Book*, 347.

were to be free, with the funds from the remaining pew rentals used to pay the minister's salary and to create a fund for repairs.[28] The church was designed to cater to a largely proletarian population, much needed in a town that only had two Anglican churches at the time (St. Anne's on Donegall Street, and St. George's on High Street).[29] Mant had begun work on the initiative in the fall of the previous year, convincing Lord Donegall to donate land and eliciting support for the project from some of the town's religious and political leaders.[30] The new church was to be located behind the Royal Belfast Academical Institution at the corner of Durham Street and College Square North. The board eventually accepted the proposal, providing a grant of £2,500 that was matched by private subscriptions from an impressive group of supporters that ranged from Lord John Beresford, the Church of Ireland's archbishop of Armagh and primate of all Ireland, to the Reverend Henry Montgomery, the influential Presbyterian minister.[31]

Christ Church had a distinctly suburban setting in its early years, a perspective underlined by the sketch of the new church included in Phillip Dixon Hardy's *Twenty-One Views in Belfast and Its Neighbourhood* (1837). It was designed with urban growth in mind, however, as textile mills and foundries were opened on the south and west side of

---

28. MacNeice, *Church of Ireland in Belfast*, 11. The Board of First Fruits was the church body that provided funds for the construction of church and glebe houses. It was replaced by the Board of Ecclesiastical Commissioners in 1834. For a crisp discussion of the development and operation of the Board of First Fruits, see Akenson, *Church of Ireland*, 113–21.

29. Christ Church was not the first of the Church of Ireland's efforts to cater to a growing population in the Belfast area. Like the Durham Street church, St. Patrick's Church in Ballymacarrett (1826–27) was built to cater to working-class men and women in a growing industrial suburb. See Royle and Campbell, "East Belfast and the Suburbanization of Northwest County Down in the Nineteenth Century," 629–62.

30. Richard Mant to William St. John Smyth, September 11, 1829, Mant-St. John Smyth Correspondence, Representative Church Body Library (hereafter RCB), MS 772/3/26.

31. *Christ Church Belfast*, 15.

2. Christ Church, 1837. Source: P. D. Hardy, *Twenty-One Views in Belfast and Its Neighborhood*.

Belfast. While the church's location was crucial to its rapid growth, this was hardly the most generous of gifts, as the donated land originally had been used as a receptacle for manure and other forms of the town's waste. Designed by the church architect William Farrell of Dublin, and built by the engineering firm Cobden and Sands, the brick church was completed in 1833 at a cost of £5,000. Christ Church was designed in a Greek revival style, with a beige sandstone façade marked by a cut-stone front and Ionic columns. Like its more famous neighbor, the Royal Belfast Academical Institution (1814), it is one of the last vestiges of Georgian Belfast.[32]

32. Dawson, "Annals of Christ Church, Belfast," 1–10; Hardy, *Twenty-One Views in Belfast*, 26–27; Larmour, *Belfast*, 8; Mant, *Memoirs of the Right Reverend Richard Mant*, 293; Pilson, *History of the Rise and Progress of Belfast*, 29. For an interesting discussion of the impact of classicism on Georgian Belfast, see Wright, "*Natural Leaders*" *and Their World*, 170–78.

The interior of the church was simple and utilitarian, designed with accommodation rather than aesthetics in mind. Lavens Ewart, a late nineteenth-century Belfast linen merchant and historian, described the church as "a plain, square building, very convenient in every respect, and not at all difficult to fill with the voice."[33] Christ Church could seat approximately 1,500 people, with nearly 1,000 on the ground floor and more than 500 in the galleries above.[34] Many of the church's more distinctive features were added in a later era, most notably its impressive church organ (1858), a stained-glass window made by the famed Birmingham craftsman Samuel Evans (1870), and a "weird and impressive" three-decker pulpit (1878). The church survived as an active Church of Ireland congregation until 1993, when a combination of bomb/arson attacks and shifts in the city's religious demography brought an end to its long history as a place of worship. In more recent times Christ Church has been restored by the Buildings Preservation Trust and is currently being used as a Centre for Information Technology Excellence by the Royal Belfast Academical Institution.

Christ Church's first minister was the Reverend Thomas Drew. Born near St. Mary's Abbey in Limerick City in 1800, he was the son of George and Sarah Drew, a baker/grocer and the daughter of the Reverend Thomas Ryan, the Church of Ireland chancellor of Emly, after whom he was named. While details from Drew's childhood are scant, we know that he attended Sunday school at St. George's Church in Limerick in 1809. The experience initiated a lifelong passion for Drew, who taught Sunday school while at university in Dublin, rising to become superintendent of the program at St. Mark's Church near Trinity College Dublin. As he put it in an 1838 letter, "I owe everything, under God, to Sunday Schools."[35] Drew's family ties in the Church of Ireland linked him to the professional networks critical

---

33. Quoted in Hardy, *Twenty-One Views in Belfast*, 26.

34. Dawson, "Annals of Christ Church, Belfast," 7; Hardy, *Twenty-One Views in Belfast*, 26; MacNeice, *Church of Ireland in Belfast*, 11; Patton, *Central Belfast*, 78–79.

35. *Christ Church Belfast*, 31–32.

to a clerical career. When his father died in 1818, he moved in with the Reverend Thomas Locke, rector of Newcastle West Parish Church, County Limerick, who proved to be a lifelong advocate and friend.[36]

In June 1819 Drew entered Trinity College Dublin, a university closely associated with two of the pillars of his life—the Church of Ireland and the Protestant Ascendancy. For Drew, it was the beginning of a lifelong association with Trinity.[37] While we do not have contemporary records from his undergraduate experience, many of his lectures and sermons make reference to faculty mentors there, particularly Joseph Henderson Singer (1786–1866), the influential Irish evangelical fellow and tutor who went on to become a lecturer, professor, and eventually the Church of Ireland's bishop of Meath. Drew's affinity for Singer certainly makes sense. With James O'Brien, another fellow at Trinity, Singer was one of the church's leading evangelical figures. Both Drew and his mentor were active leaders and participants in many of the same Anglican benevolent societies, particularly the Church Education Society, the Hibernian Bible Society, and the Protestant Orphan Society.[38]

Drew received his degree in 1826 and was ordained as a deacon the following year, leaving Dublin for the north of Ireland, where he served as curate for the Reverend William Crawford in the united parish of Skerry and Racavan in Broughshane, north Antrim. The young curate immediately put his energetic synthesis of combative anti-Catholic politics and evangelical social reform to work. A fervent opponent of Catholic emancipation, he helped to found the Ballymena Brunswick Constitutional Club in 1828, and created an impressive network of

---

36. *Belfast News-Letter*, April 9, 1864; *Irish Ecclesiastical Gazette*, July 15, 1863; Testimony of the Reverend Thomas Locke, *Testimonials to the Character and Labours of the Rev. Thomas Drew*, 17–18. It is worth noting that Drew was made executor of Locke's will when he died in 1847. Drew returned to Limerick in 1837 and 1846. See *Belfast Commercial Chronicle*, May 8, 1837.

37. Drew completed the following degrees at Trinity: BA, 1826; LL, 1841; and his MA, BD, and DD in 1842.

38. For Singer, see Lunney, "Singer, Joseph Henderson."

Sunday schools, a clothing dispensary, and other relief initiatives for the poor.[39] These efforts gained the attention of Arthur Macartney, the Church of Ireland vicar of Belfast, who with his curate, Thomas Hincks, helped to bring Drew to Belfast in November 1832 to be the perpetual curate of Christ Church. Drew remained there until 1859.

Drew did not come to Belfast alone. In 1829 he married Isabella Dalton, the daughter of a Dublin attorney. They had eleven children over the course of their forty years together: eight daughters and three sons. Two of the Drew's children became prominent public figures in late nineteenth-century Britain and Ireland. The most famous was his eldest son, Sir Thomas Drew, one of the country's leading architects. Thomas Drew Jr. learned his craft from Sir Charles Lanyon, an early Christ Church congregant most famous for designing the Custom House, Belfast, the main building of Queen's University Belfast and the Campanile of Trinity College Dublin, before moving to a storied career that saw him become the president of the Royal Institute of the Architects of Ireland, the Royal Society of Antiquaries of Ireland, the Royal Hibernian Academy, and the Royal Society of Ulster Architects. Drew designed St. Anne's Cathedral in Belfast and worked on a number of Dublin's most famous public buildings: the Four Courts and both St. Patrick's Cathedral and Christ Church Cathedral in Dublin as well as Rathmines Town Hall, often labeled his most successful building. He was the only Irish architect invited to submit proposals for the Victoria Memorial in London and Liverpool Cathedral.

One of Drew's daughters, Catharine, became a pioneering figure in British women's journalism. She began her career in architecture as well, starting as an assistant editor for the *Irish Builder* before moving to London, where she wrote a weekly column for the *Belfast News-Letter* in the 1870s and gave a notable lecture on "Women and Journalism" at the 1894 conference of the British Association of Journalists

---

39. *Belfast News-Letter*, October 28, 1828; *Christ Church Belfast*; Blackwood, *Some Biographical Notices of the Rectors of Loughinisland*, 14–15. For Drew's romanticized recollections of his time in Broughshane, see *Belfast News-Letter*, December 28, 1869.

3. Thomas Drew. Source: Portrait by Robert Gaffikin, 1839.

in Norwich. Finally, another of the Drew's daughters, Arminella Frances, married the future Orange hero William Johnston of Ballykilbeg, a short-lived union that reflected Johnston's close ties to the Drew family. The Drews' seemingly happy family life was marked by personal tragedy. No less than eight of their eleven children died before Thomas Drew passed away at his son's house at 60 Upper Sackville Street in Dublin in October 1870 (his wife Isabella had died the year before).[40] The fact that so many of Drew's children died prematurely likely contributed to his increasingly fervent religiosity in the 1850s and 1860s, and bolstered his lifelong commitment to the religious education of Protestant children.

While Drew was not a particularly coherent ideologue, he had a set of core religious beliefs anchored by a rather conventional range of conservative theological, pastoral, and religious/political assumptions and commitments. What made Drew distinctive was the extremity of his expression rather than the novelty of his ideas. To use Boyd Hilton's pithy phrase, Drew worshipped Christ the king rather than God the watchmaker.[41] His God was omnipresent, interventionist, and all-powerful. In a sermon published in the late 1830s, Drew asked his congregants to reflect on why comets failed to strike the earth more often. In his view, this was clear evidence of God's active protection. Twenty years later, he expressed this idea in more explicitly political terms: "Thus in our day, no event takes place except by the permission of the Heavenly King. The nations are in His hand, and no devices prevail when the Lord is pleased to interfere."[42] Drew's God was drawn in a kingly image.

---

40. Biographical details for the Drew family are drawn from the following sources: *Belfast News-Letter*, October 24, 1870; Leslie, *Clergy of Connor*, 311; Baxter, *Drews of Drumlohan Townland*; "Drew, Thomas (Sir)"; McGuire and Quinn, *Dictionary of Irish Biography*, 3:463, 465–68; Hamilton, "'Her Usual Daring Style,'" 39–42.

41. Hilton, "Evangelical Social Attitudes," 122; Brown, "Victorian Anglican Evangelicalism," 675–704; Hilton, *Age of Atonement*.

42. Drew, *Thoughtful Protestantism*. For two clear examples of Drew's belief in an active and interventionist God, see "The Existence of God," and "The Omniscience of God," *Sermons on Various Subjects*, 1, 11–43.

Thomas Drew was a Low Church evangelical, one of a fast-growing cohort of ministers who came to dominate the mid-Victorian Church of Ireland. Given the complexity of the nineteenth-century Irish religious landscape, I want to clarify some key terms here. As Alan Ford has noted, it is important to note the distinctive nature of the Church of Ireland, where divisions between High and Low Churchmen often were rooted in different emphases and issues than they were in the Church of England.[43] By any standard, Drew certainly had Low Church inclinations; he was highly suspicious of the High Church emphasis on episcopal authority and the right practice of public ritual. In its stead, he stressed the power of a simple and vital faith, one that focused on the promise of the afterlife and bringing the Bible actively into the lives of his congregants. As Drew advised one Broughshane parishioner whose family was going through a difficult time: "If it be true that all such trials are sent by our Heavenly father to draw us closer to him, . . . then doubtless at such times our prayers should be more present and fervent for grace as should our devotionship to God's cause should be more energetic than ever."[44]

This brings us to Drew's evangelicalism, a term that has received a great deal of scrutiny from historians of religion.[45] There was nothing original about the basic theological views of Protestant evangelicals, which were shared across a wide variety of Protestant denominations. What distinguished evangelicals from their coreligionists was the emphasis they placed on a particular set of beliefs and the warmth with which they practiced their faith.[46] The historian David Bebbington has provided the most famous definition, arguing that the

---

43. Ford, "High or Low?," 99; Nockles, "Church or Protestant Sect?," 457–63. See also Farrell, "Contested Histories," 95–107.

44. Thomas Drew to Miss Duffin, n.d. [1832], Drennan-Duffin Papers, PRONI, T.1252/39. Courtesy of the Deputy Keeper of the Records, Public Record Office of Northern Ireland.

45. For a thoughtful review of the definitional controversy, see Carey, *God's Empire*, 149.

46. For a succinct discussion, see Hilton, *Age of Atonement*, 8.

four primary characteristics of evangelical or vital religion were conversionism (a focus on the individual's experience of conversion), activism (an emphasis on the need to share one's faith with others), biblicism (a belief that the Bible provides the foundation of all faith), and crucicentrism (the idea that Jesus died for sinners on the cross).[47] In theological terms, Bebbington's formulation works well enough as a description of Drew's core attitudes and beliefs. Drew's approach to the question of activism and conversion, however, highlights the more complex ways that evangelical beliefs operated in the material world. He ardently believed that Irish Catholics needed to be rescued from Roman Catholicism if they were to be saved. His active support for conversion efforts, however, was shaped by place and proximity as much as doctrine. A militant champion of efforts to bring Catholics to the Church of Ireland in Connacht, Drew made comparatively little effort to do the same in Belfast, where Catholics were apparently to be battled rather than brought to the faith. This underlines one of the limitations of Bebbington's definition, which undervalues the importance of both political and social context in defining who is, and crucially, who is not, considered evangelical.[48] In Victorian Ulster, the term was just as likely to be used to categorize stances on questions of Protestant politics as it was on strictly theological matters. While he always maintained that true religion and politics were inextricable, there is little doubt that, for Drew, politics were foundational. The Protestant constitution was to be defended at all costs.

Drew was an educated man who participated actively in Belfast's growing network of learned societies, and an engaged public intellectual with literary pretensions. His lectures, letters, and sermons are replete with historical and theological references, gleaned from books from his own extensive library. After he received his doctorate in divinity from Trinity College Dublin in 1842, he was often known as "the

---

47. Bebbington, *Evangelicalism in Modern Britain*, 1–10.

48. Bebbington, *Evangelicalism in Modern Britain*, 5–17. For a helpful discussion of the particular attributes of Irish evangelicalism, see Akenson, *Discovering the End of Time*, 12–14, 228–29.

good Doctor Drew," a label that was used by friends and enemies alike. His intellectual affectations notwithstanding, he often argued that the church needed men of right action rather than men of book learning, a stance he shared with numerous contemporary evangelicals. As he put it in one sermon, "It is not great talent, thrilling eloquence . . . that the Church needs, but ordinary talent combined with fervent prayer, devotion, meekness and patience."[49] Despite his penchant for confrontation, Drew was an able if undisciplined speaker (Inglis described his sermons as "fervent if not talented"[50]), and both the size of his congregation and the demand for published versions of his sermons speak to the popularity of his message.

Drew's warmth and sentimentality was a significant part of his appeal. His faith was an emotional one, typically couched in a language of nostalgia and feeling. Throughout his career—and particularly in his later years—he made it clear that his God was a living God, one whose love was to be experienced in simple and emotional terms. Drew's rhetorical affections were particularly focused on the young and those who taught them: "Those who feel as pastors, parents, and friends, as Sunday and daily School teachers, will hail with thankfulness, each auxiliary thinker and writer in the work of Scriptural instruction. . . . Ministers of the gospel should ever acknowledge themselves debtors to such friends of the child. Perhaps it will yet be acknowledged, that the most ingenious and affecting modes commending gospel-truth to the human heart, is to be found in the works professedly simple, whose only object was, out of infants' mouth to train to the perfection of praise in glory!"[51] Drew often used the same language in his pastoral work, telling one congregant to "let your heart be your Redeemer of your time (as far as is compatible

---

49. Drew, *Sermons on Various Subjects*, vol. 1.

50. Inglis, *Ireland in 1834*, 248–71.

51. Drew, "Recommendatory Preface," vi–vii. See also Drew, "The Light, the Protection, and the Bounty of God," *Sermons on Various Subjects*, 2, 3–5; Reverend Thomas Drew to William Blacker, August 24, 1847, Blacker Correspondence, PRONI, T.1638/10/8; Drew, "Vision of Holy Waters," 87–94.

with domestic duties) [and] be His also."[52] There was nothing novel about Drew's sentimental register: it was the common tongue of a generation of Victorian evangelicals steeped in romanticism. In an age of atonement, religion needed to be simple if it was to be understood and felt.[53] What made Drew's warm and plaintive tone so distinctive was its juxtaposition against his fierce anti-Catholic politics. Given Drew's success at Christ Church, it seems clear that his hyperbolic oscillation between sentimentalism and sectarianism appealed to the Orange artisans of Sandy Row.

Drew's warm temperament and public orientation led him to be an energetic participant in a second, overlapping arena in Belfast: politics. Known widely as a "political pastor," he was an active supporter of the Conservative Party and a lifelong Orangeman. He was successful in both. He was chaplain to two successive viceroys in Dublin Castle (the Earl de Grey and Lord Heytesbury) under Conservative ministries in the early 1840s, and served as the chaplain for the Belfast district of the Orange Order and deputy grand chaplain for the Grand Orange Lodge of Ireland in the 1850s and 1860s.[54] Drew's politics were defined by his ardent hatred of Roman Catholicism and his consequent determination to preserve the Protestant ascendancy in Ireland. Rooted in a deeply pessimistic reading of contemporary geopolitics, Drew's remarkable ability to discern a Catholic threat (or British betrayal) was the most consistent aspect of his politics. As we shall see, even in Victorian Belfast, Drew's anti-Catholicism stood out as extreme. As he put it in an 1858 pamphlet, "We live in days when imprudent and ensnared Protestants echo the insidious cry of Romanists, and hasten to erase all remembrance of our Protestant story; to blot out all

---

52. Thomas Drew to Miss Duffin, n.d. [1832], Drennan-Duffin Papers, PRONI, T.1252/39. Courtesy of the Deputy Keeper of the Records, Public Record Office of Northern Ireland.

53. Hilton, *Age of Atonement*, 19–20.

54. *County Antrim Grand Lodge of Ireland Reports*, 1847, 1852–1859, Museum of Orange Heritage, Belfast.

laws, inscriptions and prayers bequeathed by our illustrious fathers."[55] Political activism was the only way to protect Protestant position and power in Ireland, and for Drew, that meant the Orange Order and the Conservative Party.

Neither Belfast conservatism nor Orangeism was monolithic, however, and Drew had a keen understanding that his authority and power came from his ties to both Protestant elites and his working-class supporters. Throughout his career, Drew expressed intermittent frustration with the hesitancy and inaction of Belfast conservative elites, who he felt were too moderate and not nearly "Protestant enough" in their politics. He was a mentor and a clerical precursor to the independent Orangeism of William Johnston of Ballykilbeg, part of a Protestant populist challenge to the hegemony of the conservative establishment in post-Famine Ulster politics.[56] For all his Orange populism, however, Drew remained a loyal (if difficult) Conservative. It is telling that Drew's conservatism and Orangeism were two of the primary themes emphasized at his memorial service in October 1870.[57]

Drew's political focus was a critical part of his ministry. This was more than simply being a leader/member of the Orange Order. He was an active participant and leader in a series of short-lived Protestant political associations in the 1840s and 1850s. The most famous of these was the Christ Church Protestant Association (1854–58), where Drew tilted at a wide variety of anti-Catholic windmills at meetings designed to mobilize Belfast Protestant support against the Catholic threat to Protestant safety and the British Empire.[58] An emotive and

---

55. Drew, *Protestant Anniversaries*. While Drew's rhetoric was extreme, his views reflected what Andrew R. Holmes has characterized as the "dark mood" of Protestants upset and/or bewildered by the decreasingly Protestant nature of the British and Irish state. See Holmes, "Protestantism in the Nineteenth Century," 337; Fitzpatrick, *Descendancy*.

56. Bew, *Glory of Being Britons*, 194–222; Wright, *Two Lands on One Soil*, 284–382.

57. *Belfast News-Letter*, October 25, 1870.

58. Dawson, "Annals of Christ Church, Belfast," 179–84.

wide-ranging speaker, Drew's overwrought lectures and public sermons generated both a devoted following and a great deal of mockery and frustration among a wide array of opponents. While Irish nationalists focused on his anti-Catholicism, many liberals saw Drew as the epitome of the reactionary partisanship that kept Ireland from realizing its promise. In the midst of the 1857 riots, the *Northern Whig* described Drew as an "evangelical acrobat who collects crowds while he tumbles from this to the other world, swallows (Kentish) fire, balances Jacob's ladder, juggles Church and State about, and otherwise amuses himself in a holy manner."[59] Drew was certainly easy to mock, and his fusion of evangelical religion, anti-Catholicism, and conservative politics ultimately had a toxic and destructive impact in Belfast and the north of Ireland. It was also popular in Sandy Row and other parts of the divided town and province.

Christ Church opened its doors on July 28, 1833, with an impressive flourish of Anglican respectability. The church was consecrated by Bishop Mant, a ceremonial role that seems apt given the crucial part he played in the church's creation. Services were read by Drew and Macartney before Mant delivered what the *Belfast News-Letter* described as an "admirable sermon" about the importance of coming together for public worship. Three days later, the Reverend John Brown of Aberdeen gave a sermon to raise funds for the new church before an audience that included several figures from the town's civic and commercial establishment.[60] Christ Church clearly had considerable support from both the Church of Ireland and town elites. Drew's ministry also benefitted from an active cohort of influential congregants, a core group that included Richard Davison, a prominent barrister who, like Drew, had moved from Ballymena to Belfast, and Charles Lanyon, the famous English-born architect, men who proved to be lifelong supporters. Drew's success, however, would be measured by his ability to bring the growing working-class population

---

59. *Northern Whig*, August 27, 1857.
60. *Belfast News-Letter*, July 30, 1833.

of surrounding neighborhoods into the fold. Beyond the church's central location (not an insignificant variable), Thomas Drew's largely successful efforts to build a Protestant community at Christ Church hinged on three overlapping factors: his active and controversial Conservative and Orange politics, the creation of an extensive network of schools, and his outreach initiatives for working-class families. The remainder of the chapter examines the ways these forces shaped the making of this crucial Belfast community.

CHRIST CHURCH AND POLITICS

Drew's Orangeism was a significant cornerstone of his success at Christ Church, tying the church into existing political and social networks across the town. While Orange Order membership was nowhere near as widespread as it would be in the late nineteenth century, the Orange Order had a significant toehold in Belfast by the early 1820s. The ten lodges listed on the Grand Orange Lodge of Ireland's registry of warrants in 1823 were concentrated in the weaving districts of Ballymacarrett, Brown Square, and Sandy Row, reflecting the organization's solid presence in these largely working-class areas. Orange membership increased in Belfast in ensuing years, a product of the town's growing population and conservative Protestant antipathy to Daniel O'Connell's crusade for Catholic emancipation. The order's 12th of July celebrations became increasingly contentious in the 1820s, generating outbreaks of violence in 1822, 1825, and 1828.[61] There was a seemingly symbiotic relationship between the growth of Catholic politics and the Orange Order. By the end of the decade there were twenty-seven Orange lodges listed for Belfast, and in May 1832, fifty-three lodges marched through the town center to Ballymacarrett.[62] Drew's appointment at Christ Church both reflected and strengthened

---

61. For a detailed treatment of the 1825 riot and its aftermaths, see Wright, *Crime and Punishment in Nineteenth-Century Belfast*, 19–24.

62. Registry of Warrants for the Loyal Orange Institution of Ireland, 1823, 1828–29, Museum of Orange Heritage, Belfast; Royle, *Portrait of an Industrial City*, 86.

the Orange presence in Belfast. He provided a degree of legitimacy for the association, acting, as John Bew perceptively noted, as a linchpin between elements of the town's Tory civic leadership and Drew's working-class congregants and their neighbors in Sandy Row.[63]

One of the first speakers that Drew brought to the church was the Reverend Mortimer O'Sullivan (1793–1859), an Orangeman and one of the most famous anti-Catholic controversialists of the era. A Catholic convert, O'Sullivan was an influential writer for the *Dublin University Magazine* and chaplain to the Military School in Phoenix Park in Dublin. The Orange cleric returned to Christ Church in July 1834 and was a frequent visitor throughout Drew's ministry. Although we do not have the texts of these early charity sermons, O'Sullivan's reputation and views on Roman Catholicism were well-known.[64] At a Conservative Society meeting in Dublin in September 1834, he spent nearly three hours detailing the long history of the Catholic threat in Ireland and abroad, outlining a host of contemporary Protestant grievances, and defending the Orange Order against public attack. Four of his lectures that year were published as *The Case of the Protestants of Ireland*, which quickly became something of an ultra-Protestant textbook about the dangers posed by both Roman Catholicism and a British government seemingly willing to appease the Irish Catholic majority. The following year, O'Sullivan testified before the Select Committee on Orange Lodges, arguing that the Orange Order brought peace and stability to Ulster.[65] While he failed to convince

---

63. Bew, *Glory of Being Britons*, 16, 146. Drew played the same role for Reverend Tresham Gregg and William Johnston of Ballykilbeg, providing both Orange champions with a direct conduit to Sandy Row.

64. *Belfast News-Letter*, October 25, 1833; *Belfast News-Letter*, July 25, 1834. O'Sullivan's 1837 sermon against the national schools at Christ Church was published. See O'Sullivan, *Sermon Delivered in Christ-Church Belfast*.

65. *Belfast News-Letter*, September 12, 1834. O'Sullivan, *Case of the Protestants in Ireland*; Evidence of the Reverend Mortimer O'Sullivan, *Report from the Select Committee Appointed to Inquire into the Nature, Extent, and Tendency of Orange Lodges*, 31–83, 176–97. For his services to Christ Church, Drew made O'Sullivan an honorary life subscriber to Christ Church Libraries.

the British establishment, O'Sullivan's blend of confrontational anti-Catholicism and sentimental conservatism clearly inspired Drew, who listed O'Sullivan as a mentor throughout his career.[66] More directly for our purposes, he clearly viewed the controversial Orange cleric as a significant asset for his new church.

Drew's first foray into Belfast politics was the Brown Street School controversy of 1833, an episode that underlines Drew's immediate association with Belfast conservatism as well as the central place that education occupied in his own politics. The matter concerned the prospective relationship between Brown Street School, a school founded in 1817 to provide both free schooling and scriptural knowledge for the poor, and the new national school board established by the Whig government in 1831. Most Conservatives and many evangelicals opposed the national schools, arguing that Whig efforts to create nondenominational education raised the prospect of having Protestant students taught by Catholic teachers and unfairly limited the use of the Bible in instruction. The Reverend Henry Cooke, the influential minister of May Street Presbyterian Church, led the campaign against the national school system in Belfast. Many Presbyterians were more supportive of the national schools, and both the Ulster Synod and the school board of the Brown Street School negotiated the particular terms of their potential relationships with the new national school board throughout 1832 and 1833.[67]

Things came to a head at a series of meetings of the Brown Street School's annual subscribers in September 1833. At the initial gathering,

---

66. Invitations to figures like O'Sullivan could generate controversy. In June 1849 Robert Knox, the bishop of Down, Connor, and Dromore, prohibited O'Sullivan and Reverend Henry de la Willis, the anti-Catholic incumbent in Portadown, from speaking at St. Anne's and Christ Church, respectively, because they had not received the bishop's consent. The "inhibition of Dr. Mortimer O'Sullivan" generated a moment of predictable outrage in Orange circles. See Dawson, "Annals of Christ Church, Belfast," 115–20; *Belfast News-Letter*, June 19, 1849; *Belfast Protestant Journal*, June 23, 1849.

67. See Holmes, *Henry Cooke*, 94–112.

Cooke seemed to support the board's decision that the school be transferred to the national educational board, moving the meeting's adjournment so that the question could be reconsidered. When the subscribers next met, however, Cooke had changed course, opposing the transfer of the school to the national board. According to the *Belfast Commercial Chronicle*, the meeting was attended by "great numbers of obscure persons of strong political feeling," part of an effort, it was alleged, by the Belfast Conservative Society to intimidate its opponents and block the transfer of the school to the board. They succeeded, and the body elected several new more conservative figures to the Brown Street School Committee. One of these new members was Thomas Drew, the new incumbent of Christ Church. Drew was an active supporter of Belfast conservative politics from the first days of his ministry.[68]

Drew's penchant for public controversy first surfaced at a December 1834 meeting of the Commission of Public Instruction. The commissioners were in town as part of the Whig government's ambitious plan to complete a new religious census for Ireland. The census was designed to support the new system of national schools. Drew interrupted the proceedings early in the meeting, critiquing the commission's methods and accusing officials of undercounting Belfast's Church of Ireland population in favor of Catholics and Presbyterians. While many of the town's other religious leaders attempted to soften the terms of the debate, Drew refused to back down, repeatedly pointing out what he saw as deliberate inaccuracies in the reports.[69] Drew's confrontational attitude reflected a lifelong obsession with religious demography, expressed in repeated assertions that Irish population estimates always inflated Catholic numbers. He was hardly alone in this view, which mirrored broader Anglican anxieties about

---

68. Both James McKnight and Maurice Cross testified before the 1837 House of Lords Committee on Education that the Belfast Conservative Society had led efforts to block the transfer of the school and celebrated their victory on a subsequent evening. See Holmes, *Henry Cooke*, 109–10; *Belfast News-Letter*, September 20, 1833.

69. *Belfast News-Letter*, December 12, 1834.

demographic and emigration trends in nineteenth-century Ireland.[70] Nor was this simply an Anglican matter. When the commissioners returned to Belfast two months later, the Reverend Samuel Hanna, the minister of Third Belfast Presbyterian Church, protested the partiality of the returns.[71] The complaints ultimately proved to be successful. Faced with broad dissatisfaction with the methods and the results of the 1834 religious census, the government decided to use the 1831 figures instead.

Drew's links to the sectarian riots of July 1835 underline the close relationship between Christ Church and Orange Order politics in these early years. Drew arrived in Belfast in the immediate aftermath of the successful campaign for Catholic emancipation and the passage of the Reform Act of 1832, events that transformed the basic template of parliamentary politics in Ulster. The changes raised the stakes for parliamentary and street politics, encouraging both partisan competition and popular mobilization. This process was accelerated when O'Connell began his famous campaign to repeal the Act of Union. Repeal was a step too far for many Belfast moderates, who argued that the passage of substantial reform measures between 1828 and 1834 had proved that the Union could be made to work for Ireland. Ambivalent or opposed to repeal, figures such as James Emerson Tennent, the influential politician and statesman, and James McKneight, the editor of the *Belfast News-Letter* in the 1830s, left the Liberal Party, further strengthening the ranks of a Conservative Party already dominant in Belfast. In an important book on nineteenth-century Belfast politics, John Bew has argued that the 1830s saw the growth of a new type of conservatism in Belfast, more middle-class and British than scholars traditionally have allowed. A figure like Emerson Tennent, he maintains, had little to do with the reactionary anti-Catholic politics of a man like Thomas Drew.[72]

---

70. Roddy, *Population, Providence, and Empire*.
71. *Belfast News-Letter*, February 20, 1835; *Northern Whig*, February 19, 1835.
72. Bew, *Glory of Being Britons*, 126–60.

Bew is right to say that the dominant strain of Belfast Conservatism was as much Peelite as Protestant, but it was hardly "detached from a sectarian trajectory." The campaign for—and against—Catholic emancipation had linked parliamentary and popular politics as never before, as reformers and their opponents mobilized support through often contentious public display. As a curate in north Antrim, Drew had been actively involved in this effort in 1828–29, helping to create the Ballymena Brunswick Constitutional Club in an unsuccessful effort to block Catholic emancipation. The lessons of the late 1820s were quite clear, as both O'Connell and his ultra-Protestant opponents had demonstrated the potential power and efficacy of popular mobilization. This had even more purchase in Belfast in the 1830s, since some of Drew's Orange Order supporters were now part of an expanded electorate, forged when the Reform Act of 1832 extended the vote beyond the members of the town corporation to create a uniform franchise for the borough, adding hundreds of potential voters to the rolls. Emerson Tennent and other figures may have been ambivalent about their Orange supporters, but they could not ignore them. In short, if Drew's populist Orangeism was not the dominant strain of Belfast conservatism, it did place communal constraints on a more moderate conservative establishment. Relationships had to be maintained. Conservative political success was vital for Drew, since it provided the Orange leader and his supporters with a crucial degree of ideological cover, influence, and access to resources.

This is particularly evident when we look at municipal politics. The real power of Conservative hegemony in Belfast lay at the local level, where the Tories dominated the Belfast Corporation. Such a surface account of Tory power masks significant changes in town politics. In Belfast as elsewhere in Ireland, municipal reform between 1835 and 1841 created a more representative system of local governance, transferring power from the Donegall patronage clique to the middle-class conservative elites who dominated the new town council created in 1842. Politics in this era typically are associated with John Bates, the influential town clerk and de facto party leader, whose political skill and electoral manipulation helped the Conservatives hold a virtual monopoly of power in municipal politics in the early Victorian period. This is not hyperbole. Conservatives held all forty seats on the town council between 1842 and 1855, an exceptional record in Victorian Britain, where Liberals increasingly dominated urban politics.[73] Belfast conservatism was neither monolithic nor wholly reactionary. Bates and the town council initiated a number of substantial urban improvement schemes, including the construction of new market buildings, which moved several inner-city markets to a more propitious site between the town and the River Lagan, and the creation of Victoria Street, later the site of Belfast's town hall and major commercial premises. Conservative domination did have its political costs. As Sean Connolly has argued, Belfast Conservatives' determination to exclude Catholics and Liberals from power brought a real bitterness to local politics, one that took on an increasingly sectarian edge in the 1840s and 1850s.[74] This was an atmosphere that was conducive to the rise of a confrontational Orange populist like Drew.

The increasingly contested nature of Belfast politics can be seen in the poll books for Sandy Row in the 1830s, which also make clear the neighborhood's penchant for Conservative candidates.[75] The general election of December 1832, the first openly contested parliamentary election in nineteenth-century Belfast, featured the town's first election riot, with policemen killing four men involved in a melee on

---

73. Johnson, *Middle-Class Life in Victorian Belfast*, 3. For Victorian Britain, see Gunn, *Public Culture of the Victorian Middle Class*.

74. Connolly, "Rise and Fall of a Civic Culture," 28–41. Belfast conservatism had significant factions and fractures that very much depended on time and place. When Drew attempted to introduce an anti-Whig and sectarian tone to a public meeting about Queen Victoria's 1849 visit to Belfast, John Bates and other conservatives defeated his efforts quite easily. *Belfast News-Letter*, July 27, 1849; Connolly, "Like an Old Cathedral City," 581–83.

75. Belfast Poll Book, 1831–37—Durham Street, Sandy Row, and Old Malone Road, PRONI, D.2472/1/57–59.

Hercules Street.[76] With the stakes rising, political rivalries increasingly were articulated in communal terms. In 1833, for example, the *Belfast News-Letter* categorized confrontations between Catholic and Protestant crowds in both Peter's Hill and on York Street on Christmas Day as political partisanship.[77] Confessional allegiances were being turned into political identities and Drew and Christ Church were on the front lines of that process.

This was evident in July 1835, when Christ Church was at the center of one of the town's first major sectarian confrontations. Political feelings had been running high since January, when Conservatives won one of Belfast's two parliamentary seats (they would win back the other seat in a by-election in August 1835). The 1835 riots originated in a battle over sectarian public display, the type of dispute that would become depressingly familiar in ensuing decades. Orange activists in strongholds like Ballymacarrett, Brown Square, and Sandy Row celebrated the 12th of July with a vivid ritual display, erecting Orange arches and marching with fife and drum through their own neighborhoods. One group of Orangemen marched in procession to Christ Church, where they had been invited to hear a special sermon by Thomas Drew. This was the first time that special church services had been held for members of the Orange Order in Belfast (similar ceremonies were held in St. Anne's and at St. Patrick's in Ballymacarrett). A Catholic crowd gathered at the base of Durham Street during the service, challenging their rivals by throwing up a green arch at the very edge of Sandy Row. The partisan challenge apparently enraged a group of Orangemen, who rushed down the street to confront their opponents. Magistrates called out the military—both

---

76. For various accounts, see *Belfast News-Letter*, December 28, 1832; *Northern Whig*, December 27, 1832; Hirst, *Religion, Politics, and Violence in 19th Century Belfast*, 19–35; Budge and O'Leary, *Approach to Crisis*, 32, 41–44.

77. *Belfast News-Letter*, December 27, 1833. This type of competition was not confined to electoral or street politics. In a December 1833 report, the *Northern Whig* complained about Tory efforts to push Liberals from various public bodies across the town; see *Northern Whig*, December 9, 1833.

cavalry and infantry—to prevent the riots from getting out of hand, asking both parties to take down the offending arches. The Catholic body took down their display, but a number of the Orange militants refused to do likewise, throwing a barrage of stones at the soldiers as they advanced into Sandy Row. Christ Church quickly became a central point of resistance and conflict. Members of the Sandy Row crowd refused to disperse when the riot act was read and tragedy ensued when soldiers fired, killing four people. The dead included Anne Moore, a young woman who had been watching the melee near the gates of Christ Church.[78]

Drew's links to the riots of 1835 clearly reflect the polarizing politics of sectarian contention in early Victorian Belfast. Various newspaper reports of the coroner's inquiry into Anne Moore's death show that Christ Church was already seen as an Orange space. Contemporary commentators all discussed the Sandy Row Orangemen's march to the church, although most of the testimonies make a distinction between the more respectable congregants and the rioting crowd. While the *Belfast News-Letter* failed to mention Drew by name, the *Northern Whig* singled out the Sandy Row Orangemen as the only ones who marched in procession to church and explicitly blamed Drew (among other leaders) for the ensuing affray, focusing on the reckless ways the minister incited his audience. The paper argued that Drew's efforts were part of the Church of Ireland's broader campaign to gain working-class support in Belfast.[79] While there is no direct evidence that Drew was appointed because of his Orangeism, the 1835 riot and its aftermath make two things clear: (1) Drew's open identification with the Orange Order was a key part of his appeal for a sizable section of Sandy Row Protestants, and (2) only two years after Drew's arrival, Belfast liberals already identified Christ Church as a central site of Orange extremism. For friends and enemies alike, the church

---

78. *Belfast News-Letter,* July 13, 17, 1835; *Northern Whig,* July 13, 16, 1835; Dawson, "Annals of Christ Church, Belfast," 12; Barrow, *Tour around Ireland,* 33–35. Hirst, *Religion, Politics, and Violence in 19th Century Belfast,* 43–48.

79. Hirst, *Religion, Politics, and Violence in 19th Century Belfast,* 43–48.

was seen as a kind of proto-Orange lodge.[80] This was important in early Victorian Belfast's formative years, particularly after the Orange Order was formally disbanded in 1836.

CHRIST CHURCH SCHOOLS

A commitment to Orange politics was not the only thing that brought parishioners to Christ Church. During the first four years of his ministry, Drew and his congregation undertook a series of outreach initiatives designed to put the church at the center of community life. Christ Church schools were particularly important to this project. Drew believed that religious education was a fundamental starting point of community formation; a point he underlined in an 1838 letter to the secretary of the Sunday School Society. Sunday schools had a kind of multiplier effect for a congregation, he argued, providing religious education for children, linking families more firmly to the church, and inspiring wealthy members to support other outreach initiatives.[81] Christ Church Sunday School opened a little more than three months after the first service in the church, the first of what would eventually be an extensive network of both day and Sunday schools for boys, girls, and infants.

Drew's belief in the value of religious education was hardly novel. The multipronged push to create Sunday schools was the most successful social reform movement in nineteenth-century Britain, one of the primary vehicles for the spread of evangelical values.[82] Advocates were certainly successful in Belfast; by 1900, most churches had their own Sunday schools. This was not the case in 1833, however, and Drew and his supporters worked hard to create the infrastructure for the

80. Doyle, *Fighting like the Devil for the Sake of God*, 84.
81. Drew to the secretary of the Sunday School Society, April 1838; reprinted in *Christ Church Belfast*, 31–32. Drew's understanding of the importance of this issue for a congregation can be seen in a letter to a member of prominent Broughshane area family; see Thomas Drew to Miss Duffin, n.d. [1832], Drennan-Duffin Papers, PRONI, T.1252/39.
82. Snell, "Sunday-School Movement in England and Wales," 122–68.

new schools. One of the primary obstacles was the sheer size of Christ Church District, which was nearly seventeen miles in circumference, ranging south and west from the Shankill Road across the countryside to the edges of Cavehill. Drew and his supporters met these difficulties with ambition and creativity. The church's Sunday schools initially met in the homes of respectable artisans and farmers in rural and suburban parts of the district. This was a temporary solution, however, and in 1838 construction began on schoolhouses in Bower's Hill (Huss School House), the Shankill Road (Wickliffe School House), and in Ballymurphy townland near White Rock (Luther House of Prayer and School House). Each of these modest buildings was designed to be a multipurpose religious community center, also acting as a prayer center and hosting occasional lectures and sermons.

Drew's decision to build an extensive system of church schools was motivated by a number of overlapping factors: his ambition, his anti-Catholicism, his commitment to maintaining and improving the Church of Ireland's position in Belfast, and a belief in the necessity of moral transformation. Most of these factors were detailed in the first half of this chapter, but this latter point requires further explanation. Like so many of his contemporaries, Drew's thinking on this issue clearly was shaped by Thomas Chalmers, one of the dominant figures of the Victorian age. The Scottish evangelical was an influential public intellectual and theologian whose ministerial work and writing synthesized two of the dominant cultural nodes of the era: evangelical Christianity and political economy. Chalmers was particularly famous for his pioneering urban missionary work, notably his experiments with poor relief in St. John's Parish in Glasgow. This was shaped by the belief that religious education and systematic visitation forged the kind of religious unity and social harmony that produced close-knit and self-sustaining communities. The change that Chalmers and his allies sought was moral rather than material: Bibles were more important than bread.[83]

---

83. For Chalmers and evangelical approaches to nineteenth-century poverty, see Brown, *Thomas Chalmers and the Godly Commonwealth*; Dickey, "'Going about and Doing Good,'" 38–59; Hilton, *Age of Atonement*, 55–63.

Although Drew found Chalmers's synthesis of rural nostalgia, moralist political economy, and pastoral activism attractive, it is important to note that he was not in complete agreement with the Scottish leader, opposing the Malthusian ideas on population and poverty that underscored Chalmers's evangelical economics. More directly, Drew's initiative had local precedents: the Belfast Town Mission and other missionary initiatives in the city had used similar methods from the mid-1820s. As Jonathan Jeffrey Wright has argued, however, even if Belfast evangelicals disagreed with key aspects of his thought, a wide array of the town's reformers appreciated Chalmers's clear articulation of an activist project of urban spiritual renewal.[84] Drew was clearly one of these admirers, frequently citing Chalmers's latest publications to support his own initiatives in Belfast.

The creation of Christ Church Sunday School was also shaped by broader developments in Irish education. As we have seen, the Whig government established a new system of elementary education in Ireland in 1831, providing state funding for schools that put themselves under the control of a national Board of Education. Like most Church of Ireland ministers, Drew vehemently opposed the new national school system, particularly its approach to religious instruction. The new national schools were designed to be explicitly nondenominational. Students of all religious persuasions were welcome and all religious instruction was voluntary. To this end, scripture lessons were scheduled at the end of the school day so that students of different faiths could leave if their families were uncomfortable with the nature of religious instruction being offered. As Donald Akenson argued in his influential history of Irish education, this approach reflected the consensus view of a generation of educational reformers.[85]

Where the Whigs and their supporters saw moderation and reason, Drew and his conservative allies saw betrayal. Many of Drew's

---

84. For Chalmers and Ireland/Belfast, see Gray, "Thomas Chalmers and Irish Poverty," 93–107; Wright, *"Natural Leaders" and Their World*, 221–26. Thomas Chalmers laid the foundation stone for Fisherwick Presbyterian Church in 1827.

85. Akenson, *Irish Education Experiment*, 59–122; 392–402.

sermons underlined his vociferous opposition to the national schools, featuring emotional appeals about the critical importance of providing scriptural education for Irish children.[86] The possibility that students might receive no religious instruction was anathema to Drew, who believed that there was nothing more unnatural than separating religion and education. In his pessimistic view, the increasingly secular nature of society was a "fearful national sin" and a critical factor in the declining fortunes of the nation. Drew was particularly irked that the Bible would be excluded from secular instruction, an insult to the Word of God. In his view, this was particularly pressing issue for working-class parents, whose primary duty was to "train children for the skies" and whose poverty would make them more inclined to use the national schools.[87] Secularization was not the only threat posed by nondenominational education. Not surprisingly, even the theoretical possibility that Protestant children would receive religious instruction from a Catholic teacher was reason enough for Drew to categorically reject the entire scheme.

The vast majority of Anglican ministers refused to join the new national school system. In its place, they established their own national educational network in 1839, funded and organized through the Church Education Society. Speaking at the first meeting of the association, Drew argued that he was thankful for the new national board, saying that "it was the rod that tickled them" into necessary action. He believed that fighting against the national schools was a duty that promoted the "glory of God." "Scripture," he made clear, should not be confined to the beginning or the end of the day, but "should be infused in all their instruction throughout the whole day."[88] Drew was true to his word; he was an active and dedicated member of the Church Education Society for the rest of his life, regularly attending local and national meetings and delivering charity sermons to raise funds for its schools across the island.

86. Drew, *State Education Considered*, 29.
87. Drew, *State Education Considered*, 30. For a selection of other examples, see *Belfast News-Letter*, July 9, 1839, July 31, 1840, January 5, 1849, January 7, 1857.
88. *Belfast News-Letter*, July 9, 1839.

The issue was important enough to Drew that he broke publicly with Cooke in 1840, when the powerful Presbyterian minister and the Ulster Synod joined the national system after a decade of opposition.[89] Drew argued that Cooke's decision made little sense, since the national system insulted the Bible by excluding it during secular hours and put the instruction of Irish children under the control of a Board of Education that was an "anomalous, incongruous, unholy combination" of "Protestants, Romanists, and Socinians."[90] Drew returned to the fray in March 1841, when he published a sharply worded letter supporting the Reverend Tresham Gregg's challenge to Cooke over his supposed apostasy regarding national education.[91] While Cooke and Drew worked together on a number of issues throughout the ensuing decade, their alliance often was a tempestuous one, made all the more difficult by the forces of denominational competition and the two men's tendencies to speak warmly, sharply, and in public.

The Church of Ireland's effort to create a national system of elementary education was something of a mixed bag. The Church Education Society initially attracted considerable support from Irish landlords and other elites, funds that allowed the Church of Ireland to create a truly national system of schools. While the Christ Church schools were supported entirely by local donations, they were part of this alternative network, a system that the Church of Ireland claimed had 1,870 schools and 111,952 students in 1850, including more than 15,000 non-Anglican Protestants and nearly 38,000 Catholics.[92] This was a rare instance where the Church of Ireland could maintain that it was something of a national church. On the other hand, there were very real problems. The Church of Ireland's refusal to join the new state-sponsored national system generated considerable controversy with Presbyterians and Catholics alike, sharpening both

89. Akenson, *Irish Education Experiment*, 161–87.
90. Drew, *National Education*, 2.
91. *Belfast News-Letter*, March 16, 1841.
92. *Tenth Report of the Church of Education Society of Ireland*, 10.

interdenominational and sectarian tensions throughout the 1840s. In retrospect it is hard not to see this as a lost opportunity. And, of course, it ultimately was a failed one as well. With the government adamantly refusing to provide funding for the Church Education Society, the number of schools and children in Church of Ireland schools began to decline in the late 1850s. Concerned about resources, declining facilities, and educational quality, Archbishop Beresford recommended that leaders apply for aid from the Commissioners of National Education in 1860. While Drew and other diehards opposed the move, they failed to persuade their colleagues of the need to preserve the Church Education Society. In ensuing decades, Church of Ireland schools gradually moved over to the national school system. By the turn of the century, the Anglican educational experiment was over.[93]

Drew provided a detailed portrait of his educational thinking in a sermon delivered at St. George's Church in Dublin in April 1839. The lecture was later published in *The New Irish Pulpit*, a journal that featured selected charity sermons by ministers in the Church of Ireland. Drew contended that the success of the Sunday school movement was one of the era's great achievements, saving thousands of young souls from "the den of the profligate and the office of the harlot." He argued that Christian education depended on quality instruction, cautioning that many teachers were simply not up to the task. A good teacher must be moderate in temper and stick closely to the lesson: "The closer Sunday-school work is confined to its actual duties, the safer the teacher, the more healthy the administration, the less room for discontent, or scandal, or vain display."[94] In another lecture, Drew stressed that teachers had to be well prepared but avoid preaching, since "it was a great mistake not to pay great attention to asking questions or catechizing about what had been read or committed to memory."[95] Students had their responsibilities as well and Drew recommended

---

93. See Akenson, *Church of Ireland*, 201–6; Akenson, *Irish Education Experiment*.
94. Drew, "Sunday School Teaching," 161.
95. *Belfast News-Letter*, April 6, 1867. See also Drew, *Sermon Preached at the Request of the Committee of the Protestant Orphan Society*, 7–16.

that teachers provide advanced notice about what particular passages would be taught the ensuing Sunday so that students could prepare, particularly since "the pupil should be encouraged to pass no word or passage without understanding it."[96] There is at least some evidence that Drew attempted to translate aspects of this vision into practice at Christ Church. When William O'Hanlon, certainly no friend of Drew's, visited the district in the early 1850s, he was very impressed with the infant school, particularly the ways that amusement and work were balanced in classroom instruction.[97]

Drew envisioned Sunday school as part of a broader campaign to bring Christian godliness and civility to Christ Church District. Sunday school teachers were supposed to be active and engaged members of the local community. He insisted that education must not confined to the classroom, arguing that teachers should visit their student's homes on a quarterly basis (and more frequently if illness prevailed) and interact with knowledge and warmth with both the children and their families when they encountered them on the street. A good teacher was one of the minister's strongest allies, working closely with both pastor and parents in mutual regard for the children in their care. Drew's vision for Sunday school was an ambitious one, winning souls and in the process creating "the great moral results—while proper habit, generous motive, exemplary deed and universal order are propounded, exemplified, and encouraged."[98] Moral transformation was what was important to Drew. He believed that bread without Bibles would not bring true happiness.[99] Working-class members of the congregation might have had different priorities.

It is no accident that Drew stressed love, humility, and order in his sermons and public speeches. His vision for education was a fundamentally conservative one, imbued with the condescension of class-based hierarchies. Hannah More's works on Christian self-improvement

96. Drew, "Sunday School Teaching," 161–62.
97. O'Hanlon, *Walks among the Poor of Belfast*, 29.
98. O'Hanlon, *Walks among the Poor of Belfast*, 164.
99. Hilton, *Age of Atonement*, 128.

were well represented alongside exemplary Christian biographies and classic Protestant histories in the published catalogs of both the juvenile and adult libraries established by the congregation in 1836.[100] Like More, Drew found modern education far too secular, providing "a heap of information" but little material for thought or spiritual reflection. In a published sermon on state education, he later celebrated her view that working-class people needed a basic and practical education leavened by the Word of God rather than a high literary one. He put it more forcefully at a September 1842 meeting of the London Hibernian Society, saying that teaching scientific accomplishments to poor children was like training seamen to be wealthy merchants or footmen to be "ladies of quality"; church and state had a duty to prepare working-class children for salvation.[101] Despite the jarring hyperbole, Drew's belief in the importance of providing a useful education for working-class people was broadly shared in Belfast and across Britain and Ireland, and not only by middle- and upper-class conservatives. As both Jane Humphries and Emma Griffin's research into working-class autobiographies has made clear, most British—and presumably Irish—working-class families seem to have appreciated the practical and accessible nature of Sunday school education (if not the patronizing rhetoric and tone), not least because of the reduced cost for families that could not afford full-time schooling for their children.[102]

The importance of teaching poor children discipline and other social values at the core of middle-class Victorian mores is made clear through the practical administrative details involved in setting up and running the schools. Christ Church Sunday School opened at 9:30 a.m. each Sunday, with afternoon hours available at all locations. Christ Church Day School began at 10:00 a.m. and ran until 3:00 p.m.

100. *Catalogue of the Christ-Church Library, Belfast.*
101. Drew, *State Education Considered*, 26; *Belfast News-Letter*, September 6, 1842.
102. Humphries, *Childhood and Child Labour*, 364–65; Griffin, *Liberty's Dawn*, 178–80, 183–84. Both Jane Humphries's and Emma Griffin's research also make clear the limitations of the education offered, with Humphries stressing the ubiquity of violence meted out in classrooms across the United Kingdom.

each day, and tardy students were not to be admitted.[103] Timeliness was nearly as important a virtue as godliness. Families had to pay a penny per week for day school, although discounts were available for good attendance. While not insignificant, the cost seems to have been within reach for most working families. Students were separated by both gender and age, with infant schools designed for children between the ages of three and five and separate boys' and girls' schools for those over five.[104] The vast majority of students were from Church of Ireland families, but there were a few Catholic children who attended in the early 1850s, clear evidence of the relative scarcity of educational provision in mid-Victorian Belfast.[105]

Drew's belief that the schools' impact on the community should not be confined to the classroom found its most dramatic expression in Christ Church's annual children's day. Each Easter Monday, children from the various schools marched from Christ Church to places like the Botanic Gardens, Stranmillis, and White Rock for an afternoon of food, choral concerts, and biblical verse. Initiated in 1834, the celebrations wed Drew's evangelicalism, romanticism, and love for public spectacle.[106] Similar public ceremonies were common elements of church life in the late 1830s; children's processions and call-and-response sessions were featured at the foundation ceremonies of the church's various schools and prayer stations.[107] In their reports on the festivities, both Drew and contemporary Belfast newspapers emphasized the children's piety, discipline, and self-restraint, a narrative of civility and progress that was drawn in sharp contrast to traditional "gatherings of riot and folly on Cavehill."[108] As Dominic Bryan, Sean

---

103. Dawson, "Annals of Christ Church, Belfast," 72–73.
104. Drew, *Selection of Psalms*, 88.
105. McIntyre Diary, September 1853, PRONI, D.1558/2/3/27.
106. For a more detailed treatment of Christ Church's children's day schools, see Farrell, "Feed My Lambs," 43–58; Hirst, *Religion, Politics, and Violence in 19th Century Belfast*, 41.
107. *Belfast News-Letter*, September 14, 1838.
108. *Belfast Commercial Chronicle*, April 10, 1844. See also Dawson, "Annals of Christ Church, Belfast," 45–52, 126–35.

Connolly, and John Nagle's recent work on civic identity and public space makes clear, these types of events were part of a broader civic effort to promote and enforce new, more respectable codes of behavior in early Victorian Belfast.[109]

While generally glowing accounts of these festivities doubtless were crafted from a position of evangelical and middle-class self-interest, it is equally true that "children of the loom" likely enjoyed the chance to escape the town for an outing in the country. Of course, we should not romanticize these events, for in many ways it is the limits and seeming contradictions of Drew's vision for poor children that are of interest. He was, after all, a man whose pragmatic evangelicalism combined practical support for his working-class congregants with stern lectures about the dangers of getting involved in collective action, and whose real commitment to religious education for plebeian boys and girls carried all the class assumptions of his conservative elite supporters.

There certainly was a ready market for the project. Christ Church officials claimed that 1,000 students attended church schools by the late 1830s and early 1840s.[110] While numbers reflect membership rather than regular attendance, a variety of sources chart the impressive growth of the system. The Church Education Society's annual reports indicate that enrollments grew from 300 in the early 1840s to nearly 1,100 students in 1855, a figure replicated in the 1861 *Belfast Directory*, which listed 270 students in the Day School and 900 for the Sunday School.[111] There was a degree of compulsion involved in this growth, since Christ Church congregants were expected to send their children to one of the various schools. Enrollments at the individual schools mirrored the city's broader demographic trends. Huss School on Bower's Hill (in the fast-growing, largely Protestant lower Shankill

---

109. Bryan, Connolly, and Nagle, *Civic Identity and Public Space*, 97–101.
110. *Christ Church Belfast*, 15; Dawson, "Annals of Christ Church, Belfast," 16–21.
111. Dawson, "Annals of Christ Church, Belfast," 70–71; Church Education Society, *Second Annual Report*, 94; Church Education Society, *Tenth Annual Meeting*, 61; Church Education Society, *Sixteenth Annual Meeting*, 56.

Road area) was the largest of the schools by the mid-1850s, while the Luther Daily School in White Rock barely survived.[112] On this basic level, at least, the success of the Christ Church schools is undeniable, and Drew's initiative provided a rudimentary academic and religious education for thousands of boys and girls in mid-Victorian Belfast.

These efforts did not go unnoticed. At an 1837 ceremony, Richard Davison, the congregational leader and future Conservative member of Parliament, celebrated Drew's dedication to the town's poor, saying "that as the Body without the Spirit is dead so faith without works is dead," and giving particular attention to the children in Christ Church schools.[113] Five years later, Macartney praised his educational initiatives in a written testimonial: "You saw the necessity of a scriptural education for a rising generation; and by unparalleled industry and perseverance, you raised such sums of money for the erection of schools, that those who were well acquainted with the means of the people were quite surprised by their magnitude. These schools, more especially the male, female and infant ones, attached to Christ Church, have flourished almost beyond anything that could have hoped for."[114] There were problems. While a July 1842 report praised the organization and importance of the Christ Church schools, it also outlined the difficulties in maintaining such an extensive network of schools on a narrow base of financial support (the schools only had nineteen patrons in 1842) and underlined the particular struggles of the Luther Daily School in White Rock.[115]

Many contemporaries were critical of the quality of the education provided at Christ Church. Walking through Sandy Row in 1855, the Reverend Anthony McIntyre, visiting various central neighborhoods for the Belfast Domestic Mission, questioned the civilizing impact of

---

112. Dawson, "Annals of Christ Church, Belfast," 12–15.

113. *Ulster Times*, April 1, 1837. For Davison, see *Belfast News-Letter*, February 22, 1869.

114. *Testimonials to the Character and Labours of the Rev. Thomas Drew*, 16–17.

115. Dawson, "Annals of Christ Church, Belfast," 70–73; *Ulster Times*, September 8, 1838.

Drew's Sunday school, observing two young girls playing marbles in the street and "conducting themselves very rudely." A Unitarian minister newly arrived from Dublin, McIntyre found it difficult to see any evidence of the moral improvement frequently cited by Christ Church supporters. In its stead, he found Sandy Row full of poor Anglican weaving families who took pride in the fact that they were Protestants but did not seem to have much knowledge of the Bible.[116] While McIntyre's observations were clearly shaped by his opposition to Drew's conservatism and association with the politics of sectarian confrontation, they remind us that the school curriculum was designed to strengthen the existing social order through the acceptance of class-based hierarchies and already potent notions of sectarian difference.

CHURCH EXTENSION AND OUTREACH

The creation of the Christ Church schools was part of a broader campaign to bring Belfast Protestants to church. By 1839, Drew had set up a series of prayer stations for the unchurched, a dispensary, helped to open the Ulster Magdalene Asylum, and had created a Dorcas Depot, where clothing made in the juvenile girls' school was sold at cost to parents. Drew was particularly proud of the Christ Church libraries. Amongst the nearly two thousand publications listed in the library's 1837 catalog are a number of texts that reflect Drew's pragmatic evangelicalism: books and pamphlets designed to help families struggling with aging, illness, and death—issues all too familiar to working-class families in the Hungry Forties.[117] Life was indeed quite tenuous in early Victorian Belfast; of the first seven children baptized in Christ Church in 1837, two died and three had to have private ceremonies because of "the dangerous illness of the infant."[118] These deaths must

---

116. Diary of Anthony McIntyre, December 16, 1855, PRONI, D.1558/2/3/69, 292–94.

117. *Catalogue of the Christ-Church Library, Belfast*. For overviews of these efforts, see *Christ Church Belfast*, 18–31; Dawson, "Annals of Christ Church, Belfast," 11–15.

118. Baptism Records, Christ Church, 1837, PRONI, MIC.583/23.

have had a particular poignancy for Drew, whose own daughter, Frances Anna, died in infancy in 1836.

One of the ways that working-class families attempted to see their way through difficult times was by using any of the forty-one pawn shops in Belfast by the mid-1830s.[119] Drew was concerned that many of these pawnbrokers gouged his parishioners with high interest rates. This put him a rare agreement with the prominent Belfast liberal Robert J. Tennent, and William Crolly, the Catholic bishop of Down and Connor, both of whom castigated the negative impact of pawnbrokers before the 1836 Parliamentary Commission on the Irish Poor. Inspired by the formation of a public loan office in his native Limerick, Drew wrote a public letter in May 1837 to advocate for such a scheme.[120] While this effort failed to take root, Drew already had gained a reputation as a forceful advocate for the town's Protestant working-class families. When a fever epidemic swept across Belfast in the summer of 1837, Drew recalled a recent meeting that he had with some of the town's suffering handloom weavers and their families, saying that the "starving creatures" had behaved admirably given their desperate situation. He implored town leaders to devise a more effective way to relieve the poor, arguing that fever had taken away so many heads of households that "many children, particularly females, were wandering around town unprotected."[121] Events in the 1840s would further test the boundaries of Drew's seemingly compassionate conservatism.

If Drew believed that religious education was the foundation of the Christ Church community, church extension was the project most closely associated with his name. Nearly every one of the twenty three

---

119. Kinealy and Mac Atasney, *Hidden Famine*, 22.

120. For pawnbroking in Belfast, see *Report on the Irish Poor*, 19–20; Dawson, "Annals of Christ Church, Belfast," 22–24. For Drew's public letter, see the *Ulster Times*, May 4, 1837; *Belfast Commercial Chronicle*, May 8, 1837. A week later, a "Pawnbroker" wrote in response, critiquing Drew for his many misstatements about the town's pawnbrokers; see *Belfast Commercial Chronicle*, May 15, 1837.

121. *Belfast Commercial Chronicle*, June 14, 1837; *Dublin Mercantile Advertiser*, June 19, 1837.

individual testimonials written to support Drew's 1842 nomination for a position in Birmingham attests to his creative and effective efforts to build churches and bring religion to the unchurched.[122] There was certainly nothing particularly novel about his approach, which called for the construction of new churches and the expansion of existing ones (a project well under way in Belfast by the time he arrived in 1833), increased visitation, and the creation of prayer stations and other outreach centers.[123] As Mark Smith has argued, church construction was the characteristic Anglican response to urbanization.[124] In this project, as elsewhere, Drew's primary contributions involved energy and commitment rather than innovation.

In September 1838 Drew published a public letter in the *Ulster Times*, in which he detailed the plight of Belfast's Protestant working-class families and the real need for the provision of new churches, particularly in the town's fast-growing industrial districts. Later reprinted as *The Church in Belfast*, this letter is one of the most coherent and fully developed examples of Drew's thinking on the subject. He opened the letter with a predictably pedantic critique of a recent population estimate that he believed overestimated the Catholic population in the town. Drew proceeded to outline a program of action for the Church of Ireland, citing his own congregation as kind of urban model for what could be done. Opponents had argued that the poor would not fill up its free pews—Christ Church demonstrated the falsehood of this claim. Drew claimed that his plebeian congregants gladly took their free pews and generously donated money to worthy causes, citing one woman in his congregation who sold herrings and then donated money to the poor every month. With characteristic drama, Drew argued that if "we cannot have high churches, we should

122. *Testimonials to the Characters and Labours of the Rev. Thomas Drew.*
123. For example, see the mid-1830s correspondence between Mant, Archbishop Beresford, and Thomas Hincks, curate of Belfast, Armagh Diocesan Papers, PRONI, DIO/1/25/B/20–25a. The 1833 consecration of Christ Church is perhaps the best testimony to Mant's commitment to church extension.
124. Smith, *Religion in an Industrial Society.*

have big churches."[125] To reinforce the gains wrought by church construction, he sketched a vision for a ministry that was active, energetic and practical, stating that to be successful, a minister had to be an advocate for the poor, to be "one with his flock."[126] Drew's ideal of a unified Protestant community was rooted in a conservative model of social consensus.

In the letter, Drew also called for the creation of an organization that would allow the church to better articulate its efforts at urban parish renewal. He pushed the idea at a series of public meetings, gaining the support of many of the town's ministers, most notably William McIlwaine of St. George's Church and James Morgan of Fisherwick Presbyterian Church.[127] To put institutional flesh on the bone, Bishop Mant scheduled a meeting to discuss the subject at Christ Church on December 19, 1838. The meeting gave rise to the Church Accommodation Society of Down and Connor, a body designed to mobilize resources needed to build churches that would provide for the spiritual needs of the poor. The society was, as Dawson later put it: "A practical effort to derive from private benevolence the aid which Parliament refused."[128] Although the initiative was common enough in Britain, it was more novel in Ireland, where neither cities nor Anglicans were particularly numerous.[129] The call clearly struck a nerve with the Belfast elite; £4,500 was pledged at the first meeting, which was attended by leading luminaries like Lord Donegall and Emerson Tennent as well as all of the town's Church of Ireland clergymen and several Presbyterian ministers.[130] Here was one area of public life where Thomas Drew and Belfast's largely middle-class elites could agree. An active

---

125. *Ulster Times*, February 5, 1839.
126. Drew, *Two Sermons Preached Before the University of Dublin*.
127. *Ulster Times*, September 13, 1838.
128. Dawson, "Annals of Christ Church, Belfast," 48.
129. Wolffe, *God and Greater Britain*, 85.
130. *Ulster Times*, December 20, 1838; Dawson, "Annals of Christ Church, Belfast," 48–57. Dawson's Drew-centered narrative unfairly marginalizes Mant's earlier efforts to build support for church extension.

supporter of church extension, Bishop Mant may have presided over the Christ Church meeting, but this was Drew's project. It proved to be a remarkably successful one; by the time it was dissolved in 1843, the society had raised £17,500 for church construction and poor relief, dispersing the funds for church construction through twenty grants.[131] The resultant construction of an array of architecturally plain but well located houses of worship helped to transform the city's physical, social and spiritual landscape—placing the Church of Ireland at the center of a number of working-class districts in the rapidly developing town.

Simply building churches was not enough. Working-class men and women had to be enticed to attend; a problem that bedeviled the Church of England in urban parishes across Victorian Britain. Following Chalmers's well-publicized efforts in Glasgow, a number of ambitious and energetic ministers working in urban parishes attempted to use regular visitation to create a greater sense of cohesion and community in new industrial centers. While the results of such projects were uneven at best, they were at the heart of an Anglican response to urbanization that was more dynamic than scholars traditionally have allowed.[132] Systematic visitation and outreach efforts were central to Drew's pastoral mission. Like other urban evangelicals of the period, Drew used both lay and clerical visitation to keep in close touch with his congregants and he himself was a frequent visitor to sick parishioners.[133]

Drew was no pioneer. In Belfast, various domestic or home missions had proliferated throughout the town since the mid-1820s. The first of these, the Belfast Town Mission, or Society for the Relative

---

131. Drew, *Church in Belfast*; Mant, *Memoirs of the Right Reverend Richard Mant*, 380–88; Acheson, *History of the Church of Ireland*, 152–53; Hempton and Hill, *Evangelical Protestantism in Ulster*, 112.

132. See Smith, *Religion in an Industrial Society*.

133. For one such instance, see George Posnett to Thomas Drew, March 19, 1855, Loyal Orange Order, Belfast County Minute Book, 1851–1859, Museum of Orange Heritage, Belfast. In the letter, Posnett thanks Drew for his close and constant care for his late father.

Improvement of the Poor of the Town of Belfast, was formed in 1827. Led by the Reverend R. J. Bryce, the principal of the Royal Belfast Academical Institution, this project involved a wide range of evangelical Presbyterian and Anglican ministers and businessmen (it became an explicitly Presbyterian organization in 1843). While a number of groups formed various home mission societies with differing emphases over the ensuing decades, it was the Belfast Town Mission that provided the local prototype.[134] The basic idea of the home mission was to bring religious and moral instruction to working-class families that might not otherwise see the inside of a church; to use practical Christianity to combat the various social problems associated with urbanization: drinking, gambling, and crime. This was to be achieved by the creation of what we might term a visitation culture in working-class districts. Rooms were rented to establish stations for weekly or biweekly prayer meetings or religious exercises. Ministers, licentiates, and lay scripture readers regularly visited families in their homes, distributing tracts and simply talking with men and women about the problems they faced. While there were some ministers and scripture readers who later used this as an opportunity for proselytizing, this was not a major focus of the missions in Belfast, which concentrated on making nominal Protestants "less nominal." The early Belfast Town Mission was particularly nonconfrontational. In 1828 the committee prohibited its agents from generating controversy, advising readers to carry a Douai-Reims Bible as well as Protestant scriptures with them as they walked from house to house.[135] Taken as a whole, the Belfast domestic missions were, in Janice Holmes's words, largely coordinative rather than conversionist networks.[136]

Visitation statistics suggest the remarkable energy and resources poured into these efforts. In 1836–37, one agent reported that he had made 1,989 visits (more than half of which were to the homes of the

---

134. *Report of the Belfast Town Mission*, 1828, 1830, 1833–38, Gamble Library, Union Theological College, Belfast; Sibbett, *For Christ and Crown*.
135. *First Annual Report for the Society for the Religious Improvement of the Poor*, 8.
136. Holmes, "Irish Evangelicals and the British Evangelical Community," 210.

sick), attending 315 prayer meetings and 215 reading meetings. The organization's reach expanded dramatically between 1835 and 1845, when the Belfast Town Mission reported that it distributed 32,953 religious and temperance tracts that year, sold 355 Bibles at reduced cost, and held 1,051 religious services with an estimated 60,000 people in attendance.[137] By this time, evangelical visitation and performance was an integral part of Victorian urban culture: in 1852 the Belfast Town Mission claimed that its missionaries made 34,770 home visits and held 2,176 meetings with 114,470 people in attendance. An 1855 report in the *Irish Presbyterian* claimed 31,828 visits and 1,670 meetings.[138]

Drew certainly thought that visitations were essential. Like an increasing number of Belfast ministers, Drew was a frequent visitor to the homes of his congregants, and his house visits were celebrated in the many testimonials offered to the Christ Church minister both during and after his life.[139] Drew's pastoral activism and work ethic were characteristic of a new cohort of Belfast evangelical ministers. The Reverend James Morgan, the minister of Fisherwick Presbyterian Church, walked ten to fifteen miles per day visiting sick parishioners, a duty he described as a "serious, arduous, and constant labour."[140] Given the size of his congregation and the geography of his parish, Drew could not hope to visit all of his congregants on a weekly basis. To supplement his own efforts, the church employed at least two lay scripture readers to help Drew provide this kind of regular contact, and it is clear that they were central to his vision of a successful church community.

---

137. Holmes, "Irish Evangelicals and the British Evangelical Community," 210.

138. O'Hanlon, *Walks among the Poor of Belfast*, 157–58; *Irish Presbyterian* 3, no. 34 (December 1855): 327–28.

139. From the 1842 testimonials, for example, letters from William Graham Cole, James Spencer Knox, and Arthur Macartney all highlight Drew's pastoral efforts in Belfast: see *Testimonials to the Character and Labours of the Rev. Thomas Drew*, 5–6, 12–13, 16–17. See also *Belfast News-Letter*, October 26, 1870.

140. Morgan, *Recollections of My Life and Times*, 85. For a good discussion of the intensity of the middle-class work ethic in Victorian Belfast, see Johnson, *Middle-Class Life in Victorian Belfast*, 80–90.

The ambitious minister was not content to work within the limits of his own parish, and Drew cooked up plans for a domestic mission for the Church of Ireland in Belfast shortly after he arrived at Christ Church. This was bound to create some problems. Although a number of urban missions had been created within the structure of the established church since the early 1820s, these efforts often generated tensions with more hierarchically minded High Churchmen concerned with the greater use of lay visitors and various lines of episcopal authority. This was certainly the case in Belfast, where Drew's plan for a Church Home Mission in August 1836 was rejected by Bishop Mant, who was concerned about its emphasis on itinerancy and seeming lack of respect for existing parish boundaries. Drew withdrew his initiative with relative grace and with the aid of the Reverend R. W. Bland, then rector of St. George's Church, he resubmitted a plan for a Diocesan Home Mission the following year that received the episcopal approval. This was clearly part of a broader compromise between Bishop Mant and his evangelical clergy in the late 1830s, a productive (if often turbulent) alliance that saw the creation of the Clergy Aid Society, the Church Education Society, and the Church Accommodation Society in the diocese.[141]

These visitations should not be idealized. While it may be true that many working-class families were attracted to the messages of spiritual rebirth and middle-class respectability brought into their homes by ministers and missionaries, these types of networks might also be seen as an urban Protestant parallel to the surveillance culture that accompanied the so-called devotional revolution of the post-Famine Catholic Church in Ireland. At an October 1845 meeting of the Society for the Relief of the Destitute Poor, Drew argued that ministerial visits brought other benefits to the community, saying that

---

141. Mant's opposition to home missions was made clear in his 1834 charge. See Mant, *Memoirs of the Right Reverend Richard Mant*, 305–85; Acheson, *History of the Church of Ireland*, 160.

working-class families often cleaned their homes more thoroughly in anticipation of the minister's arrival. If employers would only do the same thing with their workers, they might significantly improve public health in Belfast.[142]

There was certainly an element of social control here that was no doubt resented by the proletarian inhabitants of these neighborhoods. While we do not have working-class voices to provide direct testimony, McIntyre's diary from his visits to working-class Belfast in the mid-1850s allows us to see another problem created by the multiple domestic missions crossing working-class Belfast in search of souls and congregants: denominational competition. While McIntyre was certainly sympathetic to Belfast's communities of active practical Christianity, his diary details a corrosive competition for the unchurched. In one case, he describes how a Presbyterian town missionary cut off one widow's family's access to relief when he found out that she was sending her children to a mission school associated with Unitarianism. Another account features the story of a Protestant minister who reproved children for attending the same school. McIntyre claimed that this typified the Church of Ireland in Belfast, which enforced obligatory Sunday school for its own congregants while trying "to draft off as many from other day schools as they can."[143] Evangelical efforts to bring a sense of community and vital religion to Belfast's Protestant working class clearly had a less than savory side.

We can use the 1852 religious census of Christ Church District to get a good sense of the general contours of Drew's new church community. While the district's Church of Ireland population certainly had its share of middle- and upper-class families, the occupational data in the census largely reflects the area's working-class orientation. Given the growing importance of textiles to the industrial economy

---

142. *Banner of Ulster*, October 7, 1845.

143. Diary of Anthony McIntyre, PRONI, D1558/2/3 (T.3858/197-201; 228–29; 369–70). Courtesy of the Deputy Keeper of the Records, Public Record Office of Northern Ireland.

TABLE 2

OCCUPATIONS (>10) LISTED IN THE CHRIST CHURCH CENSUS, 1852

Occupation	Parishioners
Millworker	457
Labourer	172
Weaver	105
Servant	89
Carpenter	46
Sewed Muslin Worker	44
Shoemaker	35
Dressmaker	23
Pensioner	20
Porter	19
Dealer	18
Mechanic	17
Clerk	14
Grocer	13
Merchant	12
Flaxdresser	12
Smith	11

Source: Christ Church Census, 1852, PRONI, CR1/13D/1.

(Belfast had thirty-two linen mills with five hundred thousand spindles by 1860),[144] the domination of textile-related occupations in the district should come as no surprise.

Nearly 56 percent of the men and women listed in the census worked in occupations directly connected to the textile industry—millworkers, weavers, sewed muslin workers, and flaxdressers. Among the jobs listed, millworkers are numerically dominant, with roughly three times as many listed as any other single occupation. While there were male millworkers, the vast majority were women, often younger (in their teens and twenties), unmarried, and/or widows. Married women above the age of thirty were less common in the mills,

144. Maguire, *Belfast*, 31–33.

a pattern echoed in textile production across Victorian Britain. The Smith family of Mill Loanen in Sandy Row might be cited as a fairly representative household. In 1852 William Smith was a fifty-five-year-old weaver, whose two daughters, Margaret and Mary, ages twenty and sixteen, respectively, worked in the mills, while his wife, Margaret, lived at home. The Smiths had a lodger, Catherine McCusker, an eighteen-year-old woman who sewed muslin garments. Far more than in other parts of the United Kingdom, Belfast textile production relied on cheap female labor.[145]

Women constituted more than 50 percent of the congregants listed in the church census.[146] Christ Church seems to have been much less dependent on women than its contemporaries in Victorian Britain, where women typically made up roughly 65–70 percent of church membership in urban congregations. In the Scottish city of Stirling, often cited as an example of a hitherto underappreciated male religiosity, 59 percent of the communicants between 1848 and 1902 were women.[147] The Christ Church congregation clearly was less feminine than most of its Protestant contemporaries in Britain. Drew's combative style and ties to the Orange Order seem to have attracted a disproportionately masculine congregation in west Belfast.

Despite the dominance of the textile industry, Christ Church featured a notable degree of occupational and class diversity—the census lists 158 different occupations, including two chandlers, a professor of music, and an umbrella maker named Eliza Gaskin, a fourteen-year old girl who lived in Wylie's Place off Durham Street. Taken as a whole, the census reminds us of the relative intimacy of early Victorian Belfast as well as the gradual and sectional nature of technological change, with millworkers and other factory workers living alongside

---

145. For the Irish linen industry, see Gray, *Spinning the Threads of Uneven Development*, and Cohen, *Warp of Ulster's Past*.

146. Christ Church Religious Census, 1852, PRONI, CR1/13D/1.

147. For an interesting overview of the issue, see Brown, *Death of Christian Britain*, 156–61. Callum G. Brown's point about Stirling is based on Jeffrey, "Women in the Churches of Nineteenth-Century Stirling."

shoemakers, blacksmiths, carpenters, dressmakers, and weavers. It also reminds us that for all its reputation as a church that catered to the Protestant working class, Christ Church had important middle- and upper-class congregants. While these men and women lived in different worlds, they were in the same room at least once a week, a fact that gave rhetorical force to Drew's appeals to Protestant unity.

This was a religious census, and, accordingly, a disproportionate number of the questions had to do with that subject. Given the attention and resources various Protestant churches had put into church construction and extension since the 1830s, church attendance was clearly one of the most critical issues facing the church, and it was particularly crucial for evangelicals like Drew and his lieutenants. The publication of the 1851 Religious Census for England and Wales made this doubly important, since disappointment over plebeian church attendance figures reinforced widespread anxieties about the British working classes and led to a great deal of public criticism of the established church in particular.[148] Within the Christ Church census data, we have complete church attendance records for six of the seven districts included in the survey (and spotty data for the seventh). While they focused on the need for improvement, Drew and his colleagues should have been fairly happy with the results; 64 percent of the people listed in the Christ Church census reported that they attended church, with nearly half owning Bibles and 40 percent having prayer books.[149] This certainly compared favorably with urban districts across the United Kingdom; all eight London boroughs, Birmingham, Manchester, Leeds, Sheffield, and Bradford had church attendance records well under 50 percent.[150] Recent scholarship on the 1851 Religious Census has underlined the degree to which the census understates the importance of religion to various British populations. As Mark Smith has argued in his important study of religion and industrial development

---

148. Bebbington, *Evangelicalism in Modern Britain*, 108.

149. Christ Church Census, 1852, PRONI, CR1/13D/1; Doyle, *Fighting like the Devil for the Sake of God*, 22.

150. Bebbington, *Evangelicalism in Modern Britain*, 107–9.

in Oldham, interpreting the data is really a matter of perspective, since "when viewed as a measure of the church-going population rather than of the number of absentees [the census is], a tribute to the strength of the churches" rather than the weakness that has long been the basis of the standard "pessimistic thesis."[151] Still, the same factors which these scholars persuasively cite would hold equally true in Belfast, so 64 percent seems all the more impressive. Christ Church lay at the center of community life in west Belfast.

The fusion of anti-Catholicism, conservatism, and evangelicalism outlined in this chapter is best seen in Drew's advocacy for the Protestant Orphan Society, a Church of Ireland organization founded in Dublin in 1828 to protect orphans from poverty, illiteracy, and the dangers of Roman Catholicism.[152] The association's goal of defending and supporting vulnerable Protestant children in Ireland clearly inspired Drew. It was he who founded the Belfast auxiliary of the Protestant Orphan Society, and many of his most eloquent and extensive commentaries on childhood and education were statements of support for the organization. At one long lecture at an auxiliary society meeting in Belfast in November 1844, Drew sketched out a global history of societal commitment to fatherless children and to widows, citing the biblical narratives of Esther and Obed-Edom as well as more recent historical examples like August Francke, the German ragged school pioneer, and George Whitefield, the famed evangelical. The fact that Whitefield's Bethesda Orphanage in Savannah, Georgia, was widely criticized for the severity of its disciplinary regime serves as a nice reminder of the potential gap between Drew's rhetoric and social reality. The same talk featured multiple examples of vulnerable children in desperate need, claiming that God's favor only fell upon those nations that provided for orphans. Drew's aggressive anti-Catholicism

---

151. Smith, *Religion in an Industrial Society*, 268–69. For earlier views, see Cox, *English Churches in a Secular Society*; Joyce, *Work, Society and Politics*.

152. Cooper, *Protestant Orphan Society*, 14–17. For a model study of the seeming contradictions between the image and social experience of orphans and their families in Victorian England, see Murdock, *Imagined Orphans*.

was interwoven with these tales, perhaps most alarmingly expressed in the lecture with an extended discussion of the fifteenth-century Hussite Wars, where a proto-Protestant army opposing a papal crusade assumed the name "The Orphans," a timely reminder, Drew told his audience, for the constant need for Protestant watchmen in Ireland.[153]

This juxtaposition of weakness and vulnerability with the need for militant Protestant activism is a striking characteristic of Drew's rhetoric about the Protestant Orphan Society (and many other subjects). It certainly was not always there. In an April 1852 letter to the *Protestant Orphan Society Record*, Drew recounted the story of a daughter reunited with her mother on the quays of Belfast, bringing them home to the Christ Church congregation, where they opened a gift for the children: "The mother could not speak until she got time to inspect the beautiful box and its valuable contents. All my children were in raptures; never did the beauty of your Society shine out more touchingly than in the kindness to which that box testified. I am not ashamed to say, my own eyes filled with tears while the mother, exhibited, each gift which you had so judiciously and so thoughtfully supplied."[154]

In more public venues, however, this sentimental register of silent mothers and delighted orphans was framed alongside confrontational and explicitly political anti-Catholic rhetoric. Drew was hardly alone in this type of emotive volatility. As David Fitzpatrick suggested in *Descendancy*, shifting notions of defensive anxiety and aggressive militancy long have characterized Irish Protestant sectarian expression.[155]

Thomas Drew was an Anglican conservative with a hypersensitive and/or fantastical concern to find signs of Protestant decline and victimhood, a figure who dreamed of a revived Protestant manhood mobilized to counter the weakness of a British government that had allowed Roman Catholics to rise again in Ireland. The unfortunate

---

153. *Belfast News-Letter*, November 26, 1844.
154. Drew, *Protestant Orphan Society Record*, April 28, 1852.
155. Fitzpatrick, *Descendancy*, 13.

victims in many of Drew's grievance-fueled narratives were not illusory—if his portrait of the Catholic enemy was perverse, there was very real Protestant working-class suffering as well. In an 1840 sermon dedicated to the Protestant Orphan Society, Drew stated that nearly half of the children confirmed in his congregation in 1835 had lost both or one of their parents, a percentage that increased to nearly two thirds in 1839. In particular, he highlighted the difficulties that the absence or death of a father created for orphans (and widows), where lost wages provided a savage double blow to a family.[156] Drew doubtless underestimated the importance of women's wages and work, but his general point about the vulnerability of Protestant working-class families was clearly a central concern for Drew, and an understandable focus for the leader of a largely plebeian congregation in a rapidly changing town.

In another 1840 address intended to raise public awareness of the plight of poor Belfast weavers, Drew told the story of how a Ballymacarrett family had been reduced to destitution by the serious illness of the head of the household. While the family persevered and the weaver returned home from the lunatic asylum, they remained in debt to their landlord and lived on the brink of starvation.[157] These types of stories underlined the fact that the community and stability provided by Christ Church and other philanthropic agencies were critical resources in an era of social dislocation. If Drew's Protestant paternalism typically emphasized moral rather than material support, it was still vital in an early Victorian town that was only beginning to create a civic infrastructure to better regulate the social impact of widespread poverty. Given the power of Drew's defensive sectarianism, it is easy to see how the subject of Protestant orphans synthesized Drew's interests in working-class poverty with his binary vision of global religious

156. *Belfast News-Letter*, November 21, 1843. For the statistics on families, see Drew, *Sermon, Preached at St Peter's Church*, 13. Presumably, a fairly high proportion of the fatherless orphans were products of male abandonment rather than death.

157. *Belfast News-Letter*, June 9, 1840.

struggle. His advocacy for the Protestant Orphan Society was commonly couched in appeals to a common humanity, but it also fit his notion that Protestants needed to be more than simply anti-Catholic; they needed to support Protestants with energy and purpose. Only a proper religious education would prepare children to be the next generation of Protestant heroes, the watchmen so desperately needed if the Protestant constitution was to be defended in these difficult times. While this vision had toxic legacies in an increasingly divided town, it was not simply that, and it is clear that it was the shifting synthesis of Drew's pragmatic evangelicalism and volatile anti-Catholicism that shaped the formation of the Christ Church community.

Thomas Drew has been described as an evangelical minister who was more interested in defending the Protestant faith and restoring Protestant privilege than in generating spiritual and social change.[158] This is true in a general sense, but it is important to note that Drew saw the Orange Order as a vehicle for moral and spiritual transformation as well as Protestant politics. In his view, politics and religion were inextricably intertwined. By the late 1830s, Drew already was seen by many as a champion of the Protestant working class and the church's schools, particularly its Sunday schools, quickly became Belfast's largest single educational institution. We have few unmediated voices to gauge exactly how his congregants viewed their minister's advocacy, but they certainly voted with their feet and it is evident that Drew had successfully positioned Christ Church at the center of community life by the early 1840s. Schools were particularly critical to the church's success, helping to maintain ties to members of a Belfast civic elite often uncomfortable with Drew's confrontational Orange politics. If it was Drew's fervent anti-Catholic rhetoric that gained public notice, it was the church's location and his energetic pastoral work that created and sustained the life of a Christ Church community that was, after all, about far more than simply maintaining and strengthening a sense of sectarian difference. From his arrival in Belfast in 1833,

---

158. Doyle, *Fighting like the Devil for the Sake of God*, 20.

Drew's outreach initiatives combined with his Orange populism and a favorable location to make Christ Church the heart of a new Protestant community in Sandy Row. These same hybrid dynamics can be seen in the next two chapters, which focus on the nature and impact of Drew's evangelical Protestantism.

2

Speaking with a Clear Voice
Everyday and Political Sermons

Thomas Drew made his living and reputation with words. Sermons were particularly important to the Christ Church minister. Like most Protestant pastors, Drew saw preaching as central to his success; the most effective vehicle for expressing the gift and promise of God's grace to the members of his congregation. As he put it in a sermon published in 1839, "Every sermon we hear preached, or read, brings its claims upon us; every sermon preached, or read, is seed sown."[1]

Not all of these seeds were fruitful. Drew's public sermons were often explicitly confrontational and political in nature, featuring calls to defend Protestant Ireland against the threats posed by Roman Catholicism. Drew's most famous sermon was a violent anti-Catholic diatribe delivered to Belfast Orangemen at Christ Church in July 1857, a lecture that played a crucial part in the build-up to the unprecedented scale and destruction of the Belfast riots of 1857. Drew's performance that day was hardly exceptional. From the mid-1830s until his death in 1870, Drew regularly gave similar lectures at political meetings and churches alike, providing emotional and violent warnings about the need for Protestant vigilance in the global struggle against Roman Catholicism. Many of these were anniversary and/or occasional sermons, scheduled lectures delivered in church and attached to the holy days of the Orange ritual calendar—the 12th of

---

1. Drew, "Sermon X," *Sermons on Various Subjects*, 1:199.

July (which commemorated Williamite victories at the Battle of the Boyne and the Battle of Aughrim in 1690 and 1691, respectively), and the 5th of November (which marked the defeat of the Gunpowder Plot in 1605). Drew's Orange lectures celebrated the martyrs of the English Reformation and the Protestant heroes of the Williamite War in Ireland in the late seventeenth century to remind his supporters that they needed to fight to defend the Protestant ascendancy and keep their hard-won inheritance. It was this "Orange Drew" that dominated his public persona, celebrated for his staunch loyalty by his many friends and castigated for his fiery partisanship by his more numerous opponents. Thomas Drew's sermons consequently have been viewed as the demagogic tools of the prototypical "political pastor" or Orange cleric—a figure situated within the context of worsening communal relations in mid-nineteenth-century Belfast.[2]

While this emphasis is logical and largely persuasive, it can be misleading. For all the notoriety that Drew gained for the ferocity of his anti-Catholic rhetoric and staunch Orange advocacy, the majority of Drew's published sermons do not even mention Roman Catholicism or issues of contemporary politics, instead focusing on a rather conventional array of evangelical Protestant themes: the Bible's unmatched power to transform lives, the need for Christians to acknowledge the loving and powerful omnipresence of God and the sacrifice of Jesus Christ, the overarching importance of the spiritual life, and the need for humility, discipline, and patience in a world filled by temptation and evil. The anti-Catholicism of Drew's everyday sermons tends to be brief and comparatively sober; more condescending than the harsh and threatening rhetoric of his political public speeches and set piece Orange sermons.[3] This reflects the medium as

---

2. For examples of works that take this perspective, see Farrell, *Rituals and Riots*; Doyle, *Fighting like the Devil for the Sake of God*; Elliott, *When God Took Sides*.

3. For example, see his comment about how fortunate Protestants are to attend services where the sermons are given in a language they understand: "What a pity our poor brethren, of another Church, are still so enslaved under the absurdity of hearing what they do not understand." See Drew, "On Prayer," *Sermons on Various*

much as the message. Most of these sermons were designed for the social and spiritual reformation of his largely working-class congregation. Moreover, it should be noted that these rather conventional conservative evangelical Protestant sermons were grounded in a powerful, if often unspoken, opposition to Roman Catholicism. In mid nineteenth-century Belfast, as in many divided communities around the world, some things did not need to be said out loud. There is no shortage of evidence for Drew's powerful and ultimately destructive anti-Catholicism. It is equally clear, however, that Drew's mission was as much about the moral and social reformation of the Protestant working class as the politics of the Catholic threat. For Drew, the two were inextricably connected. As we have seen, the hybridity of his public religious expression was critical to Drew's success, allowing him to appeal to both working-class and elite audiences that had different sets of priorities.

With some notable exceptions, it was Drew's anniversary sermons that tended to be more overtly political and anti-Catholic and it is these that solidified his reputation as an ultra-Protestant champion in Belfast, Ireland, and beyond. In this regard, his preaching career reflects one of the common distinctions made in sermon studies—the difference in tone and content between everyday sermons designed to instruct congregants in Christian doctrine and the responsibilities of living a Christian life, and the "occasional" performances delivered at ritualized, set piece ceremonies to celebrate or commemorate historical, political, or religious events. It is occasional sermons that tend to have greater public impact and influence and there can little doubt that this is true of Drew's career as an anti-Catholic orator.[4] The fact that few of the published sermons of

---

Subjects, 1:173. For a discussion on the "exceptional nature" of Drew's 1857 sermon, see Dickson, *Beyond Religious Discourse*, 136–37.

4. Francis, "Sermons: Themes and Developments," 35. For the performative dimensions of Victorian sermons, see Gunn, *Public Culture of the Victorian Middle Class*, 118.

his early career even referenced Roman Catholicism, however, serves as a nice reminder that communities in Victorian Belfast were forged by positive religious associations as well as antagonistic religiopolitical ones.

This chapter examines Thomas Drew's sermons to better understand both his religious ideas and the ways they were put into practice in early Victorian Belfast. It opens with a close examination of his everyday sermons, written, performed, and published over the twenty-six years of his ministry at Christ Church. Preaching was at the heart of evangelical belief and practice, the primary mode of expressing the emotive truth of vital religion to congregant and unchurched alike. And yet, scholars have only recently begun to appreciate the critical importance of sermons as one of the central cultural and literary genres in the social life of Victorian Britain and Ireland. Sitting below a pulpit to hear a sermon was one of the only cultural experiences shared by men and women of different classes and conditions in nineteenth-century Britain, Ireland, and throughout the British Empire, a particularly important point given the cross-class nature of the Christ Church congregation.[5]

While historians have done excellent work on outdoor preaching in Victorian Belfast, comparatively little has been done on the everyday sermon.[6] Drew's published sermons sketch out the paternalist and conservative ideals of a godly society, one in which the wealthy were urged to provide charity and moral leadership for the poor. The real focus of his preaching, however, was on the poor themselves, who

---

5. For insightful introduction to the recent scholarship on sermons, see Gibson, "British Sermon," 3–30.

6. There is an insightful case study of an eighteenth-century Church of Ireland preacher in Belfast: see Gillespie and Ó Gallachóir, *Preaching in Belfast*. For two important studies of outdoor preaching, see Holmes, "Role of Open-Air Preaching in the Belfast Riots of 1857," 47–66; Doyle, "Martyrs of Liberty," chap. 9. The best study of the sermon's place in nineteenth-century Ulster religious culture is Dickson, *Beyond Religious Discourse*.

were asked to persevere in a difficult world, safe in the knowledge of God's love and the promise that the world that mattered was the next one. While we cannot be sure precisely what plebeian congregants took from Drew's messages of Christian paternalism and working-class sacrifice, the principles at the heart of these everyday sermons aligned closely with the beliefs of Belfast conservative elites who often blanched at Drew's confrontational and disruptive Orange politics. If we cannot be sure exactly what role Drew's religious and social advocacy played in the emergence of Belfast's relatively conservative Protestant working-class culture, it certainly strengthened his ties to the city's civic establishment.

This was not always the case with Drew's anti-Catholic lectures and sermons, often delivered to Orangemen and their supporters in churches and lecture halls in Belfast and across eastern Ireland. These were also a prominent part of Drew's ministry from the beginning of his tenure at Christ Church, but Drew's political performances became more frequent after 1848, when a number of factors created an atmosphere more conducive to his combative anti-Catholic performances. In these special sermons and lectures, Drew outlined the basic tenets of his religious politics, which called upon Protestant men and women to emulate the heroic actions of their ancestors to defend Protestant Ireland against the Catholic threat. Drew's speeches featured most of the standard assumptions and talking points of conservative Irish Protestant historiography: 1641, 1690, 1798, and all that. What was more novel about Drew's lectures was the extremism of his verbal violence, the sense that Ireland was a vital front in a high-stakes global battle. Throughout his career, but particularly in the 1850s, Drew used his public pulpit to keep sectarian division near the center of public dialogue. Drew's confrontational rhetoric was not designed to convince the undecided. By reinforcing already potent sectarian narratives, however, his performances helped to set the parameters of what was possible in an increasingly divided town. Drew's political ministry made it even more difficult to construct a unified civic culture in Victorian Belfast.

While Raymond Gillespie's 1997 statement that Irish historians had done little work on the history of religion in Ireland (which he contrasted with histories of institutional churches) is no longer true,[7] the nineteenth-century Church of Ireland has not been as well served by historians as its Catholic and Presbyterian counterparts.[8] Consequentially, our understanding of the overlapping registers of evangelical belief, anti-Catholicism, and doctrinal and political conservatism has not advanced much beyond the necessarily brief if insightful suggestions made by David Hempton and Myrtle Hill in their 1992 survey.[9] By examining the interfaces of evangelical religion and popular politics at Christ Church and beyond, this chapter (as well as the next) is designed to further that critical conversation.

SERMONS WITHOUT STONES:
THOMAS DREW'S EVERYDAY SERMONS

When Christ Church first opened on July 28, 1833, it was Richard Mant, bishop of Down and Connor since 1823, who preached the first sermon. A well-known scholar (he is remembered primarily for his influential two-volume *History of the Church in Ireland*),[10] Mant was more famous for his writing than his preaching, but the fact that the

---

7. Gillespie, *Devoted People*, vii. For a thoughtful review of more recent work on the subject, see McBride, "Religion," 292–319.

8. See Holmes, *Irish Presbyterian Mind*; Holmes, *Shaping of Ulster Presbyterian Belief and Practice*; Miller, "Presbyterianism and 'Modernisation' in Modern Ulster," 68–90; Miller, "Irish Christianity and Revolution," chap. 10. Pre-Famine Ulster Catholicism has been studied less than other parts of Ireland, but see Elliott, *Catholics of Ulster*, 267–370; Rafferty, *Catholicism in Ulster*, 98–134.

9. Hempton and Hill, *Evangelical Protestantism in Ulster*, 105–28. While the focus of her essay is on evangelical landlords in the 1820s and 1830s, Irene Whelan's work is quite useful here. See Whelan, "Bible Gentry," 52–82.

10. Mant, *History of the Church in Ireland*. For a recent examination of Mant's historiographical significance, see Farrell, "Contested Histories?," 95–107. While domestic chaplain to the archbishop of Canterbury, Mant published several volumes of exemplary sermons: see Mant, *Sermons for Parochial and Domestic Use*.

bishop delivered the initial sermon at Christ Church underlines both the importance of his position and his commitment to the Durham Street church he had done so much to found. A few months later, another notable speaker appeared at Christ Church to raise funds for the new church. This was the Reverend Mortimer O'Sullivan, a prominent Orangeman and infamous anti-Catholic controversialist who had won awards for his extemporaneous preaching while a student at Trinity College Dublin.[11]

While Drew could hardly compete with the status and scholarly acumen of Mant or the rhetorical pyrotechnics of an Orange firebrand like O'Sullivan, he was an effective and popular preacher. Several of his sermons were published in *The Irish Pulpit*, collected volumes of the exemplary sermons of Church of Ireland ministers particularly designed for distribution to the poor and those who ministered to them.[12] He was frequently asked to give charity sermons and was a regular lecturer at Hollymount Parish Church outside of Downpatrick from the late 1840s until his death in 1870.[13] Drew traveled extensively to give sermons and his schedule was often quite full. In 1843, for example, he preached at St. Catherine's Church, St. Mark's Church, and the Molyneux Asylum in Dublin to raise funds for the Association for the Relief of Distressed Protestants. Nearly thirty years later, at the age of seventy and only three months before his death, Drew gave charity sermons on successive weeks in Dublin, Killyleagh, Lisburn, and Kilmore, County Down.[14] Preaching was important to Drew and his sermons were a crucial part of his success at Christ Church and in the Church of Ireland.

---

11. Dawson, "Annals of Christ Church, Belfast," 10–12; Dickson, *Beyond Religious Discourse*, 26. William McIlwaine was another of the so-called premium men (1832).

12. Drew, "Rich and the Poor," 262; Drew, "Sabbath Blessings"; Drew, "Sunday School Teaching," 155–64.

13. Diaries of William Johnston, 1848–54, PRONI, D.880/2/1–6.

14. *Seventh Annual Report of the Association for the Distressed Protestants*, 16; *Downpatrick Recorder*, July 30, 1870.

In 1839, the Belfast publisher William Ferguson issued three volumes of Drew's everyday sermons titled *Sermons on Various Subjects* (unfortunately, the third volume of the collection has disappeared). Explicitly modeled on the London Tract Society's widely distributed *Cottage Sermons*,[15] the volumes were designed to help the ministers of urban congregations provide inexpensive and convenient reading material for working-class men and women. They were meant to encourage family worship at home, a key component in Drew's broader vision of a reformulated Christian household.[16] The published sermons provide a glimpse of the religious, social, and political ideas and language that Drew believed critical to his parishioners in these early formative years. While we cannot know exactly what his congregants made of his words and ideas, they were heard by thousands of men and women in Belfast. In the Christ Church Religious Census of 1852, 55 percent of the nearly four thousand people surveyed claimed that they attended church services regularly.[17] This was a point of substantial contact.

Drew's everyday sermons were designed for a working-class audience. The language and concepts of the lectures are clear and plain, full of repetition and heavy-handed signposting. Victorian preachers rarely experimented with form, and Drew was no exception.[18] His sermons were typically structured around three to five questions, clearly designed to help listeners follow the minister's discourse toward its typically dramatic and hopeful conclusion. A good example of Drew's method is "The Light, Protection and Bounty of God," where he opened his sermon with three statements about the relationship between God and the believer: what God is to the believer,

---

15. *Cottage Sermons*. For another model, see Milner, *Practical Sermons*.

16. Drew, *Sermons on Various Subjects*, 1:v–vii. Nor was Drew alone; McIlwaine described "family religion" as the most important variable in addresses to his congregation at St. George's in 1836 and 1838. See Address to Congregation, December 25, 1836, and January 1838, PRONI, McIlwaine Papers, D.2877/5/1.

17. Christ Church Census of 1852; Dawson, "Annals of Christ Church, Belfast," PRONI, CR1/13D/2/134–5.

18. Dickson, *Beyond Religious Discourse*, 21–28, 130–31.

what God gives to the believer, and the true character of the believer. Using Psalm 84:11–12 as his text ("For the Lord God is a Sun and Shield"), Drew then proceeded directly through his outline, concluding with extended reflections on the foundational necessity and transformational nature of grace, and its particular connection to the poor: "Then shall the poor man know why he was left to fill a humble lot, and be taught to understand how often the poor man's deliverer was near him, and around him in the day of trouble. Then shall every trace of jealousy, caprice, bickering and uncharitableness be known no more."[19] What is vital here is his clarion statement of one of the central tenets of evangelical Protestantism: that lives must be changed and that the power to make those changes only comes from God. Drew argued that transformation through grace was a particularly important message for the poor, whose spiritual conversion would improve their earthly lives by giving them an understanding of their social position and the eternal hope that awaited them. The importance of moral transformation was the fundamental starting point of Drew's conservatism; a message that preached working-class perseverance and support for the existing social and political order while stressing spiritual equality and the promise of true happiness for all Christian believers. These were familiar themes for Belfast Anglicans. Drew's lectures on "social" sins like pride, ambition, and anger echoed the sentiments of the mid-eighteenth-century vicar of Belfast, James Saurin, whose sermons were recently discovered in St. Anne's Cathedral.[20]

If the central frame and tone of Drew's sermons was optimistic, it was rooted in the notion that human nature was sinful, base, and corrupt. This was why religious education and moral instruction were so vital to Drew: "The mind is a great field wanting cultivation; it must

---

19. Drew, "The Light, the Protection and the Bounty of God," *Sermons on Various Subjects*, 2:17. For other explicit references to Christianity's special promise for the poor in the collection, see "The Omnipresence of God," 1:31; "Spiritual Leprosy," 1:146–47; "Spiritual Growth and Results," 2:53. See also "Rich and the Poor," 251–69.

20. Gillespie and Ó Gallachóir, *Preaching in Belfast*, 18–20.

be cherished, and sown with proper seed; without religious instruction, things rank and gross possess it; it will bring forth the latent seeds of corrupt nature all that is injurious to things around: querulousness, discontent, ill-temper, and licentious indulgences, ever flow from the neglect of mental cultivation."[21] True wisdom started from self-knowledge and the resultant fear of an all-knowing and powerful God. An emotional and open contrition and repentance was central to Drew's evangelical faith, where "every secret, envious, injurious, malicious, lustful, deadly thought—the smallest as well as the greatest, shall be revealed with a voice of thunder hereafter."[22] While Drew made clear in another sermon that God's anger was directed at sin rather than man and that the true fear of God was a filial and wholesome fear (he labeled it a holy disposition akin to that of a child being chastised by a loving father), his sermons oscillated from darkness to light and back again, moving rapidly from a dark and severe view of the human condition to the unmatched promise of salvation in God's love.[23] If Boyd Hilton is correct that it was this sentimental duality that made evangelical religion so appealing to men and women living through the transformative changes of the Victorian era, then Drew's sermons were characteristic enough of the age.[24]

The vast majority of Drew's everyday sermons were closely argued explications of a particular Biblical verse or passage. This was a common feature of nineteenth-century Irish evangelical preaching, reflecting both contemporary homiletic training and an extraordinary belief in the power of the Bible. Unlike many of his Irish contemporaries, who favored the New Testament by a 2:1 ratio, Drew selected passages from the Old Testament for the vast majority of his 1839 sermons. I do not think we can read too much into Drew's early bias, particularly since his selections were from the Old Testament books

---

21. Drew, "Rich and the Poor," 255.

22. Drew, "Omniscience of God," *Sermons on Various Subjects*, 1:35.

23. Drew, "The Fear of God," and "The Anger of God," *Sermons on Various Subjects*, 1:45–78.

24. Hilton, *Age of Atonement*, 35.

that were most popular with contemporary evangelical ministers, the prophecies of Isaiah and the Psalms, widely used by Victorian preachers for their poetic beauty and real-world accessibility. The evidence we have for Drew's later preaching career suggests a pronounced shift to the New Testament.[25]

The selection of a biblical passage was not simply a matter of choosing good subject matter; the text itself was central to the sermon. Drew's sermons often featured particularly close readings of biblical text, and it was not uncommon for him to move line by line through a particular passage to develop a sermon's central theme.[26] In a sermon delivered at Christ Church on Christmas Day 1842 and later published in *The Irish Pulpit*, Drew argued that while there were numerous arguments for and against keeping the Sabbath, "we must, however, of necessity, confine ourselves to those noticed in the text."[27] To highlight another example, in an April 1840 sermon given at Trinity Church in Dublin, Drew used Jeremiah's famous verse in Lamentations 5:3 ("We are orphans and fatherless, our mothers are like widows") to underline the necessity of supporting the poor and the vulnerable, narratives he reinforced with data from his own investigations of local life experiences. Even when he strayed from Jeremiah's words to discuss the particular challenges that women faced, he did so through another biblical verse (1 Timothy 2:15: "Notwithstanding she shall be saved in childbirth").[28] These close textual readings were also designed to serve an educational purpose, increasing biblical familiarity

---

25. Dickson, *Beyond Religious Discourse*, 101–3. In his diaries, William Johnston regularly noted the basics of the sermons Drew gave at Hollymount Church outside of Downpatrick and Loughinisland Parish Church after he moved to Seaforde in 1859. Thirty-three of the forty-five sermons he listed between 1848 and 1870 were commentaries on verses from the New Testament. See Diaries of William Johnston, 1848–70, PRONI, D.880/2/1–22.

26. Dickson, *Beyond Religious Discourse*, 61–66.

27. Drew, "Sabbath Blessings."

28. Drew, *Sermon, Preached on Behalf of the Protestant Orphan Society*, 8–13.

and/or literacy for congregants.[29] Whether or not they succeeded in doing this, of course, is another matter altogether.

The sheer volume of Drew's everyday sermons and the diversity of the subject matter make it difficult to generalize about any single thematic focus for his preaching. Not surprisingly, most of his sermons stressed the necessity of the sinner's conversion and the "wisdom and happy consequences" that stemmed from the acceptance of the gift of God's grace. Arguing against the "unnatural and false" promises of atheism in "The Existence of God" (there is little evidence that this was a particularly threatening enemy in mid-nineteenth-century Belfast), Drew stressed the notion that people needed both human reason and faith to find true happiness: it was reason that led men and women to believe in God's existence, and the acceptance of the gift of grace that allowed them to call upon God. Only from this position could happiness commence, as believers prayed for grace, for a faithful heart, and a "hand open as day to melting charity."[30] Drew insisted that a life grounded in firm Christian responsibility would be rewarded, that all laborers in the Gospel would be honored.[31]

This work was certainly needed. In nearly all of his sermons, Drew celebrated the need for Protestant action, saying that it was the primary duty of all Christians to bring people to the true church—to "invite, improve, exhort and edify now."[32] While the hopeful and positive tone of Drew's published sermons is striking, they often featured an anxious note as well, a sense that true Christians needed to redouble their efforts to create a more godly society in a world full of sin and betrayal. As he put it in "The Power, the Priesthood, and the Glory of the Lord": "True, our churches are better attended, our ministers more faithful, a greater love of family religion exhibited than in times

---

29. Akenson, *Discovering the End of Time*, 229.

30. Drew, "The Existence of God," *Sermons on Various Subjects*, 1:23–24.

31. Drew, "Light from God," *Sermons on Various Subjects*, 1:97.

32. Drew, "Man Contrite—Earth Vocal—God Merciful," *Sermons on Various Subjects*, 1:134–35. See also Drew, "Introduction," *Sermons on Various Subjects*, 1:viii–ix.

past; but more, much more is wanting."³³ In the printed sermons of the late 1830s and early 1840s, Drew argued that the social evils connected to the town's rapid growth and an absence of energy in the Church of Ireland were nearly as important a threat to true Protestantism as Roman Catholicism. These included a lack of church provision, the absence of a real work ethic among sectors of the working class, the prevalence of drink and its impact on the family, and the potential for social conflict between the rich and poor. This latter factor was especially important to Drew because of the ongoing transformation of the Belfast textile industry, where reduced wages generated widespread suffering among weaving households in Belfast and Ballymacarrett in the 1830s and 1840s.³⁴

Given Christ Church's largely plebeian congregation and the fact that these sermons were published with a working-class audience in mind, it is not surprising that Drew's lectures were particularly geared toward the poor. Christ's message was for all to hear, of course, but according to Drew, it had a special power and appeal to the poor. His thoughts were developed most fully in "The Rich and the Poor," a sermon published in an 1839 edition of *The Irish Pulpit*. Starting with a familiar text from 1 Samuel 2:7 ("The Lord maketh poor and maketh rich, he bringeth low and lifteth up"), Drew sketched an idealized portrait of a unitary human community, bound together by common interest and need: "All are taught their dependence; true philosophy bids the poor man look up to the rich man as his benefactor, and bids the rich man also to look upon the poor man as his most valuable friend. Mankind are encircled by bonds which unite them powerfully; the chain of gold may go forth from the rich, manacling the poor,

---

33. Drew, "The Power, The Priesthood, and the Glory of the Lord," *Sermons on Various Subjects*, 1:122. This call was not confined to sermons. For a contemporary example of a public address, see the report of Drew's call to action at the Great Meeting of the Diocese of Down and Connor for Church Extension at Christ Church on December 19, 1838: *Ulster Times*, December 20, 1838.

34. For a detailed examination of Drew's public response to the Ballymacarrett weavers, see chapter 4.

as auxiliary to his comforts; but equally from the poor do the getters of iron grapple the rich man and yoke him to the poor."[35] Drew often highlighted the particular desires and temptations of the rich man, exhorting him not to forget the poor, God, or himself as he surrounded himself in material possessions.[36] The acquisition of resources brought temptation and corruption and it was the Christian duty of the wealthy to use their riches to support the poor and the church. Drew consistently emphasized the benefits that came from true Christian leadership. Successful men were part of the same community as the poor, and society worked best when owners used their wealth for the benefit of the poor and the church. Drew's views on paternalism and social consensus fit well within the parameters of dominant Peelite sensibilities of British and Irish conservatism.[37]

While Drew's printed sermons regularly outlined the duties of Christian paternalism, he typically devoted much more time to instructing the poor about the benefits of living responsible Christian lives than lecturing the rich about their duties to those beneath them in the social hierarchy. Christianity, Drew asserted, brought real benefits for the poor: "It comes specially to the poor man; nay, it seems to make the poor man take precedence of the rich man, gives the poor the priority of invitation, the upper seat at its table, and the choicest (because the most needed) blessings in its gift."[38] Drew emphasized the notion that the Gospel brought both practical advantages and true happiness to working-class families. It was easy, he argued, to distinguish Christian families from those who had not seen the light. In these houses, "apartments were filthy, the wife neglectful of her person, the children in rags, disputes disturb the home and family meals." Conversely, in the Christian family home, "there is peace within; if poverty, there is submission, knowing that the Lord has a wise end

35. Drew, "Rich and the Poor," 252.
36. Drew, "Perseverance," *Sermons on Various Subjects*, 2:161.
37. Bew, *Glory of Being Britons*, 126–60.
38. Drew, "Rich and the Poor," 261. See also "Man Contrite—Earth Vocal—God Merciful," 135.

in keeping us poor."[39] This was the stark religious message of a social conservative, keen to support the existing social order and political hierarchy through the advance of Christian civility and working-class acceptance.

Religious education was particularly important to this project. Only religion could temper man's sinful nature, for "without religious instruction," the human mind would be overgrown by the "latent seeds of corrupt nature all that is injurious to things around: querulousness, discontent, ill-temper, and licentious indulgences, ever flow from neglect of mental cultivation."[40] It was a perspective that was broadly shared by Belfast evangelicals, who argued that teachings on the divine social order and the Gospel were the best guardians of social rights and stability.[41] This was clearly an emotional issue for Drew, and his appeals to provide religious education for children have an almost plaintive tone to them: "Is there on earth a more gratifying sight than that of a parent leading the little ones, given him by God, to the house of God— . . . God forbid that any of these dear lambs should be wanting to the fold, by our caprice or neglect."[42] Critics might argue about the balance of Drew's motivations (an admixture of spiritual concerns, class and sectarian anxieties, and the practical need to maintain and increase the size of the church community), but it was clear that few things were more important to Drew than bringing children into the congregation at Christ Church.

The relationship between faith and reason was another of Drew's favorite themes in these early sermons, touched on in his 1839 lectures and most fully developed in two sermons delivered at Trinity College Dublin in January 1842.[43] For all his overblown rhetoric about the appropriate curriculum for a working-class education, Drew

39. Drew, "Fear of God," 52.
40. Drew, "Rich and the Poor," 255.
41. Dickson, *Beyond Religious Discourse*, 148.
42. Drew, "Man Contrite—Earth Vocal—God Merciful," 136. For a more detailed treatment of this theme, see Farrell, "Feed My Lambs," 43–58.
43. Drew, *Two Sermons Preached before the University of Dublin*.

believed that thought and reflection were central to living a happy and productive life. The cultivation of the mind was essential if men and women were to understand the need to come to God with an open heart—and this was just as true for his congregants at Christ Church as it was for students at Trinity College. Preaching against "scholarly arrogance," Drew argued that God's word was essential for all searches for knowledge. Spiritual perception was vital for science and public affairs, for the Christian scholar must know not only his studies, but what he owes God and man. Become learned in this place, he advised students, but do not lose your perspective about what is important.[44] Drew's message that a truly Christian education focused on uniting a scholarly mind with an open and godly heart was one delivered to college students in Dublin and millworkers and their families at Christ Church alike.

If conversion brought worldly benefits to the poor, however, Drew argued that these paled in comparison to the spiritual solace and peace brought by the acceptance of God's word. Despite politicians' best efforts, poverty would exist as long as there was human sin, and in this situation, it was vital that the poor knew their proper place in God's creation. Given the poor man's material condition and his general belief that he had been treated badly by society, it was remarkable that society did not explode in anger:

> The poor man needs to feel his true position; the general opinion with regard to the relative condition of the poor man is, in many respects, wrong. The poor man generally feels as if he were hardly dealt with, especially if he cannot trace his privations to any indiscretion of his own. He feels as if the rich man only was happy—nay, as if the rich were some usurping tyrant, and he a veritable bondsman, unduly coerced to live "by the sweat of his brow;" he feels as if his condition were altogether disreputable—that he has naught to do with human sympathies—that he may be utterly and legitimately

---

44. Drew, *Two Sermons Preached before the University of Dublin*, 10–12, 38.

selfish, and that there is no sympathy demandable save from rich and poor.[45]

Like so many other Victorian evangelicals, Drew believed that poverty was more a reflection of moral character than a social problem to be solved, and here the only saving grace was religion. He argued that there was no denying the social inequalities of the material world, but that religious conversion helped working-class men and women see that they were part of a community that shared the trials of this world (albeit, Drew admitted, not in equal measure) in preparation for the next. Knowledge of the Gospel taught the poor not to envy the rich and to understand that while their social position was a subordinate one, it was not a despised one. Only an understanding that this life was all part of God's plan curbed the working man's natural anger at the material inequities of contemporary life.[46]

We do not have direct evidence about how working-class members of the Christ Church congregation received Drew's counsel to lead virtuous lives of faithful patience and perseverance. It would be wrong to assume that men and women were not attracted by the more positive elements of their minister's simple message of community and a hopeful future. As Andrew Holmes has argued, some aspects of middle-class evangelical reform brought practical benefits to working-class people. Sabbatarianism, for example, gave workers a much-needed break from the factory.[47] That said, it would be equally wrong to assume that congregants—working class and otherwise—simply accepted the messages they received from the pulpit. Drew's popularity with his Belfast congregants and Orangemen alike seems clear. Christ Church was a large and successful church, but we cannot be sure that men and women stayed because of his hard-line Protestant politics, active and pragmatic evangelical religion, or the simple fact that they lived in the neighborhood.

45. Drew, "Rich and the Poor," 258–59.
46. Drew, "Rich and the Poor," 264–69.
47. Holmes, *Shaping of Ulster Presbyterian Belief and Practice*, 75–76.

What we can be certain of is that Drew believed that both Orangeism and vital religion were central to his ministry. They were essential and inextricable. Throughout his career, he argued that the Orange Order was a vehicle for both political defence and the moral transformation of the Belfast community.[48] If Drew's efforts to bring spiritual change to Sandy Row did not gain the same degree of public attention as his confrontational anti-Catholic performances, this simply reflects the fact that his evangelical beliefs were broadly shared by the Belfast political establishment. In sermons and schoolrooms alike, Drew used his position to advocate for Orange political activism and a conservative social gospel that stressed the importance of leading Christian lives of discipline and purpose. Religion and respectability mattered here, and Drew's pastoral work and everyday sermons helped to strengthen a code of social, communal, and political norms that shaped the evolution of a broadly conservative civic culture. While more controversial, Drew's Orange sermons also played a formative role in the making of Victorian Belfast. It is to that subject that we now turn.

THE FIGHTING PASTOR: SERMONS WITH STONES

Preaching to an assembly of Belfast Orangemen at Christ Church in November 1856, Thomas Drew called upon his listeners to remember God's deliverance of the faithful and to stand strong and united in support of the Protestant principles for which their fathers had fought:

> It is an anxious and wholesome time, also, when a nation, conscious of iniquity, deprecates the wrath of an offended Lord God; "proclaims a fast and calls a solemn assembly" . . . It is a precious demonstration of gratitude to the God of our fathers, who delivered them, and by inheritance, delivered us also, from most dire calamities—from the famine hearing of the Word of the Lord, from deprivation

---

48. For a similar argument, see Sutherland, "Role of Evangelical Protestantism in the Formation of Nineteenth-Century Ulster Protestant Identity," 36–40.

of our Bible—from priestcraft and mental slavery—from the torture of the Inquisition—from the fires of the auto-da-fe—from the horrible, wholesale destruction designed by the Gunpowder Plot—from the dastardly cruelties and bigotries of James II—from the rebels of 1798—and from the more recent villainies designed at Trillick . . . Men like those of Zebulon, "which can keep rank and are not of double heart"; these now meet to glorify God for the past, and to reanimate faith in all around them, by open and resolute exhibition of their numbers and their unity.[49]

Designed to commemorate the Gunpowder Plot, Drew's sermon featured many of the central elements of his Protestant politics: his focus on historic episodes of Catholic violence and Protestant heroism, his deeply pessimistic view of contemporary British and Irish politics, the desperate need for the reformation of a sinful nation, and above all, a call for Protestant action. If remembering the past was a vital starting point, Orangemen must not stop there; they needed to stand up to defend their beliefs. It was critical, Drew argued, that they all know the "great and essential doctrines of salvation," if they were to prepare themselves for the battle made both openly and covertly by the Roman Catholic Church.[50] Delivered in church to a body of men dedicated to preserving the remains of the Protestant state in Ireland, the sermon was a clear expression of Drew's Protestant politics.

Thomas Drew was an Orangeman, an active participant and defender of the Orange Order who held various offices at local, county, and national levels throughout his life. Drew's Orangeism epitomized his belief that religion and politics were inseparable. He was a political pastor, fusing his populist brand of anti-Catholic conservatism with the moralism of Low Church evangelical Protestantism. In 1828 he helped to create the Ballymena Brunswick Club to mobilize opposition

---

49. Drew, *Sermon, Preached in Christ Church, Belfast, on the Evening of November 5, 1856*, 4.

50. Drew, *Sermon, Preached in Christ Church, Belfast, on the Evening of November 5, 1856*, 4.

to Daniel O'Connell's successful crusade for Catholic emancipation. The Brunswick Club was only the first of a series of typically short-lived Protestant political organizations that Drew created or jointed throughout his career: the Protestant Operative Society (1843–46), the Evangelical Alliance (1846–), the Ulster Protestant Association (1849–51), and the Christ Church Protestant Association (1854–58). Each of these organizations was dedicated to defending an explicitly Protestant version of British and Irish politics. All of them failed to achieve their aims. Drew's work for the Conservative interest in municipal and parliamentary politics was more successful. Led by figures as diverse as John Bates and James Emerson Tennent, the Conservatives were the dominant force in Belfast politics throughout Drew's ministry. If leaders like Tennent, Hugh Cairns (member of Parliament for Belfast in the 1850s and later solicitor general and Lord Chancellor), and Joseph Napier (member of Parliament for Dublin University [1848–56], attorney general [1852], and member of the Privy Council of Ireland) often were frustrated by Drew's boisterous anti-Catholicism,[51] conservative political success in Belfast gave Drew access to the town's establishment and a larger platform for his views.

The special sermons that Drew delivered to members of the Orange Order were one of the most controversial and influential aspects of his political repertoire. Delivered in Christ Church, and after his appointment as precentor of Down in 1859, Down Cathedral in Downpatrick, Drew's Orange sermons made him one of the Orange Order's most visible public champions. Beyond his rhetorical extremism, there was little that was novel about Drew's lectures, which rehashed familiar anti-Catholic tropes common to nineteenth-century British and Irish public life.[52] The sheer spectacle of a prominent minister of the

---

51. Writing from Italy in 1861, Napier's feelings about Thomas Drew are clear: "I have not heard from Ireland, but I observe that in your Aunt Whiteside's letters to Anne, she says that in the North of Ireland they are still pelting me about education. I suppose Drew is at the head of this." See Napier, *Lectures, Essays, and Letters of the Right Hon. Sir Joseph Napier*, 51.

52. Doyle, "Martyrs of Liberty," 149–64.

established church giving partisan lectures in a church near a communal flashpoint generated considerable outrage and support, but it was the growth of the Irish publishing industry that extended Drew's reach and reputation beyond Belfast. Many of Drew's Orange sermons were published as pamphlets and all of them were reprinted in various Irish newspapers. For Irish Catholics (and liberal Protestants), he was one of the most notorious anti-Catholic bigots of mid-nineteenth-century Ireland. For both his supporters and opponents, then, Drew's Orange performances made sure that sectarian division remained front and center on the Belfast stage.

We have seen that Orangeism was a crucial element in the making of Christ Church. In July 1835, Drew and two other Church of Ireland ministers publicly invited the Orangemen of their parishes to special 12th of July lectures, the first time that had happened in Belfast. The practice was discontinued in 1836, as British radicals forced the organization to dissolve itself in the wake of accusations that some of its leaders had been involved in a bizarre plot to place the Duke of Cumberland on the British throne after the death of King William IV. While local lodges continued to meet, the Orange Order remained largely underground until 1845, when it resurfaced as a Protestant counter to the Molly Maguires, an agrarian secret society in south and west Ulster.[53]

The Orange Order's reemergence as a public force in Irish political life was enabled by the revolutionary climate of 1848, which allowed Orange leaders to emphasize their loyalty and value as an ally to the British government in Ireland. Drew joined the local Eldon Lodge no. 7 on August 14, 1848, an elite-oriented body that included several of the town's Church of Ireland ministers and prominent figures like Hutcheson Posnett, the land agent for Viscount Dungannon and a

---

53. Kenny, *Making Sense of the Molly Maguires*, 13–44. For the complex continuities of Orange politics in these years, see Gannon, *Protestant Community in Ulster*, 142–56.

member of the town council, and Adam Hill, another local politician and future head of the Belfast Municipal Police. Drew was an active member of the lodge from the outset, nominating several of his north Antrim friends for membership.[54] His widely circulated response to the 1848 rebellion, prominent role in creating the Ulster Protestant Association in 1849, and active and loud participation in the perpetually unsuccessful campaign against the Maynooth grant quickly made Drew one of the most important figures in Belfast Orangeism.[55]

As chaplain for the district, county, and Grand Lodge, Drew regularly gave anniversary sermons for Orangemen in churches and cathedrals throughout Ulster in the 1850s and 1860s. These were lectures designed to commemorate particular events in British and Irish history: July 12 (the Battle of the Boyne, 1690, and the Battle of Aughrim, 1691), October 23 (the Irish Catholic seizure of Dublin Castle, 1641), and November 5 (the Gunpowder Plot, 1605). Anniversary sermons had a long history in Ireland. Since 1660, Church of Ireland ministers had given state-sanctioned lectures to commemorate the Gunpowder Plot and the Irish Catholic seizure of Dublin Castle in 1641, typically focusing on the sinful nature of the Protestant nation and the need for reformation, atrocity narratives that emphasized Catholic barbarity and duplicity, and God's miraculous deliverance of his chosen people. If Drew's special sermons echoed much of the content and form of traditional anniversary sermons, there were also significant differences. As James McConnel has shown, the 5th of November only became a popular festive celebration in Ulster after the passage of Catholic emancipation in 1829, joining the 12th of July as a partisan holiday

---

54. Eldon Orange Lodge (no. 7) minutes, August and September 1848, Museum of Orange Heritage, Belfast.

55. In the aftermath of 1848, Drew's work with the Ulster Protestant Association was critical in raising his profile. By January 1849 his name was one of the featured toasts (along with more celebrated figures such as the Earl of Enniskillen, Lord Roden, James Watson, James Napier, and Henry Cooke) at Orange lodge meetings in the town. See *Belfast News-Letter*, January 12, 1849.

that failed to get consistent recognition or support from the British state in Ireland.[56] If this was a tradition with a long history, it was not an unchanging one.

While he rarely spoke at Belfast's largest venues, Drew's political lectures were well-advertised and well-attended. His emergence as an Orange favorite after 1848 was a matter of changed context and opportunity rather than changed belief. The anniversary sermons he delivered to Orangemen in July and November were fiery political performances that received wide public circulation through the rapidly expanding world of print media. After 1855, this included the *Downshire Protestant*, a newspaper owned by Drew's friend, ally, and future son-in-law, William Johnston of Ballykilbeg. Drew's ties to an increasingly influential press were a vital tool in his largely successful mobilization of friends and enemies alike.[57] By the mid-1850s Drew's reputation as a Protestant champion and anti-Catholic extremist was firmly ensconced in Belfast and beyond, and Drew's highly publicized Orange lectures had much to do with that.

Like his everyday sermons, Drew's Orange lectures were simple in structure, typically organized around three to five main sections that were clearly announced in the introduction and signposted throughout. The November 1856 sermon cited earlier is a good example. Drew's lecture examined "God's gracious dealings with us in deliverances spiritual, person, and national" in five relatively short segments, using familiar historical examples to support his exclusivist Protestant politics.[58] Although the martial tone of his Orange performances

---

56. Barnard, "Uses of 23 Oct. 1641 and Irish Protestant Celebrations," 899–920; McConnel, "Remembering the Gunpowder Plot in Ireland," 863–91. For Ulster Presbyterians in the same era, see Blackstock, "Armed Citizens and Christian Soldiers," 81–105.

57. Drew was quite conscious of the importance of the press, regularly telling his audiences to support Protestant newspapers and constantly criticizing British and Irish media for their lack of support for a truly Protestant politics.

58. Drew, *Sermon, Preached in Christ Church, Belfast, on the Evening of November 5, 1856*, 5.

was certainly more threatening than his weekly sermons, Drew used the same simple language to articulate familiar stories of the ultra-Protestant mythic past. Leavened with humor and a few rather eccentric historical and religious references, "good old Dr. Drew's" message and style were clearly designed to appeal to his largely working-class Protestant audiences.

Not surprisingly, Drew's Orange sermons featured clear expressions of a binary world view dominated by the global struggle between Protestantism and Roman Catholicism and its abettors. Designed to mobilize the forces of Protestant truth against external and internal enemies, his lectures painted a negative and embattled picture of the contemporary world and were replete with verbal violence (military metaphors abound in many of his lectures) and calls for steadfast action. His infamous 12th of July lecture at Christ Church in 1857 featured a typical plea for manly efforts to save the nation: "Italy wants another Savonarola; Scotland, another Knox; and England, Another Wicliff! 'We want men!' As one looks more closely at this want of the times and the way in which latent piety and vigour are directed into wrong channels, or exhausted in mere evangelical sentimentality, we are led all the more respectfully and fervently to plead with public men, to keep before their minds the vital question for believing men, next to the great subject of salvation. Let us only imagine, what had been the result to Ireland, and indeed, to the world, had defeat befallen the arms of William."[59] Ireland required effective action and not mere sentimentality—a claim that revealed much about Drew's hierarchy of priorities. After all, this was a man who spent much of his career as an advocate for evangelical causes and celebrated a romantic rural nostalgia in many of his speeches. In Drew's hands, angels often were attacking and aggressive and an all-knowing and interactive God was constantly at the ready to deliver the faithful who were seemingly always besieged by their enemies. These were the lessons

59. *Downshire Protestant*, July 17, 1857; *Report of the Commissioners of Inquiry into the Origin and Character of the Riots in Belfast in July and September 1857*, 252.

that Protestants needed to remember if they were to truly honor their ancestors' sacrifices and protect their hard-won liberties. In sermons and political speeches throughout the 1850s and 1860s, Drew made sure that no one could ever forget.[60]

Drew's Orange sermons were dominated by his accounts of the Protestant past, featuring historical examples that served to underline the persistence and power of the Catholic threat and the need for Protestant readiness. These narratives typically pivoted on the stories of Protestant heroes in Ireland, England, and Europe: James Ussher and George Walker, Thomas Cranmer and Queen Elizabeth I, Martin Luther and Jan Hus. While Hus was a personal favorite,[61] Drew's lectures typically featured stories more familiar to his Belfast audiences; gallant King William III and George Walker, the militant rector whose determined leadership had saved the day during the Siege of Derry in the late seventeenth century. Walker seems to have been particularly important at Christ Church in the 1850s. On the one hand, this reflected the success of broader efforts to refashion the myth of the Siege of Derry in an Orange image, physically embodied by the remounting of the cannon Roaring Meg in the 1820s, the construction of the Walker Testimonial in 1828, and in 1861 the reinternment of the reputed bones of the Apprentice Boys, discovered during the renovation of St. Columba's Cathedral.[62] But there was also a personal angle to Walker's prominence at Christ Church, since Abraham Dawson, Drew's curate, had attended the reinternment of Walker's remains at Castle Caulfield, County Tyrone. On August 1, 1853, Dawson gave a

---

60. Maura Cronin has argued that the remembered (and misremembered) past played an essential role in nineteenth-century Irish popular politics, articulated in songs, published histories, and processions. See Cronin, "Irish Popular Politics," 136–38.

61. Drew's particular attachment to Hus likely stems from the latter's poverty, his willingness to suffer imprisonment and execution for the true faith, his prediction that religious reform would occur (taken by some as a prophecy about Martin Luther), and Hussite resistance to the Catholic Church. For Hus, see Fudge, *Jan Hus*.

62. McBride, *Siege of Derry in Ulster Protestant Mythology*, 50–51.

lecture, "George Walker and His Times," before the Church of Ireland's Young Men's Society in Belfast, closing with an exhibition of a plaster cast made of the Protestant hero's skull.[63] The great martyrs of the English Reformation were also celebrated frequently in Drew's discourses. Many of these figures were remembered for their humility and piety, but all were celebrated for their strength.

Drew's historical narratives often sacrificed nuance for the polemical needs of the day, something illustrated by his treatment of Oliver Cromwell. As Sarah Covington and other historians have noted, Cromwell had long been a somewhat difficult figure for Church of Ireland conservatives, who appreciated his Protestant heroism and leadership but were uncomfortable with regicide and other aspects of the commonwealth. King William III was a generally safer choice for Irish Protestants.[64] Thomas Drew had no such reservations. Echoing Thomas Carlyle's influential portrait of Cromwell, Drew celebrated the English leader as a Protestant man of action and hoped that a modern equivalent would appear to "send England's cannon to batter down the pope's castle at Rome."[65] The Orange cleric's take was more complex in an 1858 sermon, where he noted that the 1640s and 1650s had featured destructive Protestant in-fighting, something he largely blamed on Jesuit efforts to sow discord among the faithful. Singing a less than consistent tune, he then went on to celebrate the "faithful and loyal clergy" who had protected England over time.[66] Few of Drew's listeners seem to have been bothered by the seeming contradictions in his histories.

---

63. CIYMA Annual Minute Books, PRONI, D.3936/A/1/1; Dawson, "Annals of Christ Church, Belfast," 153. A phrenological examination of the skull in 1854 led Dawson to conclude that Walker had "rather a clear and controlling, than a profound or comprehensive intellect." See Dawson, "Biographical Notice of George Walker," 278.

64. Covington, *Devil from over the Sea*, 86–102.

65. Drew, *Sermon, Preached in Christ Church, Belfast, on the Evening of November 5, 1856*, 12.

66. Drew, *Sermon (on Eccl. 9:13–16)*, 14, 18.

Drew's biographies of Irish Protestant heroes were designed to personalize the struggle between truth and heresy, to emphasize the notion that Protestantism could be and must be defended, as it had been under more difficult circumstances in the past. We might not be the equal of these great men, he argued, but Irish Protestants must unite to defend the inheritance for which these heroes had sacrificed their lives. This required a determined culture of remembrance. This belief was embodied by *Protestant Anniversaries*, a fifty-seven-page calendar of important dates for Protestants that Drew compiled in 1858 for Protestant ministers, public speakers, and the heads of households:

> We live in days when imprudent and ensnared Protestants echo the insidious cry of Romanists, and hasten to erase all remembrances of our Protestant story; to blot out all laws, inscriptions, and prayers bequeathed by our illustrious fathers, and to hurl from their pedestal the Ebenezer pillars reared for the glory of God, and for the instruction of posterity. In such hapless and inglorious days, let the ABDIELS of the land proclaim everlasting commemoration of the works, times, and men of God.
>
> Let the past speak trumpet-tongued! Let the blood of the slain cry from the ground not for vengeance, but for vigilance. Let the prisons, the tortures, the burned Bibles, the nailed-up Churches, the rifled graves, and the terrific curses which were allotted to our fathers, in every land under heaven, warn us against out perils, and shame us to lively gratitude to God and to our deliverers in old time.[67]

The calendar brought together references to the events and heroes of the European Reformation, and of British and Irish history, with more contemporary and personal events like the death of Michael Sadler in 1835 and the violence at Dolly's Brae in July 1849. If some of the dates

---

67. Drew, *Protestant Anniversaries*, 5. Abdiel is a Hebrew name that means "servant of God."

were somewhat suspect, it was a powerful and vivid portrait, a defensive and muscular Protestant identity for a difficult time.[68]

Drew's portrayal of Roman Catholicism was equally simple and predictable. For the Christ Church minister, like so many Protestant evangelicals, the Roman Catholic Church was inherently authoritarian, disloyal, and heretical, a potent vehicle for Satan's work in the world. In his Orange sermons, Drew stressed the Roman Catholic Church's aggression over the centuries; this was an institution based on ignorance, intolerance, and violence. He regularly insisted that he and his fellow Protestants were not enemies to Catholics; that as much as he opposed Roman Catholicism, he was not antagonistic to individual Irish Catholics. As he put it in an 1858 sermon: "Who dares to call the true Protestant the enemy of the Romanist? . . . He is a friend—the safest, truest, and heartiest friend of the misguided Romanist."[69] If popery had ever reformed, Drew argued in his preface to *Protestant Anniversaries*, "Protestants might remit their watchfulness, and call the Romanist a friend and a brother."[70] Given the violent rhetoric and often insulting condescension of his public performances, Catholic readers (and occasional listeners) could be forgiven if they failed to recognize the distinction. In October 1848 the *Weekly Vindicator* described Drew as a "disturber of the peace" after he spoke at a Protestant meeting in the Music Hall.[71] It would become a familiar refrain.

It is true that Drew's critique often focused on historical matters as much as contemporary issues, although he certainly stressed the idea that the Catholic threat was constant and alive—"Rome is Rome ever, and Satan wills it so."[72] That said, it was the lessons of the past

---

68. Drew, *Protestant Anniversaries*, 34, 36. Sarah Covington notes that two of four dates that Drew lists for Cromwell are incorrect. See Covington, *Devil from over the Sea*, 102.

69. Drew, *Sermon (on Eccl. 9:13–16)*, 3.

70. Drew, *Protestant Anniversaries*, 5–6.

71. *Weekly Vindicator*, October 28, 1848.

72. Drew, *Sermon (on Eccl. 9:13–16)*, 13.

rather than the present that Drew typically used to draw his portrait of an unchanging Roman Catholic threat:

> The perils of Protestantism have ever been great. Not only did the caverns of the Inquisition gape for Protestant victims, but the contrivances of the Popes and Jesuits devised wholesale massacre for them. We are not to forget the crusades against the Albigenses and Waldenses; the Revocation of the Edict of Nantes, and the Dragonades; the wholesale persecutions by the Spaniards in the Low Countries; the infamously-planned and atrociously consummated massacre of St. Bartholomew's Day (on which occasion a blood-thirsty Pope had a medal struck to commemorate the slaughter, and a Te Deum was sung before him, as if God would be pleased with a deluge of innocent blood). We do not forget, and we will not consent to forget, the plot by gunpowder in 1605; nor the Irish massacre in 1641.[73]

While Victorian anti-Catholic preachers based on the British mainland might have featured less Irish material in their occasional sermons, Drew's historical sense was hardly novel, echoing the views of Anglican populists such as Tresham Gregg, Mortimer O'Sullivan, Robert McGhee, Hugh Stowell, and Hugh McNeile, ultra-Protestant champions who Drew frequently celebrated in his sermons. For Drew and his allies, the past was instructive and useful in the present, mobilizing and legitimizing the need for Protestant action. *Je me souviens.* It was context rather than content that made Drew stand out from his peers.

Despite the clarion call to action and the startling violence of his sermons, Drew nearly always cautioned his listeners that they should not use violent means to defend the faith. The language he used to do this, however, was so inflammatory that it is hard to see his call for Protestant support for the law having a moderating effect:

> We do not ask for tumultuary violence to accomplish this desirable end. We ask for no rising of Protestant men to silence the blasphemy

---

73. Drew, *Sermon (on Eccl. 9:13–16)*, 13. See also *Protestant Anniversaries.*

of the priest who adores the woman Mary, honoured though her memory be; we ask for no illegal demonstration to prohibit the priest from lifting up a morsel of bread to an insulted Heaven, and from calling on a prostrated people to adore the newly-made God. But we ask for our head magistrate, the Queen, and for legislators to take God's Word for their guide and statute-book; and we doubt not that, in their acknowledgment of its demands, no dead men would henceforth be openly worshipped—no grovelling human creatures would openly become prostrate at the tinkling of the mass-bell and at the Latin mass of the priests.[74]

While the lines between Drew's verbal extremism and communal violence are neither simple nor direct, his protestations ring hollow, an evasion of accountability for the verbal violence of his set piece performances.

A similar dynamic pervades the emphasis on prayer in his Orange sermons. In nearly every lecture, Drew emphasized and extolled the value of prayer, highlighting the fact that the lodge meetings of the Orange Order opened and closed with prayer. All was in God's hands, Drew argued, and the past showed that faithful and godly men would be rewarded: "Angels are chiefly observing, not the policy of statesmen, the march of armies, or the multitudes that assemble to hear and applaud the mere philosopher or poet: they observe sagaciously and with profound sympathy the position of god's struggling and earnest witnesses. For them a sermon has its interest, and its effective results are borne heavenward to make the 'the house of many mansions' vibrate with joy. They take cognizance of zealous and godly men, uniting in God's fear and strength for God's honour and Word. They watch for tribute to God of intellect, opportunity, wealth, prayer, and praise."[75] Writing to William Johnston in 1849 about his plans

---

74. Drew, *Sermon, Preached in Christ Church, Belfast, on the Evening of November 5, 1856*, 9.

75. Drew, *Sermon, Preached in Christ Church, Belfast, on the Evening of November 5, 1856*, 15.

for marching on the 12th of July, Drew insisted that "we need to be men of prayer, William. Any use of language or deeds unworthy of a Christian calling would do great injury to our cause."[76] These calls for prayer and thoughtful reflection, however, were undermined by their juxtaposition with his fevered rhetoric about the need for Protestant action. Mark Doyle has noted that Drew's infamous July 1857 sermon to the Belfast Orangemen at Christ Church failed to contain the usual evangelical disclaimer that true Protestants should oppose the Roman Catholic Church but treat its adherents with respectful civility. Drew's near-pornographic description of "prelates dabbled in the gore of helpless victims" and "the delicate limbs of Protestant women strained on the rack" rendered any such distinction meaningless, and the lecture's role in heightening communal confrontation that resulted in the first phase of Belfast riots of 1857 underscored the critical relationship between verbal and physical sectarian violence in Belfast.[77] If recent interpretations of sectarian rioting in Victorian Belfast have emphasized the social relationships between and within working-class neighborhoods rather than the rhetorical provocation of political pastors, there can no doubt that Drew's well-publicized Orange sermons helped to foster and legitimize a dangerous politics of communal division. These were deadly words.

---

76. Thomas Drew to William Johnston, July 9, 1849, Diaries of William Johnston, PRONI, D.880/7/1/A. Courtesy of the Deputy Keeper of the Records, Public Record Office of Northern Ireland.

77. Doyle, *Fighting like the Devil for the Sake of God*, 84–85.

3

Evangelical Protestantism in Action
The Mant Controversy, 1842–1843

Evangelical Protestantism was about far more than words. After all, Thomas Drew was not working on his own. He was part of an increasingly powerful cohort of energetic new ministers in both the Church of Ireland and the Presbyterian Church in Belfast. Figures such as Drew, Henry Cooke, John Edgar, James Morgan, and William McIlwaine transformed the town's religious landscape in the 1830s and 1840s, bringing the church and meeting house into direct contact with larger numbers of people through their public campaigns of social and spiritual reform. This created its own problems. Within the Church of Ireland in particular, the rise of a new generation of evangelical clergymen generated tension with a church leadership that was largely High Church in orientation. A few of these clashes became public in the 1840s, with Drew and his allies encouraging an increasingly confident and evangelical laity to become more involved in religious politics.

Many of these patterns can be seen in the Mant controversy of 1842–43, a seemingly arcane episode in Belfast church politics that illustrates dynamic and shifting relationships between Anglican clergymen and various lay communities in this rapidly industrializing town. The controversy was triggered by Bishop Mant's support for the

---

An earlier version of this chapter was published as Sean Farrell's "Building Opposition: The Mant Controversy and the Church of Ireland in Early Victorian Belfast," *Irish Historical Studies* 39, no. 154 (November 2014): 230–49. Copyright © Irish Historical Studies Publications Ltd 2014. Reprinted with permission.

Down and Connor and Dromore Church Architecture Society, a diocesan organization devoted to the antiquarian study of religious architecture. Linked to Puseyism and the Oxford Movement by evangelical ministers and lay congregants wary of its celebration of ritualism and externalities, the Church Architecture Society generated a contentious debate in the Belfast press that lasted several months before influential lay and religious elites quelled the controversy in late February 1843. On one level, the Mant controversy reveals the significant growth of evangelical Protestantism within the established church and the consequent tensions that influence generated within the Church of Ireland. Backed by their congregants and with the critical support of town and regional political elites, ministers such as Drew and his ally McIlwaine, minister of St. George's Church, mobilized public opinion through the press and petition to challenge Bishop Mant and his allies; a move that reflected Irish evangelicals' increased propensity to use populist methods and lay support to confront an episcopal establishment still disproportionately led by high churchmen.[1]

But the Mant controversy was more than a squabble between emergent evangelicals and powerful, if out of touch, high churchmen. One of the central arguments that Drew and his allies leveled against Mant was that he was needlessly offensive to Belfast's Presbyterian majority; that both his lectures on the "dangers of Puritanism" and his emphasis on rubrical conformity divided Ulster Protestant communities at a time they needed to be more closely aligned to face the threat posed by Irish Catholic nationalism. The controversy thus illustrates the multifaceted nature of northern anti-Catholicism, as both Mant and his opponents engaged in a kind of sectarian competition to define themselves, claiming that they were each sufficiently (or not) anti-Catholic to represent true Ulster Protestantism. This fight over the Church Architecture Society also underlines the complexity of continuing tensions between Anglicans and Presbyterians and highlights the ways in which religious controversies facilitated the use of pan-Protestant (and anti-Catholic) rhetoric, an increasingly familiar

1. Yates, *Religious Condition of Ireland*, 266–67.

4. Richard Mant, bishop of Down, Connor, and Dromore. Source: Berens, *Memoir of the Life of Bishop Mant*.

feature of religious and popular politics in Victorian Belfast and one closely associated with Drew.

The man at the center of events was Richard Mant, bishop of Connor, Down, and Dromore (added to the diocese in 1842). Born in Southampton, England, in 1776, Mant was both an energetic bishop and a prominent Anglican intellectual, one of the most learned clergymen in the Church of Ireland and author of the influential two-volume *History of the Church of Ireland* (1840), among many other titles. An orthodox clergyman who was firmly High Church in orientation, Mant's 1823 translation from Killaloe and Kilfenora in the south and west of Ireland to Down and Connor was part of a broader effort to reenergize a Church of Ireland too often characterized by lax standards of discipline and pastoral care.[2] From Mant's perspective, the challenge he faced in the diocese was made all the more difficult by both a resurgent Roman Catholicism and the extreme enthusiasm of the "Puritans" within Presbyterianism and the evangelical wing of his own church. The latter issue was of particular concern. Finding an equilibrium between orthodoxy and enthusiasm was one of the central problems faced by Anglican leaders interested in strengthening the Church of Ireland's position in early nineteenth-century Irish society.[3] Mant certainly struggled to find such a balance. As he put in an 1823 letter: "Presbyterians, you know, abound in my new charge; they are said, however, to be not very hostile to the Established Church. . . . I hope our clergy do not compromise their principles to conciliate them."[4] This was particularly fraught territory in an increasingly evangelical and Presbyterian-majority Belfast.

Mant worked hard to counter the "compromising tendencies" of his clergy and throughout his tenure he was a strong advocate for sound churchmanship, insisting on the need for discipline, hierarchy, and the enforcement of Anglican laws, standards, and traditions, a stance that generated predictable frustration from some of his more ambitious and less hierarchically oriented evangelical clergymen.[5] Mant was no simple High Church ideologue, however. While protective of episcopal authority, he was capable of creative compromise and helped to engineer the Church of Ireland's dramatic church construction project in Belfast and the region across the era. Between 1823 and 1843, Mant consecrated sixteen new churches in the diocese and rebuilt and/or extended twenty-two more.[6] This should come as no

---

2. Yates, *Religious Condition of Ireland*, 63–98.

3. Yates, *Religious Condition of Ireland*, 67.

4. Richard Mant to Edward Berens, June 3, 1823, quoted in Mant, *Memoirs of the Right Reverend Richard Mant*, 159.

5. Hempton and Hill, *Evangelical Protestantism in Ulster Society*, 67–69.

6. Yates, *Religious Condition of Ireland*, 98–99.

surprise. After all, it was Mant who secured funding and support for the construction of Christ Church.

While Mant is remembered for his association with the church's early Victorian urban renewal, the church accommodation project also revealed growing tensions between the bishop and Drew and his evangelical allies. From their perspective, Mant seemed overly concerned with matters of hierarchy and form that paled in importance with the calling of bringing vital religion to the urban masses. These tensions were not new for Mant, whose abiding interest in matters of public worship and efforts to implement oft-neglected church rubrics had generated conflict with evangelicals throughout his career in England and Ireland. As early as 1812 he had provoked their ire with his critique of the evangelical rejection of the doctrine of baptismal regeneration and his general distrust—*evangelical* is "a word too often used"—is clear in his official biography.[7] For Mant, rubrical conformity and the use of consistent, legitimate forms of public worship were crucial matters because they distinguished the Church of Ireland "from other classes of Protestants," a factor made all the more important by the rise of evangelicalism in a town with a substantial Presbyterian presence. Many of these tensions can be seen in a clash between Drew and Mant over plans to create a diocesan mission for Belfast's extensive unchurched population in the mid-1830s.

The idea of a domestic mission was certainly not a new one in the town. The Belfast Town (later City) Mission was founded in 1827, part of the broader effort to bring scripture and greater civility to the urban poor.[8] The Belfast Town Mission was nondenominational, however, and a number of the town's Church of Ireland ministers wanted a specifically Anglican initiative, part of the effort to carve out a larger space for the established church in the predominantly Presbyterian town. The initial result of these efforts was the Church Home Mission

---

7. For the controversy over baptismal regeneration, see Nockles, *Oxford Movement in Context*, 229–35. For a more general account, see Bebbington, *Evangelicalism in Modern Britain*, 9–10.

8. See Sibbett, *For Christ and Crown*, 1–10.

Society, but this was quickly dissolved in 1834, when Mant opposed the project because it involved ministers operating outside of the bishop's authority.[9] Two years later, Drew and a number of his allies took up the project again, meeting at the home of the Reverend Robert Bland, curate at St. Anne's Cathedral, to craft a plan they thought might meet with the bishop's approval.[10] When Drew brought the plan to Mant, however, he rejected it outright, calling it an unauthorized interference with his jurisdiction.

Some of the issues involved in this controversy can be seen in Mant's 1836 charge, "The Church, the Guide of Her Ministers' Conduct and Teaching," a not-so-subtle assertion of episcopal authority. In it, Mant sketched out the need for an Anglican via media between the errors of Roman Catholicism and the dangers of heterogeneous Puritanism, a course that underlined the importance of episcopal authority, rubrical conformity, and clerical discipline.[11] Regarding the latter, Mant made clear his support for church extension efforts where clergymen brought their ministry to places outside of church, as long as those sites were properly licensed. Accordingly, when Drew brought a revised plan that was more sensitive to Mant's sense of episcopal authority and existing parochial boundaries, Mant gave his consent and the plan was implemented in 1838. While the rift had been resolved and a productive compromise established, the episode highlights the differences between the establishment-minded Mant and his energetic and independent evangelical lieutenant.[12]

---

9. Mant, *Memoirs of the Right Reverend Richard Mant*, 293.

10. Mant, *Memoirs of the Right Reverend Richard Mant*, 340–43; Dawson, "Annals of Christ Church, Belfast," PRONI, T.2159/1, 26–28.

11. Mant's efforts to maintain a firm distinction between the Church of Ireland and Dissenting churches generated a response from the Reverend Henry Cooke, who warned Mant that only the opponents of the established church would benefit from a polemical war between Anglicans and Presbyterians in Ireland. See Henry Cooke to Richard Mant, October 7, 1836, Mant Correspondence, National Library of Ireland, MS 15,361 (1).

12. Mant, *Memoirs of the Right Reverend Richard Mant*, 313–51; Acheson, *History of the Church of Ireland*, 152–53. Drew also ran afoul of the church establishment when

In many ways, this clash was as much a matter of political temperament and style as theology, something underlined by a July 1842 letter that Drew wrote to James Emerson Tennent, the influential Conservative member of Parliament for Belfast: "Mant is an Ultra; honest, learned, active in bookwriting and unsurpassed in letter writing but timid—too isolated."[13] This contrast between the Bishop's scholarly and elitist orientation and Drew's action-oriented populism underlines a broader tension that all is too apparent in Belfast church politics from 1835 on. For all his formal support for church extension in Belfast, the fault lines between Mant and his evangelical clerics were clear by the time the Mant controversy erupted in late 1842.

THE MANT CONTROVERSY, 1842–1843

While Mant long had taken a scholarly interest in the history of the Anglican Church, his advocacy for a society dedicated to the study of church architecture was inspired by a more recent emergent group in the Church of England. This was the Cambridge Camden Society, an organization founded in 1839 by Cambridge undergraduates John Mason Neale, Alexander Hope, and Benjamin Webb to promote "the study of Gothic Architecture and Ecclesiastical Antiques."[14] Also known as the Ecclesiological Society, the group quickly gained adherents and influence with its core argument that the corruption and ugliness of Victorian Britain could best be countered by an attempt to recapture the piety and beauty of medieval church architecture.

---

he tried to increase his income through celebrating marriages and christenings of men, women, and children who did not reside in his district. See Edward Stopford to Primate Beresford, February 5, 1836, Church of Ireland Diocesan Papers, PRONI, DIO/1/125A/17B.

13. Thomas Drew to J. Emerson Tennent, July 29, 1842, Emerson Tennent Papers, PRONI, D.2922/C/12/3. Courtesy of the Deputy Keeper of the Records, Public Record Office of Northern Ireland.

14. For an overview of the history of the Cambridge Society, see White, *Cambridge Movement*.

The Cambridge Camden Society was closely associated with John Henry Newman's Tractarian movement, an effort to renew the theology, ecclesiology, sacraments, and liturgical practices of the Church of England. The long-term impact of the Cambridge Camden Society is undeniable; by the end of the nineteenth century, the society's standards for church architecture had become the norm, effectively reinventing the design of parish churches across England. In the short term, however, reaction to the organization was divided, with many British and Irish Protestants hostile to the Cambridge Camden Society's romanticized vision of the medieval church. The image of this association and its links to the Oxford Movement was a particularly powerful weapon for Belfast evangelicals and their allies, who argued that the Church Architecture Society acted as a kind of beachhead for the Catholic invasion of Protestant Belfast. In nineteenth-century Ulster, where sectarian lines of division seemingly were always awaiting reinvention, this kind of controversialist rhetoric crackled with potentially explosive power.

The first meeting of the Church Architecture Society made the group's sympathy with the aims of the Cambridge Camden Society quite explicit. According to one account, Mant argued that the society had a positive role to play in the diocese, for "whatever tends to add dignity and majesty to 'the houses of God in our land,' provided it be free from all superstitious admixture, is deserving of our encouragement: whatever tends to diminish these qualities, is deserving of censure and reprobation."[15] It would be difficult to find a more lucid statement of the Cambridge Camden Society's goals linking architectural and spiritual beauty. Mant illustrated the importance of spiritual aesthetics with a story about a local church, where a beautiful ancient pulpit and reading desk made of black oak had recently been painted a muddy yellow. James Saurin, archdeacon of Dromore and rector of Seagoe Parish

---

15. *Report of the First Meeting of the Down and Connor and Dromore Church Architecture Society*, 13. For a detailed examination of the topic across the Victorian era, see McBride, "Bishop Mant and the Down and Connor and Dromore Church Architecture Society, 1837–1878."

Church, quickly asserted his innocence in the commission of this particular aesthetic sin,[16] but Mant's general point was clear—external beauty and tradition mattered, and parish churches should reflect the majesty and splendor of the established church.

Saurin's letter of denial was the first printed in response to Mant's address. It was not the last, however, as public reaction to the creation of the Church Architecture Society quickly grew heated and the organization soon became a controversial touchstone. Shortly after the meeting, McIlwaine got into a fierce argument with the staff of the *Ulster Times*, furious that they would not print his letter on the spot (the newspaper maintained its support for Mant and the fledgling architectural society for the first few months of the controversy).[17] Given his leadership of the ensuing campaign against the Church Architecture Society, McIlwaine's argument that the *Ulster Times* was actively provoking Belfast Presbyterians and flaunting Puseyism was telling.[18] McIlwaine moved his own critique to the more sympathetic *Belfast Commercial Chronicle*, and both opponents and defenders of the new organization rushed into the breach and an emotional public discussion quickly emerged across the Belfast press. Although Mant attempted to quiet the controversy at the organization's second meeting in early November, arguing that attacks on the society were based on a fundamental misunderstanding of the group's goals, it was too late and rhetorical temperatures continued to rise throughout the winter of 1842 and 1843.[19]

16. *Ulster Times*, October 15, 1842.

17. *Ulster Times*, October 11, 1842. This struggle was not picked up in either of Belfast's major newspapers, the *Belfast News-Letter* and the *Northern Whig*, a fact that underlines the key role played by McIlwaine's public journalism in widening the sphere of debate.

18. *Ulster Times*, October 11, 1842. The subject seems not to have been a passing one for St. George's rector; McIlwaine's second lecture before the Church of Ireland's Young Men's Society in 1851 was titled "Some Thoughts on Church Architecture and Ecclesiastical Remains," *Annual Reports of the Church of Ireland Young Men's Society*, PRONI, D.3936/A/1/1.

19. *Ulster Times*, November 3, 1842.

5. William McIlwaine, rector of St. George's Church. Source: Walker, *History of St. George's Church Belfast*; original portrait in St. George Archives. Courtesy of Brian M. Walker and Rev. William Odling-Smee, curate of St. George's Church.

William McIlwaine was the person most responsible for ratcheting up both the heat and scale of the debate. Born in Dublin in 1807, he arrived at St. George's Church in 1836 after short stints in Balteagh, County Londonderry, and Cloughjordan, County Tipperary. One of Drew's closest allies, McIlwaine seemingly shared his friend's ability to generate conflict, actively participating in controversialist anti-Catholic street preaching in the late 1840s and 1850s and bitterly breaking with the Church of Ireland Young Men's Society in the mid-1860s (an organization he had helped to found in 1850).[20] In October 1842 these clashes were still far in the future, however, and McIlwaine's invective was focused on the High Church novelties of the Church Architecture Society. Writing in the *Belfast Commercial Chronicle* under the pseudonym "Clericus Connorensis," McIlwaine wrote a series of nineteen public letters titled "What Is Puseyism?", a reference to Edward Bouverie Pusey, one of the leading figures in the Oxford Movement. Later published as *Ecclesiologism Exposed*, McIlwaine's vitriolic journalism helped to keep the controversy in public view for nearly half a year.[21] Since his arguments effectively reflected the main tenets of evangelical and popular opposition to the society, it is worth examining these letters in some detail.

20. For McIlwaine, see Ritchie, "William McIlwaine and the 1859 Revival in Ulster," 803–26. For the relationship between street preaching and sectarian violence in the 1850s, see Holmes, "Role of Open-Air Preaching in the Belfast Riots of 1857," 47–66. For his break with the Church of Ireland's Young Men's Society, see McNeilly, *First Hundred Years*. According to J. B. Leslie, McIlwaine was the first clergyman in Belfast to have hymns sung, to hold early morning Holy Communion, preach in the surplice, and to hold Harvest Thanksgiving Service. See Leslie, *Clergy of Connor*, 469. McIlwaine's increasing interest in High Church forms late in career underlines the danger in assuming that *High Church* and *evangelical* are necessarily oppositional terms in the Church of Ireland.

21. The letters were published in the *Belfast Commercial Chronicle* from mid-October 1842 to the end of February 1843. They were later published in pamphlet form as McIlwaine, *Ecclesiologism Exposed*. For simplicity's sake, further references to McIlwaine's letters will be to this single publication. This is available at: https://archive.org/stream/a625113202cleruoft#page/n1/mode/2up.

McIlwaine's extended critique of the Church Architecture Society was rooted in the notion that the society's emphasis on external form strayed too far from the principles of true Protestantism. Simply put, Puseyism was popery, and even if many of the new organization's members were well-intentioned, he argued that the association reflected a dangerous effort to move the established church closer to Roman Catholicism. Throughout the series, McIlwaine equated the new organization with both the Cambridge Camden Society and the Oxford Movement, moving back and forth between local lectures on medieval church architecture and John Henry Newman's controversial *Tract Number Ninety* on the church's foundational Thirty-Nine Articles of Religion. His critique of Newman was particularly trenchant: "That more false and libellous glosses on Gospel truth, and more derogatory to the doctrine of England's national faith, never came from the pen of an open or concealed enemy."[22] Constantly referring to the Oxonian cant of his opponents, McIlwaine's basic message was clear; this was Catholicism in disguise, and needed to be opposed as such by all true Ulster Protestants.

More particularly, McIlwaine and his allies argued vociferously that Mant's emphasis on church architecture was a waste of money and effort. What was needed was an unrelenting drive to bring true religion to Belfast's lamentably large population of unchurched men, women, and children. As Drew put it: "In my humble opinion, with architecture we clergymen have little to do; . . . nor have we hitherto wanted the assistance of an architect of acknowledged generosity [Charles Lanyon]; under his direction our buildings were becomingly constructed and adapted to the real wants of the people—namely—CHURCH ACCOMMODATION."[23] A number of commentators framed their critiques of the Church Architecture Society by detailing its negative impact on the Church Accommodation Society, a valuable organization undermined by both a loss of "sufficient subscribers"

---

22. McIlwaine, *Ecclesiologism Exposed*, 16.
23. *Belfast Commercial Chronicle*, January 16, 1843.

and the "moral taint" attached to the Church Architecture Society. As Abraham Dawson later put it in "The Annals of Christ Church, Belfast," this more valuable society was dissolved because of the "baneful influence of the Romanizing party in the Church of England," particularly those people concerned with the architecture and ornamentalism of churches.[24] This was by no means a unanimous opinion. Richard Arthur Agar, curate of Drumgath Church near Rathfriland, County Down, argued that "the fact is, he [McIlwaine] either is ignorant, or affects to be so, of our real objects when he argues thus absurdly."[25] Another correspondent failed to see the connection between the two societies, wondering how "one body of men [was] to be hindered in building churches, because another body of men would wish them to be built in a peculiar way?"[26] However plausible, this argument failed to convince many Belfast evangelicals and their supporters, who continued to see the Church Architecture Society as a potentially heretical association that diverted scarce resources away from church accommodation. In the seventeenth letter of his series, McIlwaine asked why the church was spending money on stained glass for the new Kilwarlin church near Hillsborough, when so many people remained ignorant of the primary tenets of the Bible.[27] In short, even if this new association was harmless, it drew time and resources away from the central project of Belfast Protestantism: spreading the Gospel.

Not surprisingly, there was an important theological element to this argument. For McIlwaine and his many fellow evangelicals, Puseyism was heresy; its emphasis on external factors was an unwanted distraction from the central truth of the Reformation and of

---

24. For a sampling, see *Ulster Times*, October 18, 1842, January 12, 1843; *Belfast Commercial Chronicle*, January 16, 1843; McIlwaine, *Ecclesiologism Exposed*, 44, 47–49. See also Dawson, "Annals of Christ Church, Belfast," 76. Opponents of the Church Architecture Society placed this point at the center of their petition to Bishop Mant; see *Ulster Times*, February 2, 1843.

25. *Ulster Times*, November 29, 1842.

26. *Ulster Times* December 22, 1842.

27. McIlwaine, *Ecclesiologism Exposed*, 50–52.

Protestantism—that true religion was justified by faith alone. Using Richard Hooker's *Discourse on Justification* as the Anglican standard on the subject, McIlwaine argued that justification by faith only had long been the common denominator of Protestantism, and that Puseyism, with its emphasis on human tradition, physical edifice, and centralized episcopal authority, created needless division between Protestants. Even if the movement's adherents were not aiming to return the Church of England to Rome, McIlwaine was certain that Puseyism was a threat to God's truth and that the Tractarian advocacy of these Popish innovations inevitably led to the Eternal City.[28] Ornate tradition could not replace the simple truth of faith in God's word. As he put it, "I love the chaste and beauteous structure of my National Church" and he did not want to change them, particularly not by "groping amid old ruins for the deformed remains of a rude age."[29]

Finally, opponents of the Church Architecture Society grounded their critique in a popular British historical narrative that featured the Protestant heroes and enemies of the English Reformation. As scholars such as J. C. D. Clark and Linda Colley have made clear, this Protestant historical narrative was central to eighteenth- and nineteenth-century notions of national identity throughout the British Isles. These stories retained a vibrant relevance in mid-nineteenth-century Ulster even as the power of anti-Catholicism faded somewhat in Great Britain.[30] McIlwaine's frequent references to sixteenth- and

---

28. For the main tenets of McIlwaine's theological argument against Puseyism, see McIlwaine, *Ecclesiologism Exposed*, 9–13, 15–18, 26–28, 31–38, 45–47, 52–54. For a solid introduction to Richard Hooker's notions of justification, see Simut, *Richard Hooker and His Early Doctrine of Justification*, 1–12. For Hooker and historiography, see Brydon, *Evolving Reputation of Richard Hooker*.

29. McIlwaine, *Ecclesiologism Exposed*, 19.

30. For religion and English and British nationalism, see Clark, *English Society*; Colley, *Britons*. Linda Colley has rightly been criticized for understating the denominational fractures within British Protestantism. For searching critiques of Colley's treatment of religion and nationalism, see Pincus, "Review of Linda Colley's *Britons*," 132–36; Newman, "Nationalism Revisited," 124; Kidd, "North Britishness and the Nature of Eighteenth-Century British Patriotisms," 364–81.

seventeenth-century historical figures make it clear just how vital it was for evangelicals to portray themselves as the true inheritors of the English Reformation. In his first letter, McIlwaine tellingly opened with the story of Archbishop William Laud, wielded here as a powerful warning against those who supported the novelties of the Oxford theologians and their allies.[31] This historical claim was not limited to McIlwaine, as one clerical correspondent in the *Ulster Times* made clear when he argued that no one connected with the Cambridge Camden Society should be allowed to hold office to protect "the pure principles of the Reformation for which Cranmer, Latimer and Ridley suffered martyrdom."[32] Simply stated, McIlwaine and his allies argued that the Tractarian veneration of artifice, tradition, and the medieval past was suspicious and downright Catholic, a narrative rooted in a resonant morality tale of principled Protestant heroes and base Catholic treachery. By equating the Church Architecture Society with Laud and King Charles I, he made it clear that the new organization and its sponsors were on the wrong side of British and Irish history.

If McIlwaine believed that Puseyism posed a real threat to true religion, he remained confident that the common sense and faith of the Ulster Protestant laity would see these innovations for what they were. To counter the "popish threat," Belfast evangelicals mobilized their congregants against Puseyism, a populist strategy that Mant and other elites clearly viewed with distaste. Across the spectrum, evangelicals consistently contrasted their faith in the true Protestant

31. McIlwaine, *Ecclesiologism Exposed*, 9–10. While there are references to various seventeenth-century English figures throughout McIlwaine's letters, letter 17 contains an extended treatment of this theme, focusing on early Tractarian critiques of Jewel, Luther, Cranmer, Ridley and Latimer. See McIlwaine, *Ecclesiologism Exposed*, 50.

32. *Ulster Times*, January 14, 1843. Of course, these martyrdoms remained a critical symbolic power within certain conservative narratives of the Ulster past and present. Drew, for example, scheduled special services at Christ Church to commemorate the tercentenary anniversaries of the sixteenth-century martyrdoms of Cranmer, Latimer, and Ridley in 1855 and 1856. See Dawson, "Annals of Christ Church, Belfast," PRONI, T.2159/185 and /195.

impulses of the laity with the hierarchical and authoritarian distrust of the people displayed by their opponents.[33] As the editor of the *Belfast Commercial Chronicle* opined: "The Laity of our Church are now called upon to make a move—let them do so with firmness and determination—let them act with the temperance which becometh their Christian profession, the zeal of men who recognize the magnitude of the interests at stake; not for the purpose of achieving a vain triumph, but the noble object of resolutely maintaining the liberty with which Christ has made them free."[34] McIlwaine used similar language in the introduction to his *Ecclesiologism Exposed*; the lay movement against heresy proved that those who believe their "poorer brethren are unable to form an opinion on the merits of an issue" were quite mistaken.[35]

The clearest expression of the evangelical faith in the Protestant zeal of the laity came in an effort to draw up a memorial to the bishop of Down and Connor. The first notice of this effort appeared in a mid-January report of the *Belfast Commercial Chronicle*, which argued that the laity had finally begun to stand up against the ruinous mixture of ecclesiology and for much-needed church accommodation, reporting that "many of the most influential and respectable gentlemen of Belfast, all subscribers and friends of the Church Accommodation Society," had recently met to take a firm stance against the Church Architecture Society.[36] The mechanism they chose was a petition, a widely used tool in nineteenth-century British and Irish political life.[37] In this case the memorial was drawn up and circulated throughout parts of Belfast and the surrounding villages of Counties Antrim

---

33. McIlwaine makes reference to an awakened laity in letters 7, 9, 18 and 19. See McIlwaine, *Ecclesiologism Exposed*, 25–28, 52–55. In addition to the petition controversy described below, see *Belfast News-Letter*, November 18, 1842; *Belfast Commercial Chronicle*, January 18, 1843.

34. *Belfast Commercial Chronicle*, January 9, 1843.

35. McIlwaine, *Ecclesiologism Exposed*, vii.

36. *Belfast Commercial Chronicle*, January 18, 1843.

37. For the petition as a crucial part of nineteenth-century British political culture, see Huzzey and Miller, "Politics of Petitioning," 221–43.

and Down. It was this circulation that drew the sharpest comment. Richard Davison, a leading Christ Church congregant and one of the members of a committee appointed by the leaders of the Church Architecture Society to examine the relationship between the organization and the Cambridge Camden Society, clearly was angered by the methods employed to obtain signatures for the petition: "One thing that is offensive is the effort to raise the laity in opposition to their bishop, without solid evidence. I'm not charging those who signed the petition with this offense, their motives were pure—but the others, who hawked it through Antrim and Down villages for signatures from the humblest people in life and saying that they should sign against Puseyism."[38] Other supporters accused opponents of running a misinformation campaign against the bishop. One minister complained to the Marquess of Downshire that in Dundrum he knew "that signatures were asked for the memorial because of the alleged intention of the Bishop to introduce candles on the Communion Tables of the several churches!"[39] For all the complaints about their methods, the petition against the Church Architecture Society certainly garnered a significant degree of popular support; more than 1,300 people signed the memorial, which was formally presented to Mant on February 1, 1843, by a deputation led by Colonel John Ward, Conway Dobbs, and W. G. Johnston, a former member of Parliament.[40]

The petition appeared in the February 4 issue of the *Belfast Commercial Chronicle*, with a complete list of signatories and Mant's response. The list was topped by an impressive array of northern elites, including

---

38. *Ulster Times*, February 28, 1843. Chosen in early February, the committee consisted of Davison, Mant, Colonel William Blacker, Colonel F. Crossley, and the Reverend J. S. Monsell. See *Belfast Commercial Chronicle*, March 1, 1843.

39. W. Smyth Cummings to the Marquess of Downshire, March 3, 1843, Downshire Papers, PRONI, D.671/C/209/19. Courtesy of the Deputy Keeper of the Records, Public Record Office of Northern Ireland.

40. See Colonel John Ward to the Marquess of Downshire, January 26 and February 5, 1843, Downshire Papers, PRONI, D.671/C/209/10–12; Dawson, "Annals of Christ Church, Belfast," 79–82.

the Lord Mayor of Belfast and fifty-one justices of the peace from across the province. This was not simply an elite campaign, however, and a brief analysis of the social background of the signatories provides a window into emergent cross-class networks in early Victorian Belfast. By cross-referencing the 1843 petition with data from an 1852 religious census of Christ Church District in Belfast, we get occupational data on a sample of fifty-one of the men who signed the petition.[41] The participants reflect the social range and makeup of this crucial Anglican community in Belfast: twelve were laborers and eleven were weavers, while three carpenters, two sawyers, two merchants, and two publicans signed. Although we cannot be absolutely sure that any of the individual names that appear on both lists are not duplicates (i.e., it is quite possible that there may be two different men named Hamilton Wardlaw), the broad contours of the results seem incontrovertible—significant numbers of middle- and working-class Belfast Anglican men signed the petition against the Church Architecture Society.

The memorial itself was a relatively simple document; one that neatly reflected the publicly expressed concerns of leaders like Drew and McIlwaine. After highlighting the long history of "unity and amity" between clergy and laity within the diocese and emphasizing the value of recent organizations such as the Church Accommodation Society, the petition expressed "alarm and apprehension" at the spread of the dangerous ideas associated with "Tracts for the Times" and the Cambridge Camden Society. Although the memorialists were convinced that these doctrines had not yet made significant progress in the province, they argued that this wrongheaded association had undermined church accommodation efforts and "that the same evil effects will be speedily and fatally felt, in paralyzing the operations of our other Diocesan Institutions." The petition concluded by asking Mant to "withdraw his countenance" from the Church Architecture Society.[42] In short, the memorial was a direct challenge to Mant's authority, and his interest in, and support for, the fledging organization.

---

41. Christ Church Census, 1852, PRONI, CR1/13D/1.
42. *Ulster Times*, February 2, 1843; *Belfast News-Letter*, February 4, 1843.

Mant's reply to the memorial only exacerbated the conflict. While thanking the memorialists for the opportunity to openly explain his views on these subjects (for "to answer anonymous calumniators has been morally impossible"), both the tone and much of the substance of his answer reinforced evangelical and popular opposition to the bishop. Most of the letter is respectful and measured in tone and content, as Mant thanked the respectable gentlemen who brought him the memorial for providing him the opportunity to explain his views on these matters. Along these lines, Mant provided a detailed refutation of the charge that the Church Architecture Society was a Catholic or proto-Catholic organization. He tried to counter this argument by asserting his own anti-Catholic credentials, highlighting recent diocesan charges that had warned against "some of those false doctrines that you have lamented as being promulgated by the 'Tracts for the Times.'" Moreover, he underlined his longtime support for the Church Accommodation Society, arguing that it had been designed as a temporary association, but expressing a willingness to reconstitute a society based on similar principles if that is what was needed and desired.[43] Above all, Mant called for respectful and rational discussion, exhorting his parishioners to "put their confidence in their Bishop," to look with "charity and brotherly love" on their brethren and to study and learn the actual principles and workings of the Church Architecture Society rather than depending on the emotional hyperbole that had dominated public discourse.[44]

Unfortunately, for many of his readers, less temperate sections of Mant's public letter overwhelmed this moderate and almost academic call for the reasoned study and debate of the issues surrounding the Church Architecture Society. Clearly angered by the challenge to his position, Mant opened with a robust assertion of episcopal authority,

---

43. Mant clearly was serious about this point, writing the British Prime Minister, Sir Robert Peel, about the issue; see Richard Mant to Sir Robert Peel, December 12, 1843, Peel Papers, General Correspondence, vol. 357, ff. 433–ff. 23, British Library, London.

44. *Ulster Times*, February 2, 1843.

critiquing clergymen for not giving him "the respect due to my office" and arguing that among those who deviated from the Church of Ireland the real danger came from those with "anti-episcopal, anti-liturgical, anti-ritual [beliefs] and irregular zeal" rather than the High Church ritualism of the Tractarians.[45] This was not a message likely to soothe evangelical hearts and minds and was particularly disturbing to those concerned about growing tensions between Presbyterians and Anglicans.

Anglican-Presbyterian relationships in Belfast in the early 1840s were replete with seeming contradictions. On the one hand, the increased presence and influence of evangelicals within the Church of Ireland created something of a common language for members of the two denominations and enhanced opportunities for tangible alliances, a tendency most famously embodied in the storied career of the Reverend Henry Cooke. This was reinforced by both the demographic growth of Belfast Catholics and the rise of organized Irish Catholic nationalist politics, elements that helped create an environment seemingly ripe for pan-Protestant cooperation. But denominational tensions remained high in both Ulster and across the British Isles, with traditional Anglican anxieties sharpened by Presbyterian and other Dissenting churches' dramatic growth in urban centres. In the early 1840s, these tensions found expression in the heightened anti-Dissenter rhetoric of high churchmen (doubtless shaped by the rise of evangelicals within their own established church), an 1840 Anglican challenge to the validity of Presbyterian marriages that remained controversial until its resolution in 1844, and, of course, that continual theme of denominational strife—religious education.[46]

45. *Ulster Times*, February 2, 1843.
46. See, for example, Dr. James McKnight's fierce anti-Drew editorial on national education: *Banner of Ulster*, September 4, 1849. For a helpful overview of these tensions, see Wolffe, *Protestant Crusade in Great Britain*, 204. Presbyterian perspectives are examined in Reid and Killen, *History of the Presbyterian Church in Ireland*, 3:485–88; Hall, *Ulster Liberalism*, 85–87; Miller, "Demise of the Confessional State in Ireland," 116–17. For Cooke, see Holmes, *Henry Cooke*.

In many ways, these seeming contradictions were embodied in Thomas Drew's career. Drew was a natural ally for evangelically minded Dissenters and throughout his tenure at Christ Church he worked with Presbyterian leaders like John Edgar and James Morgan on questions of social and moral reform ranging from temperance and anti-slavery to animal cruelty and famine relief. Despite these cooperative and productive relationships, Drew struggled to maintain interdenominational harmony with his colleagues, intermittently provoking clashes with Presbyterian ministers sensitive to establishment-minded critiques (and at times, his conservative and Orange politics). Part of this was a product of Drew's agenda of institutional growth, and as we have seen, his efforts to carve out a larger Protestant space in Belfast through the creation of denominationally specific initiatives in church outreach, domestic mission, and education generated tension with non-Anglicans and Anglicans alike. The Orange historian R. R. Sibbett clearly had Drew in mind when he later blamed such efforts for rising interdenominational tensions in the early 1840s.[47] But it was not simply Drew's commitment to the strengthening the Church of Ireland's place in Belfast that triggered controversy—his heavy-handed interventions on both national (particularly education) and local issues in the late 1830s and early 1840s did little to foster cooperative relationships between Anglicans and Presbyterians.[48]

Although Drew's bombastic public rhetoric continued to generate sporadic clashes with even like-minded evangelical Presbyterians,[49] by

---

47. Writing in an era where the importance of pan-Protestant unity was a more firmly established element in Ulster Unionist rhetoric, Sibbett lamented the ways that heightened interdenominational strife made mission work much more difficult. See Sibbett, *For Christ and Crown*, 71–72.

48. Drew generated a particularly emotive controversy in 1840 with remarks he made in Annalong, County Down, and Glynn, County Antrim, blaming Presbyterians for the current state of interdenominational strife, a speech that generated at least two bitter responses from ministers angered by Drew's "gratuitous attack." See *Belfast News-Letter*, August 25, 1840, September 8, 1840; *John Knox and the Reverend Thomas Drew*.

49. At one meeting dedicated to bringing relief to Belfast's poor population, Cooke was exasperated by Drew's long-winded attack on the use of soup for relief,

late 1842, he and his conservative and evangelical allies maintained that Mant was the problem, that he was far too antagonistic toward Ulster Presbyterianism. In a letter to Emerson Tennent, Drew argued that what was needed now was someone would soothe rather than provoke conflict between the city's two largest Protestant denominations, an approach that likely was as much a matter of tactics as ideology.[50] Nor was Drew alone in this belief. In a January 1843 report, the *Belfast News-Letter* was quite critical of Mant for needlessly giving offence to Presbyterians and other Dissenters with his sharply worded warnings about the dangers of Puritan excess.[51]

For all his anti-Dissenter rhetoric, however, Mant's real fury was directed at the people who had circulated the memorial throughout the diocese, "as if the object to be attained were the carrying of a contested popular election by a mere numerical majority of clamorous voices." What made this populist mobilization particularly offensive to the bishop was what he called the "quality" of many of the signatories—"Persons disqualified by their age, and habits, and station in life, and defective knowledge—rather, I may say, by their utter ignorance—of the points in question, for forming a proper judgment concerning them."[52] This elitist tirade only reinforced Mant's reputation for being "isolated" from his parishioners and generated a number of angry letters in the Belfast press in February 1843. Even Lord Downshire, a man inclined to "place confidence in our Bishop," argued that Mant needed to be made more aware of the strength of public opinion on this issue.[53]

---

saying that he was not as fearful as soup as Drew and that he believed the speech was "political claptrap." As so often happened with Drew, Cooke's anger here reflected Drew's personality and style as much as belief. See *Ulster Times*, June 30, 1842.

50. Thomas Drew to J. Emerson Tennent, July 29, 1842, Emerson Tennent Papers, PRONI, D.2922/C/12/3.

51. *Belfast News-Letter*, January 20, 1843.

52. *Ulster Times*, February 2, 1843.

53. The Marquess of Downshire to Richard Davison, February 17, 1843, Downshire Papers, PRONI, D671/C/209/14.

While disagreements over the enforcement of liturgical conformity continued throughout the remainder of Mant's tenure,[54] the controversy over the Church Architecture Society quickly faded from public view in the early spring of 1843, as the town's political and religious leaders worked to quell the conflict. At a late February meeting of the Church Architecture Society, board member Richard Davison reported that the organization had been cleared of the charges of Puseyism. Like Mant, Davison deplored the mobilization of the laity in church politics. With delicious irony, the report also highlighted Drew's own inconsistency, making note of the stained-glass window in his own Chapel of Ease, while he had critiqued the same (a stained-glass window that featured the diocesan arms) in the newer Magdalene Asylum Chapel.[55] Davison's report certainly did not go unanswered; the *Belfast Commercial Chronicle* launched a rhetorical assault on the lawyer, citing "the effable horror which seizes him [Davison] when he discovers the monstrous fact that, absolutely, many of the humbler Episcopalians in Belfast and throughout the diocese have attached their names to it."[56] For all the rhetorical fury, however, reconciliation won the day, as Davison and other political elites, most notably Lord Downshire, endeavoured to reconcile the two parties, recommending that the Bishop dissolve the connections between the local Church Architecture Society and the Cambridge Camden Society. As Lord Downshire put it in a letter to Davison: "Although I have been unable to approve or join in some of the means which have been taken to express the dislike of those who have protested against the Church Architecture Society—I am disposed upon principle to place confidence in our Bishop, but I also wish to be of service to our Bishop, and above all, to our Church, and I therefore have willingly joined with those who deemed it their

---

54. For an overview of the controversy stemming from the bishop's 1843 charge that focused on enforcing liturgical conformity, see Drew's public remonstrance against the "occult mode of instituting the Diocesan Church Architectural Society": *Ulster Times,* July 22, 1843.

55. *Ulster Times,* February 28, 1843.

56. *Belfast Commercial Chronicle,* March 1, 1843.

duty to make his Lordship acquainted with the general feeling of the Established Church in his Diocese."[57] The *Ulster Times* also trumpeted the need for calm, arguing that while it was important to have fair and free discussion, "it now believes that further conversation on this subject can only result in further division, at a time when all Protestants need to unite to face down Popery."[58] At a meeting held on February 27, 1843, Mant agreed to cut all ties with the Cambridge Camden Society, and while tensions between Mant and evangelical figures like Drew and McIlwaine continued to play themselves out in public over other issues, the Mant controversy itself was over.

On one level, this seemingly minor episode in early Victorian Belfast religious politics had little tangible effect. After all, Mant retained his position and quickly regained the support of conservative elites interested in Anglican unity. While some of the issues at play cropped up in congregational disputes in Ballymoney and Hillsborough in 1845 and 1846, these were relatively minor affairs, and Mant even remained quite active in the Down and Connor and Dromore Church Architecture Society (renamed the Harris Society in 1845), presenting a number of papers until 1846.[59] If Mant weathered the rhetorical storm easily enough, however, the episode does provide a number of

---

57. See Lord Downshire to Richard Davison, February 17, 1843, Downshire Papers, PRONI, D.671/C/209/14. Courtesy of the Deputy Keeper of the Records, Public Record Office of Northern Ireland. Downshire, a devoted and deeply conventional Anglican, had battled with Walter B. Mant, archdeacon of Down, over the latter's supposed Puseyite tendencies in the 1830s and was a key player in an 1845 clash in Hillsborough. See Yates, *Religious Condition of Ireland*, 287–89, and Maguire, *Downshire Estates in Ireland*, 81.

58. *Ulster Times*, February 14, 1843. For another letter calling for an end of the recent clerical controversies, see *Ulster Times*, March 4, 1843.

59. The Mant family, both the bishop and his sons, were central to the workings of the local society, presenting a sizeable proportion of the society's published papers between 1842 and 1846. See "Stray Papers on Diocesan History and Antiquities, Read before the Down, Connor and Dromore Architecture Society and the Harris Society, 1842–46," Reeves Manuscripts, DIO1/24/12, PRONI. My thanks to Fred Rankin and Brian M. Walker for this reference.

important insights into the shifting nature of religious politics in this transitional period.

The Mant controversy illustrates evangelical religion's rapid rise to prominence in Victorian Britain and Ireland and the tensions that this growth brought to the complex mosaics of Belfast and Ulster Protestantism. By the late 1830s and early 1840s figures such as Drew ministered to substantial communities of middle- and working-class Anglicans attracted by their assertive syntheses of practical Protestantism, anti-Catholicism, and populist evangelical faith in well-placed urban churches. Throughout the early Victorian period these evangelical ministers attempted to leverage their greater congregational numbers and links to broader communities in Belfast and beyond in an effort to challenge the High Church establishment within the Church of Ireland, mobilizing support through the populist instruments of the press and petition. The Reverend Henry Cooke's effective use of public opinion has been noted by a number of scholars,[60] but the Mant controversy shows that a new generation of Anglican ministers were also adept at such tactics and it is clear that Mant struggled to respond effectively in this new landscape.

While ministers and other social elites led the challenge, this was not simply a top-down initiative; beyond this rhetorical struggle over the Church Architecture Society, there are clear signs that efforts to impose High Church rituals, rubrics, and standards angered substantial numbers of lay Anglicans. At a January 1843 meeting of the Church Accommodation Society designed to bring unity to Belfast Protestantism, the *Belfast News-Letter* reported that Drew and McIlwaine received enthusiastic applause from the large crowd ("not less than a thousand men and women") that attended the meeting.[61]

Nor was this confined to Belfast. In 1845–46, two years after the Mant controversy had subsided, Mant's own domestic chaplain, the

---

60. For a recent view, see Miller, "Demise of the Confessional State in Ireland," 109–24. See also Hempton and Hill, *Evangelical Protestantism in Ulster Society*, 69, 98–99, 205–6.

61. *Belfast News-Letter*, January 20, 1843.

Reverend Canon William St. John Smyth, faced sharp opposition from his Ballymoney congregation over what some congregants saw as unwarranted innovations in the order of the church service, the wearing of the surplice, and the positioning of the font. According to one of the leaders of this challenge, these changes had been made by Bishop Mant's brother Robert when he was rector in the mid-1820s and the congregants wanted to go back to their traditional mode of service. When Smyth and his curate, the Reverend James Dunseath, refused to make sufficient concessions, a number of the congregants boycotted church services, with one family placing a padlock on a church pew to prevent others from using it in their absence. The dispute continued for more than a year and the correspondence between Smyth and his congregants reveals lay voices that are sharply critical and confident, quite willing to challenge ministers on matters of religious practice. Charles O'Hara, one of the leaders of the protest, admitted that his efforts had been inspired by a similar (and successful) effort by Hillsborough Anglicans against the Reverend Walter B. Mant, archdeacon of Down and the bishop's son. Smyth eventually conceded to most of the demands before his death two months later, in November 1846.[62] By the 1840s, evangelical Protestantism was not a movement at the margins; its belief, language, and practice had spread widely enough throughout the Church of Ireland in Ulster that lay congregants felt confident in refusing the imposition of what they saw as dangerous High Church novelties.

It would be wrong, however, to see opposition to the Church Architecture Society in strictly evangelical or even religious terms. The sheer fluidity between evangelicalism, conservative politics, and a more generalized attachment to tradition was one of the keys to the success of "political ministers" like Cooke and Drew, and it was certainly at work here. It is true that McIlwaine and other ministerial leaders were evangelicals and that a number of participants labeled

---

62. Mant-St. John Smyth Correspondence, Representative Church Body Library, MS. 772/6/1–17.

their opposition as *evangelical*, but that term was often used as code for a true or pure Protestantism as much as a description of a particular set of theological beliefs. In short, the boundaries between evangelical and conservative are difficult to establish here, and many of the organization's foes were doubtless conservative Protestants offended by change as much as religious principle. In this regard it is worth noting that Drew, McIlwaine, and others often emphasized the physical and visual elements of Mant's proposals and that in both the Ballymoney and Hillsborough disputes, boycotting opponents demanded an end to "innovations" like the wearing of the clerical surplice, the order of the service, and the Prayer for the Church Militant. Each of these factors had theological dimensions, of course, but part of the populist appeal of such opposition was that it was both evangelical and conservative, and the fact that the majority of lay participants in Ballymoney and Hillsborough couched their objectives in terms of going back to the way that things were before Mant's efforts to enforce rubrical conformity underlines the wisdom of a more cautious approach.

If it would be wrong to describe lay activism in these struggles as simply top-down—it is also important to underline the key roles played by political and social elites in this controversy. In Belfast, McIlwaine, Drew, and other ministers used the press to mobilize their supporters, and middle- and lower-class Protestant men signed the petition against the Church Architecture Society, but it was the town's political elites who led the delegation to present the petition to Bishop Mant. McIlwaine and his allies, moreover, never lost an opportunity to emphasize the breadth and respectability of elite participation in the campaign. This episode also illustrates the complexity of these relationships, as figures such as Davison and Lord Downshire attempted to stake a middle course of reconciliation in the crisis, critiquing Mant's High Church elitism and hierarchical isolation from his parishioners while deprecating the more radical popular mobilization used by Mant's opponents in their efforts to excoriate the Church Architecture Society. In this case, their efforts ultimately worked to dampen down intra-Anglican conflict in Belfast church politics. Prominent landowners played even more dominant leadership roles in later disputes, with Lord Downshire and O'Hara leading the opposition in Hillsborough and Ballymoney, respectively. If leaders like Davison shared Mant's distaste for populist challenges to episcopal authority, other political elites were not so unequivocal, wielding popular opposition to affect conservative religious change. The success of the populist movement against the Church Architecture Society clearly was dependent on the support and advocacy of leaders with substantial political and social authority.

Finally, the Mant controversy illustrates how conflicts over religious matters could foster cross-class movements that brought together influential political elites, evangelical ministers, and substantial lay communities of middle- and working-class Anglicans in early Victorian Belfast and beyond. Figures such as McIlwaine and Drew acted as crucial linchpins in the creation and mobilization of these networks. Christ Church, located between the industrial suburb of Sandy Row and the more respectable neighborhoods and institutions of the town core, acted as a particularly important meeting place for seemingly divergent social groups. In an era when the Orange Order was not particularly strong in the town, Christ Church's role as a site of intra-class Anglican interaction was all the more crucial.[63]

While the importance of pan-Protestant rhetoric and cross-class networks to late nineteenth-century Belfast Protestant politics make it tempting to draw out the political implications of the Mant controversy, there is no evidence that the particular coalition brought together in the winter of 1842–43 had any lasting political impact. While Church of Ireland ministers such as Tresham Gregg and Drew attempted to mobilize populist support for a more explicitly Protestant politics in the 1840s and 1850s, respectively,[64] they had rela-

---

63. Focusing on the 1850s, Mark Doyle has termed Christ Church as kind of makeshift Orange Order lodge in an era where Orange processions were banned. See Doyle, *Fighting like the Devil for the Sake of God*, 84.

64. For Gregg's Protestant Operative Society, see Crawford, "'Overriding Providence,'" 157–68. For a brief treatment of Drew's Christ Church Protestant Association, see Doyle, *Fighting like the Devil for the Sake of God*, 26–27.

tively little success, and it would be the Orange Order, comparatively weak in Belfast until the late 1850s and 1860s, that eventually brought together many of these strands to more political effect.[65] The clash, however, does illustrate the blurred lines between religion and politics in early Victorian Belfast, since much of the heat generated by opposition to the Church Architecture Society stemmed from the fact that the organization (and what it supposedly represented) could be portrayed as a move in the direction of Roman Catholicism. David Hempton and Myrtle Hill suggested that sectarianism might have helped Ulster evangelicalism to gain support in working-class communities, evidenced by the ways that sectarian conflict kept religious issues in public view in the Victorian city.[66] The controversy over the Church Architecture Society certainly shows the complex operation of sectarianism in Ulster society.

Mant clearly was sensitive to the dangers of being labeled "soft on Catholicism," and at the very least, it is evident that his evangelical opponents used their self-defined status as anti-Catholic champions to define and police the boundaries of acceptable practice within the Church of Ireland. For all of McIlwaine's fire and Mant's ineffectual protestations, however, it was reconciliation that won the day in February 1843, as conservative lay and religious elites patched over this clash with relative ease. Even Drew, a frequent participant in many of Victorian Belfast's rhetorical clashes, soon called for perspective and unity, arguing that strife over these types of matters (church rubrics) was "deadening to the soul."[67] Although few disagreed with Drew's sentiment, even this brief examination of the Mant controversy reveals that for all that seeming simplicity of the contest, religious politics in early Victorian Belfast often was anything but simple.

---

65. For a vivid example, see William Johnston's campaign to repeal the Party Processions Act. See Farrell, "Recapturing the Flag," 52–78. For a different perspective on Johnston's career, see Bew, *Glory of Being Britons*, 194–222.

66. Hempton and Hill, *Evangelical Protestantism in Ulster Society*, 123.

67. *Ulster Times*, July 22, 1843.

CONCLUSION

Thomas Drew's sermons feature the language of evangelical Protestantism, an increasingly powerful code in Victorian Belfast and beyond. Historians long have noted the multifaceted roles played by evangelical religion in providing some working-class men and women a greater sense of belonging to an increasingly dominant Victorian culture of liberal respectability.[68] Particularly in the late-developing northern capital, church was a vital cross-class contact point in the early Victorian era; it was, clearly, one of the crucial venues for social integration. This was not a simple, top-down process; there is no evidence that Christ Church congregants accepted Drew's conservative ideals of godly respectability on his terms, messages that often featured a palpable tension between the minister's hierarchical condescension and his populist inclinations. That said, there is significant evidence that these norms were increasingly accepted by members of the Protestant working classes in later nineteenth-century Belfast. At a minimum, they became important markers of status and respectability, particularly after 1850. The mutability as well as the potency of this language is on display throughout the events described in the previous two chapters.

Sectarian fractures further complicated this process in urban centers like Belfast, and, to a lesser extent, Liverpool, divided by significant and complex ethno-religious lines.[69] At the outset of the previous chapter, I noted David Hempton and Myrtle Hill's provocative idea that anti-Catholicism offered evangelicals an entrance point for the diffusion of broader evangelical ideals among working-class Protestants. The successful campaign waged by evangelicals like Drew and McIlwaine against the Church Architecture Society to mobilize support

---

68. Hempton and Hill, *Evangelical Protestantism in Ulster Society*; Smith, *Religion in an Industrial Society*; Foster, *Class Struggle in the Industrial Revolution*; Joyce, *Work, Society and Politics*; Koditschek, *Class Formation and Urban Industrial Society*.

69. The classic study here is Neal, *Sectarian Violence*. For a more recent treatment, see Belchem, *Irish, Catholic, and Scouse*.

against Mant (and the breadth of that support) seems to provide evidence for that insight. Perhaps opposition was as much a matter of religious conservativism as evangelicalism in a technical sense, but there can be no doubt that anti-Catholicism was the primary touchstone used to mobilize popular opposition to High Church "innovation" in Belfast and the region. The power of this language became more evident after 1848, as the binary rhetoric of Catholic-Protestant division featured more frequently in public debate in Belfast and beyond. As we will see, Drew played no small part in creating this more contentious environment, helping to create a series of Protestant political associations in the late 1840s and 1850s. If these organizations failed to gain much political traction, they did use an increasingly competitive newspaper industry to keep an aggressive and confrontational anti-Catholicism in public view, something that generated angry opposition from both an emergent Belfast Catholic population and a range of more liberal-minded voices across the diverse communities of Belfast Protestantism. In this more heated atmosphere, Drew (and others, such as McIlwaine) came to epitomize a particularly aggressive and destructive form of anti-Catholicism, a portrait reinforced by his widely publicized occasional sermons. The fact that some of these sermons were delivered in churches rather than the city's contentious public spaces sharpened the portrait that Drew was unnecessarily extreme and confrontational, someone whose verbal violence transgressed acceptable norms of sectarian performance. It would be these Orange sermons that defined Drew's public legacy, obscuring the more conventional Victorian reality of his everyday advocacy of conservative evangelical Protestant religion and respectability. Tragically, it was unemployment and famine rather than clashes over religion and ritual that dominated the Hungry Forties, social challenges made more deadly by the characteristic ideological fusion of evangelicalism, political economy, and sectarianism. The next chapter examines Drew's efforts to navigate these difficult waters, efforts that highlight the seemingly contradictory elements of his commitment to Protestant paternalism and social conservatism.

4

A Trustee of the Poor?

Thomas Drew and the Hungry Forties

Speaking at a meeting of the Christ Church Protestant Association in June 1855, Thomas Drew called upon Belfast employers to support Protestant workers and their families suffering through the vicissitudes of a wartime economy. Calling himself a trustee of the poor, he criticized manufacturers who simply left Belfast after making their fortunes, saying that it was appalling that such men forgot the workers who helped them earn their livelihoods:

> A man starts up here, and constructs a mill or manufactory; . . . in a few years, this prosperous man finds himself possessed of £50,000, or even £200,000, and retires from business. In the meantime, what of the tens of thousands who have come at his summons? They have made no increase, . . . in worldly substance. Some are growing old and helpless; some delicate girls have pined in sickness, . . . of the change of temperature from the warm mill to the rain and sleet of the open highway, and they died. Some are maimed by accidents and are useless. Some are young and need instruction: no few orphans abound and need protection. Let us ask, does all responsibility cease when the successful merchant withdraws, and leaves a legacy of many thousands of souls to the overburdened clergy to look after, when prosperous alchemy has transmuted flax into gold?[1]

---

1. *Belfast News-Letter*, June 8, 1855.

If Belfast businessmen failed to support the working men and women who so deserved their pity, Drew called for the "blight of God" to descend upon "their pillared mansions and broad acres," saying that "Belfast gold [should] have no blessing when wrung from Belfast men."[2]

Drew quickly tempered his argument, making it clear that he believed that most employers were benevolent and that he was thankful that unemployed workers had borne their suffering with "good conduct and patience."[3] There was a performative dimension to Drew's occasionally trenchant but ephemeral critiques of commercial excess, which were almost always followed by appeals for order and patience. Drew was a social conservative who was consistently supportive of traditional social hierarchies and whose populist rhetoric had clear and very real limits. Even if these sharply worded appeals rarely translated into material action, however, Drew's vocal support for Protestant working-class families was a critical part of his image—that of a forceful public advocate for his plebeian congregants and Orange brethren alike.

What exactly are we to make of Drew's advocacy for the Protestant working classes? To what extent did Drew act as a tribune for the Protestant poor? How did this fit within his broader mission at Christ Church? This chapter examines the ways that Drew's fusion of nostalgic Tory paternalism, evangelical economics, and reactionary politics operated in early Victorian Belfast. Drew's beliefs centered on a defensive Protestant populism rooted in anxieties about both the Catholic threat and the moral, religious, and social challenges posed by unregulated capitalism in an emergent urban landscape. It is difficult to assess exactly what Christ Church congregants made of these sentiments, but Drew's success in building and maintaining one of the largest Anglican Church communities on the island suggests that

---

2. *Belfast News-Letter*, June 8, 1855.

3. *Belfast News-Letter*, June 8, 1855. Drew listed a few expatriate businessmen whose commitment to Belfast workers' material and spiritual welfare he celebrated: George Tombe, William Wilson, and the Joy family, but stressed that while he would like to mention more individuals, he could not think of any others.

most were at least ambivalent toward his conservative advocacy for working-class Protestants. Given the consistency with which he delivered such sentiments (despite the cost to his career within the Church of Ireland), Drew's hyperbolic populism seems to have been genuine as well as opportunistic. The late 1830s and 1840s were fluid and formative years in Belfast, featuring both tremendous social dislocation and the gradual creation of the town's basic public infrastructure and civic culture. These changes created a difficult environment for an ambitious and public-minded minister whose congregation was rooted in the textile districts of west Belfast. Drew navigated this terrain with characteristic bombast and energy, efforts that skirted potential tensions with his own supporters and generated conflicts with members of the town's political and religious establishments. Drew's commitment to Protestant working-class families and Orange loyalty ultimately saw him through the turmoil of the 1840s. If anything, both the Christ Church congregation and Drew's reputation as Belfast's leading advocate for plebeian Protestants were stronger as the 1850s began, aided by Anglican migration to the city and the island's increasingly contentious religious politics.

After sketching out the primary tenets of Drew's Tory paternalism, his attitudes toward poverty, work, and the family, I move on to examine his response to the dominant social crises of the 1840s: the distress of Belfast and Ballymacarrett weaving families caught in the ongoing transformation of the textile industry and the tragedy of the Great Irish Famine. Drew's reaction to these calamities highlights some of the contradictions in his thinking about poverty, emigration, and poor relief. Drew's beliefs reflected some of the dominant strands of Victorian social thought, celebrating the distinction between the deserving and undeserving poor, and venerating the patriarchal family as the natural foundation of the social order. Like many of his contemporaries, he was clearly anxious about the emergence of a market-driven urban society and struggled to apply his conservative Christian mores to the landscape in which he lived and worked. Drew's rhetoric about the poor was anything but consistent, alternating between severe statements that contested workers' claims of need and strident public advocacy for famine victims. Drew's efforts to position himself as a tribune of the poor were critical to both his ministry and his populist vision of Protestant politics. These years again remind us that Drew's largely successful leadership of the Christ Church community was rooted in a potent and ever-shifting mix of evangelical religion, Tory paternalism, and anti-Catholicism, one where words often spoke louder than actions.

AN EVANGELICAL TORY PATERNALIST
IN EARLY VICTORIAN BELFAST

In his pioneering study of evangelical religion and economic thought in early nineteenth-century Britain, Boyd Hilton argued that the rise of Christian economics was both a reaction against and part of the vogue for political economy that dominated mid-Victorian British political culture. In Hilton's view, evangelical Protestantism's dual focus on depravity and salvation, the anxious oscillation between optimistic and pessimistic registers and uncertainty about "whether happiness or misery best testified to God's efficient governance of the mortal world," made it particularly well-suited for the ambiguities of early nineteenth-century British society.[4] Featuring a shifting blend of high Tory rural romanticism and a moderate variant of the era's dominant political economy, Thomas Drew's brand of Orange paternalism exemplified the complexity of early Victorian evangelical economics. He certainly saw himself, and was seen by many, as a champion of the Protestant working classes, an image rooted in his defensive anti-Catholicism, his evangelical desire to save souls, and his populist conservative politics. Like most middle-class Victorians, Drew was ambivalent about the emergence of a market-driven society, celebrating its productive prowess while worrying about the corrupting impact of its material focus.[5] Style was as important as substance here,

---

4. Hilton, *Age of Atonement*, 34–37.

5. Roberts, *Making English Morals*, viii; Searle, *Morality and the Market in Victorian Britain*, 3–5.

for in many ways Drew's reputation stemmed from his blunt-spoken willingness to speak out about the problems faced by the Protestant poor as much as the particular ideas that governed his philanthropic endeavors. If there were real limits to Drew's proletarian advocacy, however, his support for Protestant working-class families should not be dismissed as merely rhetorical, a fact reflected in his energetic work for famine relief and his strong if inconsistent support for moderate factory reform and urban improvement.

At the same time, the confrontational language of his anti-establishment outbursts has led some observers to mislabel Drew as a kind of radical.[6] A boisterous and emotive speaker by inclination and temperament, Drew's working-class advocacy was grounded in a broader paternalist conservative vision that renders such a label misleading. Not surprisingly, he strongly opposed working-class efforts to improve wages and working conditions through collective action. Like most Victorian conservatives, his view of an ideal society featured a stable and hierarchical agrarian social order, and he looked to an idealized ultra-Protestant narrative of the British and Irish past. Drew opened his *Protestant Anniversaries* by quoting Edmund Burke: "No people will look forward to posterity who do not look back to their ancestors."[7] While critical of both the secular and heartless nature of the policies driven by more mechanistic applications of political economy, Drew was wary of state intervention in economic relationships, constantly emphasizing the need for extensive private philanthropy rather than expensive public outlay. This was not just a matter of keeping the rates down; Drew believed that state support fostered a culture of dependence that should only be risked in a time of crisis. While he acknowledged the roles that structural issues played in creating societal inequality, Drew believed that poverty was primarily a matter of individual character whose antidote was moral reformation rather

---

6. Brewer and Higgins, *Anti-Catholicism in Northern Ireland*, 68–69.
7. Drew, *Protestant Anniversaries*, 1.

than material change.[8] Of course, this interpretation of Irish poverty was shared by many contemporaries. When the social investigator William O'Hanlon wrote about the lives of the poor he encountered in the slums of post-Famine Belfast, he made clear that he believed it was the prevalence of indolence and drink that led to pauperism.[9] Drew agreed.

Drew was not a Tory radical like Richard Oastler, but he did use a synthetic language of Tory paternalism and moderate political economy to articulate his ideas about most social issues.[10] His concern for the welfare of the poor was rooted in a conventional British conservative model of social consensus, a view that aimed to restore "a properly functioning, hierarchical society structured around patrician obligation and plebeian deference, with private philanthropy as its vital social cement."[11] Drew often attributed his social thinking to his urban surroundings and the influence of Michael Sadler, who moved to Belfast in 1834 and was a member of the Christ Church congregation before his death the following year.[12] Sadler was one of the era's most famous and influential conservative advocates for industrial reform; his 1832

---

8. Drew, *Sermons on Various Subjects*, 2:80–81.

9. O'Hanlon, *Walks among the Poor of Belfast*, 8–9. For two insightful commentaries on conceptions of poverty, charity, and relief in nineteenth-century Ireland, see Crossman, *Poverty and the Poor Law in Ireland*, 13–32; McCabe, *Begging, Charity, and Religion in Pre-Famine Ireland*, esp. 187–260.

10. Richard Oastler (1789–1861) was a "Church and King Tory" who doubled as a prominent leader in the movement for factory reform. Known as "Parson Bull," George Stringer Bull was an Anglican minister from Bradford who helped to mobilize support for factory reform. See Furse-Roberts, *Making of a Tory Evangelical*, 187–203; Weaver, *John Fielden and the Politics of Popular Radicalism*.

11. Lawrence, "Paternalism, Class, and the British Path to Modernity," 148.

12. According to Sadler's biographer, Drew gave "an impressive sermon" at Sadler's funeral service; see Seeley, *Memoirs of the Life and Writings of Michael Thomas Sadler*, 552. For synopses of Sadler's place in a broader English political context, see Hilton, *A Mad, Bad, and Dangerous People?*, 372–438, esp. 406–11; Furse-Roberts, *Making of a Tory Evangelical*, 198–203.

report on children's working conditions in industrial Britain typically is seen as one of the foundations of the factory reform movement. A fervent opponent of Catholic emancipation and a fierce critic of full-blown Malthusian political economy (which featured "pallatives [sic] that fall like punishments"), Sadler argued that Thomas Malthus's theories on overpopulation were both morally and statistically unsound, references that regularly appeared in Drew's later sermons and publications. In 1828 Sadler authored a book on Ireland's social problems, arguing that English working-class conditions could not be improved without simultaneously improving the situation of the Irish worker. For Sadler, compulsory poor relief was needed to create greater social stability. He argued fervently against the exceptionalism of Irish poverty and cited the prosperity of densely populated Ulster as proof that Malthus's theories of overpopulation were incorrect. Offering a relatively coherent Christian conservative critique of the excesses of industrial capitalism and inhumane liberal abstraction, Sadler's appeal and utility to a man like Drew was natural. He is one of seven people memorialized in the church with a tablet or window.[13]

While Drew's approach to the social problems of his day was nowhere near as coherent or consistent as his famous English congregant, he shared a number of beliefs with Sadler and his Tory paternalist colleagues, opposing the Irish Poor Law Act of 1838 and supporting moderate factory reform in the mid-1840s.[14] Drew's attitude toward the dominant political economy of the era was complicated. Like Sadler, he opposed Malthusian ideas about population (too

13. Sadler, *Ireland, Its Evils and Remedies*. For Sadler's influence on Drew, see *Speeches of the Rev. Hugh Stowell*. Besides Sadler, the others are Drew, William and Harriet Byrtt, Charles Lanyon, and James and Mary Stuart. See Clarke, *Gravestone Inscriptions*, 163–66. For Sadler, see Gray, *Making of the Irish Poor Law*, 63–64.

14. Drew was hardly alone. His good friend William McIlwaine also supported the Ten Hours Act and other measures of factory reform. See McIlwaine, *Dressmaker*, 40–41. For influential arguments about paternalism and nineteenth-century British society, see Joyce, *Work, Society and Politics*; Koditschek, *Class Formation and Urban Industrial Society*, esp. 414–44.

abstract and godless), but he was sympathetic with some of the fundamental tenets of early Victorian political economy—the primary importance of private philanthropy and the ideal of a limited state. While he wanted manufacturers to act in a Christian manner, to treat their workers humanely, and to support their families in times of need, he made it clear that there was nothing wrong with businessmen making a profit: "Nor let the morose, unkind idea go forth, that the gospel wars with wealth and industry; the gospel only adds responsibility to the one and would check and keep within due bounds the exercise of the other; nay, where the owner of much wealth is a child of God, recognizes his responsibility and for God's sake and the interests of true religion makes blessed use of his means for himself and for others, then is wealth made glorious and hearts made happy."[15] It was an issue of balance, of avoiding the moral corruption that came from seeking profit for its own sake and recognizing that the profits of a business were derived from the labor of working men and women. For Drew, riches were made godly by their use, ideally driven by a sense of Christian purpose, responsibility, and action. His philanthropic ideals were shared by the majority of Belfast's middle-class elites. In February 1855, for example, he organized a public lecture "on the duty of giving in proportion to means and income" with the Reverend John Edgar, the influential Belfast Presbyterian evangelical, and John Workman, a prominent Presbyterian businessman and philanthropist.[16]

Drew's populist paternalism should not be overstated or romanticized; wealthy men who gave generously to the Church of Ireland and supported its philanthropic efforts to bring true religion and a degree of material comfort to the poor had a friend in Drew. As we have seen, the primary stated focus of Drew's ministry was to prepare men and women for the next life, and his emphasis on the virtues of forbearance and perseverance upheld a vision of society that was stable

15. Drew, *Sermons on Various Subjects*, 2:161.
16. *Northern Whig*, February 17, 1855. For a good discussion of middle-class philanthropists and their relations with the working class in Belfast, see Johnson, *Middle-Class Life in Victorian Belfast*, 162–72.

and firmly hierarchical. While Drew clearly looked to society's "natural leaders" for leadership, the fact that he regularly emphasized the need for Christian businessmen to fulfill their responsibilities to the poor clearly appealed to working-class Protestants struggling with the effects of urban and industrial transformation.

This same perspective guided his attitude toward work. Like so many Victorian commentators, Drew stressed the importance and value of work, urging employers to recognize that their profits came from the labor of their employees. His model again emphasized social consensus; truly Christian manufacturers understood that both they and their employees had a stake in the success of their concern and treated their workers accordingly. Drew opened an 1839 sermon with the notion that every man must procure a living in the world and that perseverance and labor were productive and admirable qualities, as long as they did not cut short life or distract from what was really important: salvation.[17] He made a similar argument in "The Rich and the Poor," a sermon published in *The Irish Pulpit*: "All are taught their dependence; true philosophy bids the poor man look up to the rich man as his benefactor, and bids the rich man also to look upon the poor man as his most valuable friend. Mankind are encircled by bonds which united them powerfully; the chain of gold may go forth from the rich, manacling the poor, as auxiliary to his comforts; but equally from the poor do the fetters of iron grapple the rich man and yoke him to the poor."[18] There was a clear political dimension to Drew's rhetoric. As he stated in another lecture, much of his career had been spent trying to counteract the divisive work of "the chartist, the socialist, and the demagogue."[19] Drew's beliefs certainly aligned well with other Belfast conservatives. As Vincent Geoghegan's work on Owenism makes clear, Belfast conservatives were willing to see the cooperative efforts of respectable working men as legitimate philanthropy, but

---

17. Drew, *Sermons on Various Subjects*, 2:161.
18. Drew, "Rich and the Poor," 252.
19. *Belfast Commercial Chronicle*, November 18, 1843.

viewed the collective action and radical politics of trade unionism as anathema.[20] If Drew's vision of social consensus and his appreciation for the value of labor naturally appealed to some of his working-class followers, there is little doubt that his balance was tilted firmly toward employers and social elites. It was clearly better to have chains of gold than fetters of iron.

Through both his sermons and Christ Church's extensive networks of prayer stations, Sunday and day schools, libraries and lecture series, Drew stressed the importance of the familiar values of middle-class respectability: discipline, forbearance, frugality, humility, and sobriety, calling idleness and indifference the deadliest of all habits.[21] He exhibited little sympathy for workers' efforts to improve their wages and working conditions and made clear that he believed that most state efforts to provide employment for distressed workers were counterproductive, undermining private employment and philanthropy. The poor man should look on the rich man in friendship, and the rich man should cherish the poor man's soul if not his life.[22] If Drew's populist outbursts occasionally offended establishment conservatives, it was his tone rather than content that rankled. His advocacy for the poor was romantic, reactionary, and conventional, never seriously challenging the social order. Drew might have seen himself as a trustee for the poor, but he was a servant of the rich.

Drew's views on poverty and poor relief were similarly orthodox. His opposition to the Irish Poor Law was rooted in a mélange of conventional critiques of the new welfare regime: its impact on private philanthropy, its failure to recognize the spiritual roots of social life, and its cost to local taxpayers.[23] Drew's views on poor relief centered on that most Victorian of ideas, the distinction between the deserving and undeserving poor. His humanitarian impulses clearly were

20. Geoghegan, "Robert Owen, Cooperation and Ulster in the 1830s," 6–26.
21. Drew, "The Omniscience of God," *Sermons on Various Subjects*, 1:41–43. See also Drew, *Sermons on Various Subjects* 2:151.
22. *Ulster Times*, January 2, 1840.
23. Gray, *Making of the Irish Poor Law*, 244–45, 249–51, 255–56.

directed toward the former, who, like most of his contemporaries, he defined as women, children, the elderly, and the injured.[24] Drew certainly could be harsh to those he deemed undeserving. At one February 1847 meeting in the midst of the Great Famine, Drew used these categories to savage effect, calling for the expulsion of itinerant beggars from Belfast, a move blocked by his evangelical ally, John Edgar.[25] Vagrancy was a particularly powerful site of anxiety. Drew believed that movement was the ultimate sign of the undeserving poor. Many British and Irish political elites clearly agreed, reflected in the passage of the Vagrancy (Ireland) Act of 1847, which made begging and homelessness punishable by a month of hard labor in jail. Drew was more supportive of homeless men, women, and children who were both demonstrably local and unable to support themselves. Speaking in support of the creation of the Night Asylum for the Homeless Poor in Belfast in January 1841, for example, Drew argued that anxieties that the institution would attract itinerants and increase crime were exaggerated.[26] He certainly agreed with an 1839 editorial in the *Ulster Times* that the challenge for any viable relief scheme was to maintain the distinction between a "vagrant and an honest man overtaken by want in seeking for labour."[27] Drew's philanthropy had fairly strict if conventional limits.

Drew was determined to protect the sanctity of the patriarchal family, arguing that it was the essential starting point of all social relationships: industry, economy, government, and education. Like so many middle-class Victorians, he believed that both modern urban

---

24. Ciarán McCabe's recent work underlines how Irish people of different classes and religious beliefs shared overlapping conceptions of poverty and poor relief, particularly the distinction between the deserving and undeserving poor; see McCabe, *Begging, Charity, and Religion in Pre-Famine Ireland*, 255–56. For the classic study of Victorian ideas about poverty, see Himmelfarb, *Idea of Poverty*.

25. See Kinealy and Mac Atasney, *Hidden Famine*, 78.

26. *Ulster Times*, January 19, 1841.

27. *Ulster Times*, January 3, 1839.

society and the growth of the state posed threats to the family.[28] It was this belief (along with his anti-Catholicism) that lay behind his fervent opposition to the national schools. Parents, not the state, should control the lives of their children. In an 1840 sermon delivered on behalf of the Protestant Orphan Society at St. Peter's Church in Dublin, Drew made this point with particularly clarity: "Parents," he argued, "are the best teachers of children," adding that "our universities groan under unnatural monastic instruction" and hoping that "our universities to teem with men who feel as parents."[29]

It was Drew's belief in the primacy of the family that led him to publish his multivolume *Sermons of Various Subjects* in 1839, a cheap primer designed to promote family worship among working-class parishioners. Daily or regular family prayer sessions were common in Victorian Britain, particularly in middle-class households. They typically were led by the male head of household, who recited or read prayers before or after work. Scholars have long seen the pervasiveness of family prayer as a powerful demonstration of the widespread influence of evangelicalism in Victorian Britain.[30] Using personal correspondence and family Bibles kept at May Street Presbyterian Church, Alice Johnson has detailed how important and potentially enlivening these sessions could be for middle-class families in Victorian Belfast.[31] We do not have the same type of evidence for working-class households, and it is all but certain that such practices were less prevalent in plebeian circles. That said, this ideal was clearly central to Drew's notion of community, one he underlined repeatedly in sermons. Family worship strengthened the Christian household, helping to insulate it from the temptations of urban commercial life. The patriarchal family was more than an essential building block for civil society, it

---

28. Searle, *Morality and the Market in Victorian Britain*, 152–65. See also Scranton, "Varieties of Paternalism," 235–57.
29. Drew, *Sermon, Preached at St. Peter's Church*, 10.
30. Tosh, *Man's Place*, 36–37.
31. Johnson, *Middle-Class Life in Victorian Belfast*, 191–92.

was a metaphor for God's relationship with humanity. In Drew's view, God was the ideal father, powerful, loving, and vigilant: "We, poor earthly fathers, are not, at all times, employed in thinking of our children, our love is not always exercised in the same degree; we are not sure, that in chastening them, we are wholly free from the vile passions of our nature, and that we are not rather indulging our anger, rather than using loving correction, for our children's good—not so with the heavenly Father."[32] God was a parent who paid attention all the time and whose children should honor their father's love with what Drew termed a filial fear.

Not surprisingly, Drew's vision of family celebrated the Victorian ideal of a companionate marriage, fundamentally based on emergent notions of a remade manhood: sober, God-fearing, and strong. In households where a filial fear of God predominated, temperate husbands and fathers led their families in prayer, inculcating and modeling good habits of diligence, and order, and leading generally happy lives. By contrast, he argued that it was easy to see homes lacking the foundation of faith, where filthy apartments were marked by frequent disputes, children in rags, and women who failed to take care of themselves. This was a deeply conservative vision of family, of course, for true happiness only occurred in the hereafter, with poor families submitting to their worldly station in the comforting knowledge that it was part of God's plan.[33] Anna Clark has shown how conservative gender and marriage norms crowded out more radical alternatives in Glasgow, Lancashire, and London in the 1830s and 1840s, enshrining a family ideal that was based upon a breadwinner's wage that was out of the reach of most working-class families.[34] Drew's work clearly had the same object. And, of course, the savage gap between ideal and reality would have been much wider in mid-nineteenth-century Belfast,

---

32. Drew, "The Fear of God," *Sermons on Various Subjects*, 1:49.
33. Drew, *Sermons on Various Subjects*, 1:52.
34. Clark, *Struggle for the Breeches*.

where standards of living were lower and high percentages of women worked in low-paying textile jobs. Drew rarely talked about women's factory work, an instructive silence given the preponderance of female millworkers in his west Belfast congregation. Drew's social critique typically became less pointed as the subject became more local.[35]

Drew's take on women's roles in society was also well within the bounds of the emergent and soon to be dominant middle-class gender norms in Belfast and across Britain and Ireland. While Christ Church seems to have been less dependent on female participation than most nineteenth-century British churches, Drew regularly emphasized women's crucial but subordinate importance to the family, community, and nation. In an 1840 sermon, he articulated his view of a woman's role within marriage: "Woman's destiny is two-fold: she is destined to pain and sorrow (Genesis iii, 16) and to subjection. She is to reverence her husband and he is to cherish and protect her. When rightly understood, this difference of position is scarcely felt. Still, if man has protracted toil as his lot, the pangs of childbirth (the severest pangs that fall to the lot of mortality) are woman's dowry."[36] Drew emphasized that properly expressed and understood, these patriarchal bonds should be "scarcely felt," but his emphasis on female subordination was clear enough. And he believed that these realities had a real impact on female religiosity: it was easy to see that women were more pious than men, attending church more frequently and coming more frequently to the Lord's table.[37]

Drew's conservative view of gender norms clearly was shaped by class and familial expectations. In a November 1891 interview, his daughter Catharine, a pioneering female journalist and writer who moved to London after her father's death, gave credit to her father

---

35. Drew's relative silence on women's factory work contrasts sharply with the emphases of other Victorian moral reformers. See Searle, *Morality and the Market in Victorian Britain*, 165.

36. Drew, *Sermon, Preached at St Peter's Church*, 12.

37. Drew, *Sermon, Preached at St Peter's Church*, 12.

for her enduring love of books and education. She insisted that he had "advanced ideas" on what women should know and taught her "various branches of study that were then supposed to be suited only to boys."[38] Drew's commitment to Catharine's education certainly paid dividends in her impressive writing career, but it was atypical at Christ Church, where there was little evidence of advanced views about female education in the curriculum and/or organization of schools.

While it was a woman's special role to keep her husband on a firm and virtuous path, Drew argued that women should participate in public life to help improve moral standards and support the oppressed: "Let women discountenance not merely what is immoral, rude or presumptuous, but also what is unprincipled in politics and unsound in public life and that will give succor to the oppressed cause to true religion. It would be absurd to suppose where the interests of the young, the ignorant and the poor were concerned that woman should be a silenced and forbidden spectator of wrong and that her sex should be precluded from a defence of the revealed principles of truth and eternity."[39] William McIlwaine made a similar case in an 1846 essay, in which he urged middle- and upper-class women to learn more about the working conditions faced by dressmakers and milliners so they could better use their influence to improve this "national sin."[40] Scholars have noted that this type of conservative argument for women's participation in discussions of public morality opened up arenas for female philanthropic endeavor in nineteenth-century Britain.[41] If the political spaces it created were relatively limited in Victorian Belfast, middle- and upper-class women at Christ Church seem to have leveraged these arguments into public action, raising funds for clothing

38. *Belfast News-Letter*, November 14, 1891.
39. Drew, *Thoughtful Protestantism*, 13.
40. McIlwaine, *Dressmaker*, 43–45.
41. Colley, *Britons*, 237–82; Luddy, *Women and Philanthropy in Nineteenth-Century Ireland*. More recently, Alice Johnson has shown how a number of middle-class women in Belfast defied societal expectations in pursuit of educational and intellectual fulfilment. See Johnson, *Middle-Class Life in Victorian Belfast*, 220–73.

societies and signing petitions on religious education and other issues.[42] Drew's ideal here was seemingly Lady Harriet Forde, whose philanthropic work for the poor near the family's Seaforde estate first took Drew to south Down in 1836.[43]

Many of Drew's gender ideals found expression in his support for the Ulster Magdalene Asylum and Episcopal Chapel. Located on Donegall Pass, the asylum was designed to rehabilitate women who had become pregnant out of wedlock, been involved in prostitution, or convicted of petty crimes. Initially a multidenominational project, Presbyterian supporters bowed out amidst increasing denominational competition in the mid- to late 1830s. Like the Magdalene asylums associated with other religious denominations throughout Ireland, rehabilitation was built on a routine centered on discipline, piety, and work—a combination that appealed to Drew's hybrid Tory paternalism and social conservatism as well as his passion for church extension. The project received £1,000 each from the Church Accommodation Society and George Tombe, a prominent barrister and member of the Christ Church congregation, who gave Drew an additional £1,200 to complete construction. Drew placed a particular importance on aristocratic women's efforts to raise funds for the institution, noting that Ladies Donegall, Bangor, Bateson, and Forde were all members of the committee to build the new institution.[44] The Ulster Magdalene Asylum and Episcopal Chapel opened in 1839, and Christ Church leaders clearly saw its formation as part of Drew's church extension work. As Abraham Dawson would later write of the effort, "Besides the refuge provided for lustful passion, another clergyman, another church and a school for scriptural instruction contributed to relieve the wants

---

42. For one such example, see *Ulster Times*, March 24, 1842, April 12, 1842. In these reports, the newspaper claimed that 539 women signed a petition against National Education that "emanated from the females of Christ Church congregation." For the impact and importance of evangelical networks for women's public action, see Dickson, "Evangelical Women and Victorian Women," 700–725.

43. Drew, "Annals of Loughinisland," 161.

44. *Ulster Times*, May 16, 1839.

of the community."⁴⁵ Drew donated a little over £1 annually to the asylum and chapel and was secretary to the Board of Trustees in its early years. Despite some early turmoil, the church survived, and by the late Victorian period, the asylum was known colloquially as "The Steamer" for its association with its steam laundry. The laundry closed in 1916.⁴⁶

Drew was in many ways a conventional Irish Protestant conservative. Fiercely anti-Catholic, he was a consistent supporter of the landlord interest and had a romanticized view of an idyllic rural order. His seemingly strident public advocacy for the poor, expressed intermittently before supportive audiences, and his support for evangelical moral and social reform, were equally conventional. It is the shifting synthetic nature of these beliefs and their implementation, however, that is of interest here. Drew was not a simple anti-Catholic reactionary; he was not simply anything, and this contingent ideological fusion was critical to his appeal and success at Christ Church. The events of the late 1830s and 1840s revealed many of the potential tensions between the hybrid Tory paternalism and political economy of Drew's pragmatic evangelicalism and his working-class congregants—this was a difficult environment that required almost constant negotiation. Despite his very real commitment to Protestant working-class families and his often sharp rhetoric, when push came to shove, Drew eventually aligned himself with the conservative establishment on nearly every issue; political stances that never seemed to cost him significantly with his own largely plebeian constituency. To get a better sense of the ways that Drew applied his social thinking to the major issues of his day, the remainder of this chapter examines how Drew responded to two of the socioeconomic crises of the Hungry Forties:

---

45. Dawson, "Annals of Christ Church, Belfast," PRONI, T.2159/1, 60–63; *Ulster Times*, May 16, 1839.

46. For the history of Magdalene Societies in Ireland, see Luddy, *Prostitution and Irish Society*, 76–123; Smith, *Magdalene Laundries and the Nation's Architecture of Containment*.

the difficulties faced by Belfast and Ballymacarrett handloom weavers in the early 1840s and the horrors of the Great Famine.

THE LIMITS OF HIS ADVOCACY: THOMAS DREW AND THE BALLYMACARRETT WEAVERS, 1842–1843

The tragic demise of the handloom weavers is one of the classic narratives of nineteenth-century British social history. The basic outlines of the story are well-known and can be briefly summarized here. Between 1815 and 1840, handloom weavers living in industrial cities and villages across Britain lost their jobs, status, and wages as the advent of technological change, the shift from domestic to factory production, and global trade networks remade the textile industry. The plight of the handloom weavers featured prominently in pessimistic interpretations of the Condition of England question, narratives that detailed industrialization's negative impact on working-class men and women in early nineteenth-century Britain.[47] Even in recent work that is comparatively positive about the effects of industrialization on plebeian lives, the basic narrative about the handloom weavers remains relatively unchanged, featuring stories that highlight the cyclical unemployment, suffering, and uncertainty that workers experienced in the 1830s and 1840s.[48]

While textile production in the north of Ireland was part of this famous British story, the industry there had its own distinct patterns of development. Unable to compete with their more highly capitalized English rivals, Ulster's cotton manufacturers largely were displaced

---

47. For the most influential of these works, see Engels, *Condition of the Working Class in England*; Hammond and Hammond, *Village Labourer*; Hammond and Hammond, *Town Labourer*; Hammond and Hammond, *Skilled Labourer*; Hobsbawm, "British Standard of Living," 46–68; Thompson, *Making of the English Working Class*. For a more recent interpretation that emphasizes the global reach of the textile industry, see Beckert, *Empire of Cotton*.

48. Griffin, *Liberty's Dawn*, 37–38; Hunt, *Building Jerusalem*, 20–44.

by 1830, often shifting to linen and leaving behind a vulnerable and declining array of small-scale and household producers. Domestic handloom production remained more prevalent in mid-nineteenth-century Ireland than England or Scotland, particularly in a linen industry where mechanization was slower to take hold.[49] This was certainly the case in Ballymacarrett, the Belfast industrial suburb just east of the Lagan. Surveying the history of suburban development in East Belfast, Stephen A. Royle and T. J. Campbell estimate that in 1819 nearly every home in Ballymacarrett's Lagan Village had at least one person spinning for one of four local manufacturers. More than a decade later, the Reverend J. H. Potts, curate of St. Patrick's Church on Newtownards Road, made clear that the "dense mass" of his parishioners relied on the loom for subsistence. Crowded into poor-quality housing, Ballymacarrett's mostly Protestant textile workers suffered through boom-and-bust cycles in the 1820s and 1830s, receiving lower and lower wages for their handiwork.[50] In short, despite significant regional variation and Ireland's comparatively late industrial development, the broad narrative of relative decline featured in nineteenth-century British historiography seems appropriate for the north of Ireland. Historians might debate the extent to which Irish textile workers' real wages fell between 1815 and 1840, but there is no doubt that depressed wage levels and declining work status left thousands of households increasingly vulnerable in pre-Famine Ulster.[51]

49. For a brief overview of the nineteenth-century context, see O'Hearn, "Irish Linen," 161–90.

50. Royle and Campbell, "East Belfast and the Suburbanization of North-east County Down," 640; *Belfast News-Letter*, February 12, 1830.

51. Liam Kennedy has argued that the declining wages and living standards of northern handloom weavers were exaggerated, as households would have been compensated in part by declining food and housing prices, particularly in rural areas. See Kennedy, "Rural Economy," 1–61; James, *Handloom Weavers in Ulster's Linen Industry*, 30–36. For a more conventional view stressing wage and status decline, see O'Connor, *Labour History of Ireland*, 6–27.

6. Barefoot Irish girl, York Street Mill. Portrait by William Makepeace Thackeray (1842), in Thackeray, *Irish Sketch Book, 1842.*

The dilemma faced by the region's handloom weavers and their families had been the subject of public conversation long before the crisis years of the late 1830s and 1840s. In both 1826 and 1828, Belfast philanthropists created funds for the families of distressed weavers.[52] In February 1830 Potts organized a charity sermon to raise funds for the relief of the "wretched weavers, . . . brooding, pale and haggard, over the doom of their unprovided families." Nearly £150 was promised

52. *Belfast News-Letter*, May 10, 1826, February 22, 1828.

at the ensuing meeting, led by substantial donations from the Marquess of Donegall, Narcissus Batt, and workers at the local foundry.[53] When the parliamentary commission on handloom weaver petitions did its work in 1835 (one of several official investigations into the Irish textile industry between 1825 and 1840), three days were spent gathering evidence in the northern capital, with formal testimonies given by John Boyd, a handloom weaver, and Alexander Moncrieffe, a Belfast muslin manufacturer.[54] The plight of textile workers in late Georgian Belfast was no secret.

Things were particularly bad in Ballymacarrett. Situated on low-lying alluvial land along the shores of Belfast Lough and the east bank of the River Lagan, Ballymacarrett's rapid nineteenth-century growth was driven by industrialization both in the village and in nearby Belfast. Although home to several industrial sites from the late eighteenth century, it was the growth of the textile industry that fueled Ballymacarrett's expansion. *The Ordnance Survey Memoir* estimated that three thousand people lived in the industrial suburb in the 1830s, a population that grew by 17 percent between 1831 and 1841. Most of the new inhabitants lived in clustered villages of whitewashed one-story stone cabins with earthen floors. Many of the homes were so poor that they were exempt from ratable valuation. Interspersed between the industrial villages were the suburban villas of several substantial businessmen and local landowners. The most prominent of these was William Coates, owner of the Lagan Foundry and sundry other businesses, who lived at his Snug Brook estate (renamed Glentoran in 1854). It was the Coates family that developed the northwestern industrial core of the fast-growing east Belfast suburb. One commentator described the majority of Ballymacarrett's occupants as "industrious but poor," while a lifelong resident later recalled that several of the villages were "as a rule almost always bordering on poverty."[55] While the family

53. *Belfast News-Letter*, February 12, 1830, February 16, 1830.
54. *Select Committee on Hand-Loom Weavers' Petitions*, 105–43.
55. Campbell and Royle, "East Belfast and the Suburbanization of Northwest County Down," 638–41. See also Lewis, *County Down*, 17–18.

wages paid by the linen merchants who employed most of the inhabitants of Ballymacarrett were comparatively high in the mid-1830s, they collapsed in the trade depression of the late 1830s and early 1840s, leaving an already poor population increasingly at risk of starvation and disease.[56]

Given his reputation as an advocate for the Protestant poor, it is no surprise that Drew quickly became a spokesman for the region's distressed weavers. He first stepped forward in the summer of 1839, when rumors spread that the Whig government was prepared to support James Emerson Tennent's bill for regulating Irish cotton, hempen, and linen manufactures. Most Belfast and Ballymacarrett workers opposed the measure, saying that it sided unfairly with employers. Moreover, the men claimed that Emerson Tennent had betrayed an 1838 agreement forged under the auspices of local magistrates. The operatives did not stand alone in opposition. A diverse array of influential liberal and nationalist leaders opposed the bill in parliament, including William Sharman Crawford and Daniel O'Connell, who received a direct appeal from the Ballymacarrett Weavers Committee.[57] It was not only radicals, liberals, and nationalists. According to Drew, a group of weavers asked him to intercede on their behalf to make sure the bill was not going forward. Drew quickly confirmed this in correspondence with Richard Muggeridge, assistant Poor Law commissioner.[58] Emerson Tennent's bill never received a second reading. Drew's intervention had nothing to do with the bill's failure to secure passage, of course, but it does illustrate his status as a kind of self-appointed tribune for the Protestant working classes.

Drew's response to the continuing difficulties faced by Belfast and Ballymacarrett weavers in the early 1840s was more ambivalent,

---

56. Kinealy and Mac Atasney, *Hidden Famine*, 17.

57. Henry Crone, Secretary, Linen and Cotton Weavers of Belfast, to Daniel O'Connell, July 20, 1839, *Correspondence of Daniel O'Connell*, 6:261–62; *Vindicator*, August 3, 1839, August 7, 1839; *Northern Whig*, August 13, 1839; *Belfast Commercial Chronicle*, August 19, 1839.

58. *Ulster Times*, August 29, 1839.

highlighting both the limits of his advocacy and some of the potential difficulties he faced in maintaining relationships with his working-class supporters. This was particularly apparent in the summer of 1842, when a severe trade depression led to further wage cuts and mass unemployment in textile districts across the United Kingdom. In August, as many as a million men participated in a general strike in Britain, an action made all the more threatening to political and social elites by the mass mobilization of the Chartist movement. Thousands of workers engaged in direct action, breaking machines and marching into industrial centers like Manchester to demand higher wages and political reform. The state responded in kind, and violent confrontations occurred throughout Britain. These became known as the Plug Plot Riots, so named because of labor activists' efforts to stop work in the mills by removing the plugs from boilers. At least ten men were killed in riots in Halifax and Preston, and thousands were brought to trial in the strike's aftermath.[59] While matters were much less confrontational in Belfast, the crisis of 1842 was a crucial backdrop for northern events, raising the stakes and sharpening the potential for social conflict.

In early April, an estimated two hundred weavers and their supporters met at the Police Buildings in Belfast to plead their case and discuss the possibility of assisted emigration to Canada.[60] The Reverend Henry Cooke took the lead on the issue, outlining the situation in a letter published across the Belfast press and at a series of public meetings that followed. At various sites, Cooke assured audiences that the weavers' plight was real, that half of the Ballymacarrett weavers were out of work with little prospect for employment. While Cooke made clear his general opposition to assisted emigration, he argued that it

---

59. The historiography on early to mid-nineteenth-century popular politics in Britain is too immense to detail here. See Chase, *Chartism*; Navickas, *Protest and the Politics of Space and Place*; Stedman-Jones, *Languages of Class*; Thompson, *Chartists*.

60. *Belfast News-Letter*, April 12, 1842, April 19, 1842, April 26, 1842, May 17, 1842. The call for a Ballymacarrett Emigration Society, complete with a list of supporters, was printed in the April 9, 1842, issue of the *Ulster Times*.

seemed to be the most logical solution in this case, and hoped that Belfast philanthropists would help him raise much-needed funds for the distressed weavers. If the conservative minister's initial response seemed sympathetic, it also quickly underlined the limits of Victorian philanthropy. Cooke made clear that inquiries would be made into the character of any weavers who wanted to emigrate and that they would be responsible for at least half of the money for their passage across the Atlantic. The plea for funds, however, certainly found a ready audience; £150 was raised at the first meeting and £1,000 was subscribed to the fund by July. While Drew was unable to attend the first two meetings, he was an initial subscriber and was named to a committee created to help raise additional funds for the potential emigration of distressed weavers and their families.[61] The committee eventually used some of the money raised to support soup kitchens in Smithfield and Ballymacarrett, and helped to send 170 men, women, and children to Quebec aboard the *Independence* in June 1842.[62]

The weavers did not simply wait for such help. On May 2 an estimated four hundred men met with their supporters at Adam's Point near Ballymacarrett, where they issued a sharp challenge to their opponents, resolving to use all lawful means "to resist any further reductions in their wages, as the sum at present received was entirely inadequate to support themselves and their families." The men also refused to work for a "certain manufacturer" unless he increased wage rates to match other "respectable manufacturers in town." The company in question was John R. Vance and Son, muslin manufacturers and merchants based in Rosemary Street in Belfast. Vance's son, Gilbert, quickly responded to the Ballymacarrett men in a public letter, accusing them of making libelous statements about business practices and wage cuts, accusations that generated a predictably bitter exchange in the *Belfast News-Letter* over the next few weeks. The weavers' clear

---

61. *Belfast News-Letter*, April 16, 1842, April 19, 1842; *Ulster Times*, April 16, 1842, April 19, 1842.

62. Royle, *Portrait of an Industrial City*, 66.

statements of a moral economy of sorts received little support from their supposed tribunes.[63] Drew later took the Ballymacarrett men to task, saying that at least these tendencies seemed to be confined east of the Lagan, a claim that contradicted the obvious point that the same issues reverberated across his own largely proletarian district. Despite the seeming tension, there is no evidence that Drew or his conservative allies' antipathy to collective action lost them significant working-class support, a point to which we will return at the end of this chapter.

The issue of assisted emigration was a more complicated matter for Drew. Like Cooke and many of his Irish evangelical contemporaries, Drew had an ambivalent attitude toward emigration. Always wary of what he considered excessive state expenditure, Drew typically argued against the idea that emigration was a solution to Ireland's problems, part of a group of Protestant clergymen who consistently opposed the use of state-assisted emigration as a form of poor relief.[64] In the Ballymacarrett case, Drew's opposition to emigration was sharpened by the fact that he was loath to see Protestants leave Belfast and Ireland. Like Cooke, Drew supported assisted emigration as a possible measure of last resort. In this case, however, he believed that the situation had not reached that point. His attitude grew more severe as the crisis of 1842 deepened. In late June, Richard Davison wrote a public letter detailing the mounting desperation of Belfast weavers, claiming that 2,400 people were now living in destitution. The future Conservative member of Parliament outlined three potential solutions to the problem: emigration, providing work (preferably at home), and

---

63. *Belfast News-Letter*, May 3, 1842, May 6, 1842, May 10, 1842, May 13, 1842. For the applicability of moral economy to nineteenth-century Irish developments, John Cunningham, "Popular Protest and a 'Moral Economy' in Provincial Ireland," 26–48.

64. Roddy, *Population, Providence, and Empire*, 27–50. It interesting to note that there is no evidence that Drew participated in the Protestant Colonisation Society, an organization active in the early 1830s that shared his ultra-Protestant concerns about assisted emigration.

providing food (soup kitchens). While Davison made clear that there were drawbacks to each of these modes of relief, he argued that emigration seemed to offer the most effective and permanent solution.[65]

His minister was not convinced. At a meeting in July, Drew again used Sadler's work to advance the idea that Ireland was capable of supporting twice its current population. In the meantime, he argued that what was needed was caution and patience for better times, not shipping off the young and able-bodied sections of the population. Drew's arguments for caution were clearly rooted in anxieties about loyal Protestants leaving Ireland. It was not simply a matter of anti-Catholicism, however, and at that same July 1842 public meeting Drew's admixture of fiscal conservatism and sentimental paternalism was on clear display:

> The case of the poor weavers was to be most tenderly dealt with; he would not have them leave the meeting under the impression that they were cordially pitied—but the meeting, at least the legislative part of it, must deal with them as fathers with children, desperate as was their condition. They must not let these poor men, with their helpless families, find a certain death in the Canadian wildernesses, and a shroud in the snow-wreaths of that fearful climate. Besides, the poor weaver, from previous habits, was ill fitted to grapple with the rough work which fell to the lot of the hewer of the wood, or with the perils of the forest.[66]

As much as he disliked emigration, however, Drew agreed to send them away from their native land, but only as a last resort. At this point, however, it was too late in the season to contemplate traveling across the Atlantic. A month later, he gave a similar speech, arguing that "the harvest was approaching" and "there were symptoms of better days" ahead. In 1842 Drew's argument that the weavers would have

---

65. *Belfast News-Letter*, June 28, 1842.
66. *Belfast News-Letter*, July 29, 1842; *Ulster Times*, July 30, 1842.

to wait for state-assisted emigration seemed to have won the day (with ratepayers, at least).[67]

In August and September, Belfast newspapers were filled with reports of the general strike in Britain.[68] Despite the continuing depression, matters were relatively quiet in Belfast. This was not the case across the region. In north Down, weavers organized under the mythic leader "Tommy Downshire" to protest the low wages they received from local linen manufacturers. Although Lord Downshire and a local magistrate managed to diffuse the crisis, Tommy Downshire's Boys engaged in a sophisticated and relatively effective campaign to improve their position (forty-one area manufacturers signed a public agreement to raise wages).[69] There was, however, no equivalent movement in Belfast. There was a public meeting in Ballymacarrett in late November 1842, but it was designed to celebrate British military victories in China and India. Two prominent leaders of the Ballymacarrett Weavers Committee, Thomas Carson and Henry Crone, spoke at the meeting, detailing their belief that imperial successes would lead to higher wages and employment and calling for celebratory "illuminations" across the district. The meeting's chairman, William Coates, made clear that he would have no part in such excesses and that they seemed premature given the continuing distress in the textile industry.[70]

Coates's point was well taken, since a soup kitchen in Ballymacarrett was feeding an estimated seven hundred to nine hundred people at the time.[71] Although the economy improved in the New Year, thousands of weavers remained unemployed. The question of assisted emigration again was taken up again at a series of meetings in May 1843. The gatherings were generated by petitions asking the Poor

---

67. *Ulster Times,* July 30, 1842.

68. *Belfast News-Letter,* August 19, 1842, August 26, 1842, August 30, 1842, September 6, 1842, September 13, 1842, September 20, 1842.

69. Blackstock, "Tommy Downshire's Boys," 125–72.

70. *Belfast News-Letter,* December 2, 1842.

71. *Northern Whig,* November 29, 1842.

Law commissioners to raise funds to help distressed members of the community leave Ireland for the British colonies. Despite his opposition to the potential tax increase, Drew, supported by the prominent Belfast liberal Robert J. Tennent, successfully moved that a committee be formed to consider the letters and petitions of people wanting to emigrate.[72] It soon was clear Drew's support for an investigation did not reflect any kind of sudden liberality toward the workmen. When he chaired the ensuing meeting the following week, Drew argued against providing state support for most of the witnesses. His arguments were blunt and severe. Drew repeatedly stressed the need to document family rather than individual wages—a standard argument designed to reduce public outlay. More personally, Drew told one petitioner that he had been foolish to move to Belfast and urged him to move back to central and north Antrim, where Drew had never known one poor person.[73]

The tone of Drew's committee report to the town meeting was more measured but firmly against raising the rates to provide for assisted emigration. He argued that as much as the committee sympathized with the industrious workers who came before them and recognized that a few of the individuals were truly desperate and deserving, most of the applicants had family wages that were too high to qualify for support from Poor Law resources. With no real demonstrated need, want of employment, and the potential for better days ahead, Drew's committee found that there was no case for providing public money for the petitioners.[74] The workers present might be forgiven if they came away from the meeting thinking that Drew's compassion was more firmly focused on the next life than this one.

While Drew's doctrinaire and rather unsympathetic tone on these issues seemed to run counter to his reputation as a public advocate for the town's Protestant workers, it should be stressed that his views were

72. *Belfast Commercial Chronicle*, May 20, 1843.
73. *Belfast Commercial Chronicle*, May 27, 1843.
74. *Belfast Vindicator*, June 3, 1843.

well within the norms of a Belfast philanthropic culture that emphasized the necessity of industry, thrift, and self-help. Drew's cautious conservatism echoed that of much of Belfast's civic leadership, which was notoriously reluctant to use public funds to support the poor. As Allison Jordan and other scholars have shown, the efforts of even the most humanitarian philanthropists in the Victorian town were structured by the concepts and language of political economy. In 1829, for example, Dr. Robert Tennent (the father of Robert J. Tennent), by all accounts a more thoughtful and liberal-minded man than Drew, argued against raising funds for distressed cotton weavers for fear that it would distort the local labor market.[75] The Great Famine would bring these tensions to their tragic apotheosis.

Drew rarely remained in such potentially unpopular spaces for very long. In 1843 he was aided by an improving economy and trends in local and national politics, as O'Connell's campaign to repeal the Act of Union quickly displaced the Ballymacarrett weavers from the headlines. While public support for repeal in Belfast lagged behind the rest of the island, the movement gained momentum in the northern capital with the formation and growth of the Belfast Repeal Association (BRA) in late 1842 and early 1843. Led by members of the town's nascent Catholic middle class, the BRA used well-publicized weekly meetings to garner substantial working-class support.[76]

Repeal's increased local and national public profile generated a rather predictable response from Protestant opponents in Belfast, who formed the Protestant Operative Society in April 1843. Organized by the famous anti-Catholic controversialist, the Dublin-based evangelical Reverend Tresham Gregg, the association was designed to mobilize working-class Protestant opposition to repeal. The organization had an immediate impact on communal relations, generating sectarian clashes in and around the Exchange Rooms in its initial meetings in

---

75. *Belfast News-Letter*, June 29, 1829. See Jordan, *Who Cared?*; Connolly and McIntosh, "Whose City?," 244.

76. For the early history of Repeal in Belfast, see Hirst, *Religion, Politics and Violence in 19th Century Belfast*, 52–67; O'Luain, "Young and Old Ireland," 38–53.

early April. Although Gregg's tumultuous visit was widely condemned in the Belfast press, the Protestant Operative Society quickly garnered substantial support in Sandy Row and Ballymacarrett.[77] It is difficult to get a clear sense of the association's private workings, but the organization's public face was clear enough, reflected in the reports of a deputation sent to an anti-repeal meeting held just outside of Belfast in June 1843, and a petition against repeal that featured seventeen thousand signatures. The exact nature of Drew's involvement with the Protestant Operative Society is unclear. He was certainly sympathetic to the organization's goals, and at least one of its most prominent leaders, David Alderdice, a publican from Durham Street, was a member of the Christ Church congregation.[78] If Drew was not an active participant, the Protestant Operative Society was certainly an organization akin to the Protestant political associations he worked with his whole career.

The rise of repeal transformed Belfast politics. As we saw in the mid-1830s, increased political competition and polarization could generate communal clashes in west Belfast. Opposition to repeal in Ballymacarrett, Brown Square, and Sandy Row was nothing new, of course. When Daniel O'Connell visited Belfast in January 1841, he was greeted by opponents who attacked the hotel where he was staying as well as the homes of priests and prominent Repealers. While authorities managed to contain the situation, O'Connell's departure was celebrated as a victory in loyalist neighborhoods. With both parties better organized in 1843, the situation proved even more difficult to manage and the July marching season saw the most extensive sectarian riots yet in Belfast. The 12th of July riots featured intermittent crowd violence that ranged across various west Belfast neighborhoods for two weeks. By all accounts, the riots were initiated by working-class

---

77. Reports of W. Molony, Resident Magistrate, Outrage Papers, County Antrim, April 4-5, 1843, National Archives of Ireland; *Belfast News-Letter*, April 7, 1843.

78. Reports of W. Molony, Resident Magistrate, Outrage Papers, County Antrim, June 21 and 27, 1843, National Archives of Ireland; Christ Church Census, 1852; Hirst, *Religion, Politics, and Violence in 19th Century Belfast*, 45.

Protestant attacks on Catholic homes in the Pound and Sandy Row, violence that generated retaliation. Catherine Hirst has argued that the riots were the product of local Protestant opposition to an increasingly public demand for repeal.[79] The political markers of contention were certainly clear in July 1843: crowds in Sandy Row and the Pound burned effigies of Daniel O'Connell, the Catholic temperance advocate Father Theobald Mathew, and William of Orange. Whatever the motivation, the violence continued for two weeks, featuring attacks on both Catholic and Protestant homes in the boundary zones of west Belfast, assaults on young millworkers, and stone-throwing melees in open fields and streets. Although both Catholic and Protestant participants were found guilty at later trials, a subsequent investigation into the July riots led the *Vindicator* to accuse the Belfast police of Orange favoritism.[80]

Although Drew was not directly involved in the violence, Christ Church lay at the center of the Belfast riots of 1843. Durham Street was one of the primary battlefields in July, and at least two of the people found guilty at the trials in late July were members of the congregation when the religious census was taken in 1852.[81] More importantly for our purposes, the growth of sectarian contention reduced the chance that serious class tensions would develop within Drew's constituency. With the threat of repeal at the forefront of political discussion,

---

79. Hirst, *Religion, Politics, and Violence in 19th Century Belfast*, 70.

80. *Vindicator*, September 20, 1843. Interestingly, the leader focused on "Sunday harangues" by Presbyterian ministers, a focus that reflects Cooke's leadership of conservative religious politics. Reports of the riots and the ensuing trials can be found in all of the Belfast newspapers throughout the summer and fall of 1843. For the trials, see *Northern Whig*, July 29, 1843, September 14, 1843. See also Reports of W. Molony, Resident Magistrate, Outrage Papers, July 12, 13, 16, and 21, 1843; September 17, 1843, National Archives of Ireland. For the most detailed account of the riots, see Hirst, *Religion, Politics and Violence in 19th Century Belfast*, 67–70.

81. Christ Church Census, 1852. The two were George Elliott, a thirty-five-year-old printer who lived at 162-3 Stanley Street, and James McDowell, a sixty-six-year-old weaver who resided at 154-5 Fox's Row. It is worth noting, of course, the possibility that these could be different men with the same name.

Drew quickly returned to his well-established reputation as a Protestant champion, a standing only strengthened by his role in the Mant controversy. This was no simple matter of Orange anti-Catholicism replacing Drew's conservative working-class advocacy. Throughout the 1840s Drew continued to celebrate his self-defined role as public champion of Belfast's poor, hosting a meeting in favor of factory reform in January 1847,[82] acting as secretary of the Belfast General Relief Fund, and frequently writing public letters on various issues concerning Irish (and Belfast) poverty to a range of Belfast newspapers. Ultimately, however, it was Drew's anti-Catholicism and Orange politics that defined his public reputation. The "good Doctor Drew" always returned to his characteristic synthesis of true-blue Protestantism and Tory Paternalism. While Drew's response to the Ballymacarrett weavers in 1842–43 shows that this support could be more rhetorical than real, his muscular anti-Catholicism and reputation as a Protestant champion helped him retain and strengthen ties to his Orange working-class supporters in Belfast in the 1840s and beyond. While there are a number of reasons for Drew's success, he was greatly helped by the heightened sense of communal difference that emerged in the late 1840s and early 1850s, fostered in no small part by the tragedy of the Great Famine.

THOMAS DREW AND THE GREAT IRISH FAMINE

Recent histories of the Great Irish Famine in Belfast have underlined the severe impact the famine had on the town as well as some of the ways those experiences were erased in its aftermath.[83] These same patterns can be seen at Christ Church, where the famine experience was silenced and/or recast as something that largely happened outside

---

82. *Belfast News-Letter*, January 26, 1847.
83. Kinealy and Mac Atasney, *Hidden Famine*. For the ways that the famine experience was excised from the dominant strands of Ulster Protestant collective memory, see Miller, Boling, and Kennedy, "Famine's Scars," 36–60; Farrell, "Providence, Progress and Silence," 101–13.

of the northern capital. Thomas Drew played a prominent role in famine relief in Belfast, serving as secretary to the Belfast General Relief Fund and a member of the governing committee of a specifically Church of Ireland effort. Over the five months of the fund's operation, Drew and others raised over £9,000 for famine relief, funds that were distributed across the island. This generated substantial controversy in Belfast, as prominent subscribers to the General Relief Fund argued that the town's needs should receive priority in the allocation of relief. While the two sides reached a compromise that maintained the all-island nature of the relief effort, the public dispute continued in the Belfast press, where the town's two leading liberal newspapers disparaged Drew for comparing Belfast to his native Limerick. The debate over the fund's so-called Drew policy underlined his controversial position in Victorian Belfast and the ways that the famine experience strengthened notions of regional difference in the northern capital. This was anything but a simple matter, as the idea of Belfast and/or Ulster exceptionalism was shared by both Drew and his opponents. The mythic notion that the Great Famine was something that happened "out there" only increased in future years, a silence reflected in the treatment of the famine in "The Annals of Christ Church, Belfast," the unpublished church history completed in 1858 by Drew's own curate, the Reverend Abraham Dawson. By largely writing the famine out of the Christ Church experience, both Drew and Dawson's work illustrates the ways that providence, progress, and silence shaped the ways that the famine was remembered and forgotten in various circles in the north of Ireland.

Drew's first public pronouncement about the Great Famine came at a meeting held in the town hall on April 8, 1846, to discuss the need to create a relief committee in Belfast. The issue at hand was another crisis in Ballymacarrett, where hundreds of men and women were said to be on the verge of starvation. When the potato crop failed in 1845, the British government immediately recognized the potential danger in Belfast's poorest suburb, providing two grants in aid for the local relief committee. By 1846 the Ballymacarrett committee had ordered 1.5 million tons of Indian corn, but more resources were needed. One of the problems was related to boundaries, since Ballymacarrett lay within the Belfast Poor Law Union but was considered by many town councilors to be outside of the town.[84] The April meeting was largely the product of the advocacy of Charles Troup, the Scottish editor and owner of the *Banner of Ulster*, which, almost alone amongst Belfast newspapers, published stories on the growing crisis in the north Down village. After John Kane, Belfast's mayor, and the Reverend Charles Courtenay, rector of the parish church in Ballymacarrett, opened the meeting by outlining the deteriorating situation, Drew quickly intervened, asking if local authorities could provide a statistical profile of destitution in east Belfast. If the inquiry proved that distress existed to the extent that had been claimed, he argued that the committee should put together a case that "would draw iron tears from the most hard-hearted of our merchants." That case, however, had not yet been established.[85]

If Drew's skeptical attitude toward the claims of poverty was not clear from his opening remarks, his ensuing comments left no room for doubt. He warned listeners about the potential tax increases that came with relief and suggested that the Ballymacarrett weavers had hurt themselves through their own efforts to increase their wages through collective action. He made clear that he believed that relief should not be provided to people whose poverty stemmed from industrial action or their own improvidence. After all, he argued, Sandy Row's textile workers had not made similar complaints.[86] After Troup defended the weavers, Drew relented somewhat, nevertheless reading a government circular that insisted that relief committees apply the distinction between the able-bodied poor and those unable to support themselves. There was certainly no shortage of need; the Ballymacarrett committee employed nearly 200 people in stone-breaking (providing wages that supported nearly one thousand men, women,

---

84. Grant, "Great Famine in County Down," 354–55; Kinealy and Mac Atasney, *Hidden Famine*, 46–51.

85. *Banner of Ulster*, April 10, 1846.

86. *Banner of Ulster*, April 10, 1846; *Belfast Commercial Chronicle*, April 11, 1846.

and children) and handing out rations of coal and food to those "without any means of subsistence or any prospect of getting employment." Somewhat reluctantly, the assembly agreed to form a relief committee in Belfast. Drew did not volunteer for the new body, but he was hardly alone in his less than sympathetic attitude toward the Ballymacarrett poor. When 150 people asked the newly formed Belfast relief committee for help in emigrating to Upper Canada through the newly formed Ballymacarrett Emigration Society, the committee refused their appeal, saying they did not have the funds to pay for emigration. While the government provided another grant of £100 to Ballymacarrett in June 1847, the funds ran out within a month.[87]

Drew's attitude toward famine relief was anything but consistent, oscillating between warm advocacy for those in need and cruel pronouncements about the failings of Irish character. His primary engagement with the Great Famine and famine relief was through his work as one of the two secretaries to the Belfast General Relief Fund (Thomas McClure, the future Liberal member of Parliament for Belfast, was the other). The fund was created in January 1847 to provide relief for the distressed poor in both Belfast and Ireland. The prime mover behind the project was the Reverend John Edgar, the seceding Presbyterian minister and professor of theology at the Royal Belfast Academical Institution. Most famous for his work as a temperance advocate, Edgar published *A Cry for Connacht* in November 1846 after a proselytizing tour through the west of Ireland. Overwhelmed by the suffering he encountered, Edgar used the pulpit and the Belfast press to mobilize support for efforts to relieve western distress. His emotional plea for support at a speech at May Street Presbyterian Church generated widespread attention: "I hope soon to have an opportunity of directing public attention to spiritual famine in Connaught, but our effort now is to save the perishing body; and whether our countryman and brother be a Protestant or Romanist, we acknowledge the claim which, in this day of his deep distress, he has on our purses and our

---

87. Kinealy and Mac Atasney, *Hidden Famine*, 47–51.

hearts. Our brother is starving, and, till we have satisfied his hunger, we have no time to inquire whether he be Protestant or Romanist."[88] While Edgar's fusion of social concern and sectarian sentiment led many Catholics to charge him with souperism (the practice of providing relief in exchange for religious conversion, an accusation made against evangelical Protestants during and after the Great Famine), there can be little doubt about the success of his work mobilizing support for famine relief in Belfast,[89] where he helped to create the Belfast Ladies Association for Connacht and the Belfast General Relief Fund.[90] The latter fund's subscribers and participants soon included a wide array of Belfast business, political, and religious elites, who contributed more than £7,000 between January and May 1847.[91]

If Edgar was the individual most responsible for the creation of the fund, Drew was an early subscriber and part of an inner circle that first met on January 2, 1847, to initiate relief efforts. The group created three basic guidelines for the creation and operation of the fund: (1) that relief was to be provided "to alleviate the present distress, without restriction to any locality"; (2) that funds raised would be entrusted to a committee elected by and from the fund's subscribers; and (3) that the money would only be spent on food. The group created a governing committee that featured Drew; Edgar; the Reverend Cornelius Denvir, the Roman Catholic bishop of Down and Connor; and a range of other figures representing the town's business, civic, and religious establishments. It was Drew who proposed the idea that the next step

---

88. Killen, *Memoir of John Edgar*, 218–19.

89. For Edgar's place within Irish Presbyterian and Great Famine historiography, see Frogatt, "Rev. John Edgar (1798–1866)"; Holmes, "Religion, Anti-Slavery and Identity," 378–98; Miller, "Irish Presbyterians and the Great Famine," 169–73; Moffitt, *Soupers and Jumpers*; Whelan, "Stigma of Souperism," 135–54.

90. For the Belfast Ladies Relief Association for Connacht, see Luddy, *Women and Philanthropy in Nineteenth-Century Ireland*, 187–88.

91. Drew presented the Belfast General Relief Fund's final report to a public meeting in January 1849, published widely across the town's press. See *Belfast News-Letter*, January 5, 1849. For a solid overview of the fund's history, see Kinealy and Mac Atasney, *Hidden Famine*, 114–20.

was to call for a town meeting to give people a chance to voice their opinions about famine relief. The others agreed, and the new Lord Mayor, John Harrison, called for a public meeting on January 15.[92]

The first town meeting was an impressive affair, drawing a wide array of Belfast's business, political, and religious leaders to the Large Room in the Commercial Buildings. Proposing the third resolution, Drew made a long and rambling speech to gain support for the fund, which he argued was needed both to provide much-needed support for the Irish poor and to demonstrate that Belfast and Ireland could take care of their own to an English public that was increasingly skeptical about Irish claims of need. Citing both a recent trip through his native Munster and letters he had received from clergymen throughout the country, Drew catalogued the severe distress of the people living in the south and west. Action was needed; people were dying.

Drew called for higher wages for Irish rural laborers, quoting O'Connell's famous claim that the Irish laborer was the worst clothed, fed, and lodged in all of Europe. Why, he, argued, should Irish laborers be paid less than their English counterparts? Drew provided several examples of north Down landlords who provided their tenants and workers with good wages and housing, critiquing those who would not raise wages for fear of upsetting the "labour market," an odious term favored by political economists that reminded Drew of the "slave market." Higher wages would transform Ireland. As he put it: "Pay the labourer throughout Ireland as you pay him in the North of Ireland, and I promise you, by God's blessing, you will see Ireland another country." Continuing in this populist mode, he praised the sacrifice of his own era's "fur coat brigade," noting that the gentlemen of the Down Hunt had recently canceled their gathering in Newtownards, sending money instead to two relief committees: "Now I say long life (not to the Down Hunt!) to the gentlemen of the Down Hunt; and if they will only sell the dogs and send the proceeds—we will be more

---

92. *Northern Whig*, January 7, 1847; *Vindicator*, January 9, 1847.

obliged to them."[93] Edgar followed Drew with a less dramatic appeal, making clear that Belfast applicants were eligible for support from the fund. All in all, Drew's performance was an effective one, featuring a mix of broad humor, emotive paternalism, and hyperbolic rhetorical radicalism. Drew received plaudits for the speech, which was reprinted in nearly every Belfast newspaper. The *Belfast Protestant Journal* called it one of the best speeches that had been delivered in Ireland during the Great Famine while one *Northern Whig* correspondent wrote that he had never heard a better or more appropriate speech from a clergyman.[94] The appeal generated an immediate response; by January 26 the fund had received over £4,600 from subscribers.[95] Drew quickly became one of the public faces of famine relief in Belfast, which proved to be something of a mixed blessing.

Edgar's late intervention at the January meeting presaged one of the most contentious issues raised by the Belfast General Relief Fund—the question of how relief should be distributed and whether or not applications from Belfast should receive priority. The issue was raised at a committee meeting by two prominent Belfast liberals, John Francis Ferguson and Robert J. Tennent, who called for a general meeting of subscribers to reconsider the way the fund operated. Drew opened the well-publicized March 19 meeting with a detailed review of the committee's work, reporting that supporters had subscribed nearly £7,000. Over the first three months of the year, the committee had approved 124 grants, sending over £2,800 to applicants across the island to purchase food. Fifty-five of these grants had been made to

---

93. The *Belfast Commercial Chronicle* provided the fullest account of Drew's speech. See *Belfast Commercial Chronicle*, January 16, 1847.

94. *Belfast Protestant Journal*, January 23, 1847; *Northern Whig*, January 19, 1847. Drew's speech also inspired one Belfast resident to write a public letter to him, suggesting that the town's wealthy inhabitants should hold a public exhibition of their privately-held art to raise funds for famine relief. See *Belfast News-Letter*, January 26, 1847.

95. *Belfast News-Letter*, January 5, 1849.

applicants from Ulster, including a recent donation of £1,000 to the Belfast Soup Kitchen, which Drew claimed would have closed without the support. The secretary closed his opening remarks by stating that the committee was now receiving six to seven applications per day, requests that featured harrowing descriptions of the suffering wrought by the crisis.[96] Drew's argument was clear. Conditions were getting increasingly desperate across Ireland, and the fund needed to retain its island-wide focus.

Not surprisingly, Drew's report generated a spirited discussion about the distribution of the fund's resources. Ferguson, a prominent linen merchant, argued that rapidly deteriorating conditions in Belfast and the government's recent amendment of the Irish Poor Law to allow local districts to establish relief committees and borrow money had transformed the situation. Money primarily raised in Belfast should now stay in the town to help alleviate local distress. With this in mind, Ferguson and Tennent proposed that the committee deal more liberally with Belfast applications and limit the amount of relief sent to "remote parts" of Ireland. Several subscribers moved quickly to defend the committee's work, arguing that all of the island's poor deserved support and reminding participants that Belfast (and Ulster more generally) had received the lion's share of funding thus far. Drew was the most outspoken of these speakers, arguing that while conditions were bad in Belfast, they were far worse in the south and west of Ireland. He went on to assert that such a move would be a stain on Belfast's honor: "And he did hope that no resolution would be that day passed by Belfast merchants, lest in future instead of Belfast, it might be called hold fast." If the resolution was passed, Drew argued that he would be ashamed to visit his "native Limerick." Others quickly moved in to soften the terms of discussion. And while the rhetoric was dramatic, the argument was a rather semantic one. As fellow committee member Dr. S. S. Thomson pointed out, "There was a very little difference of opinion, if all parties understood each other. Mr. Ferguson

---

96. *Belfast News-Letter,* March 23, 1847.

did not want the money exclusively for Belfast; and the other side had no wish to exclude Belfast." While a "long and desultory conversation followed," a compromise of sorts was negotiated. While the final resolution made explicit mention of the new law and Belfast's particular needs, the committee retained the discretion to make grants across the island.[97] On the surface, at least, nothing seemed to have changed.

The meeting's seemingly peaceful resolution did not mean an end to public controversy. The *Banner of Ulster* and the *Northern Whig* provided spirited critiques of Drew's "anti-Belfast policy," responses that were sharpened by Drew's negative reputation in Presbyterian circles as much as the fund's alleged discrimination against the Belfast poor. The *Northern Whig* was particularly adamant about the issue, arguing that Dr. Drew and his supporters wanted to prevent the Belfast poor from receiving relief: "We must take leave to insist, that upon this fund our own poor have the first claim."[98] The tone of the debate was sharpened by the committee's rejection of a grant application by the Belfast Ladies Association that would have allowed doctors to distribute relief through an industrial school supported by the organization. While the committee eventually reevaluated its initial decision under political pressure, providing the organization a grant of £100, the initial rejection provided fodder for those arguing for a more Belfast-centered approach to famine relief.[99]

If the *Northern Whig*'s polemic was in some ways merely a continuation of the argument about the use of the remaining resources of the fund, the newspaper took up the regional dimensions of the disagreement with a vengeance, wielding Drew's comparison of Belfast to Limerick to savage effect: "We beg to tell him, that he should feel ashamed, and hang his head, at the notion that Limerick, with its fair city, the third in the kingdom—a city which is sufficiently proud, and is ever ready to babble about nationality and independence, should be

97. *Belfast Commercial Chronicle*, March 23, 1847.

98. *Northern Whig*, March 23, 1847. For a similar argument, see *Banner of Ulster*, March 23, 1847.

99. Kinealy and Mac Atasney, *Hidden Famine*, 118–20.

gaping, as a beggar, to catch alms from Belfast. . . . And yet, Dr. Drew ventures to talk of being 'ashamed' of Belfast, if a part of the money that ought to go to the support of our own poor, be not handed to him, for the benefit of his 'native Limerick.'"[100] In another article, the *Northern Whig* continued its critique of what it termed *the Drew policy*, sarcastically urging the committee to send more money to County Mayo rather than support the suffering poor at their own doors. Writing under the moniker "Justice," another correspondent took up a similar line of argument, adding that it was no wonder that the people of Belfast were angry about the issue when the relief committee rejected the Belfast Ladies Association and sent money to exotic places like "Cape Clear and Dingle-a-Cooch."[101]

Drew's advocacy for all-Ireland relief gained him some surprising, if temporary, allies. Defending Drew and the committee, the *Vindicator* argued that their approach represented true philanthropy against the circumscribed charity of their opponents. The nationalist paper called for a united approach to take care of the poor, critiquing the provincial airs of the Belfast-first faction: "If we have honour and charity at heart, all will subscribe . . . If we cannot, let us come down from conceited greatness and go a begging decently."[102] A later letter writer tackled these regional dimensions directly, arguing that Drew had many faults, but apparently the worst of these was that he had "the unparalleled indiscretion to have been born in Limerick," which, he added, was apparently not nearly far enough north for the *Northern Whig*.[103]

There is certainly no tangible evidence that Drew and his committee discriminated against the Belfast poor in favor of their southern Irish compatriots. Drew's reports on the distribution of the fund's grants make it quite clear that the vast majority of all moneys went

100. *Northern Whig*, March 23, 1847.
101. *Northern Whig*, April 6, 1847. "Dingle-a-Cooch" is a reference to Thomas Moore's poem "If and Perhaps."
102. *Vindicator*, March 24, 1847.
103. *Vindicator*, April 7, 1847.

to Belfast and its surrounding northern counties. His final report, however, also reflects the committee's sensitivity to the charge that they had neglected Belfast, listing grants made to the Belfast Soup Kitchen, the Industrial School of the Belfast Ladies Association, and the town's day asylum and the Destitute and Sick Society. Drew also highlighted the committee's grants to emigrants aboard the *Swatara*, a fever-stricken ship forced into Belfast Lough by bad weather in March 1847. Medical authorities inspected the ship and its nearly three hundred passengers, who were forced to stay in lodgings on Waring Street for a month while the *Swatara* was fumigated and repaired. Food for the emigrants, many of whom were from Roscommon, was purchased with funds from the Belfast General Relief Fund as well as a subscription raised by a local emigration officer. In his final report, Drew stressed the committee's role in allowing the emigrant ship to leave Belfast for the United States, an emphasis that doubtless reflected civic fear about the potential spread of typhus.[104]

The Belfast-first crowd was certainly on strong ground when it emphasized the increasing need for famine relief in the northern capital. While it may have been partially hidden by Belfast's urban landscape, the famine was hardly something "out there," a point underlined by recent historians and any number of contemporary sources. In November 1846 the town's two soup kitchens dispensed 1,500 quarts of soup and more than 2,000 pounds of bread per week. By February 1847 that had increased to 20,000 quarts of soup and 4,000 pounds of bread, no doubt aided by the grant from the Belfast General Relief Fund.[105] The minutes of the Belfast Poor Law Board of Guardians show that weekly admissions to the workhouse increased from a range of 5–20 in January 1846 to 150–300 in May 1847. A February 1847 medical attendant's report underlined the pressure that increased

---

104. *Belfast News-Letter*, January 5, 1849. The *Swatara* was forced to come ashore at Derry after leaving for Belfast. Dozens died before the ship finally arrived in Philadelphia. See McMahon, *Coffin Ship*, 79–80; Kinealy and Mac Atasney, *Hidden Famine*, 87–88.

105. Kinealy and Mac Atasney, *Hidden Famine*, 61, 65, 73.

numbers placed on the workhouse system, arguing that "each week is likely to become epidemic among us. It is admitted by everyone acquainted with the arrangements of hospitals, that the more crowded the sick are, the higher is the rate of mortality and in this infirmary there are 100 in a space that should not admit more than 65."[106]

Perhaps the most tangible markers of the Great Famine's impact on Belfast were the town's cemeteries, which, by 1847, no longer had enough room to hold the bodies of the dead. Public controversy over the issue surfaced in the summer of 1847, when a variety of political and religious leaders complained vociferously about the state of the town's three cemeteries. Drew was one of these advocates, pushing for the establishment of a public cemetery at a town meeting on August 23: "He knew himself that they were very badly off for burying ground, for he had seen the way that Shankill graveyard was choked up with the dead. The system of breaking up skulls, and sinking spades in the coffins, and dead bodies, rendered it intolerable in any Christian community, and actually pestiferous to the ministers and priests who had to perform the offices for the dead in it."[107] While matters were not as dire in Belfast as they were in west Cork or Kerry, the impact of the Great Famine was real enough in Belfast.

If the regional dimensions of the Belfast General Relief Fund's famine relief efforts generated controversy, there were no such divisions over the question of what to do with the itinerant poor—those paupers from England, Scotland, and other parts of Ireland who had traveled to Belfast for relief, an issue that dominated conversation across a range of associations and institutions devoted to poor relief in the northern capital. While Drew had justified grants to the day asylum and the Destitute and Sick Society because of their work with paupers from out of town, he was often callous toward the itinerant poor, arguing at a February 1847 meeting that the suppression of street

---

106. Medical Attendant Report, February 3, 1847, Belfast Poor Law Union Board of Guardians, PRONI, BG/7/A/5/183–4. Courtesy of the Deputy Keeper of the Records, Public Record Office of Northern Ireland.

107. *Belfast News-Letter*, August 24, 1847.

begging needed to be made a higher priority.[108] In his final report for the Belfast General Relief Fund, Drew thanked John Holden of the Ulster Railway Company, which transported 11,608 people who had received varying degrees of relief in Belfast "a portion of their journey homewards" to other parts of Ireland—a gesture that the men and women shipped out of town might have viewed with less warmth. It is important to note that Drew's views on the mobile poor were not controversial amongst his fellow philanthropists. For Drew and the vast majority of his Belfast colleagues, paupers who were strangers deserved sympathy and a measure of Christian charity, but not extended support—a notion that had deadly provenance throughout Ireland during the Great Famine.[109]

The Belfast General Relief Fund wound up its work with little fanfare in May and June 1847. Although no public explanation was offered, the combination of the controversies over the distribution of relief and the passage of the Poor Law Amendment Act of 1847 are the most likely reasons for the fund's rather unceremonious end. Drew doubtless was relieved, since a number of accounts celebrate the long hours that he and his fellow committee members spent raising funds and evaluating grant proposals.[110] While Drew, Edgar, and their allies had successfully maintained the fund's all-Ireland framework, press coverage suggests that public opinion in Belfast largely had shifted against them. The motivations behind Drew's commitment to the fund's island-wide framework were complex. There was a personal connection for the Limerick native, of course, but it is worth noting that all of the ministers who dominated the committee work worked from templates that combined the need for humane social action with an evangelical desire to convert Catholics to Protestantism. Given both the sensitivity of the subject and Drew and Edgar's support for

108. *Northern Whig*, February 23, 1847.

109. Crossman, *Poverty and the Poor Law in Ireland*; Crossman, "Attitudes and Reponses to Vagrancy in Ireland," 264–79.

110. *Belfast Commercial Chronicle*, April 24, 1847; *Belfast News-Letter*, January 5, 1849; Dawson, "Annals of Christ Church, Belfast," 110.

proselytism, it is worth noting that there were no charges of souperism connected to the fund.

Drew was involved in another relief effort that was explicitly conversionist in its aims: the Fund for the Temporal Relief of the Suffering Poor of Ireland through the Instrumentality of the Clergy of the Established Church. Founded on January 4, 1847, just two days after Drew helped to create the Belfast General Relief Fund, the fund was established by a group of Church of Ireland ministers and their supporters to distribute relief and take advantage of "an opening that has been made for conveying the light of the Gospel into the darkened mind of the Roman Catholic peasantry thus severely suffering."[111] The association was immediately critiqued by the *Banner of Ulster*, the *Northern Whig*, and the *Vindicator*, which all accused the Belfast clerics of needlessly politicizing the tragedy.[112] Although Drew was not as active in the group as some of his colleagues, he was a member of the fund's governing committee, sharpening his negative reputation in Catholic and liberal circles. The controversy did not seem to inhibit the Anglican evangelicals, who raised £2,000 by March 16, 1847, distributing the majority of the funds to clergymen in Munster, Connacht, and West Ulster. Despite efforts to merge the fund with the Belfast General Relief Fund, the two organizations were kept distinct.[113]

The debates over the General Relief Fund's distribution of aid illustrate some of the complex ways that notions of northern difference influenced the ways that people responded to the Great Famine. Both Drew's arguments and those of many of his opponents rested on the idea that the north of Ireland, and particularly Belfast, stood apart from the rest of the island. Even Drew's case for raising the wages of rural laborers rested on the idea that such a move would remake Ireland in an Ulster image, a perspective he reinforced with his argument that comparatively prosperous Belfast had a duty to support the rest of

111. *Belfast News-Letter*, January 8, 1847.

112. *Banner of Ulster*, January 8, 1847; *Northern Whig*, January 7, 1847; *Vindicator*, January 13, 1847.

113. Kinealy and Mac Atasney, *Hidden Famine*, 133.

the island. While Belfast-first supporters clearly were driven by deteriorating conditions in the northern capital, their arguments were just as clearly shaped by notions of provincial superiority, seen in the *Northern Whig*'s mockery of Drew's Limerick connections and its critique of the committee's seeming commitment to exotic and isolated locales in Cork, Kerry, and Mayo. These types of narratives were hardly new, of course, but they were strengthened immeasurably by the Great Famine (and dramatically politicized by the 1848 rebellion), a fact that can be seen by briefly charting the ways that Drew and his colleagues discussed the impact of the famine on Christ Church District.

Drew rarely mentioned the prevalence of local distress amongst his own congregants. When he talked about Belfast poverty during the Great Famine, it was either in general terms, lacking the types of specifics he lavished on reports from Cork and Limerick, or focused on paupers from outside Belfast, a narrative that reinforced a general sense that the famine was something "out there." The overwhelming pressure placed on the Belfast workhouse, the soup kitchens, and other institutions designed to serve the thousands of men, women, and children who needed relief belied this effort to silence the suffering of the Belfast poor during the famine. These deaths often were quite close to Drew. On July 21, 1847, for example, the *Belfast Commercial Chronicle* reported that James Noble, one of Christ Church's scripture readers, had died the previous day of typhus fever.[114] Even in Drew's own works, we get glimpses of horror through the cracks of this protective facade. In the "Annals of Loughinisland," an unpublished manuscript he wrote in the 1860s about the local history of the south Down parish and his own ministerial career, he recounted the impact of the 1847 fever epidemic in Belfast by discussing the death of a mother and her daughters, one of whom was a teacher at the Christ Church Adult School.[115] In public, however, Drew's famine narratives featured graphic but firmly distant tales of horror.

114. *Belfast Commercial Chronicle*, July 21, 1847.
115. Drew, "Annals of Loughinisland," 200.

The silencing of local suffering is evident in the Reverend Abraham Dawson's "The Annals of Christ Church, Belfast." Born in County Tyrone in 1827, Dawson became curate at Christ Church in 1851, a year after he had received his degree at Trinity College Dublin. By all accounts, Dawson was an energetic and effective administrator. He engineered the church's 1852 religious census and was an active participant in both the Christ Church Protestant Association and the Church of Ireland's Young Men's Society, where he gave lectures on George Walker, the militant cleric who led Protestant resistance at the late seventeenth-century Siege of Derry. After leaving Christ Church in 1857 to become the rector of Knocknamuckley Parish Church near Portadown, Dawson enjoyed a successful clerical career that culminated with his selection as dean of Dromore. He died in Belfast in 1905.[116] Dawson clearly had a scholarly bent, publishing several articles in the *Ulster Journal of Archaeology* as well as his unpublished book on Christ Church.[117] In the midst of this useful local history, Dawson includes a nineteen-page discussion of the Great Famine, a rather conventional famine narrative that leans heavily on the work of Sir William Wilde.[118] After a brief introduction to the history of potato, he provides a detailed statistical account of the dead and a largely optimistic portrait of an Ireland that would be remade by this horrific tragedy. What is striking about Dawson's portrait of the famine, however, is the complete absence of local suffering. There is no mention of Sandy Row or Christ Church beyond his celebration of Drew's hard work to raise funds for famine relief. In Dawson's 1858 retelling, the Great Famine was something that happened elsewhere.[119]

Many of these same dynamics can be seen in the rate-in-aid controversy of 1849. In February of that year, Prime Minister John Russell

---

116. For a more detailed discussion of Dawson and his portrait of the Irish Famine, see Farrell, "Providence, Progress and Silence," 101–13.

117. Dawson, "Biographical Notice of George Walker," 129–35, 261–77; "Terrier of the Parish of Seagoe," 224–26; "St. Patrick's View of the Braid Valley," 113–19.

118. See Gray, "Accounting for Catastrophe," 50–66.

119. Dawson, "Annals of Christ Church, Belfast," 142–61.

proposed a new for famine relief in Ireland. This was a national tax to be paid in support of bankrupt Poor Law unions that were almost entirely in the south and west of Ireland. There was widespread opposition to the proposal in Ulster, where figures from across the political spectrum inveighed against a scheme that they claimed (falsely) discriminated against the comparatively prosperous north. Drew was one of the loudest voices against the measure, speaking at a series of public meetings in March. Drew's opposition was rooted in a rather unattractive amalgam of conservative critique of the Poor Law and notions of regional superiority and civic pride. At a March 2 meeting, for example, Drew claimed that the rate-in-aid would be ruinous for two counties in Ulster (Antrim and Down), where landlords were already granting sizable remissions on their rents. No place, he continued, had done more for Connacht and Munster than Belfast, which, he claimed, had raised £15,000 for the districts of the south and west.[120] Days later at a meeting on the need for sanitary reform in Belfast, he argued that the rate-in-aid scheme would reduce prosperous Ulster to the poverty of the south and west in a matter of years.[121]

But Drew's argument was not simply about geography. He also maintained that the extravagance of the Irish Poor Law had damaged the national character, teaching Irishmen that they could rely on state handouts rather than their own initiative. "The government," he argued, "should tell Paddy that, after a certain day, he must work for his bread." He continued in this vein by lambasting northern politicians as "sleeping beauties" who had done nothing for Ulster since he had come to the province. It was high time that these men "did something for us," actions that would only be taken if audience members got involved in politics, a sign of Drew's intermittent frustration with the conservative establishment.[122] This line doubtless brought cheers from the crowd, but the hollowness of Drew and his northern

120. *Belfast News-Letter*, March 6, 1849.
121. *Banner of Ulster*, March 9, 1849.
122. *Belfast News-Letter*, March 6, 1849. See also Drew's public letter to Lords Lyndhurst and Brougham: *Belfast Protestant Journal*, March 24, 1849.

allies' claims was revealed soon enough. The government's bill easily passed the House of Commons shortly thereafter. British politicians heard northern arguments about the injustice of the rate-in-aid bill as self-interested complaints rather than patriotic and loyal sentiment.[123] Drew's rhetoric may have played well in Orange circles in Belfast, but it was simply not effective outside of Ireland. This lesson would be repeated throughout the next decade.

CONCLUSION

Thomas Drew clearly cherished his reputation as a champion of the Protestant poor. This was not simply a matter of self-aggrandizement. Supporters and critics alike celebrated his devotion to those in need. Drew was often a fierce if conservative advocate for the Belfast and Irish poor. He provided educational opportunities and support for plebeian households through Christ Church's extensive networks of schools and social and spiritual outreach programs, supported moderate measures of factory and sanitary reform, and worked diligently to raise funds for famine relief. He was, in some ways, a tribune of the Protestant poor. And yet, as this chapter has shown, there were real limits to Drew's advocacy. He often opposed working-class claims of poverty in blunt and moralistic terms and rarely supported state-funded initiatives to provide poor relief. A public letter published in the *Belfast Protestant Journal* during the rate-in-aid controversy of 1849 epitomized, albeit in extreme form, Drew's opposition to such programs. Calling the Irish Poor Law "extravagant, poverty-creating, and demoralizing," Drew went on to state that "no Poor Law in Ireland ought to contemplate other objects than the helpless aged, the sick, the lame, the blind, the deaf and dumb, the fatherless, and the widow."[124] It is hard to imagine a more stringent statement of the Victorian distinction between the deserving and undeserving poor.

123. Grant, "Great Famine and the Poor Law in Ulster," 45.
124. *Belfast Protestant Journal*, March 24, 1849.

Yet such beliefs hardly distinguished Drew from his Belfast contemporaries, most of whom were notoriously reluctant to raise taxes to support the poor. Perhaps this is one of the factors that helps to explain why Drew's frequently less than sympathetic responses to Protestant working-class difficulties in the 1840s had such little impact on plebeian support for the "good doctor." Philanthropic endeavor in Victorian Belfast nearly always combined a genuine concern for the poor with an aim to strengthen the values of industry, thrift, and self-help. Charity in the northern capital, as Sean Connolly and Gillian McIntosh have argued, was a prisoner of its social context.[125] If Drew opposed initiatives to expand the social safety net beyond a limited definition of the deserving poor, he was hardly alone. The Society for the Amelioration of the Working Classes, a Belfast reform organization founded by members of the town's civic establishment in 1845, featured an educational program of lectures on subjects such as political economy.[126] In early Victorian Belfast, Drew's track record of rhetorical and real support for Protestant working-class families was sufficient to maintain his reputation as the champion of Sandy Row. There were seemingly few alternatives.

There is little that is distinctive about Drew's various initiatives to appeal to working-class Anglicans, which neatly parallel the efforts of socially active evangelical ministers from Glasgow to Oldham and Shuttleworth. But Belfast is not Oldham, and the northern capital's potent ethno-religious divisions help to explain Drew's successful navigation of the troubled waters of the 1840s. For all the limits of his plebeian advocacy, it was primarily Drew's vociferous anti-Catholicism and his well-earned reputation as a champion of Orange and Protestant politics that helped him maintain ties with his working-class supporters. The deepening sectarian politics of the 1840s, epitomized by the Belfast riots of 1843 and sharpened by both the Great Irish Famine and

125. Connolly and McIntosh, "Whose City?," 244.
126. Minute Book of the Society of the Amelioration of the Working Classes of Belfast, February 1845–61, PRONI, D.1860/1.

the 1848 rebellion, made Drew's task much easier, as the rising utility of anti-Catholicism constrained the formation of alternative collectivities in the rapidly growing town. As this chapter has shown, debates over the distribution of famine relief and particularly the Ulster rate-in-aid controversy reflected these dynamics, featuring narratives of regional difference that were often rooted in potent and none-too-subtle anti-Catholic codes. This was comfortable ground for Drew, who had been a prominent anti-Catholic controversialist and stalwart supporter of the Orange Order since his arrival in Belfast in 1833. It was a reputation that would only grow in the ensuing decade.

5

Belfast's Populist Political Parson
Thomas Drew and Anti-Catholic Politics

Thomas Drew's reputation as a political minister largely stems from the period after 1848, when he was one of Belfast's loudest anti-Catholic voices, a role that both reflected and strengthened the sharpened sectarian politics and growing presence of the Orange Order in the burgeoning industrial city. Drew's public notoriety as Belfast's leading Orange cleric stemmed in part from newspaper coverage of the meetings of the Christ Church Protestant Association, an organization he founded in 1854 to educate and mobilize the Protestant working classes against a Catholic threat made all the more dangerous in his mind by British appeasement and ineptitude. Drew also was closely linked to the Belfast riots of 1857, which many attributed in part to a caustic anti-Catholic diatribe he delivered to Belfast Orangemen gathered at Christ Church to commemorate the 12th of July that year. The controversial minister's long-standing reputation as a dangerous and divisive public speaker was only strengthened by the government investigation that followed the riots, which placed much of the blame for the unprecedented scale of that summer's urban violence on Orange partisan display and the provocation of evangelical street preaching. It was the Belfast riots of 1857 and their contentious aftermaths that led many to view Drew as the epitome of the north of Ireland's destructive party politics. By the time Drew left Christ Church to become rector of Loughinisland Parish Church and precentor of Down in 1859, he was one of the most notorious anti-Catholic preachers in all of Ireland.

Drew was unrepentant about his politics. Answering those who preferred their pastors to steer clear of such matters, he made it quite clear that he did not see his ministerial position as an inhibition on political activity: "It was useless to say that he, as a minister, should not interfere in politics. Had he not as much interest as any man in the town in having a proper representative in Parliament? Had he not an interest in having a free Bible and a free constitution, as well as any other? And why should he then be told, that when he became a minister, he ceased to have any interest in the welfare of his country."[1] While the partisan nature of Drew's ministry was attacked by his many opponents, this political emphasis never waned. Even his most sympathetic observers highlighted the Christ Church minister's advocacy for Conservative and Orange politics as one of his primary legacies.[2] This was no small matter. Throughout Drew's career, but particularly in the decade following the Great Irish Famine, his provocative politics played no small part in keeping sectarian division at the center of public attention in Belfast.

Drew's often ferocious anti-Catholic polemics had a Janus-faced impact on mid-Victorian Belfast politics and society. On the one hand, Drew's political extremism placed very real constraints on his influence and effectiveness. Volume and activity are not necessarily good indicators of influence, as a number of other studies of Orangeism and ultra-Protestant politics have made clear.[3] Drew was an energetic and effective minister and a popular speaker for ultra-Protestant audiences, but the same anti-Catholic diatribes that made him an Orange champion alienated constituencies of more moderate conservative opinion that dominated Belfast and Irish Protestant politics. Many within these civic networks shared Drew's anti-Catholicism in the broadest sense, but there were significant ideological and tonal variations within the

---

1. *Belfast News-Letter*, October 4, 1855.

2. For a clear example, see the Reverend Robert Hannay's sermon at Drew's funeral: *Belfast News-Letter*, October 25, 1870.

3. See Wolffe, *Protestant Crusade in Great Britain*, 198–289; MacRaild, *Faith, Fraternity, and Fighting*.

town's anti-Catholic politics. Jonathan Jeffrey Wright has drawn a useful distinction between moderate anti-Catholicism and a more extreme or sectarian variant in his work on the career of James Emerson Tennent. While Emerson Tennent and Drew often used a similar vocabulary, the British political leader's anti-Catholicism was shaped by lingering enlightenment critiques of Roman Catholicism rather than the emotive sectarian fury of a blustery Orange bigot or evangelical controversialist. In Emerson Tennent's case, these beliefs were shaped by his extensive interactions with Catholics outside of Ireland, both on tours of the European continent and in South Asia, when he was colonial secretary in Ceylon. While such categories should not be seen as watertight, Wright's examination of Emerson Tennent's career has the great virtue of treating anti-Catholicism as a complex historical subject, something more than a monolithic atavistic tradition.[4]

While most Protestants in Victorian Belfast had a well-worn knowledge of the language of anti-Catholicism, its basic histories, tenets, and rhetorical flourishes, many found the divisive opinions and confrontational performances of a figure like Drew a step too far in normal times. The *Irish Presbyterian*'s October 1857 description of Drew as a warmhearted and energetic cleric whose bitter politics generated and sustained factional division is a characteristic reflection of the broad center of Belfast Protestant opinion.[5] Even the generally sympathetic *Belfast News-Letter*'s coverage echoed these same themes; Drew was a stout champion of the Protestant interest who regularly overstepped the bounds of conservative civility. The *News-Letter*'s critique of William Johnston paralleled its treatment of Drew: too often, the paper lamented, both of these men put their Protestantism before their Conservatism.[6] This distinction helps to explain why Drew had

---

4. Jonathan Jeffrey Wright, "'Perverted Graduates of Oxford,'" 127–48.

5. *Irish Presbyterian* 5, no. 53 (October 1857): 256–57.

6. *Belfast News-Letter*, October 18, 1856. This characterization came in the midst of a long diatribe against the "Downshire Dunce," an epithet the paper gave Johnston after he provided Drew with hyperbolic support after the minister critiqued the way that newspapers operated.

relatively little positive influence outside his own communities of support (which were admittedly extensive); it was only during times of regional or national crisis that Drew spoke to anything like a national audience. As we shall see in the next chapter, Drew's status as a problematic figure is all too clear in the heated aftermath of the 1857 riots.

Drew's relatively marginal status within Belfast establishment politics did not mean he had a marginal impact on popular politics in the northern capital. He was an activist leader of important and substantial Protestant constituencies in the early Victorian town, and his influence and impact grew dramatically in the 1850s. If many of Belfast's leaders had little sympathy for Drew's boisterous anti-Catholic politics, they had to account for the influence he had with Orange working-class supporters and his own substantial congregation. Drew's religious work acted as a crucial bridge here. Although Drew lacked the evangelical bona fides of Henry Cooke or even Hugh "Roaring" Hanna, his commitment to church extension and religious education helped Drew maintain positive relationships with the town's conservative establishment. And he did have more active supporters amongst Belfast's business and political elites, influential figures like Richard Davison and William Coates.

Ultimately, however, Drew's political influence was greatest in a negative sense. His politics were not particularly complicated for the majority of Belfast Catholics, for whom Drew's name and reputation were synonymous with Orange bigotry and intolerance. This was evident in the Belfast riots of 1857, which Drew helped to initiate by giving a controversial and well publicized anti-Catholic lecture at Christ Church that accelerated tension in west Belfast. Even when Drew was not directly involved in events, his toxic reputation could have a real impact on the ground. In August 1857, when the Church of Ireland's Belfast Parochial Mission attempted to preserve the peace in Belfast by suspending the anti-Catholic street preaching that was at the center of increasing controversy, the town's principal nationalist newspaper, the *Ulsterman*, commented sarcastically that it was worried about Drew, since the Church of Ireland had "'shut up' the fanatic parson and bridled his rancorous tongue for the present." While Drew was

7. Thomas Drew. Lithograph by Dominique Fabronius, circa 1850. © National Library of Ireland, EP DREW-TH (1) III. Courtesy of the National Library of Ireland. The portrait is undated but was almost certainly completed in the early 1850s, as Fabronius moved to Philadelphia in 1855.

on the group's board and was a fierce supporter of open-air preaching, he had not been particularly active in the movement. In early September, local activists again used Drew's name to mobilize public opinion, falsely claiming that Drew was going to preach on the steps of the Custom House (it was actually Hanna, the young minister of Berry Street Presbyterian Church).[7] By 1857, it was clear that for Irish Catholics and many British and Irish liberals, Thomas Drew was the archetype of the Orange cleric, an embodiment of the worst aspects of militant Protestantism in Belfast, its virulent anti-Catholicism, and the presumed alliance between Orangeism and local government officials. While other ministers would fill these shoes in future years, it was Drew who was Belfast's first populist political parson, a symbol of the city's seeming inability to escape the madness of sectarianism.[8]

This does not mean that Drew's role in the making of Victorian Belfast was simply symbolic. He was, after all, a Church of Ireland minister who had built an extensive community at Christ Church and an Orange leader whose public advocacy and support provided a sense of legitimacy and protection for hundreds if not thousands of working-class brethren. Drew was well positioned to become a spokesman for ultra-Protestant alienation that emerged as a significant force in the aftermath of the government inquiry into the Belfast riots of 1857. The riots also made clear just how much his work and words mattered, particularly in a post-Famine city where population growth, an increased Catholic public presence, and an increasingly competitive newspaper market created an atmosphere more conducive to his

---

7. *Ulsterman*, August 31, 1857; *Belfast Daily Mercury*, September 7, 1857; Doyle, *Fighting like the Devil for the Sake of God*, 92–93. Hugh Hanna (1821–92) was a Presbyterian minister famous for his provocative open-air sermons in Belfast. He served as minister of Berry Street Presbyterian Church and St. Enoch's Presbyterian Church in Carlisle Circus, where a memorial statue to Hanna stood until it was damaged by an IRA bomb in 1970.

8. For an argument that emphasizes the roles played by the state and local civic leaders in the construction of Victorian Belfast's dysfunctional politics, see Morris, "Reading the Riot Commission," 194–219.

factional demagogic talents. The next two chapters chart Drew's career in Protestant politics between 1848 and 1859, when he left Belfast for a new position in Loughinisland, County Down. Drew was a successful minister of one of the largest congregations in the city, and a partisan Orange leader whose vitriolic public performances strengthened the communal division that was increasingly seen as a defining characteristic of the Victorian city. If his extremism (both real and imagined) kept him from obtaining public positions he apparently craved, it had a very real impact on the streets of the northern capital.

CHRIST CHURCH AND PROTESTANT POLITICS

A potent fusion of anti-Catholicism and populist conservative politics had always been central to Drew's ministry at Christ Church. He was a lifelong Orangeman, regularly acting as chaplain to the Grand Orange Lodge of Ireland and district grand chaplain of the county lodge, positions that gave him close ties to Protestant working-class communities across Belfast. These relationships were extremely important to Drew, as he made clear in a letter published in in the *Belfast News-Letter* in October 1856: "I am likely to know the mind of Protestants more than most men. I mix with the masses as much as any clergyman. I am the minister of a district of 30,000 souls, two thirds of which are Episcopalians and Presbyterians. I am proud to say that I hold sundry offices among the Orangemen, that bring me more into contact with the Orangemen of Ireland than any other clergyman or layman in Ireland."[9] While the religious elements of Drew's evangelical belief are important on their own terms, his religion frequently had an overtly political dimension. By the late 1840s, Drew's status as one of Belfast's leading anti-Catholic controversialists made him a symbolic champion of a certain kind of Protestant politics, a standing strengthened by both his reputation as an advocate for Protestant working-class families and his public commitment to the Orange

9. *Belfast News-Letter*, October 11, 1856.

Order. This was reinforced by Drew's activity in Belfast Conservative politics, his energetic public support for candidates like the successful lawyer and Conservative member of Parliament for Belfast, Richard Davison, who he once described as having "the honour, whatever it is, or the discredit of being my only patron."[10] As a minister and a political conservative, Drew's position depended on his efforts to maintain a delicate balancing act between the volatile forces of Orange populism and the more conventional elite-oriented politics of the conservative establishment. Like many of his successors in Ulster religious politics, he was not always successful in this endeavor.

The primary framework with which Drew viewed the world was one of binary struggle; a global fight between the heroic forces of Protestant truth and the dangerous and heretical apostasy of the Roman Catholic Church. This had straightforward political implications for Drew: true Protestants worked to uphold the Protestant constitution against both the constant threat posed by Roman Catholicism and the British and Irish political leaders (both Whig and moderate Conservative) who believed that Catholic and nationalist interests needed to be appeased. While Drew's hypersensitivity to the Catholic threat was exceptional (and its impact sharpened by his position at the heart of an increasingly divided town), there was nothing particularly original about his political-religious beliefs, which featured tropes that were standard for most British and Irish ultra-Protestants in the Victorian age: the sheer and destructive nature of Roman Catholicism as a politico-religious system, the ambition and power of the Roman Catholic Church, the corresponding need for Protestant watchfulness and readiness, and the danger posed by naïve elites who believed that Irish Catholics could be safely integrated into the British and Irish polity. The violence of Drew's rhetoric certainly placed him at the edge of Victorian anti-Catholicism. In the 1850s relatively few Belfast (let alone British and Irish) clergymen shared his belief that Catholic emancipation should be reversed. That said, while Drew placed

---

10. *Belfast News-Letter*, March 12, 1857.

greater emphasis on *Irish* historical narratives and contemporary controversies, in its general contours, the anti-Catholicism articulated at Christ Church in the 1850s was similar in content (if not in tone) to the popular anti-Catholicism that was a prominent feature of life in Victorian England and Scotland.

What made Drew's politics more novel were Belfast's sectarian geopolitics and his position as minister of Christ Church and a leader of the Orange Order, which provided him with popular constituencies to mobilize for the Protestant cause; ties to influential political and religious elites; and a measure of clerical legitimacy in an urban setting where the Catholic threat was seemingly manifest. Drew's Presbyterian contemporary, the Reverend Henry Cooke, was a more powerful and sophisticated figure, but as Belfast's leading Anglican minister in politics, Drew's ties to the state and membership in the Orange Order provided him with political advantages over his Presbyterian colleague.[11] At the same time, however, what is striking here are the constraints on the extent of the cleric's political power; like Cooke (and, for that matter, politically minded Catholic religious leaders such as John MacHale), Drew largely floundered when he ventured outside his tribe.

In some ways, Drew's closest parallel in Irish Protestant politics was the Reverend Tresham Gregg, who in 1841 created the Dublin Protestant Operative Society to mobilize the Irish capital's Protestant working class to fight against municipal corruption and nationalist efforts to repeal the Act of Union. Gregg traveled to Belfast in April 1843 to initiate a Belfast chapter for the organization, but the meetings generated more sectarian and interdenominational animosity than membership. Much of this was shaped by Gregg's confrontational style, which managed to offend Catholics and Presbyterians in equal

---

11. For Cooke as the paradigmatic political parson, see Holmes, *Henry Cooke*, 208. The parallels with Cooke are intriguing: both mobilized lay public opinion to defeat clerical opponents and both were relative failures when they stepped outside their own relatively narrow constituencies (Ulster Presbyterianism for Cooke; Christ Church and Belfast and Ulster Orangeism for Drew). See Miller, "John MacHale, Henry Cooke," 109–24.

measure, albeit for different reasons. Given Gregg's reputation as one of the island's most fearsome anti-Catholic controversialists (most famously on display in his weeklong 1838 dispute in the Rotunda in Dublin with the Catholic priest Father Thomas Maguire),[12] the reasons for Catholic opposition are easy enough to understand. In May 1841, the *Vindicator* labeled Gregg a "furious maniac" after he was arrested for an assault on a convent in the capital. The Belfast Catholic paper later nicknamed him "Thrash'em Gregg," and together with figures like Drew and William McIlwaine, he came to personify what many British and Irish contemporaries viewed as a particular kind of aggressive and irrational ultra-Tory anti-Catholicism within the Church of Ireland.[13]

Seemingly never content with one enemy, Gregg regularly provoked more liberal-minded Protestant constituencies with his stout defence of the privileges of the established church and pointed barbs against what he saw as dangerously conciliatory Presbyterian attitudes about the subject of national education. When Gregg visited Belfast in April 1843 to organize a local chapter of the Protestant Operative Society, an angry Catholic crowd disrupted the meeting, forcing Robert Coulson, the town's superintendent of police, to lead his men into the fray to protect the Dublin minister. The *Belfast News-Letter* editorialized against the personal motives behind what it termed the "Greg-arious invasion," noting that it had no support from the city's conservative establishment.[14] While only twenty five people signed up for the new organization at the initial meeting, the chapter soon gained popular support in Sandy Row and Ballymacarrett, doubtless aided by the threat of Daniel O'Connell's crusade for repeal. Catherine Hirst

---

12. *Authenticated Report of the Discussion between the Rev'd T. D. Gregg and the Rev'd Thomas Maguire.*

13. *Belfast Vindicator*, May 5, 1841, May 8, 1841.

14. *Belfast News-Letter*, April 4, 1843, April 7, 1843, April 21, 1843. For the best overview of Gregg's Protestant Operative Society, see Crawford, "'Overriding Providence,'" 157–68, and Maguire, "Church of Ireland and the Problem of the Protestant Working-Class of Dublin," 196.

has argued that the Protestant Operative Society was an important early manifestation of Belfast Protestant working-class politics, citing the key leadership roles played by evangelical ministers and Durham Street grocers and publicans, who organized both public meetings and a petition drive against repeal.[15] While the organization clearly was an important prototype, the Protestant Operative Society proved to have little long-term traction in Belfast and disappeared from view in Dublin by 1846, as the threat of repeal receded and conservative Protestants across the island moved back to a reestablished Orange Order.

While Drew steered clear of some of Gregg's more eccentric views (late in life he apparently believed in his own immortality), the two were kindred spirits who attempted to mobilize working-class Protestants with a spiky rhetoric of vociferous anti-Catholicism and Tory radicalism. At a meeting in Belfast more than a decade later, Gregg called Drew his "brother or should I say father in Christ" and claimed a remote paternity for the Christ Church Protestant Association.[16] There was a great deal of truth in the statement. Drew and Gregg both championed a populist-oriented mobilization of Protestant politics, while their aggressive commitment to the defence and expansion of the Church of Ireland and tendencies toward rhetorical excess led both to regularly offend members of other Protestant denominations as well as Irish Catholics. Gregg's efforts to organize a local chapter of the Protestant Operative Society also illustrate the difficulties faced by anyone interested in creating a popular Protestant political association in mid-Victorian Belfast: the sensitive terrain of interdenominational rivalries, the need to balance populist and establishment conservatism, and the seeming impossibility of creating independent organizations outside of the long-established Orange Order.

Drew's emergence as one of Ireland's leading anti-Catholic figures in the 1850s occurred in a political and religious environment that was much more amenable to populist Protestant politics. Ireland

---

15. Hirst, *Religion, Politics and Violence in 19th Century Belfast*, 45.
16. *Belfast News-Letter*, February 20, 1856.

was transformed between 1845 and 1854, as a million Irish men, women, and children died in the Great Famine and an estimated two million emigrated across the decade. Many British and Irish evangelicals interpreted these events as a divine cataclysm brought on by the improvident lives of Irish Catholic men and women, a narrative that only strengthened notions of northern difference. As noted in the previous chapter, these notions of Ulster exceptionalism silenced the very real suffering experienced by northern men and women during the Great Famine, but they were nonetheless influential in liberal and conservative Protestant circles across the province, underlining a growing sense of regional separation that had obvious cultural and political consequences.[17]

This interpretation of regional difference was only amplified by the 1848 rebellion. For Drew and many Irish conservatives, the rebellion provided unassailable proof of the need for a more active and energetic defence of the Protestant constitution. Drew made this clear at a March 1848 meeting of the Evangelical Alliance in Belfast's Music Hall. Individual Catholics might be honest and benevolent (he singled out the conciliatory Cornelius Denvir, bishop of Down and Connor, as a prime example), Drew intoned, but until Catholics publicly renounced "the horrible doctrines of their church, and disowned the atrocious butcheries by their ancestors," Irish Protestants would view them with a measure of suspicion. And who could blame them when they looked at the current state of the country: "Thank God we have still a government able and willing to put down sedition—and if the traitors—for traitors they are—do rise *en masse*—if they do come on, with their barricades and broken bottles—why, the Protestants of Ireland will meet them, and prove, as they have proved before, strong and victorious, by the blessing of God!"[18] The *Belfast News-Letter* echoed Drew's "eloquent" call, describing the Orange yeomen of Ulster as "the impregnable citadel of Protestantism and the British

---

17. A brief survey of Ulster exceptionalism can be found in Nally, *Human Encumbrances*, 84–85.

18. *Belfast News-Letter*, March 28, 1848.

connexion" against "the hundreds of thousands of armed traitors in train throughout the other three provinces."[19]

When the rising finally occurred in July 1848, reality fell far short of these lurid fears. British state forces managed things with relative ease, epitomized by William Smith O'Brien's ignominious surrender to local police at Ballingarry, County Tipperary, on July 29. Drew and other ultra-Protestants nevertheless attempted to mobilize loyalist sentiment into political action, creating the Belfast (later Ulster) Protestant Association, a body dedicated to the demonstration of Protestant loyalty to the British constitution. Although leaders claimed that seven hundred people had signed up by the end of July, and conservative press reports celebrated the large audiences that attended lectures by Tory stalwarts such as the Earl of Roden, Drew, or McIlwaine, the organization failed to gain momentum as a political force, again underlining the difficulties faced by figures interested in sustaining popular Protestant political associations outside the structure of the Orange Order.[20] If more moderate voices came to the fore as the temperature cooled, however, the 1848 rebellion allowed figures like Drew to update the historical architecture of their sectarian narratives with performances that entertained and offended in equal measure. The performative aspect of these types of political meetings was important in an era of constrained opportunities for working-class leisure. At the same time, this was not simply a matter of spectacle, as anti-Catholic diatribes generated a comforting sense of continuity, legitimacy, and patronage for plebeian Protestants living in a turbulent and emergent industrial urban environment.[21] Reports of the rebellion certainly generated increased support for the Orange Order in Belfast. An October 1848 Antrim County lodge committee report claimed that the ranks had nearly doubled over the previous year.[22]

19. *Belfast News-Letter*, March 28, 1848.
20. *Belfast News-Letter*, July 28, 1848.
21. Doyle, *Fighting Like the Devil for the Sake of God*, 27.
22. GOLI, Antrim County Report, October 1848.

Drew's trenchant opposition to Irish nationalist politics was made all the more powerful by his anti-Catholic religious beliefs, a distinction between religion and politics that he and his supporters would have rejected. These types of blurred lines were hardly novel; the notion that Irish Catholics answered to a foreign power was one of the touchstones of mid-nineteenth-century Irish Conservative politics.[23] Fears and anxieties about Roman Catholicism loomed particularly large in the evangelical imagination in the 1850s, driven by the reestablishment of the Roman Catholic hierarchy in England and Wales in 1850 (the so-called Papal Aggression) and opposition to British governmental support for St. Patrick's College and Seminary at Maynooth in Ireland. The growth of anti-Catholic sentiment led to the government's passage of the Ecclesiastical Titles Act in 1851, and to the renewal of loud but ineffective public campaigns against the Maynooth Grant.[24] Drew was active in the latter movement, speaking at Protestant meetings in Downpatrick and at the Rotunda in Dublin in February 1852.[25] At the Dublin meeting, Drew made it clear that Protestants needed to unite and boldly work together until the mental pollution and disloyal threat of Maynooth was destroyed: "What was Protestantism—true, evangelical Protestantism—in its character of truth? Protestantism was a series and harmony of principles which have God for their author and the Bible as their witness. Active Protestantism is the legitimate maintenance and propagation of these truths. Protestantism loves the Bible, and would fain love all that is accounted precious therein. It loves truth and kindness, order and liberty, benevolence and loyalty. It has a fine and comprehensive motto, supplied by one who loved Christ, and served him faithfully—'Honour all men; love

---

23. Shields, *Irish Conservative Party*, 81.
24. Wolffe, *God and Greater Britain*, chap. 2.
25. *Belfast News-Letter*, February 2, 1852, February 23, 1852. Wallis, "Revival of the Anti-Maynooth Campaign in Britain," 527–47; Wolffe, *Protestant Crusade in Great Britain*, 198–210, 262–80. For an insightful portrait of the broader importance of anti-Catholicism in Mid-Victorian English society, see Paz, *Popular Anti-Catholicism in Victorian England*.

the brotherhood; fear God; honour the King.'"[26] While such speeches had little tangible effect on British and Irish politics, Drew's calls to mobilize Protestant activists against Maynooth burnished his reputation as a Protestant champion and anti-Catholic demagogue.

Maynooth's importance as a catalyst and symbolic marker in conservative politics can be seen at the local level in Orange lodge records. Historians long have understood that the Orange Order was a crucial element in garnering Belfast Protestant working-class support for the Conservative Party in late nineteenth-century city and national politics.[27] The lodge minutes allow us to document the early formation of these political networks. In May 1852 the Reverend Thomas F. Miller, the Church of Ireland's vicar of Belfast, addressed the county lodge on the known strengths of the longtime Conservative member of Parliament, W. J. Johnston, and talked at greater length about a new Conservative candidate, Richard Davison, the prominent barrister and one of the leaders of the Christ Church congregation. Miller told the membership that he had sent Davison a letter asking him to answer three questions that he saw as vital to representing both Protestantism and Orangeism in 1852:

1. Do you oppose the grant to Maynooth?
2. Do you oppose the repeal of Ecclesiastical Titles Bill?
3. Will you support the principles of the Orange Association in Parliament?

While Protestant clergymen like Miller and Drew doubtless placed greater emphasis on the substance of these matters than their plebeian brethren, the questionnaire underlines the key role that Maynooth and other religious issues played in legitimizing a more respectable Orange politics for conservatives who might be uncomfortable with the noisy populism of the marching tradition. In this case, Davison's

---

26. *Belfast News-Letter*, February 23, 1852.

27. For a succinct version of this view, see Walker, "1885 and 1886 General Elections in Ireland," 36–40.

affirmative replies to each of these questions were enough for Miller, who in turn told Orange leaders to advocate for Davison within each of their local lodges.[28] While we cannot be sure how individual Orangemen exercised their voting rights (and the right to vote would hardly be universal in 1852 within an organization whose membership was largely working class), Davison was elected, and remained a Conservative member of Parliament for Belfast for the remainder of the decade.

If anti-Catholicism had a greater prominence in British and Irish political discourse in the 1850s, Belfast's dramatic population growth helped to ensure Drew a larger audience. Between 1831 and 1861, the city's population more than doubled, rising from 53,000 to nearly 120,000. More important for Drew's strengthened position in the mid-Victorian city, the Church of Ireland population of Shankill Parish rose from an estimated 16,000 to nearly 29,000, a story told more dramatically by the increased number of baptisms at Christ Church, which rose from 116 in 1845 to 596 in 1858.[29] While the Church of Ireland remained the church of a substantial minority of Protestants in Belfast (Presbyterian numbers grew at a similar rate and other Protestant denominations grew even more quickly), its growth in Belfast provided Drew with greater influence and leverage within a larger if still somewhat discrete community.

These factors provide the immediate context for the formation of the Christ Church Protestant Association (CCPA), founded on May 23, 1854. Like its predecessors in Belfast Protestant politics and so many of its contemporary anti-Catholic associations across Britain and Ireland, the CCPA hoped to use political action (discussion, education,

---

28. County Lodge Minutes, May 25, 1852, Museum of Orange Heritage, Schomberg House, Belfast.

29. The 1831 figures are from Liam Kennedy and Kerby A. Miller's important research project on Irish religious demography. See Miller et al., *Immigrants in the Land of Canaan*, 670. For baptism, marriage, and burial statistics, see the Annual Returns in the Appendix in Dawson, "Annals of Christ Church, Belfast," PRONI, T.2159/1).

and petition) and prayer to mobilize true Protestants against the twin threats of Roman Catholicism and Irish nationalism.[30] In practical terms, the organization simply provided Drew with another pulpit to call for Protestant action from both his local, and—through newspaper reports—regional/national networks of supporters. The message was certainly a familiar one. Combining claims of strength and vulnerability in equal measure, Drew's grievance-centered defence of ascendancy dominated the organization's meetings, articulated through frequent calls for an assertive Protestant community response to combat the Catholic threat and British political weakness. As Drew argued at an early session, Protestantism was not only about remembering the truths in the Bible but also involved living in resolute determination to sustain and uphold those truths.[31] The CCPA's monthly meetings consistently featured this type of confrontational language, providing fodder for Drew's liberal and nationalist foes and sharpening sectarian tension in the city.

The CCPA's initial membership numbers were relatively modest, with twenty-six people signing up at the first meeting. The association's first annual report argued that this had been a matter of choice, stating rather optimistically that the organization was "a little band who sought of God guidance in the proposed movement. Growing insolent from the unwise and unscriptural concessions made to them by Protestant statesmen, the Romanists had become at once more extravagant in their demands, and more subtle in the use of schemes by which to forward their designs, hostile to the welfare of the empire, and our safety as Protestants; . . . We have not sought to fill the books

---

30. Dawson, "Annals of Christ Church, Belfast," 159–64. Drew clearly drew inspiration from the Protestant Association, a largely Anglican and Conservative organization founded in 1835 to protect the Protestant character of the British state. There is no indication that the CCPA was formally linked to the Protestant Association. For that organization's early history, see Wolffe, *Protestant Crusade in Great Britain*, 90–102.

31. *Belfast News-Letter*, August 9, 1854.

with a multitude of names. We desired not names but men."[32] Membership numbers did increase. There were fifty-three members signed up after the first meeting in June 1854 and the association reported 132 members in early 1855. Like other anti-Catholic associations in Victorian Britain and Ireland (the Orange Order in Ireland being the exception), the CCPA's membership remained relatively modest in size.[33] The CCPA helped to sponsor special events that often attracted much larger Belfast audiences. When Gregg spoke at a Protestant Association demonstration chaired by Drew in November 1854, for example, an estimated 1,200 people filled Victoria Hall to hear Gregg admonish British political leaders for their weak commitment to Protestant principles.[34]

A number of scholars have written about the CCPA, typically seeing it as a reflection of the hardening sectarian divide in mid-Victorian Belfast.[35] In the most compelling treatment to date, Mark Doyle described the CCPA as Drew's vehicle to mobilize and educate working-class Protestants about what he believed were the dominant issues of the era.[36] The association's membership seems to have been predominantly male and working class; Drew repeatedly stressed the humble background of his followers, arguing on one occasion that "they did not court the patronage of the aristocracy. They had the support of honest, sincere working men and he said to them: 'Go on and prosper.'"[37] Drew's penchant for rhetorical excess aside, there seems to have quite a bit of truth to his claim. The majority of identifiable individuals who signed an 1854 CCPA petition to Dublin Castle were

---

32. Dawson, "Annals of Christ Church, Belfast," 159–64; 179–84; 184; *Belfast News-Letter*, August 8, 1855.

33. Wolffe, *Protestant Crusade in Great Britain*, 6–7.

34. *Belfast News-Letter*, November 15, 1854; Dawson, "Annals of Christ Church, Belfast," 170.

35. Doyle, *Fighting like the Devil for the Sake of God*, 26–27; Hirst, *Religion, Politics and Violence in 19th Century Belfast*, 44.

36. Doyle, *Fighting like the Devil for the Sake of God*, 27.

37. *Belfast News-Letter*, August 8, 1855.

from firmly lower-middle and working-class occupations: pensioners, shoemakers, textile workers, and the like. While a number of the petition's signatories were Drew's congregants, CCPA members came from across the town, attracted by the Orange minister's reputation and hard-line politics.[38]

The CCPA's claim that it "did not court the patronage of the aristocracy" was a bit more tenuous, as it managed to secure a significant level of support from conservative political, religious, and social elites across Ulster and Ireland. Drew served as president, and his curate, the Reverend Abraham Dawson, was secretary until his 1857 departure from Belfast. A number of Church of Ireland ministers and a few business and political elites were made honorary vice presidents and/or members of the CCPA's executive committee, most notably the Reverend Theophilus Campbell, Francis and William Coates; Davison, Gregg, William J. Gwynne, and the future Orange hero, William Johnston of Ballykilbeg. With the exception of Drew and Johnston, few of these men were particularly active members, although both Davison and Gregg gave lectures at CCPA meetings. Elite involvement, however, provided the organization with a measure of legitimacy and access to political capital and resources that might be lacking otherwise.

Drew was the dominant figure throughout the CCPA's brief history; he was the primary speaker at nearly all the organization's public meetings, which were reported thoroughly in the pages of an increasingly competitive Belfast press. Given the breadth of coverage and Drew's propensity for rhetorical excess, it is easy to exaggerate the impact and influence of the association. Meetings typically were dominated by a narrow circle of figures, most notably Drew, Dawson, Johnston, and Christopher Mallin, another prominent member of the

---

38. CCPA Petition to the Lord Lieutenant, in Thomas Drew to Sir John Young, October 12, 1854, National Archives of Ireland, Registered Papers, 1854/19289; Belfast and Ulster Streets Directory, 1852 and 1858; Henderson's Belfast Directory, 1852, http://streetdirectories.proni.gov.uk; Christ Church Religious Census, 1852, PRONI, CR1/13D/1.

congregation and assistant secretary of the CCPA.[39] Moreover, while reports indicate that meetings were well attended, monthly gatherings were held in Christ Church's Mission Rooms, a space that could only fit a relatively modest audience. Audiences for the CCPA's quarterly meetings were much larger, with members and nonmembers alike gathering for sessions at the Victoria Hall.

The CCPA was an organization dedicated to support Protestant action against what Drew and his allies viewed as an increasingly aggressive and dangerous Roman Catholic Church. In its second annual report, Drew described the organization in no uncertain terms: it was, he argued, an association designed to unite earnest Protestant men of all ranks for prayer, encouragement, and protection. Protestant watchmen were needed, Drew stressed, because both British and Irish history showed that "Rome was vigilant, designing and destructive," the primary obstacle to human liberty.[40] In this face of this historic threat, true Protestants needed to be active and resolute in their politics. For the CCPA, political action involved public resolutions and the presentation of petitions to Dublin Castle and the British Parliament. At the organization's first meeting in June 1854, members signed a petition against the "illegal" adoption of ecclesiastical titles by Roman Catholic bishops, a document presented in the House of Commons by Davison. Other CCPA petitions focused on a wide array of ultra-Protestant hobby horses, calling for the repeal of Catholic emancipation, the withdrawal of the Maynooth Grant, the abolition of convents, the denial of Catholic priests' access to prisoners, and an end to the appointment of Catholic chaplains in the Royal Navy.[41]

The Maynooth Grant featured prominently in nearly every CCPA meeting. For Drew and his supporters, the idea that the British government would provide funding for the education and training of Roman

---

39. Mallin worked at McTear and Co., a prominent felt manufacturer in Belfast, and was superintendent of Christ Church Sunday School.

40. *Belfast News-Letter*, May 16, 1856.

41. Dawson, "Annals of Christ Church, Belfast," 161–64; *Belfast News-Letter*, March 7, 1856.

Catholic priests in Ireland embodied everything that was wrong about contemporary British and Irish politics. Sessions combined vivid and fantastical descriptions of the education provided at Maynooth with stubbornly optimistic assessments of the English ultra-Tory politician Richard Spooner's annual crusades to eliminate the grant in Parliament.[42] In March 1856 Drew devoted an entire meeting to the recent report of a royal commission of inquiry into Maynooth (similar commissions had examined matters at Cambridge University, Oxford University, and Trinity College Dublin). The report found little to be worried about, but for Drew, this only proved that the whole effort had been "cooked," and the commission's wide ranging focus on the nature of papal authority and confessional practice, particularly those involving sexual matters, gave ultra-Protestants a wealth of material for polemical use.[43] Using a recent pamphlet by the prominent anti-Catholic controversialist, the Reverend Robert J. McGhee, to make his case, Drew presented an exhaustive survey of Maynooth's "fearful teaching and unfaithful teachers," the use of ultramontane textbooks, the suppression of evidence, and the interference of Archbishop Cullen.[44] A report distributed later that year claimed that nine hundred people had signed the CCPA's petition to the House of Commons against the hated Irish Catholic college.[45] On this issue, there was simply no room for compromise.

For Drew and his compatriots, the threat posed by Irish Catholics was no distant matter of history or abstract principle; contemporary events showed that Protestant readiness was required for survival.

---

42. For the campaign against Maynooth in Britain and Ireland, see Wolffe, *Protestant Crusade in Great Britain*, 198–210, 277–80; Wallis, "Revival of the Anti-Maynooth Campaign," 327–48; Shields, *Irish Conservative Party*, 116–23, 152–57.

43. Corish, *Irish Catholic Experience*, 200–201.

44. *Belfast News-Letter*, March 7, 1856. Characteristically, Cullen used the royal commission to exert the control over Maynooth. See Corish, *Irish Catholic Experience*, 200, and Larkin, *Making of the Roman Catholic Church in Ireland*, 343. For McGhee—rector of Holywell, Wales, and a former minister of Harold's Cross Church in Dublin—see Bowen, *Protestant Crusade in Ireland*, 69, 113–21.

45. *Belfast News-Letter*, May 16, 1856.

While the Young Ireland rebellion of 1848 had certainly updated an historical template that traced its lineage back to the mid-seventeenth century, it was a contemporary attempt to assassinate the Earl of Enniskillen and his supporters at Trillick, County Tyrone, that exercised Drew and his followers in the CCPA in the late months of 1854. On September 15 of that year, William Cole, third Earl of Enniskillen and grand master of the Grand Orange Lodge of Ireland, had visited Derry for a day of Protestant celebration with an estimated eight hundred supporters, taking a specially designed excursion train for the occasion. Returning on a railway line that had just been opened the previous month, the train was derailed near Trillick, driven off the tracks by the seemingly deliberate placement of three large boulders. Two men were killed and several injured as they jumped from the train. Seven Catholic railway workers (six navvies and a mason) were arrested, but after spending ten months in jail, the men were released when insufficient evidence was found to support the murder charge, a decision that generated outrage in Irish Conservative and Orange circles.[46] Linking the assassination attempt to the Gunpowder Plot of 1605, Drew celebrated the providential deliverance of the noble earl and his followers, but castigated both local Catholics for their allegedly inhumane treatment of victims and survivors, and the Irish Catholic member of Parliament and attorney general William Keogh, for his supposed legal incompetence and religious bias. Following Drew, Mallin drew a political lesson from the outrage, which had been caused by the "Pseudo Protestants" who dominated British and Irish politics. As Mallin saw it, Trillick and its legal aftermath only outlined the need for men to stand for truths that might be initially unpopular. The Protestant Associations, like William Wilberforce before them, he argued, would champion what was right rather than what was popular and expedient.[47] Protestants need not ever be slaves.

---

46. For Trillick, see Farrell, "Trillick Railway Outrage," 217–40; Fitzgerald, "Trillick Derailment of 1854," 31–47.

47. *Belfast News-Letter*, August 9, 1855. Drew also spoke about the Trillick outrage to a County Down meeting in November 1854, where he argued that he had

The idea that Protestant vigilance was constantly needed was reinforced by a rich sense of legal grievance.[48] In this view, Irish Catholics were not only disloyal and out to destroy the Protestant population; they also received favorable treatment before the law. The Orange Order's parades on the 12th of July were a particularly sensitive subject, an issue that would propel Drew's future son-in-law William Johnston to a successful political career in the late 1860s.[49] Party processions had been made illegal again in 1850 in the aftermath of the atrocities at Dolly's Brae in 1849, legislation that the British state only enforced in areas where partisan marches were likely to generate conflict. While Orange leaders reluctantly acquiesced in the new legislation, they watched Irish roads and lanes closely for evidence of preferential treatment.[50] In September 1854 the CCPA sent a petition to Dublin Castle, protesting a Catholic sacerdotal procession that had taken place in Tuam, County Galway. For Drew and his compatriots, these activities were an open insult to Protestants in the north of Ireland, where the law against party processions allegedly was enforced in its full severity.[51] When Dublin Castle officials refused to make a

---

documentary evidence that Rome had approved the murder. See Diaries of William Johnston, November 10, 1854, PRONI, D.880/2/6.

48. This is a kind of mirror image to the Irish nationalist tendency to see themselves as the "Most Oppressed People Ever" (MOPE). Perhaps the ultra-Protestant equivalent would be the "Most Aggrieved People Ever" (MAPE?). See Kennedy, *Colonialism, Religion and Nationalism in Ireland*. David Fitzpatrick has noted the importance of an emotive sense of grievance in his more recent *Descendancy*.

49. Johnston's diaries make clear how close he was to Drew, who was a frequent correspondent with the future Orange hero, who asked for Drew's political advice in 1851 and regularly visited the Drew's Belfast home. These ties were particularly obvious after Johnston's mother died in 1852. When Drew traveled to Lecale to comfort the young man, Johnston's grateful admiration was clear, calling Drew "Paul-like" in his "zeal, affection," and ability "to be all things to all men"; see Diaries of William Johnston, February 10, 1852, PRONI, D.880/2/5.

50. For Johnston's political campaign, see Farrell, "Recapturing the Flag," 52–78.

51. Drew to Young, October 12, 1854, National Archives of Ireland, Registered Papers, 1854/19289; *Belfast News-Letter*, September 15, 1854. Drew had been in Tuam

full investigation into the events in Tuam, Dawson again drew a sharp contrast between the government's support of Archbishop MacHale and his Roman Catholic minions with the treatment allotted to the loyal Orangemen of Ulster. While the incident was raised briefly in a debate in the House of Lords, both English and Irish law officers argued that the event was legal since there was no violation of the peace. The matter was dropped.[52]

Maynooth and events like Trillick and Tuam resonated with particular power because they combined two of the most powerful enmities in Ulster Protestant politics: Roman Catholicism and the British government. Time after time, speakers at the CCPA's monthly meetings lambasted the expediency of British politicians, unwilling or unable to stand firm for the Protestant principles they believed were responsible for the past glories and future possibilities of the British nation. Both the coalition government of Lord Aberdeen (1852–55) and the first Palmerston ministry (1855–58) that followed received fierce critiques at Christ Church, the former for its seeming lack of unity and inept management of the Crimean War, the latter for its failure to support the established church and its continued appeasement of Irish Catholicism.[53] Nor was Catholicism the only religion that members targeted in their surveys of contemporary religious politics. Mallin described Palmerston's effort to pass Jewish emancipation as the "Jew Bill" and derided the prime minister for his reliance on an unholy trinity of radicals, Catholics, and Jews.[54]

---

for a confrontational meeting on religious conversion in June 1853, a connection that doubtless fostered his focus on this particular issue. See Dawson, "Annals of Christ Church, Belfast," 139.

52. The official correspondence and related material on the Tuam incident and investigation can be found in the Registered Papers at the National Archives of Ireland: NAI, Registered Papers, 1854/19289; 1855/141; 1855/1247. See also *Belfast News-Letter*, February 9, 1855.

53. *Belfast News-Letter*, August 9, 1854, February 9, 1854, March 9, 1854, July 5, 1854, September 6, 1855, May 16, 1856, June 11, 1857.

54. *Belfast News-Letter*, June 11, 1857.

Mallin's antisemitic remark reflected a more general trend. At a CCPA meeting in October 1856, the Reverend J. N. Woodroffe, rector of Glanmire Church and a member of the Cork Protestant Association, provided a prophetic interpretation of the "recent war," arguing that the Jews would gather in Palestine and fight on the side of the Antichrist against true Christians in the upcoming apocalypse.[55] Drew shared the antisemitism of his evangelical and ultra-Protestant compatriots, frequently attending meetings of the Society for Promoting Christianity Among the Jews. This rhetoric certainly was present in Drew's sermons. In William Johnston's diaries, he discusses an 1848 sermon that Drew gave at Hollymount Church near Downpatrick, County Down, that featured a rather extended meditation on "Jewish error," and Drew's published 1862 sermon on state education contains a similar critique of Jewish exclusivity and unfriendliness. Such sentiments were broadly shared by most British conservatives in the 1850s, a decade that featured some of the most virulent antisemitic rhetoric of the Victorian era.[56]

If Peelite, Whig, and Radical politicians came under predictable fire at CCPA meetings, Conservative leaders fared little better. For Drew and his allies, Lord Derby and Benjamin Disraeli's failures to live up to the ultra-Protestant promises they had made on the hustings were nothing short of rank betrayal. Calling for their dismissal from the leadership, Drew, Johnston, and others claimed that Lord Derby and Disraeli's hypocritical politics highlighted the need for new truly Protestant Conservative leaders, or in more radical moments, the need for a separate Protestant Party. As Drew put it in August 1856: "Protestant supremacy is dear to us—we don't wish to interfere with any man's liberty, . . . but we demand that our liberty be guaranteed

---

55. *Belfast News-Letter*, October 22, 1856.

56. Johnston Diaries, January 16, 1848, PRONI, D.880/2/1; Drew, *State Education Considered*, 16–17. For antisemitism in Victorian Britain and its links to anti-Catholicism, see Paz, *Popular Anti-Catholicism in Victorian England*, 15, 71; Clark, *Albion and Jerusalem*; Rubinstein, *History of the Jews in the English-Speaking World*.

and fortified."[57] Only British and Irish politicians who consistently and publicly supported Protestant initiatives—men such as Richard Spooner, Joseph Napier, and Richard Davison—came in for consistent praise at CCPA meetings. Of course, this was not always a matter of principle or political beliefs. Although the organization supported Hugh Cairns, the Conservative member for Belfast and future British Lord Chancellor, Drew sarcastically noted his seeming inability to find the time to speak at Christ Church, gently making fun of his relationship with Mary Harriet McNeill and praising his father's superior record of bringing Episcopalians and Presbyterians together.[58] Drew's critique did not seem to have a negative impact on Cairns, who remained a prominent conservative defender of the Church of Ireland in a political and legal career that lasted well into the 1880s.[59]

International and imperial issues loomed large in the mid-1850s, dominated by the Crimean War in 1854–56 and the Indian Rebellion of 1857. These matters were widely discussed at the organization's meetings, showing both a lively interest and awareness of imperial crises and a resolute and often creative determination to interpret these events in light of firmly domestic British and Irish matters.[60] Like most of their contemporaries, speakers were sharply critical of Lord Aberdeen's management of the Crimean War. At a meeting in February 1855, Drew opined that while war was always a curse, the

57. *Belfast News-Letter*, August 9, 1856. After a CCPA meeting in February 1855, William Johnston noted in his diary that he had spoken out against Derby's proposed junction with Gladstone and company; see Diaries of William Johnston, February 6, 1855, PRONI, D.880/2/7.

58. *Belfast News-Letter*, October 11, 1856. Drew's critique of Cairns brought a sharp rebuke from the *News-Letter*, which argued that Drew's time would be better spent bringing Conservatives together rather than fomenting division.

59. Tellingly, Cairns was one of the figures who supported Drew's nomination for vice-regal chaplain in 1866. See chapter 7 for a brief discussion of the Drew chaplaincy scandal.

60. For two thoughtful examinations of these issues, see Doyle, "Sepoys of the Pound and Sandy Row," 849–67; Bender, "Ireland and Empire," 343–60.

recent destruction of British regiments was particularly tragic because it had occurred because of governmental incompetence rather than enemy gunfire.[61] On this point at least, Drew was not far wrong; only 10 percent of the British soldiers who died in the Crimean War were killed in action. The fact that so many of these deaths were the result of cholera would have made the conflict all the more poignant across Victorian communities that had suffered from the same affliction.[62] These traumatic associations were just as powerful in Belfast as they were in Liverpool and London.

Opposition to the Crimean War was not simply a critique of military tactics and political leadership—it was also a moral question. British theological justifications for the war, expressed by various members of the clergy at the outset of the conflict, were rooted in a sense that Britain had a special national mission, rooted in the inheritance of the special relationship with God enjoyed by the Israelites of the Old Testament. As John Wolffe has shown, however, this narrative could be a double-edged sword, since military failures often were judged as a reflection of God's displeasure with his chosen people. This was an argument that had a particular resonance with Drew and like-minded northern Protestants.[63] For members of the CCPA, British military failures in the Crimea were linked inextricably to the appeasement of Roman Catholicism. As Davison put it: "We are engaged in a two-fold war; one abroad, the resistance of Russian aggression, which if not met by the united power of England and France, would destroy the balance of power and the future peace of Europe; the other, Papal Aggression at home, which aims at the extermination of Protestantism, and the consequent extinguishment

---

61. *Belfast News-Letter*, February 9, 1855.

62. Markovits, *Crimean War in the British Imagination*, 3, 9, 29. See also Huddie, *Crimean War and Irish Society*.

63. Wolffe, *God and Greater Britain*, chap. 2, sec. 2. For a pioneering comparative study of covenantal mindsets on political and cultural identity, see Akenson, *God's Peoples*.

of that free and glorious liberty, which our Constitution allows."[64] Less moderate voices were more explicit about the connection. British military failure, Drew argued, was God's punishment meted out to an unfaithful nation. In an 1856 sermon to mark the twenty-third anniversary of Christ Church's opening, Drew hoped that future British subjects would remember the men sacrificed to incompetence and ambition in a conflict that seemingly defied history and logic: "To make common cause with France on behalf of Muslims was at best a strange alliance: 'Protestantism and Popery allied to maintain the power of infidelity.'"[65] Anti-Catholicism was only part of this picture, of course, and Mallin took the populist line that the war had revealed the rotten core of the British aristocracy.[66]

Mallin's sarcastic jibe at Quaker opposition to the war ("peace men—too good for the world"[67]) makes it clear that their opposition to the war was as much about politics as principle. If Drew and his allies wielded a confident and generally supportive language of empire, however, there was a fairly consistent note of ambivalence to CCPA rhetoric about imperial violence. The body sent out a number of petitions of sympathy and support for imperial troops,[68] but this was not a simple support group for war and empire. If principled opponents of imperial war were mocked, there was no corresponding celebration of the brave Christian soldier, doubtless a reflection of the unpopularity of

64. *Belfast News-Letter*, August 9, 1854.
65. Drew, *Thoughtful Protestantism*, 10.
66. *Belfast News-Letter*, February 9, 1855, September 6, 1855. Discussing the royal proclamation of a national day of humiliation and prayer in April 1854, Abraham Dawson critiqued business owners (who made their employees work in factories and on the railways), Catholic priests (who kept loyal Catholics from marking the day), liberal Presbyterians, and Quakers for ignoring their sovereign's request to spend the day in prayer and observance for the widows and children of British soldiers in the Crimea.
67. *Belfast News-Letter*, February 9, 1855, September 6, 1855.
68. *Belfast News-Letter*, October 25, 1854; Dawson, "Annals of Christ Church, Belfast," 197–99.

the Crimean War in Britain and Ireland. This ambivalence may also, however, have been shaped by shifting evangelical attitudes toward war in mid-nineteenth-century Britain.[69]

The other great imperial crisis of the decade, the Indian Rebellion of 1857, was a simpler matter for interpretation at Christ Church, where it was portrayed as a kind of modern imperial redux of the Irish Rebellion of 1641. In an August 1857 lecture, Drew surveyed the history of India since the mid-sixteenth century before settling into a vivid description of the atrocities committed against British men, women, and children. Like so many Victorian commentators in the late summer of 1857, Drew lingered on images of women's bodies, describing how female victims were "stripped naked, flogged through the streets, and finally hacked and hewn to pieces."[70] Shifting from a kind of pornography of violence to its more local impact on the Christ Church community, Drew mentioned the missionaries murdered in the rebellion, listing the men and women that he and his friends in the Church of England's Society for the Propagation of the Gospel knew, a reminder of the ways that missionary networks brought the empire home to religious communities.[71]

But if imperial matters were frequent topics of conversation, this lecture was primarily about Ireland, and Belfast in particular. The CCPA meeting occurred on the evening of August 24, 1857, as reports of controversial street preaching and the formation of a gun club in Catholic west Belfast kept sectarian tensions alive in the aftermath of the first phase of the Belfast riots of 1857. Drew claimed that Indian modes of torture were remarkably similar to those employed in Ireland in 1641, as described in both the depositions and Sir John Temple's famous history of the Irish Rebellion. He was particularly critical

---

69. Markovits, *Crimean War in the British Imagination*, 1–11; van der Veer, *Imperial Encounters*, 85.

70. *Belfast News-Letter*, August 26, 1857.

71. For the Society of the Propagation of the Gospel, see Carey, *God's Empire*, 84–111.

of politicians who advocated for the appeasement of "these fiends." Drew made his point with an historical tale, mocking the members of the Irish Parliament, who, he claimed, meeting in the aftermath of 1641 massacre, had not wanted to stigmatize participants by calling them "rebels" or "murderers." Drew brought his remarks quickly into the present, defending evangelical street preachers against the attacks of Catholic opponents and their liberal Protestant abettors.[72] Writers at the *Northern Whig* took great offence at Drew's parallel between the events of the Irish Rebellion of 1641 and the Indian Rebellion of 1857, calling his conduct and remarks "lamentable," particularly since they were made in front of a "thoughtless and ignorant audience."[73]

The redolent connections drawn between 1641 and 1857 seem simple enough, but Drew's comments again were a bit more complicated than simply supporting a righteous war against an evil communal foe. He closed his lecture by asking the association to pray for their "imperilled countrymen." God, Drew insisted, would show British leaders what needed to be corrected and he prayed that England's armies would not take "bloody vengeance upon the vile ones who have done so wickedly."[74] This was a characteristic rhetorical technique for Drew, who often concluded intemperate lectures with more moderate and conventional conservative and religious reflections. Given the vivid nature of his comments about Indian and Irish modes of torture, it is difficult to imagine that his conclusion had a particularly calming effect. At the same time, it is worth noting that Drew's lecture came two days after the first British reports of the tragedy at Cawnpore, which only strengthened an already furious Victorian campaign for retribution. Unlike so many of the letters to the *Times* in August 1857, Drew's sermon on India was no clarion call for imperial violence; as

---

72. *Belfast News-Letter*, August 26, 1857. For Temple's influence, see Gillespie, "Temple's Fate," 315–33.

73. *Northern Whig*, August 27, 1857.

74. *Northern Whig*, August 27, 1857. For the complexity and diversity of British responses to 1857, see Herbert, *War of No Pity*; Malik, *War of Independence or Clash of Civilisations?*.

always, it was primarily about Belfast and Ireland.[75] Drew's ambivalence about imperial expansion and war in India was underlined the following year in his *Protestant Anniversaries*, in which he stated that the East India Company's 1856 annexation of Oudh had been unjust and that the advent of British direct rule over India in 1858 was a hopeful sign of better days to come.[76]

The CCPA's stated goals were to educate and mobilize working-class Protestants to recover ground lost in the struggle for Protestant Ascendancy, Protestant truth, and freedom from Catholic tyranny. In terms of its tangible aims, of course, the CCPA was a spectacular failure: the Catholic Relief Act of 1829 was not overturned, and the British government grant to Maynooth remained firmly in place. It is difficult to assess exactly what working-class Protestants took from the meetings. While newspaper accounts and Dawson's unpublished history provide reports of both what was said and how many people attended the meetings, we simply do not have sources that reveal how the largely working-class membership made sense of Drew and his cohort group's performances. The meetings do reflect the pervasive rhetoric and stereotypes of Victorian anti-Catholicism, which provided an interpretative language for integrating diverse events like the Maynooth Grant, the Crimean War, and the Indian Rebellion of 1857 into compelling historical narratives and morality plays with tangible local relevance. By highlighting the need for constant vigilance against a common foe and providing a heightened sense of continuity and communal solidarity, this shared language may have reduced the

---

75. On July 15, 1857, Nana Sahib ordered the massacre of approximately two hundred women and children as British forces approached Cawnpore, bodies that were stuffed into a local well and/or thrown into the Ganges River. According to Christopher Herbert, exaggerated reports of the massacre unleashed a national call for retribution and vengeance. This only fed British military atrocities in the field, which included cannonading and forcing prisoners to clean up after executions, a clear violation of high-caste Hindu notions of ritual pollution. See Herbert, *War of No Pity*, 4–5, 99–101. See also Wagner, *Skull of Alum Bheg*, 175–90.

76. Drew, *Protestant Anniversaries*, 17, 41.

potential for social and political conflict in a rapidly changing city.[77] At the same time, it is hard to imagine that anyone was converted at the organization's monthly meetings, which seem to have had little positive impact outside of Orange and Conservative circles. Like so much of Drew's work, the organization is best viewed as a defensive network—albeit an aggressive one with an offensive impact, focused on shoring up the faithful rather than making new allies and friends. It was successful enough on those terms.

What is clear is that reports of the meetings of the Christ Church Protestant Association confirmed Drew's status as one of the town's leading anti-Catholic figures among Belfast Catholics. There was certainly nothing new about Drew's reputation for anti-Catholic invective. At an 1841 speech at the English Catholic Institute in London, for example, Daniel O'Connell mocked recent statements made by "my good friend" Thomas Drew, arguing that despite all of the Protestant claims of conversion, Roman Catholicism did not seem to be going away.[78] With Gregg and McIlwaine, aggressive anti-Catholic controversialists like Drew became emotive symbols of a particularly violent and destructive mode of anti-Catholicism. Clerical politicians served as invaluable touchstones for the writers of an emerging Belfast Catholic press interested in creating and mobilizing a marginalized civic community. Not surprisingly, Cooke, Drew, Gregg, and McIlwaine were all featured prominently in the pages of the *Vindicator* in the 1840s and the *Ulsterman* in the 1850s. The fact that they were all members of the Orange Order (with the notable exception of Cooke) made them even more useful. Endlessly quotable and relentlessly caricatured, they became critical oppositional figures for an emergent Catholic community struggling to play a more public role in the life of Belfast.

---

77. This somewhat speculative idea (to my mind at least) lies at the center of the work of Peter Gibbon and Henry Patterson's analyses of Ulster proletarian politics. See Gibbon, *Origins of Ulster Unionism*; Patterson, *Class Conflict and Sectarianism*.

78. *Vindicator*, May 19, 1841.

Drew came to personify extreme anti-Catholicism in the city in the mid-1850s, particularly through the vivid reports printed in the pages of Dennis Holland's *Ulsterman*, which delightedly reported his seemingly inexhaustible stores of anti-Catholic bombast at the public meetings of the CCPA, the Irish Church Missionary Society, and other organizations. In October 1856 Holland argued that "the oratorical Doctor of erratic vision" was so extreme that he must be a Jesuit in disguise, "an emissary of Rome especially committed to sap the foundations of Protestantism, and destroy the great evangelical bulwarks of this mighty empire."[79] If Drew aimed to shore up the faithful with his emotional declarations of Protestant truth, his efforts mobilized Belfast Catholics in defensive opposition, making the minister himself a powerful symbol of the city's hardening sectarian lines of division. Clearly on display at the meetings of the CCPA, Drew's divisive and confrontational behaviour and reputation would have tragic results in the summer of 1857. A similar dynamic can also be seen in Drew's involvement with a much more powerful organization in British and Irish religious politics: the Orange Order.

THOMAS DREW AND THE ORANGE ORDER

In *Twenty Reasons for Being an Orangeman*, Thomas Drew outlined the motivations behind his lifelong commitment to the Orange Order. His arguments were remarkably similar to the principles and statements he had outlined in a career of public oratory: the desire to live in Protestant truth with his brethren, his belief that Roman Catholicism was a system of mental slavery that was committed to the destruction of Protestantism, and the need to push for true Protestant government

---

79. *Ulsterman*, October 24, 1856. See also *Ulsterman*, October 6, 1856. For a telling example of the conflation of the ministers of the "Evangelical Alliance" with "the demon of Orangeism" in the Belfast Catholic press, see the leader in *Vindicator*, February 11, 1846. The Belfast riots of 1857 only solidified such images of "Orange ministers" like Drew and McIlwaine.

in Britain and Ireland, particularly in an era when "the nation was imperilled" due to the "downward progress of British legislation."[80] Drew's pamphlet certainly featured positive sentiments about Orange fellowship, living in Protestant truth, and the evangelical need to bring Protestant truth and enlightenment throughout Britain, Ireland, and the British Empire. That said, what is notable about Drew's argument here is the definition of the Orange Order as an essentially defensive organization designed to protect Protestants from the threat of Roman Catholicism and to shield the United Kingdom from God's wrath. To friends and enemies alike, it was a familiar message.[81]

If the song remained the same, however, the institution made all the difference. The Orange Order had both a history and membership numbers that were unmatched by any other organization in Irish Protestant politics.[82] The order had genuine plebeian roots across Ulster and in Belfast, a real advantage in fast-growing Protestant working-class districts in Ballymacarrett, north Belfast, Sandy Row, and the Shankill Road area of west Belfast.

After a decade (1835–45) in official abeyance, the Orange Order made its public reappearance at an August 1845 meeting in Enniskillen. The order was led by Lord Enniskillen, who argued that both the expiration of the Party Processions Act and Molly Maguire activity in Cavan and Leitrim justified the organization's rebirth.[83] The 1848

---

80. Drew, "Twenty Reasons for Being an Orangeman," *Ulster Observer*, December 17, 1863. My thanks to Mark Doyle for the reference.

81. The *Ulster Observer* called Drew's statement "an outrage on decency and truth." See *Ulster Observer*, December 17, 1863.

82. The historiography of early and mid-nineteenth-century Orangeism is not overly crowded. For the most insightful treatment, see MacRaild, *Faith, Fraternity and Fighting*. For Irish developments, see Fitzpatrick, *Descendancy*, 21–40; Senior, *Orangeism in Ireland and Britain*.

83. Evidence of the Earl of Enniskillen, *Report of the Commissioners of Inquiry into the Origin and Character of the Riots in Belfast* (hereafter *1857 Belfast Riots Inquiry*). While banned, local lodges continued to meet and were certainly active in local elections and public rituals. Between 1837 and 1845, Lord Roden was technically grand master of the order but was relatively inactive. It was the Earl of Enniskillen who

rebellion provided both further impetus and political cover for the Orange Order, which was soon embroiled in controversy over the Dolly's Brae conflict of 1849, a sectarian clash near Castlewellan, County Down. Triggered by an Orange procession routed provocatively through a contested pass, the violence left an estimated thirty Catholics dead, many of them noncombatants. The investigation that followed underlined the features that made the Orange Order such a difficult organization for British governance in Ireland; its assertive and overtly sectarian public rituals, the communal hostility and violence its marches often triggered, and its connections to local landlords who often doubled as government officials. In the aftermath of the clash, three of Drew's allies and close friends in the organization—Francis and William Beers, and Robert Jocelyn, third Earl of Roden—lost government commissions for their roles in the conflict, a decision that generated predictable outrage from Orange conservatives and their supporters.[84] More seriously for the order, however, the furore over Dolly's Brae led to a decline in overall membership, as many upper-class supporters withdrew their support for an organization that was again proving to be more trouble than it was worth.

If the sectarian atrocities at Dolly's Brae appalled most British and Irish observers, they did nothing to halt the organization's advance in Belfast, where it grew dramatically in the 1850s and 1860s. While certainly an important presence in the pre-Famine town, the Orange Order's Church of Ireland orientation had always limited its potential for growth in the northern capital. The increased movement of rural Catholics into Belfast from the 1830s and the subsequent growth of

---

initiated the "rebirth" of the order, a fact reflected in his ascension to the position of grand master of the Grand Lodge of Ireland in 1846. See Curran, *Protestant Community in Ulster*, 147–56. For the sectarian dynamics connected to the Molly Maguires, see Kenny, *Making Sense of the Molly Maguires*, 27–31.

84. The Ulster Protestant Association held a considerable meeting in the Music Hall to honor Roden and protest the dismissal of the Orange magistrates; see *Belfast News-Letter*, November 2, 1849. For Dolly's Brae and the Orange mythologies that were created in its aftermath, see Farrell, "Writing an Orange Dolly's Brae," 90–106.

the urban Protestant population in the 1840s and 1850s created the basic conditions for Orange growth in Belfast.[85] While Presbyterians largely remained outside of the organization until the late nineteenth century, Anglican in-migration and the growth of evangelicalism and conservative politics made Belfast a more sympathetic arena for the Orange Order. This can be seen in the dramatic growth in the number of official Orange lodges in the city, which rose from thirty to ninety between 1853 and 1861, with the overall membership tripling between 1851 and 1870.[86] The warrant registries held at the Museum of Orange Heritage in Belfast underline this consistent growth pattern: an 1849 County Antrim Report indicates that were thirty-six lodges, while an 1856 report lists forty-two lodges.[87]

County lodge records allow us to chart both the social composition and the geography of Orange growth in the city. On a basic level, we can track the physical growth of the Orange Order in Belfast in the 1850s by constructing a map of local lodge masters and their deputies using county lodge records and addresses from various Belfast street directories. The resulting map provides few surprises, with Orange leaders generally living in two parts of town: Sandy Row and Brown Square/Shankill Road in west Belfast, and a broad area north of town center bounded by Great Patrick Street to the north, Carrick Hill/Queen Street to the west, and Ann Street to the south. Ballymacarrett also had a significant Orange presence.[88] Christ Church lay in the heart of Orange west Belfast. At least twelve lodge masters and their

---

85. Doyle, *Fighting Like the Devil for the Sake of God*.

86. Belfast County Orange Lodge, *Centenary Official History*, 15, 27; Budge and O'Leary, *Approach to Crisis*, 92–93; Doyle, *Fighting like the Devil for the Sake of God*, 27–28.

87. Registry of the Loyal Orange Institution of Ireland, 1856, Museum of Orange Heritage, Belfast (hereafter MOH); County Antrim Grand Orange Lodge of Ireland Report, 1849, MOH.

88. County Orange Lodge, 1849 Report, Grand Orange Lodge of Ireland, Belfast; Grand Orange Lodge of Ireland, County Antrim Report, August 1853, MOH; Belfast Street Directories, 1840–66.

deputies lived within easy walking distance of the Durham Street church and the vast majority of the congregation lived in neighborhoods that provided the Orange Order with much of its membership.[89]

This raises the question of the social composition of the Orange Order in early Victorian Belfast. With a disproportionately Presbyterian middle class remaining largely outside the order until the Home Rule Crisis of the 1880s, Orange membership was rooted in the rural and urban Anglican working-class population, with national and regional leadership positions largely taken by conservative Anglican landlords and ministers. The relative weakness of middle-class Orangeism undercuts more reductionist Marxist models of top-down unionist development. It is true that nineteenth-century Orangeism certainly acted as a vital conduit for the spread of conservative politics and evangelical values to Anglican working-class men and women, but it did not do so on strictly elite terms—this was not a simple matter of hegemonic bourgeois social control.[90] There was a real independence to Protestant working-class culture and populist interests often placed severe constraints on elite direction, boundaries perhaps best epitomized by a fervent plebeian commitment to Orange public processions that caused no end of headaches for Orange leaders.

What this social model meant was that local lodge masters and Church of Ireland ministers like Drew occupied critical linchpin positions in the association, tightening connections between a socially and geographically distant elite leadership and its working-class members. Lodge records clearly indicate that local leadership was largely drawn from the lower middle class, artisans, and the upper echelons of the

89. Christ Church Census, 1852, PRONI, CR1/13D/1. Unfortunately, the second volume of the census (which contained information from Millfield, Boundary Street, Falls Road South and North, Shankill, and the "country districts" of Springfield, Legoniel, and White Rock) has disappeared from PRONI.

90. The most sophisticated articulation of this argument is Miller, "Belfast's First Bomb," 262–80. For approaches that largely echo my own thinking on this crucial issue, see Doyle, *Fighting like the Devil for the Sake of God*, 28–29; MacRaild, *Faith, Fraternity and Fighting*, 25–29.

working class. Of twenty lodge masters who can be identified in Belfast street directories from the 1850s, only three or four were clearly upper- or upper-middle class, including Drew's own lodge master, Francis Hull, co-owner of a flax-spinning company who lived on the lower Falls Road. Hull's deputy master was Drew's close friend Hutcheson Posnett of Donegall Pass, the master of chancery for Antrim and Down and the land agent for Arthur Trevor-Hill, third Viscount Dungannon, an ultra-Protestant Tory once denounced by O'Connell as "the meek and modest representative of the clergy of Durham."[91] More typical, however, was Hugh Laverty, master of Lodge 486 (County Lodge 14), a grocer and publican who resided at 47 Stanley Street, just southwest of Christ Church.[92] While hardly dominant, grocer-publicans were the largest single occupation group among the lodge masters, followed by men working in various aspects of textile production and the clothing trade. These social details are fragmentary evidence of a largely working-class association operating in a city where the textile industry was the dominant engine of growth. While there were certainly tensions between the drinks trade and the evangelical and Protestant nature of the Orange Order, the key roles played by publicans should not surprise, a phenomenon with clear parallels in both Irish nationalist and working-class associational life across the British Isles.[93]

Mid-Victorian Belfast Orangeism's plebeian orientation is also reflected in both the reports of the Antrim Grand Lodge and the

91. Norgate, "Arthur Trevor-Hill."

92. County Antrim Lodge Report, 1849, MOH. To generate this social profile of the Belfast lodge masters, I used the various digitized Belfast Street Directories (1840–66) now helpfully housed at the PRONI website: http://streetdirectories.proni.gov.uk/. For a similar argument, see Doyle, *Fighting Like the Devil for the Sake of God*, 43–44n55. Given the fact that one volume of the 1852 Christ Church survey is absent and we do not have lodge membership lists, it is impossible to construct a detailed profile of the number of Christ Church congregants who were in the Orange Order, but at least three lodge masters (a sawyer and two laborers) seem to have been members of Drew's church.

93. For the most recent view, see Kadel, *Drink and Culture in Nineteenth-Century Ireland*.

Belfast county lodge minutes. One of the most important functions of these meetings was to formally record the addition of new members and/or hear cases regarding the suspension of membership and/or expulsion of a member for various offences. While there were extraordinary cases involving the expulsion of members for marrying Catholics, and in two particularly interesting instances, for supporting the repeal of the Act of Union, the vast majority of expulsions involved the nonpayment of dues—a solid indicator of Orangeism's working-class base. To take one admittedly dramatic example, the November 25, 1851, meeting heard twenty-four suspension cases—twenty-three of them involved the nonpayment or arrears of dues. In the other case, James Stevenson was kicked out of the order for desertion from the army.[94] Many of the other cases certainly echo the vulnerability of working-class people living in a turbulent economic climate; embezzlement and fraud were not uncommon, and in one case in November 1856, John MacGowan and George McClenaghan were suspended seven years for pawning their lodge flag.[95] These findings certainly echo Donald MacRaild's portrait of the Orange Order in northern England.[96] For all its ties into the powerful networks of the Irish elite, Belfast Orangeism in the 1850s was firmly proletarian in terms of membership.

This same working-class orientation can be seen in efforts to create a special benefit society for widows and orphans in 1851. The creation of mutual aid societies was one of the hallmarks of nineteenth-century associational life. Across the British Isles, such efforts accelerated in the 1850s, a trend reflected in the passage of an annually renewable Friendly Societies Act in 1855, legislation made permanent twenty years later. In the Belfast county lodge, the district master, Robert Waring, a woolen draper who lived on Donegall Street, pushed for the creation of an Orange widows and orphans' benefit fund in

---

94. These cases are all drawn from the 1851 County Minute Book, MOH.
95. Antrim Grand Lodge Report, November 1856, MOH.
96. MacRaild, *Faith, Fraternity and Fighting*, 109–55, 200–241.

February 1851. While there was some support for the idea, a majority of members did not want to hold a special meeting on the issue and the idea fell by the wayside at a meeting in late March,[97] likely undermined by the organization's relatively weak capital base. The creation of an Orange benevolent fund would have to wait for another day. This did not mean that efforts to support the bereaved were not made; they were just handled on a case-by-case basis. At three consecutive meetings in the spring of 1854, for example, the county lodge voted to give three widows ten shillings each to help cover expenses.[98] While they lacked the financial resources of British friendly societies such as the Foresters or the Oddfellows (or the later Orange Order, for that matter), members of the Orange Order in Belfast clearly shared the proletarian tendency to pool resources collectively to help their membership through the myriad difficulties of working-class life.

The sense of community implicit in this commitment to mutual aid was a key part of the Orange Order's appeal, a phenomenon with obvious parallels to Vincent Comerford's portrait of the social dynamics of Fenianism.[99] The minutes make quite clear that the lodges acted as crucial circles of friendship and support. After two of Drew's children died within two weeks of one another in October 1852, the Christ Church minister, district grand chaplain at that point, thanked the Orangemen of the district for their sympathy and kindness in his time of need. Likewise, when Posnett, deputy master of lodge 7, fell seriously ill in late 1854 and eventually died in early 1855, it was Drew who comforted the family, spending several days and nights in Posnett's Donegall Pass abode. Posnett's son, George, later wrote Drew saying that his father's warmest and best friends had been in the organization. Posnett gave particular thanks to Drew for "the consolation to know that his last moments were soothed by the kind offices of his best friend and Brother Orangeman to whom all our family feel most

---

97. County Minute Book, February and March 1851, MOH.
98. County Minute Book, March, April, and May 1854, MOH. That same year a burial committee was formed to mobilize support for the creation of a burial fund.
99. Comerford, *Fenians in Context*.

deeply for the kindness he manifested."[100] The minutes make clear the fact that the sociability and support members found in the lodges was an important part of the Orange Order's appeal.

The issues that dominated discussion in the county lodge minutes involved matters common to almost any club or society: splits and divisions over internal matters, fundraising for special projects, and seemingly endless discussions about the association's rules and regulations. Many of the county meetings in 1851 and 1852 focused on the efforts of four lodges to leave the Belfast County Lodge and establish a second district lodge within Belfast. Although there appear to have been genuine differences over organizational issues (the district was becoming too large, too many meetings were being scheduled, etc.), personal/political motivations seem to have been at least as important. Matters centered on lodge 486. At a meeting in August 1851, the lodge master, Hugh Laverty, proposed a vote of censure against Waring for his publication of a pamphlet on the use of crosses in churches, a controversial touchstone issue within Belfast Protestant politics since the Mant controversy. Since only two people had apparently read the pamphlet, the matter was tabled until the next meeting, with the majority of participants showing their support for Waring by walking out long before a vote could be held.[101]

Before the next meeting, however, Laverty published his charges against the county master in the *Banner of Ulster*, and with three other lodge masters, brought grievances against the county lodge, saying they wanted to leave to form their own lodge. The stakes had been raised and the tone of the November meeting was clearly tense and sharp. Laverty's key supporter was James Wilson, the former owner of the *Belfast Protestant Journal*. They argued vociferously that the district was too large to be manageable, that members were forced to

---

100. County Minute Book, January–March 1856, MOH. William Johnston also noted that "poor Isabella Drew has been taken away," musing that she had just been at Ballykilbeg House the year before. See Diaries of William Johnston, October 17, 1852, PRONI, D.880/2/5.

101. Diaries of William Johnston, August 1851, PRONI, D.880/2/5.

spend time at too many meetings, and that they did not feel as if the county lodge represented their sentiments. In particular, they highlighted the case of Laverty's lodge mate Thomas McCullogh, who had been suspended for publishing documents "injurious" to the organization. For all of their passion, Laverty and Wilson were defeated quite easily within the meeting, as Waring and his deputy district master effectively circled the wagons, charging Laverty with slandering the officers and organizations. For his part, Waring promised to visit every lodge in the district over the next month to take the temperature of the membership. The four dissenting lodges had their warrants revoked and McCullogh was suspended from the organization for ninety-nine years by the Antrim County Lodge in 1852. One of the dissenting lodges returned to the fold within a year, making a public apology, and lodge 486 is listed again in the 1856 warrant register. Laverty was no longer its lodge master.[102]

While this convoluted story has its own Belfast and Orange peculiarities and the clash is replete with anti-Catholic rhetoric, the crucial point here is that this conflict could have happened in any organization in the nineteenth- and twentieth-century world. The issues at stake were both organizational and personal in the main; it was a petty power squabble that was, above all, local. It was also quite human, a dimension too often absent from scholarly and popular accounts of Orangeism and one that an associational focus puts front and center.

Given its largely working-class composition in the early 1850s, it is perhaps no surprise that a great deal of the Orange Order's time and attention was spent on fundraising. The major project of the county lodge was to raise funds for a Protestant Hall; discussion began in 1851 and continued until 1854, when the organization decided to purchase the old Deaf and Dumb Institution at a discounted price for its use as a hall. Even this more modest arrangement created some problems;

---

102. This account is drawn from various sources held in the Museum of Orange Heritage, Schomberg House, Belfast; County Minute Book, August, November, and December 1851 meetings, the May, June, July, and September 1852 meetings; County Antrim GOLI meeting, October 1852 and the Warrant Registry, 1856.

when Drew and George Posnett went to the home of George Matthews, who was holding the money raised by the "Protestants of Belfast" for this purpose, he at first refused to hand over the funds, saying that individual subscribers would have to sue him to get the money.[103] Matthews's opposition was quickly overcome and the association could quickly return to its seeming true passion: formulating the rules and regulations for the use of the new building. A grandiose Orange Hall was built on Clifton Street in Belfast in 1883, when the Orange Order was quickly becoming a very different organization.

One of the standard narratives in the literature on the late nineteenth-century emergence of Ulster Unionism is that both Orangeism and evangelical Protestantism played key roles in the so-called taming of the Protestant working classes.[104] Recent scholarship has quite rightly made quick work out of the more reductionist and static formulations of this argument, but we can see tensions between those who attempted to place moral improvement closer to the center of Orange life and those who resisted such a change. Even within his own organization, Drew's influence had its limits. Such a dynamic is certainly evident over the various debates about the closing hours of the dining halls. There certainly was a tension between working-class practice and even the most pragmatic evangelical ideals reflected in the almost constant curfew violations by lodge members participating in their parties and meetings. This became such an issue by 1858 that the county lodge called a special meeting, at which an exasperated Drew argued that at the very least the hours should not be extended. While taking their beloved chaplain's opinion into account, the gathering proceeded to allow lodges to have the privilege of using the hall for their soirees twice a year, saying that they could stay until two o'clock in the morning on those special occasions.[105] Orangemen may have been largely conservative and certainly respectful of

103. County Minute Book, August 2, 1854, MOH.
104. For a thoughtful review of this issue, see MacRaild, *Faith, Fraternity and Fighting*, 25–27.
105. County Lodge minutes, November 2, 1858, MOH.

the moralistic platitudes of evangelical Protestantism; they were also, however, members of a largely working-class organization, and there were limits to how far they would curtail their activities.

The various dynamics outlined in this chapter—the tightly linked growth of populist Protestant politics and the increasingly contentious sectarian atmosphere in Belfast in the 1850s, the increased volume and scope of Drew's Protestant politics and the limits those politics placed on his influence outside of Christ Church and the Orange Order, the plebeian nature of Belfast Orangeism and the relationship between the Orange rank and file and their veteran cleric—are on full display in both the events and aftermath of the Belfast riots of 1857. Tragically, they also highlight the ways that Thomas Drew's reputation and his polemics could have a very real and deadly impact on people's lives and communal relations in the increasingly divided city.

6

Thomas Drew and the Belfast Riots of 1857

The Belfast riots of 1857 were one of the most significant episodes of violence in nineteenth-century Ireland. Seemingly initiated by a virulent anti-Catholic sermon that Thomas Drew had given to Belfast Orangemen and their supporters at Christ Church to celebrate the 12th of July, the riots were a complex series of clashes that involved sizable Catholic and Protestant crowds, policemen, and soldiers, ranging across the city in two linked phases in July and September 1857. While there were remarkably few fatalities, hundreds of men, women, and children were injured. Families were displaced from disputed frontier zones in Sandy Row and the Pound, forced out of wrecked homes targeted by communal activists. Mark Doyle has argued that the riots marked a notable shift from the highly ritualized sectarian confrontations of the Ulster countryside to the larger-scale, and ultimately more deadly, forms of communal violence that marked the late nineteenth-century city. Rioters greatly strengthened the basic outlines of Belfast's sectarian geography in 1857, driving both communal, and, to a lesser extent, political opponents from west Belfast neighborhoods. The house expulsions gave a particular intimacy to the violence, embedding the abstract binaries of communal difference into the everyday lived fabric of working-class households, increasingly polarized around the actions of extremists in both communities. There were other consequences, as the 1857 riots and the subsequent inquiry transformed British thinking about crucial aspects of governing Belfast, persuading officials of the necessity of significant police reform, the strategic value of using overwhelming force to contain and curtail crowd violence, and the need to limit street preaching, which was viewed in increasingly negative terms (part of the state's increased willingness to limit free access to public space to better maintain the public peace in a divided city).[1]

In the most thorough and compelling accounts of the riots to date, both Catherine Hirst and Mark Doyle have emphasized the proletarian nature of sectarian conflict in Belfast, arguing that while political and religious leaders such as Drew and Hugh "Roaring" Hanna played critical roles initiating sectarian confrontations in July and September, the riots primarily were driven and sustained by social relationships between and within Belfast's working-class communities.[2] An important corrective to earlier interpretations and persuasive in the main, this focus on working-class violence nevertheless undervalues the roles that Drew and other clerical leaders played in the long-term political and social formation of these communities as well as the ways that the 1857 riots made Drew and other "Orange clerics" powerful symbols of Belfast's supposedly foundational communalism. In short, it was not simply that Drew's divisive career as a political pastor and Orange zealot helped to create the environment that enabled and sustained these riots. Perhaps more important were the ways that outsized narratives of Drew and other ministers' roles in the Belfast riots of 1857 were consolidated and amplified in newspaper accounts and the government inquiry that followed. These portrayed Drew as the epitome of a simplified and irrational sectarianism that became one of the primary lenses through which Belfast was viewed. In many ways, then, the shadows of Drew and/or Hanna and the 1857 riots have loomed over the historiography of modern Belfast, shaping and constraining British and Irish thinking about the Victorian city's past, present,

---

1. Doyle, *Fighting like the Devil for the Sake of God*, 76–106; Morris, "Reading the Riot Commission," 208–16; Bryan, Connolly, and Nagel, *Civic Identity and Public Space*, 71–110.

2. Doyle, *Fighting like the Devil for the Sake of God*, 76–106; Hirst, *Religion, Politics and Violence in 19th Century Belfast*, 157–64. See also Farrell, *Rituals and Riots*, 143–50.

and future. Given the comprehensive analysis of the riots provided by recent scholarship, there is little need to provide another detailed account of the Belfast riots of 1857. What follows instead focuses on Drew's relationship to the sectarian violence that summer, the ways that it reflects both the tangible impact of his anti-Catholic politics and the peculiar nature and legacies of that influence.

R. J. Morris has argued that the Belfast riots of 1857 occurred in five linked but relatively distinct phases: a first period in July of accelerating ritualized confrontations between Catholic and Protestant crowds in the boundary zone between Sandy Row and the Pound; an intermittent period in August marked by increasing controversy over evangelical Protestant street preaching and the formation of the Catholic Gun Club; the more wide-ranging and destructive violence in September, triggered by the controversialist street preaching; the government investigation into the 1857 riots; and subsequent clashes in 1858.[3] While Morris focuses on the inquiry, his approach epitomizes one of the welcome features of more recent work on sectarian violence: a close attention to the shifting nature and geography of conflict.[4]

On July 12, 1857, Thomas Drew gave a highly anticipated lecture to a large body of Belfast Orangemen and their families at Christ Church. The idea for the gathering originated at an Orange Order district meeting in late May, where it was suggested that Belfast Orangemen should meet at Christ Church on the 12th since the holiday fell on a Sunday that year. There was recent precedent. On November 5, 1856, Drew had given a special sermon to the Orangemen of Belfast to commemorate the anniversary of the Gunpowder Plot of 1605. The *Belfast News-Letter*'s report of the event stressed the large audience in attendance at Christ Church, with the lower half of the church filled with Orangemen wearing the emblems of several lodges. The talk, a rather well-worn call for Protestants to remember, and be worthy

---

3. Morris, "Reading the Riot Commission," 194–97.

4. See accounts by Doyle and Hirst. For an important earlier study of street preaching, see Holmes, "Role of Open-Air Preaching in the Belfast Riots of 1857," 47–66.

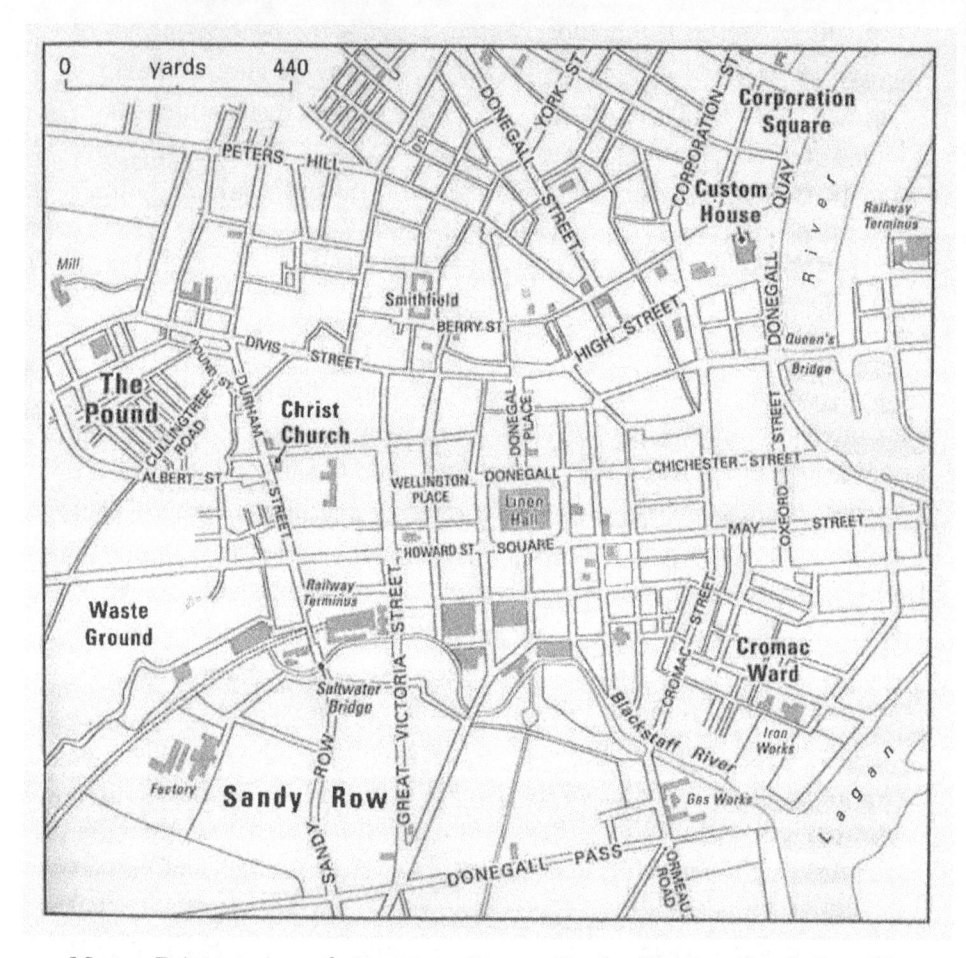

Map 4. Primary sites of 1857 riots. Source: Doyle, *Fighting like the Devil for the Sake of God*, 77. Courtesy of Mark Doyle and Manchester Univ. Press.

of, God's deliverance, was later published due, it was claimed, to high demand in Orange circles.[5] Drew agreed to deliver another anniversary sermon in 1857 so long as any funds raised by the event were given to the Protestant Orphan Society. Orange leaders quickly agreed to

5. *Belfast News-Letter*, November 6, 1856; *Morning Advertiser*, September 11, 1857; Drew, *A Sermon Preached in Christ Church, Belfast, on the Evening of November 5, 1856.*

his terms. Word of the lecture spread through Orange networks and news circulated quickly throughout Belfast.

Publicists did their work well. On the early evening of the 12th, a large body of Orangemen and their supporters converged on Christ Church,[6] many marching in procession from Sandy Row and sympathetic districts across the city. In an effort to uphold the literal terms of the Party Processions Act of 1850, the marchers only donned Orange sashes and lilies upon entering the church, a technicality that surely made little difference to their opponents but drew a great deal attention from commentators afterward. Drew's sermon that night was the second of the day for many of the Orangemen, who had attended morning services at Malone Church (St. John's) outside of town.

The Orange celebrants were not alone. While Belfast had been relatively quiet in the approach to the 12th in 1857, rival crowds gathered at the edge of Sandy Row and the Pound to observe the spectacle of Orangemen marching to the centrally located church. Thomas Lindsay, chief constable of the municipal police, positioned policemen outside the constabulary barracks on the corner of Albert Street and Durham Street (right across from Christ Church) to manage the crowds, a strategy that seemed to work well enough.[7] Reading the evidence given before the riots commission, the pervasive presence of young people is striking, a reminder of both the recreational element in these public confrontations as well as the fact that they involved entire communities.[8] In his testimony, Sub-Inspector Harris Bindon highlighted the number of six- and seven-year-old boys and girls who had come to see

---

6. William Johnston reported that 2,500 people were present for Drew's sermon, a number that seems inflated given that Christ Church's capacity was 1,500. See *Downshire Protestant*, July 17, 1857.

7. County Lodge minutes, May 26, 1857, June 30, 1857, Museum of Orange Heritage, Belfast (hereafter MOH). Report, *1857 Belfast Riots Inquiry*, 3–4; evidence of William Tracy, *1857 Belfast Riots Inquiry*, 20–21; evidence of Thomas Lindsay, *1857 Belfast Riots Inquiry*, 35–39; evidence of John McLaughlin, *1857 Belfast Riots Inquiry*, 113; evidence of Thomas Ward, *1857 Belfast Riots Inquiry*, 185.

8. Bryan, Connolly, and Nagle, *Civic Identity and Public Space*, 96.

the Orangemen enter the church. This would have tragic consequences later that week—the three people shot and wounded in the first phase of the riots were two boys playing marbles and a young female millworker named Mary Ann Tynan.[9] Despite the tense confrontation, the service began without particular incident.

Drew's lecture seemingly met the expectations held by audiences inside and outside the church that evening. Opening with a celebration of the living voice of Jesus, he quickly moved to identify the Roman Catholic Church as the primary source of intolerance in the world. He recalled the torture and violence of the Inquisition in a lurid passage later reprinted by newspapers intent on portraying Drew as the living embodiment of Ireland's primordial sectarianism: "Of old time, lords of high degree, with their own hands strained on the rack, the delicate limbs of Protestant women; prelates dabbled in the gore of helpless victims; and the cells of the Pope's prisons were paved with the calcined bones of men and cemented with gore and human hair!" This was not simply a matter of history, Drew insisted, as the contemporary world was plagued with rank injustice that was too often linked to Roman Catholicism. The three events that Drew selected for his lesson that evening formed a rather peculiar, if ultimately familiar trinity: Catholic Austria's efforts to prevent Italian liberty; Napoleon III's active support for the pope; and the continuing evil of slavery in the United States.[10]

Despite this global framework, Drew's lecture focused on Irish matters, providing a quick survey of late seventeenth-century events that celebrated William of Orange's deliverance of loyal Irish Protestants from the oppression of King James II and "the fierce Tyrconnell." As we have seen, Drew believed that true Protestants had to constantly

---

9. Evidence of Harris Bindon, *Belfast Riots Inquiry of 1857*, 50. All three—Mary Ann Tynan, Patrick Murphy and Adam Ward—were most likely hit by incidental gunfire. See *1857 Belfast Riots Inquiry*, 6.

10. *Downshire Protestant*, July 17, 1857; *1857 Belfast Riots Inquiry*, appendix no. 1, 248.

keep these stories in their hearts, examples to live by for loyal men and their families. After all, the world remained a dangerous place, and the only "position of the true Protestant is one of earnest vigilance." The defence of Protestant truth required men of action with a bold, honest, and unselfish spirit: "We want men! Men of might, men of intelligence, men of valour, and men of God! . . . Our cities want men like Walker and his clerical brethren of Derry (both church and dissenting). Our princes want prelates like Latimer and Ridley to stand at their sides." If the British government would not defend Protestantism, Irish Protestants had to stand up like these heroes of the past. Drew closed by asking his listeners to remember Protestant orphans, the boys and girls "who will soon take our places, and cherish their father's Bible and the good old Orange Institution."[11] His lecture was a clear and emotional call for Protestant action to combat the threat posed by Catholicism in Ireland and across the world.

The text of Drew's sermon received a great deal of attention in the aftermath of the July riots and beyond. In the long term, Catholic and liberal newspapers in Belfast and Dublin as well as British officials came to see the veteran minister's "indiscreet" performance as a significant event in the summer's unprecedented urban violence. More immediately, however, Belfast newspapers treated Drew's Christ Church lecture to Belfast Orangemen as a relatively ordinary occurrence, which, in a sense, it was. Both the *Belfast News-Letter* and the *Banner of Ulster* published accounts of the "annual event" on July 13 and 14, respectively, focusing their reports on the more respectable religious elements of Drew's sermon. Other newspapers were more critical. On July 13 the *Ulsterman* noted with alarm that Orangemen had marched in military array to Christ Church. More substantially, on July 18 (after several days of rioting had occurred), the *Belfast Daily Mercury* inveighed against Drew for "preaching to the Sandy Row ruffians," keeping "detestable animosities alive" by "pandering to

---

11. *Downshire Protestant*, July 17, 1857.

a blood-thirsty feeling."[12] Both Hirst and Doyle have pointed to the ideological and social cover that Drew's lecture provided for working-class Protestant activists, assuring Sandy Row Orangemen that they had the support of a powerful patron.[13] The opening flourish of Drew's speech that evening had a particularly violent quality to it and there is no doubt that the lecture's virulent anti-Catholicism contributed to the summer's mounting sectarian tension after it was published in full in the *Downshire Protestant*.[14] Drew's sermon was central to the interpretative lens through which the Belfast riots of 1857 would be understood. It was not, however, the text that mattered in the short term. Rather, it was the anticipation, the spectacle, the spread of rumor, and, above all, the geography of the performance that drove events forward in July. Christ Church was located right across from the conflict zone (what would now be called a flashpoint) between the Pound and Sandy Row. Widely advertised and deliberately scheduled at the height of the sectarian calendar, the visual and physical spectacle of men walking two by two up Durham Street or Botanic Avenue into College Square to attend a performance by Belfast's most famous anti-Catholic cleric was what mattered.

For all its drama and notoriety, Drew's sermon did not lead to sectarian rioting in the immediate sense. Orangemen and their supporters left the church quietly, marching home with relative ease.[15] Even James Simms, proprietor and editor of the *Belfast Daily Mercury* and no

---

12. *Belfast News-Letter*, July 13, 1857; *Belfast Daily Mercury*, July 18, 1857. See also *Banner of Ulster*, July 14, 1857; *Ulsterman*, July 13, 1857.

13. Doyle, *Fighting like the Devil for the Sake of God*, 85; Hirst, *Religion, Politics, and Violence in 19th Century Belfast*, 157.

14. *Downshire Protestant*, July 17, 1857. John McLaughlin, the owner of the *Ulsterman*, attended Drew's service that evening. See evidence of John McLaughlin, *1857 Belfast Riots Inquiry*, 118.

15. While there were reports of the abuse given to some Orange participants, no serious outbreaks of violence occurred. McLaughlin testified that the Orangemen had a police escort from Christ Church, a telling comment about Catholic beliefs about the partisan nature of the town's police force. Evidence of John McLaughlin, *1857 Belfast Riots Inquiry*, 109.

friend to Drew or the Orange Order, later wrote that "no matter how reprehensible Dr, Drew's conduct was, . . . in permitting party emblems in church and giving such an inflammatory sermon, . . . we must still admit the truth that the Orange men were quietly in Church."[16] The only notable incident that night occurred when members of a Catholic crowd mistakenly identified John Loughran, the young and seemingly drunk son of a prominent Catholic merchant in town, as a Protestant antagonist (for reasons known only to him, he was wearing an orange lily in his hat). Police rescued Loughran from the crowd, arresting him for disturbing the peace and carting him safely away to jail.[17]

While nothing further happened that evening, matters deteriorated in west Belfast over the next few nights, with both Catholic and Protestant activists preparing for conflict in their respective neighborhoods. The July riots began in earnest on the evening of the 14th, with the clashes taking on a wearyingly ritualized pattern over the next few nights, with battles between Catholic and Protestant crowds that gathered after work on the waste ground between the Pound and Sandy Row. While rioters shot and wounded two children and a young millworker, participants typically used more earthly weapons, attacking opponents with brickbats, cobblestones, and their own fists. The ensuing violence often was dangerous but rarely deadly, although three local policemen were nearly beaten to death by rioters who pulled them from a shop. The most widely discussed event of the July riots was an attack on houses owned by William Watson, a Catholic businessman who had purposefully rented to a mixed clientele in an effort to reduce the threat of communal violence. Watson's ecumenical approach failed to pay off, as Protestant rioters smashed windows and drove both Catholic and Protestant tenants out of at least twenty of his houses on Albert Crescent, Brooke Street, and Quadrant Street, all

16. *Belfast Daily Mercury*, February 15, 1858.
17. Evidence of James Bell, *1857 Belfast Riots Inquiry*, 189. For a detailed account of the Loughran episode, see Doyle, *Fighting like the Devil for the Sake of God*, 76–78.

located within a few blocks of Christ Church.[18] In so doing, combatants enforced binary communal definitions that would be one of the most powerful legacies of Belfast's late nineteenth-century riots. For example, Biddy Burke, a Catholic mill worker who had boarded with a Protestant man in Sandy Row for four years, testified that Protestant crowds had told her landlord to "throw out the Papish whore or they would throw down his house."[19] It is vital to note that the July violence was confined to "the disturbed districts" of west Belfast: the working-class neighborhoods that lay between the Pound and Sandy Row. Rioting only stopped on July 19, a full week after Drew had delivered his controversial sermon.

The first phase of the riots that summer was halted in part by an emerging state strategy of containment, as policemen and soldiers were posted in force at potential contact points between the two working-class neighborhoods. Although the weeklong rioting had been contained within the city's western industrial districts and no one had been killed, the cost had been quite high. In the short term, three young people were seriously wounded by gunfire, and countless others doubtless sustained injuries that went unreported. Dozens of families were driven from their homes.[20] While it is difficult to get an exact sense of the extent to which Christ Church members were involved, it is worth noting that the church's 1852 census lists at least two families living in Watson's houses: a family of five headed by George Armstrong, a forty-year-old laborer, and a family of eight led by Sarah Irwin, a forty-two-year-old widow.[21]

We can also use the Christ Church census data to sketch the basic outlines of the congregation's relationship with another key

---

18. Evidence of William Tracy, *1857 Belfast Riots Inquiry*, 20–31; evidence of Harris Bindon, *1857 Belfast Riots Inquiry*, 49–58; evidence of William Watson, *1857 Belfast Riots Inquiry*, 126–27.

19. Evidence of Biddy Burke, *1857 Belfast Riots Inquiry*, 124–25; Hirst, *Religion, Politics, and Violence in 19th Century Belfast*, 159.

20. Doyle, *Fighting like the Devil for the Sake of God*, 83–88.

21. Christ Church Census, 1852, PRONI, CR1/13D/1.

participant in the summer's riots: the municipal police. This was a subject of no small controversy. Throughout the 1850s the radical gadfly John Rea waged a war against the Tory-led town council, alleging that the local police force was partisan and sectarian. Not surprisingly, Rea continued this attack at the riots inquiry. His colleague Alexander O'Rorke linked the allegations more tightly to Christ Church, saying that Drew had provided recommendations for the force. In his study of the Belfast Town Police (nicknamed "the Bulkies"), Brian Griffin has argued that the force's sectarian reputation was more a matter of appearance (it was almost entirely Protestant) than behavior.[22] While O'Rorke failed to provide evidence to support his allegation, there was a pronounced police presence in the Christ Church congregation: ten constables are listed in the surviving census data. Some of this was undoubtedly a matter of geography, since Head Constable Joseph Henderson and two other constables lived in the police barracks across the street from Christ Church. That said, the fact that ten policemen were congregants of Belfast's most notorious Orange preacher certainly lent credence to Rea and O'Rorke's assertions of bias. Moreover, Police Superintendent Adam Hill had once been the master of Drew's local lodge before resigning from the Orange Order in 1855.[23] Taken in conjunction with the six other policemen who owned up to being former members of the Orange Order, appearances alone make it easy to see why Belfast Catholics saw the municipal police as partisan.[24]

If local and state authorities had brought the initial riots under control, sectarian rhetoric and rivalry remained high throughout late July and August. While Christ Church ceased to be at the center of events, Drew's name and reputation were seemingly ever present in

22. Griffin, *Bulkies*, 116–34.
23. Report, *1857 Belfast Riots Inquiry*, 6; evidence of Thomas Lindsay, *1857 Belfast Riots Inquiry*, 40; evidence of Joseph Henderson, *1857 Belfast Riots Inquiry*, 200–205; Christ Church Census, 1852, PRONI, CR1/13D/1.
24. While underlining the force's problematic Protestant composition, Brian Griffin makes the important point that working-class Protestants had no great love for the local police force either. See Griffin, *Bulkies*, 124.

the continuing controversies, playing a key and revealing role in triggering the second and more destructive violence of the late summer. The critical precipitating factor in late August was the controversialist preaching of evangelical Protestant ministers. There was nothing new about open-air preaching, which had become a familiar part of the Belfast streetscape by the mid-1850s. In the charged atmosphere of the summer 1857, however, open-air preaching came to represent larger issues of political and religious identity for increasing numbers of Belfast residents—the Protestant right to religious liberty or yet another insult to a Belfast Catholic community weary of such slights. The developments that led to the crisis that summer originated at a meeting in December 1856. Responding to the seeming success of Presbyterian street preaching and their own corresponding insecurities about their relative position within the town, several of Belfast's Church of Ireland ministers moved to create the Belfast Parochial Mission.[25] The organization's stated goals were to "meet the urgent and acknowledged spiritual wants of the parish" by providing "additional divine services in destitute localities" and the creation of "free schools, wherever practical." Drew and two prominent members of the Christ Church congregation—Richard Davison and Charles Lanyon—were on the organizing committee, which featured a coterie of Anglican ministers and much of the Belfast conservative establishment.[26]

While Drew was on the board and fiercely supported the Protestant right to preach in public spaces, he was not a particularly active member of the new organization, which announced its first schedule of public sermons on July 19, 1857. The initial speaker was to be

25. The increased use of open-air preaching can be charted through the reports of the *Irish Presbyterian* (1853–58). See Holmes, "Role of Open-Air Preaching." Comparing the situation in Belfast and Liverpool, Mark Doyle argues that the British state was remarkably indulgent to evangelical Protestant preachers. See Doyle, "Martyrs of Liberty," 149–64.

26. *1857 Belfast Riots Inquiry*, appendix no. 7; Dawson, "Annals of Christ Church, Belfast," PRONI, T.2159/1.

his good friend William McIlwaine, rector of St. George's Church. While McIlwaine later stressed the fact that he and others had deliberately chosen noncontroversialist subjects for their lectures, his reputation as an anti-Catholic controversialist more than made up for the lecture's substance. McIlwaine had been involved in widely publicized contests with Catholic priests since the late 1840s, and his confrontational attitude toward Roman Catholicism is underlined by the title of his 1857 Lent lectures: "Is Popery Christianity?"[27] Given the violent context of that week, magistrates asked the ministers to delay their series and the Belfast Parochial Mission complied, rescheduling McIlwaine's lecture for August 9 on the steps of the new Custom House.[28] While the police were readied for a fight, McIlwaine's sermon went off relatively quietly, as did another lecture the following week. There was a dynamic media response, however, that foreshadowed an increasingly contentious press discourse about street preaching that certainly hindered efforts to reduce the temperature in Belfast. Responding to the "detestable McIlwaine", the *Northern Whig* lamented the threat to public disorder posed by the Church of Ireland body's decision to hold the series: "We hear a great deal . . . about Sabbath desecration; but it seems to us a queer kind of "Sabbath observance" which risks street rows."[29] When Thomas Roe's August 23 service generated some public opposition, the Belfast Parochial Mission canceled the remainder of the series. Taking this as an egregious insult to the Protestant right to preach the gospel, Hanna took up the challenge against the wishes of the synod, delivering a sermon on Sunday, September 6, that initiated the second outbreak of

27. Evidence of the Reverend William McIlwaine, *1857 Belfast Riots Inquiry*, 74; *1857 Belfast Riots Inquiry*, appendix no. 6, 254–55.

28. Both McIlwaine and the Church of Ireland bishop of Down, Connor, and Dromore, Robert Knox, were in close contact with both local magistrates and Dublin Castle throughout July and August 1857. See Larcom Papers, National Library of Ireland (hereafter NLI), MS 7624/14–20.

29. *Northern Whig*, August 13, 1857.

violence that summer, a weeklong conflict that ranged across several Belfast neighborhoods, featuring tragically fatal violence and more widespread house-wreckings.[30]

Given Drew's central place in later narratives of Belfast riots of 1857, his relatively marginal presence in the second phase of the riots is worth noting.[31] If Drew was physically absent, however, his name and reputation were seemingly ubiquitous throughout August and early September, a reflection of his public career as an anti-Catholic figure and the utility of his name for Belfast Catholic activists determined to resist Orange aggression in the town. This is reflected clearly in the pages of the *Ulsterman*, which repeatedly referred to Drew's 12th of July performance and used him to castigate evangelical Protestant street preaching. Drew's name was particularly potent in this case because he linked street preaching, a complex phenomenon whose practitioners ranged across the political and religious spectrum, with the Conservativism and Orangeism that the paper's editor, Dennis Holland, and other Catholic leaders blamed for the oppression of Belfast Catholics. It was not simply Drew. Henry Cooke and William McIlwaine, two other "political ministers," also served this purpose. In a particularly vivid editorial, Holland described Cooke as a "senile" man of a bygone era, and was hopeful that better days were ahead despite "the sanguinary outrages of Sandy Row, and the fanatical insanities of the Drews."[32] When the Church of Ireland canceled its outdoor lecture series, the paper called on its readers to pity Drew,

---

30. Government officials tried to get leading Presbyterian evangelicals like Cooke and Edgar to restrain Hanna, an effort that failed. See Larcom Papers, NLI, MS 7624/ 41–43, 53. For the best account of the September violence, see Doyle, *Fighting like the Devil for the Sake of God*, 88–101.

31. Doyle, *Fighting like the Devil for the Sake of God*, 93. The power of Drew's reputation and its impact on the ensuing narrative of sectarian contention is illustrated by the number of scholars who incorrectly list him as being involved in the Custom House violence. See Hirst, *Religion, Politics and Violence in 19th Century Belfast*, 164; Griffin, *Bulkies*, 116.

32. *Ulsterman*, September 2, 1857.

who would now be "constrained to confine his inflammatory addresses to his followers within the walls of his own preaching-house."[33]

The campaign to use Drew's name to mobilize opposition to street preaching did not end with the Belfast Parochial Mission. When Hanna announced his determination to preach outdoors in early September, the *Ulsterman* made the "mistake" of reporting that it was Drew was scheduled to give a lecture on the steps of the Custom House:

> Dr. Drew is to be "out" next Sunday. It is his turn, in the arrangement of the Church of England clergy, who are with energetic zeal popularizing the establishment by disturbing Belfast; and Dr. Drew, we all know, is not a man to back out of a sacred duty of disorder from any fear of the martyrdom which become so renowned a saint. Apostolic blows and knocks are certainly in prospect; but the reverend man courts the peril and defies the mob, which may tend to reciprocate howling harangues with sermons in stones. . . . [The police] will be there to protect Dr. Drew, while he inflames the passers-by into the bad blood which it pleases this Christian pastor, a leech-like purifier of Popery, to draw out.[34]

A week later, Catholic activists distributed a similar call to arms on a placard they had secretly printed in the *Ulsterman*'s offices: "Down with Open-Air Preaching. Down with Fanatic Drew, the Squinting Divine! The Enemy of Tranquility and Peace."[35] When a Catholic crowd came to the Custom House, they found that the offending

---

33. *Ulsterman*, August 31, 1857. Dennis Holland was not alone. That same week, the *Northern Whig* critiqued "deranged Drewism." See *Northern Whig*, August 29, 1857.

34. *Ulsterman*, August 27, 1857. The *Northern Whig* made a similar report on August 27, 1857.

35. *1857 Belfast Riots Inquiry*, appendix no. 5, 253; *Northern Whig*, September 24, 1857. The squinting description refers to a controversy initiated when Drew described Irish Catholics as less aesthetically pleasing than their Protestant counterparts. The *Northern Whig* replied by wondering whether Drew's squint-eyed face was the new standard for Orange beauty.

services had been moved to nearby Corporation Square and that Hanna would be speaking rather than Drew. It did not matter. When a body of men began to heckle the minister, they were attacked by forty to fifty Protestant shipyard workers, recruited by Hanna to defend his congregation.[36]

The deadly September phrase of the riots initiated by the clash at Corporation Square lasted a full week and ranged across Belfast, bringing house-wrecking and violence to neighborhoods that had been quiet in July—the Cromac District east of city center and Donegall Pass to its south. A great deal of the violence in September occurred in the familiar confines of the Pound and Sandy Row, led again by relatively small groups of activists. It was not only urban geography where we can see the expanded scope of the second phase. The September violence was more sustained and involved whole communities, a point nicely illustrated by Mark Doyle's analysis of the degree to which women were involved as both participants and victims in both home-wreckings and in campaigns of intimidation and violence directed at millworkers of "the wrong sort" both inside and outside factories. At a later trial, a lawyer claimed that hundreds of Catholic girls had been driven or forced out of Belfast's mills and that some were now starving because of the lost wages.[37]

Thomas Drew was almost entirely absent from the scene. He made at least one public appearance when he led a funeral procession through a Catholic crowd on September 6, but according to the *Ulsterman*'s report, Belfast Catholics offered no disrespect—"even to Dr. Drew." Christ Church congregants were apparently not so fortunate, and the Belfast Police Committee decided to post a constable to

---

36. Hanna was added to the list of offensive clerical divines who came to emblemize Belfast sectarianism for Irish Catholics and liberal British officials. He was not a member of the Orange Order, a distinction that made little difference to the *Freeman's Journal*, which described him as "the inflated and inflammatory divine" who "reminds the Orange furies" of the need "to defend Blood-bought rights." See *Freeman's Journal*, September 12, 1857; *Ulsterman*, September 7, 1857.

37. Doyle, *Fighting like the Devil for the Sake of God*, 94–100.

protect men and women attending services at Christ Church, College Square Presbyterian Church, and Fisherwick Presbyterian Church. The following Thursday, word spread amongst Belfast Catholics of an impending attack on St. Malachy's Church, a false rumor that presaged the church's central place in sectarian contention in the future.[38] The rioting subsided after a week, but not before hundreds of men, women, and children had been injured and/or driven from their homes.

More than anything, it was the government investigation that followed the riots that forever linked Drew's name to the Belfast riots of 1857. The riots commission first met at the Belfast Court House on September 14 and heard testimonies from a wide array of men, women, and children over the following two weeks. Headed by David Lynch, a Dublin lawyer who was a Catholic Whig and close friend of Thomas Larcom, undersecretary of state for Ireland, the inquiry was part of a government effort to foster reconciliation in the divided city. In his opening statement, Lynch announced that the riot commission was a public court of inquiry designed to establish what had happened that summer so that government officials and political leaders could devise and implement policies and practices that led to the better protection of the peace and the safety of the city.[39] In reality, however, the inquiry also operated as another phase of the riots, as various lawyers and government officials used the court as a public arena to establish partisan narratives about who and what were responsible. Catholic and Liberal lawyers were more effective than their Tory and Orange opponents in the inquiry, crafting a compelling narrative of Belfast exceptionalism that emphasized Orange and evangelical Protestant provocation and Catholic victimization.

This became the established story of the Belfast riots of 1857, a framework that informed (and constrained) British and Irish thinking about communal relations in modern Belfast.[40] The figure of the

38. *Ulsterman*, September 7, 1857; *Belfast News-Letter*, September 8, 1857; Doyle, *Fighting like the Devil for the Sake of God*, 94–95.
39. David Lynch, *1857 Belfast Riots Inquiry*, 17.
40. Morris, "Reading the Riot Commission," 194–219.

evangelical preacher or Orange cleric was an important component in this construct, a potent symbol of Belfast's supposedly fundamental sectarian irrationality. Nowhere was this clearer than in *Punch*'s September 1857 "The Ballad of Roaring Hanna," which laid the blame for the deadly violence in Belfast on the provocations of Protestant ministers who should know better.

> Reverend Drew and Cooke and Roe,
> Roaring Hanna
> Where Orange hates and Papist glows,
> Roaring Hanna
> In Church 't were wiser, if more slow,
> Roaring Hanna
> To preach "the word" without "the blow,"
> Roaring Hanna . . . [41]

Although the British comic newspaper's focus was on Hanna, its use of Drew and Cooke in the opening line was telling, reflective of their symbolic power and long careers as anti-Catholic orators in Belfast. The notion that the emotional harangues of evangelical clergymen fostered sectarian violence in the north of Ireland was, of course, not new. Earlier that year, Thomas D'Arcy McGee, the former Young Irelander, celebrated the moral courage of the Catholic bishop of Derry, Edward Maginn, by contrasting his quiet strength with the enthusiastic political sermons that prepared men for violence by celebrating "bloody deeds delivered in the name of religion," a clear reflection of a well-established trope about Ulster's ranting clergymen.[42] The Belfast riots of 1857, however, gave unprecedented scope to this view and

---

41. "The Ballad of Roaring Hanna," *Punch*, September 26, 1857.
42. McGee, *Life of the Reverend Edward Maginn*, ix. It is tempting to think that the author had Drew in mind, but there is no tangible evidence. McGee visited Belfast for a few days in 1856, but he had plenty of experience with anti-Catholic preachers, and his comments likely reflected this general phenomenon. My thanks to David A. Wilson for providing his expertise on this matter.

it was perhaps here that Drew played his most important role in the making of Victorian Belfast.

Resident Magistrate William Tracy, the first witness called to provide evidence at the inquiry, began his testimony by detailing the events that occurred at Christ Church, recalling efforts to contain the crowds who had gathered to witness the spectacle. He argued that it had been "very indiscreet" for Drew to preach such a fiery partisan sermon and was one of many who held Drew responsible for the ensuing violence. Throughout Tracy's testimony, as well as that of two policemen who followed, O'Rorke and Rea, the two lawyers representing Belfast Catholics at the inquiry, continually referenced Drew, linking the minister to the municipal police, evangelical street preaching, and the Orange Order, three factors that ultimately would be blamed for the riots. O'Rorke repeatedly asked witnesses whether Drew had worn an orange scarf over his black clerical robes while he delivered his infamous 12th of July sermon (he had not). Christ Church also featured prominently in the testimony of John McLaughlin, owner of the *Ulsterman*, and John Hacket, an overseer at a Falls Road bakery who chaired the first meeting of the Catholic Gun Club, a largely plebeian association formed in late July and August 1857 to defend Belfast Catholics from sectarian attacks. Both had attended Drew's sermon and provided rich details of the insignia worn by the majority of the audience. While McIlwaine reminded the commissioners that Drew's name had been misused by the Belfast press to stir up trouble in late August and September 1857, his testimony failed to counter an established narrative that featured Drew as a central player in the summer's violence.[43]

Irish newspapers provided saturation coverage of the investigation, providing a national audience for these stories. A simple search

43. Evidence of William Tracy, *1857 Belfast Riots Inquiry*, 20–37; evidence of Thomas Lindsay, *1857 Belfast Riots Inquiry*, 38-45; evidence of Harris Bindon, *1857 Belfast Riots Inquiry*, 55; evidence of Thomas Green, *1857 Belfast Riots Inquiry*, 65; evidence of William McIlwaine, *1857 Belfast Riots Inquiry*, 75; evidence of John McLaughlin, *1857 Belfast Riots Inquiry*, 109–22; evidence of John Hacket, *1857 Belfast Riots Inquiry*, 134–35.

of the British Library's newspaper archive shows that seventy-two Irish newspapers mentioned Drew in 463 articles in September and early October 1857. References to Drew came particularly thick and fast during the first week of the inquiry, as Tracy and other officials recounted the events of the July phase of the riots. While Belfast newspapers provided the most frequent coverage of the riots commission, Dublin was not far behind.[44] On September 19 *Freeman's Journal*, the influential nationalist newspaper, argued that Belfast had not known a day without "riot, bloodshed, battery, and house-wrecking" since that "memorable day on which the Rev. Dr. Drew had preached to the Orangemen at Christ Church."[45] Conservative and liberal newspapers in Belfast took a more nuanced line, with both the *Belfast News-Letter* and the *Belfast Daily Mercury* emphasizing the fact that the Orangemen in Christ Church went home quietly that evening.[46] This interpretation, however, did not seem to diminish Drew's role in the dominant narrative that emerged from the inquiry. When the Lord Lieutenant wrote to Thomas Larcom to commend the work of the investigation, he reminded himself to get "the extract from Dr. Drew's sermon mentioned in the report."[47] Months later, the *Freeman's Journal* was still focused on Drew, arguing that it was his "hot stimulant" that transformed "drum-beating, fife-squeaking, and marching in Sandy Row" into something far more serious.[48]

The publication of the commission's report in February 1858 brought renewed attention to the 1857 riots. In the report, Lynch

44. *Belfast Mercury* led the way with thirty-nine hits, followed by *Northern Whig* (thirty-four), *Dublin Daily Express* (thirty), and *Belfast News-Letter* (twenty-four). Drew received significant coverage in three of Dublin's most important Catholic and nationalist newspapers: *Freeman's Journal* (sixteen), *Catholic Telegraph* (thirteen), and *Dublin Evening Post* (thirteen).

45. *Freeman's Journal*, September 18, 1857.

46. *Belfast Daily Mercury*, September 25, 1857; *Belfast News-Letter*, September 18, 1857.

47. Earl of Carlisle to Thomas Larcom, November 30, 1857, Larcom Papers, NLI, MS 7624/73.

48. *Freeman's Journal*, February 10, 1858.

and Smythe outlined a series of factors they believed were responsible for the riots. The account underlined just how thoroughly Belfast Catholics and Liberals had "won the inquiry," blaming the aggression of the Orange system, the rhetorical excess of the Belfast press (the *Ulsterman* was singled out), the irresponsible behavior of evangelical Protestant ministers, and, above all, the continuing power of sectarian partisanship within the Pound and Sandy Row for the violence of that summer.[49] Frequently mentioned in the evidence, Drew was not named in the report, although he was one of the people implicated in the report's pointed critique of the Orange Order: "The celebration of that festival by the Orange party in Belfast, is plainly and unmistakably, the originating cause of the riots. . . . Popular confederacies are perilous, because they generally become unmanageable."[50] Clearly, it was not only Belfast Catholics who found Drew's extremism unpalatable.

The riots commission and its report quickly entered ultra-Protestant and Orange lore as another example of liberal appeasement—the loyal Protestant watchmen—attacked again. The subject of the riots, and the supposed calumnies poured on Drew and the Orangemen of Belfast, was taken up at three separate meetings of the Grand Orange Lodge of Ireland County Lodge in the late summer and fall of 1857. On July 28, "Dr. Drew paid the lodge a visit and closed the proceedings with prayer and afterwards explained away his conduct during the recent riots and the false reports that had gone forth and also that the Orangemen were found to have been participants in the late disgraceful disturbances." The following week the lodge held a special meeting to put together a public address of support for Drew and later that year pledged to hold a special soiree as a kind of testimonial to the beloved doctor.[51] Drew kindly refused the honor, at least until the Grand Lodge had met on the matter.

49. Report, *1857 Belfast Riots Inquiry*, 2–14.
50. Report, *1857 Belfast Riots Inquiry*, 8–10.
51. GOLI, County Minutes, July 28, 1857, August 8, 1857, October 16, 1857, MOH.

While Drew was consistently critical of the summer's "disgraceful" riots, he certainly never exhibited any remorse for his own role in the controversies—quite the contrary. Arguing that his July sermon had been misrepresented, Drew gave the lecture again in Christ Church on February 14, 1858, a week after the publication of the commission's report. In a letter to the undersecretary in Dublin Castle, Tracy reported that he had never seen a larger or more excited congregation at the church and that Drew had promised his audience that he would give similar sermons on Sunday evenings to come. This, Tracy made clear, could only lead to trouble in the future.[52] A month later, Drew told district leaders that a recent article in the *Downshire Protestant* outlining how Orangemen should act in court should be distributed at the local lodge level.[53] If British and Irish commentators blamed Drew for the violence of 1857, he did not seem to mind, clearly reveling in his role as Sandy Row's Orange champion.

The publication of the 1857 report failed to bring cloture to the streets of Belfast, which saw the return of large-scale sectarian attacks in late May and early June 1858. The precipitant event was a funeral procession on May 30 for the daughter-in-law of John Hacket, former leader of the Catholic Gun Club. As the procession passed Sandy Row on the way to Friar's Bush Graveyard, Protestant residents began to trade blows with Catholic marchers and a stone-throwing melee soon broke out at the newly christened Boyne Bridge. While magistrates and police managed to separate the parties, the fight initiated a cycle of sectarian attacks across the city over the next few days. Both Catholic and Protestant activists were involved. Two Presbyterian ministers were assaulted by a Catholic crowd on May 31 while Protestant rioters attacked a series of Catholic and Liberal sites in the town: Bernard Hughes's bakery on Fountain Lane, the *Northern Whig*'s offices, and

---

52. William Tracy to Thomas Larcom, February 15, 1858, Larcom Papers, NLI, 7624/85; Dawson, "Annals of Christ Church, Belfast," 221.

53. GOLI Belfast County Minutes, March 30, 1858.

two Catholic churches: St. Malachy's and St. Patrick's. On June 2 the *Belfast News-Letter* claimed that the town was in worse shape than it had been the previous year.[54]

The newspaper was hardly alone in its anxiety. Both McIlwaine and Drew wrote missives to the new Tory Lord Chancellor, Sir Joseph Napier, deploring the "revival" of rioting and asking for effective action from Dublin Castle. Drew's letter started on a cautious and thoughtful note, warning Napier that military displays often provoked as many problems as they solved, an argument that reflected a growing sense of resentment about state action, particularly about policing and enforcement of the law outlawing party processions, among working-class Protestants. He closed with a polite but stinging critique of local magistrates, asking for the appointment of stipendiary magistrates to take control of military forces in Belfast: "They [resident magistrates] are excellent, honourable, and kind hearted men, I cannot, however, but deplore their indecision and hesitation to enforce the law in September, from whence such an excess of turbulence occurred. And judging from what I witnessed on last evening, I would say, no time can safely be lost in appointing determined, cool, and experienced men to save us from further calamities."[55] As time would make clear, Drew's opinions about the state's application of force and enforcement of the law very much depended upon who was being targeted.

Dublin Castle soon responded with a show of hitherto unseen force, ordering an infantry regiment, a calvary regiment, and one hundred reserve constables north to Belfast. Military officers and two additional resident magistrates were given detailed instructions on how to use these additional forces to end the unrest. By June 4, there were more than 300 constables, 170 cavalrymen, and 1,000 infantrymen

54. *Belfast News-Letter*, May 31, 1858, June 2, 1858, June 3, 1858; *Ulsterman*, May 31, 1858; Doyle, *Fighting like the Devil for the Sake of God*, 144–48.

55. Thomas Drew to Sir Joseph Napier, June 1, 1858; William McIlwaine to Sir Joseph Napier, June 2, 1858, Larcom Papers, NLI, MS 7624/94–5. Courtesy of the National Library of Ireland.

patrolling the streets of Belfast.[56] Two days later, the city was quiet. The Belfast riots of 1857 were finally over. Or so it seemed.

CONCLUSION: TRANSLATING ANTI-CATHOLICISM INTO SECTARIANISM

The historian John Wolffe has stressed that there is "nothing inevitable about the translation of Protestant-Catholic difference into Protestant-Catholic conflict."[57] The Belfast riots of 1857 illustrate the complex process of translation involved in turning anti-Catholic sentiment into sectarian contention. Despite the understandable focus on the graphic language of his 12th of July sermon, Drew's relationship to the outbreak of violence was less direct than often assumed. Despite the anticipation of conflict, the gathered Orangemen marched out of Christ Church and returned to their homes in Sandy Row with relative ease, aided by the strategic placement of police at critical flashpoints. Drew's emotional harangue did not whip up his listeners into an anti-Catholic frenzy that translated directly into violence. This should not surprise, since there was little that was novel about Drew's sermon, which did not differ radically from the anniversary sermons and political lectures he had been giving in Christ Church and throughout Belfast for more than a decade. This does not mean that the report commissioners were wrong when they linked Drew to the outbreak of the riots. It is impossible to disagree with William Tracy's assessment that "it was very indiscreet of Dr. Drew to preach that sermon."[58] What was different this time, however, was context rather than content; reputation, reception, and response as much as religious prejudice.

Thomas Drew was influential with both his Christ Church congregation and his Orange brethren and their supporters across the

---

56. Doyle, *Fighting like the Devil for the Sake of God*, 146.
57. Wolffe, "Exploring the History of Catholic-Protestant Conflict," 1–21.
58. Evidence of William Tracy, *1857 Belfast Riots Inquiry*, 31.

Protestant working class in Belfast. But the exact nature of the influence is what is of interest here. Too often analysts have taken a simple top-down perspective on these issues, giving figures like Drew far more control over events than they actually possessed. As the previous chapter's brief examination of the Orange Order in the 1850s illustrates, Drew could not simply take his working-class brethren where he wanted them to go. He certainly had substantial influence, solid ties built through his public advocacy for the Protestant working class (and opposition to Roman Catholicism), his commitment to the Orange Order and patronage and support of its members, but his ideological and political influence was supportive and coordinative rather than creative; his anti-Catholicism reinforced and legitimated already existent and potent beliefs. Both his speeches at the meetings of the Christ Church Protestant Association and his work with Orange Order were meant to mobilize and defend rather than convert; his confrontational commitment to the Church of Ireland and extreme anti-Catholicism typically alienated Ulster Presbyterians and more moderate Irish Protestants alike. Drew's populist ties to the Protestant working class may have crowded out the development of alternative collectivities that might have transcended the sectarian binaries that Drew and his ultra-Protestants celebrated, but they did not do so on simple middle-class terms; this was not a simple process of "taming the working classes."

Drew played a more direct role in the making of Victorian Belfast through the organization of anti-Catholic spectacle; his creation of a widely advertised set-piece confrontation in the streets outside of Christ Church in July 1857. While the public rites surrounding his 12th of July sermon did not lead directly to violence, the ritual display and territorial assertion did provoke a reaction from local Catholics, helping to create an emotive and increasingly threatening confrontational cycle that sparked fear and violence across the Pound and Sandy Row. Drew's reputation as a divisive anti-Catholic polemicist and advocate for the Orange Order was essential to this mix, a fact underlined by the wrongful use of his name to mobilize Belfast Catholics against the insult of open-air evangelical preaching in September

1857. Mark Doyle is undoubtedly correct to say that Drew was a "symbol of all that was threatening about militant Protestantism" in Belfast.[59] If Drew's extremism and working-class populism limited the reach of his influence within Belfast and Irish Protestant politics more than contemporaries realized, the depth and consistency of Drew's career in anti-Catholic politics helps us to understand why many Irish Catholics saw him as the worst man in all of Ulster.

59. Doyle, *Fighting like the Devil for the Sake of God*, 93.

7
A Clerical Watchman
Life after Belfast, 1859–1870

On July 10, 1859, Thomas Drew gave a special 12th of July sermon to the Orangemen of Lecale District at Down Cathedral in Downpatrick. The lecture was one of Drew's first public performances after a promotion led him to leave Christ Church, delivered to a large and enthusiastic audience of supporters who had crowded into the cathedral.[1] Speaking from Galatians 4:16—"Have I now become your enemy by telling you the truth?"—Drew roused the partisan audience with a vivid and familiar harangue, describing the unchanging nature and heretical threat of Roman Catholicism in thick and evocative detail, celebrating God's deliverance of the Protestant people, and underlining the need for a militant culture of active remembrance, epitomized by the "watchful, intelligent and brave men" who sustained the Orange societies in Ireland and throughout the British Empire. While Drew closed with a more sympathetic plea that Protestants must hold the cause of the widow and the fatherless close to their hearts, Drew's core message was a clarion call of an aggrieved and muscular ultra-Protestant politics: "Shall we cease to remember the days and men of

---

1. William Johnston's enthusiastic report in the *Downshire Protestant* estimated that two thousand people were in attendance for the sermon while the *Belfast News-Letter* stuck to the comparatively sober "to the Orangemen of Lecale." See *Downshire Protestant*, July 15, 1859; *Belfast News-Letter*, July 11, 1859. For the history of the cathedral, see Rankin, *Down Cathedral*.

Derry? Never."[2] Following the sermon, William Johnston and other members of the county's ultra-Protestant gentry collected funds for the Protestant Orphan Society and the audience slowly filed out of the cathedral to the strains of "God Save the Queen."[3] Not all observers were so positively moved by the Orange spectacle in Down Cathedral. In a letter to the *Northern Whig*, one writer complained that it was "disgraceful that houses of worship should be turned into Orange lodges, and pulpits into platforms for the use of language which, if held in a public place, and before a mixed assemblage, would, inevitably, lead to a breach of the peace."[4] While Drew had left Belfast, he had certainly not lost his ability to mobilize friend and foe alike.

Drew's departure from Belfast began in January 1859, when Robert Knox—bishop of Down, Connor, and Dromore—appointed him rector of Loughinisland Parish Church, a position that also made him precentor of Down Cathedral, and the rural dean of Mourne. Knox, a Whig evangelical unpopular in ultra-Protestant circles for his politics and his conciliatory and pragmatic approach to a range of church issues, received high marks for Drew's promotion in the conservative and Protestant press, which credited Knox for recognizing Drew's merits despite their opposing views on politics.[5] The two men certainly had close personal ties. The bishop's uncle was Edmund Knox, the longtime bishop of Limerick, and one of his first positions in the Church of Ireland had been at St. Munchin's Parish Church in Limerick, where the younger Knox took care of Drew's mother while she was dying during a cholera outbreak in 1847. Speaking at a meeting in

---

2. For the full text of Drew's sermon, see *Downshire Protestant*, July 15, 1859.

3. William Johnston of Ballykilbeg; John Waring Maxwell of Finnebrogue; William Keown of Ballydurgan House, Downpatrick; and Spencer Perceval were the leading figures mentioned.

4. *Northern Whig*, July 27, 1859.

5. R. B. McDowell's description of Knox's diocesan career is worth quoting: "Knox, with calm tenacity, maintained his Whig principles in an unsympathetic environment." See McDowell, *Church of Ireland*, 8; Acheson, *History of the Church of Ireland*, 175.

Downpatrick in November 1860, Drew praised Knox in the highest terms, thanking him for both his friendship and the promotion.[6] He was not alone in his newfound happiness. Citing Drew's close ties to the region, his long experience as an effective pastor, and his support for Orangeism and pure Protestantism, Johnston's *Downshire Protestant* made it clear that the people of Seaforde were delighted with the selection of this Protestant champion and "familiar friend."[7] Thomas Drew had found a new home.

It is easy to understand why Drew accepted the position. Throughout his career, Drew occasionally talked about wanting to leave Belfast, citing the relatively low pay and the high demands of the position. Notably, the Loughinisland rectorship was worth more than £400 annually (significantly more than Christ Church) and it no doubt appealed to Drew's rural nostalgia and sense of history. Situated amidst the beautiful countryside eight miles southwest of Downpatrick, Loughinisland Parish Church is located in Seaforde village, featuring picturesque views of the Mourne Mountains and overlooking the demesne lands of the Forde estate. The Forde connection was a crucial one for Drew. Lady Harriet Forde long had been an active supporter of his, with whom she shared an active interest in vital religion and philanthropy for the poor. Drew had preached regularly at the Forde's Hollymount Church on the outskirts of Downpatrick since it opened in 1840, a practice that he maintained for the remainder of his life.[8] Lady Forde was related to the Reverend Henry Maxwell, sixth Baron of Farnham, linking her to one of the chief families involved in the so-called Second Reformation of the 1820s.[9] These networks serve as a nice reminder of the intimate circles of the Church of Ireland

---

6. For Drew's praise of Knox's treatment of his mother, see *Belfast News-Letter*, November 29, 1860.

7. *Downshire Protestant*, January 10, 1859.

8. Diary of William Johnston, 1848–54, PRONI, D.880/2/1–6.

9. For the Farnham's conversion effort at their Kingscourt estate in County Cavan, see Whelan, *The Bible War in Ireland*, 172–76; Akenson, *Discovering the End of Time*, 219–20.

evangelical and military families that nurtured and sustained clerical careers. When Lady Forde died in February 1868, Drew officiated at her funeral at Hollymount, calling her an "angel of piety and benevolence," and celebrating her as an evangelical ideal; a woman who comforted the poor and sick in the county infirmary and "yearned for holiness."[10]

If Drew's Seaforde parishioners were delighted with their new minister, the members of his old congregation, his Orange brethren, and the Belfast conservative establishment were sorry to lose the man who had done so much to build, expand, and sustain the Christ Church community (or at least they said so in public). In a characteristic review of Drew's impact on the city, the *Belfast News-Letter* emphasized his hard work in creating and fostering a largely working-class congregation, celebrating his advocacy for the poor, and the creation of schoolhouses and mission rooms throughout Belfast. The Christ Church congregation was losing, it reported, "a kind friend, an able and talented preacher and a zealous and efficient minister."[11] His Orange brethren certainly agreed. Speaking at a reunion of the Drew Lodge (LOL 684), a man named McQuitty celebrated Drew's pastoral activity, the affection with which he was held by his congregation, and his unflinching support of the dignity and brotherhood of the Orange Order.[12]

Other reactions were more equivocal. While the *Belfast Daily Mercury* admitted that Drew was an effective pastor who served the poor energetically and faithfully, the paper highlighted the damage done by Drew's divisive public politics: "He did considerable mischief by inflaming religious animosities, and keeping alive an insane spirit of party. That he was wrong-headed but conscientious, we never doubted. Simply in his ministerial character he was most estimable and laborious, while as a party politician he presented a marvelous contrast,

---

10. *Downpatrick Recorder*, February 22, 1868.
11. *Belfast News-Letter*, January 4, 1859.
12. *Belfast News-Letter*, July 14, 1860.

for he was the very antipodes of what a Christian minister should be."[13] The paper went on to congratulate both Drew and Knox for the appointment, arguing that Drew had never received the rewards he deserved from the party that he had served so actively through the years.[14] His congregants clearly agreed, and it was soon announced that Richard Davison, Charles Lanyon, and other leading members of the Christ Church congregation were raising money for a tribute fund for Drew.

The testimonials began in early June, when a group of congregants and teachers gave Drew an elaborate set of canonicals and furnished the study of his new home.[15] A week later, Charles Lanyon presided over a formal meeting at Christ Church, where it was announced that the testimonial committee had raised £1,000 to honor the former Christ Church minister, a substantial proportion of which came from members of the Belfast conservative establishment. The congregation's printed public address celebrated Drew's pastoral activism and outreach work, particularly his efforts to bring religious education to the Belfast poor through cottage lectures, missions, and schools. In a printed reply, Drew stressed his own unworthiness for such a kindness, saying that he feared that this "farewell address" gave him too much credit and overlooked his many mistakes. That said, Drew was thankful for their words and hoped they would continue to work together in the same great cause:

> By the memory of our past sorrows and joys, our united testimonies, our Protestant platforms, our common rations, our oft-blended supplications, I ask your prayers and intercessions for every work and labour of love which we have shared together; for the new Pastor, that God may bless him richly, and with all honour; that years of

---

13. *Belfast Daily Mercury*, January 5, 1859.

14. *Belfast Daily Mercury*, January 5, 1859. It is notable that the *Ulsterman* provided little commentary on the departure of the man who been such an emblematic figure in their coverage of Belfast politics.

15. *Belfast News-Letter*, June 17, 1859.

prosperity and a great harvest of souls may be given to him; that he may escape the snares of Satan and rejoice amidst the blessings of the old, the young, the sick, the poor – the widow and the fatherless, ..., of all who look up to him for words of life and consolation.[16]

Drew closed his public letter by asking his old parishioners to pray that as he enjoyed the comparative quiet of rural society, he would be able to move forward in the "evening of his life" toward a place where "no enemy came in and no friend goes out."[17] Drew and his family moved to south Down in the middle of May. With characteristic energy, he began his new position with a series of outreach initiatives, holding a prayer meeting in Seaforde Courthouse and giving lectures in various schoolhouses across the area. The *Belfast News-Letter* applauded the "healthy and practical tone" of Drew's lectures, seeing them as an effective conservative counterpunch to the dangerous religious enthusiasm of the 1859 revival.[18] The new rector's ambition and popularity soon led to other initiatives as well, most notably the expansion and renovation of Loughinisland Parish Church. Funded by the Church of Ireland's Ecclesiastical Commission as well as private donations from Colonel William Brownlow Forde, Drew, and his new congregation, the church reopened in December 1862, featuring a new transept; a memorial window dedicated to Forde's father, the Reverend William Brownlow Forde; and a new chancel, pews, and pulpit designed by Thomas Drew Jr. A ceremony to celebrate the reopening of the church featured women from the Christ Church

---

16. *Downshire Protestant*, July 1, 1859.
17. *Downshire Protestant*, July 1, 1859.
18. *Belfast News-Letter*, July 2, 1859. While Christ Church was not at the center of Belfast revivalism, it was not exempt from controversy. When Denis Browne, dean of Emly, argued that he saw no evidence that the "finger of God" was involved in the physical manifestations at the heart of the revival, an estimated one hundred people walked out of Christ Church. See *Belfast Morning News*, July 13, 1859. For the historiography of the revival, see Holmes, "Ulster Revival of 1859," 488–515.

congregation in Belfast, who, according to one report, formed a kind of amateur choir for the day, performing "various chants and psalms with excellent effect."[19] The architectural reviews of the renovations were equally positive, and the *Downpatrick Recorder* enthused that the reopened parish church was one of "the most beautiful and well arranged" churches in the diocese.[20]

Throughout the final decade of his life, Drew remained active in many of the same causes that had dominated his public career in Belfast, acting as a forceful advocate for the Orange Order and ultra-Protestant and conservative politics. Drew continued to be an active participant in a host of associations dedicated to moral and social reform, with a particular focus on Sunday schools and the Protestant Orphan Society. In public meetings throughout the 1860s, he reveled in his newfound role as the stalwart senior voice of conservative principle and experience, providing largely predictable commentary on some of the decade's most dramatic events: the Belfast riots of 1864, the Fenian Rising of 1867, and the disestablishment of the Church of Ireland in 1869. Even in his final decade, Drew remained something of a wild card, exemplified by his vocal support for William Johnston and land reform in the election of 1868. He retained powerful connections to Belfast, regularly traveling there to give lectures and sermons at Christ Church and other venues.

Orange politics continued to dominate his public persona—in both a positive and a negative sense. On August 12, 1862, Drew returned to Belfast to attend the Great Protestant Demonstration, where thousands of Orangemen crowded into the recently opened Ulster Hall to hear Orange favorites like Johnston, Hugh "Roaring" Hanna, and Sir William Verner inveigh against the British government's lack of appreciation and support for the Orange Order. Drew took his turn

---

19. *Belfast News-Letter*, December 17, 1862.

20. *Downpatrick Recorder*, December 20, 1862; Blackwood, *Some Biographical Notices of the Rectors of Loughinisland*, 14–15.

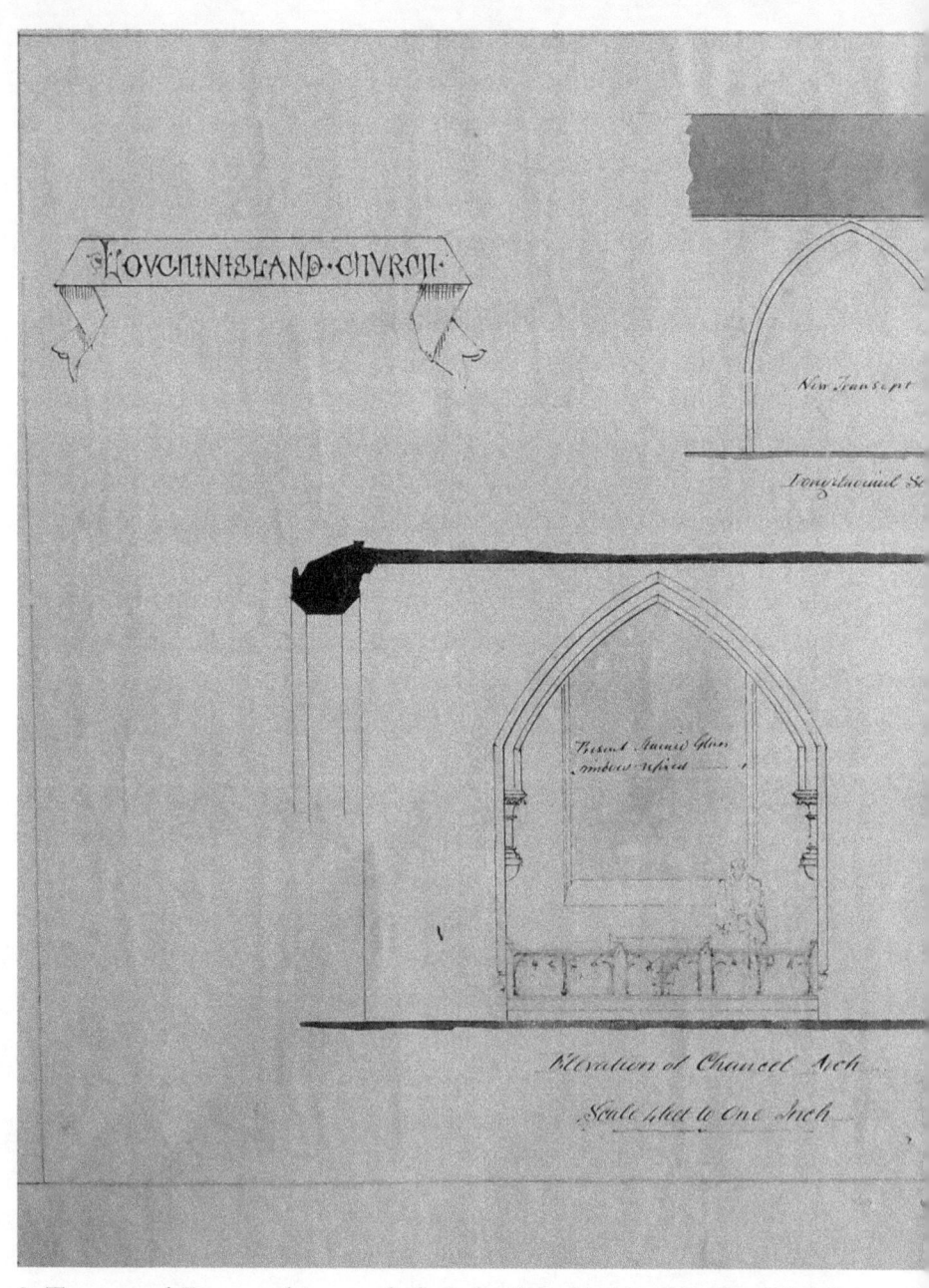

8. Turner and Drew architectural plans for Loughinisland Parish Church, 1862. Representative Church Body Library, Architectural Drawings, Portfolio 11. © Representative Church Body Library.

Transverse Section thro' Vestry and Chancel

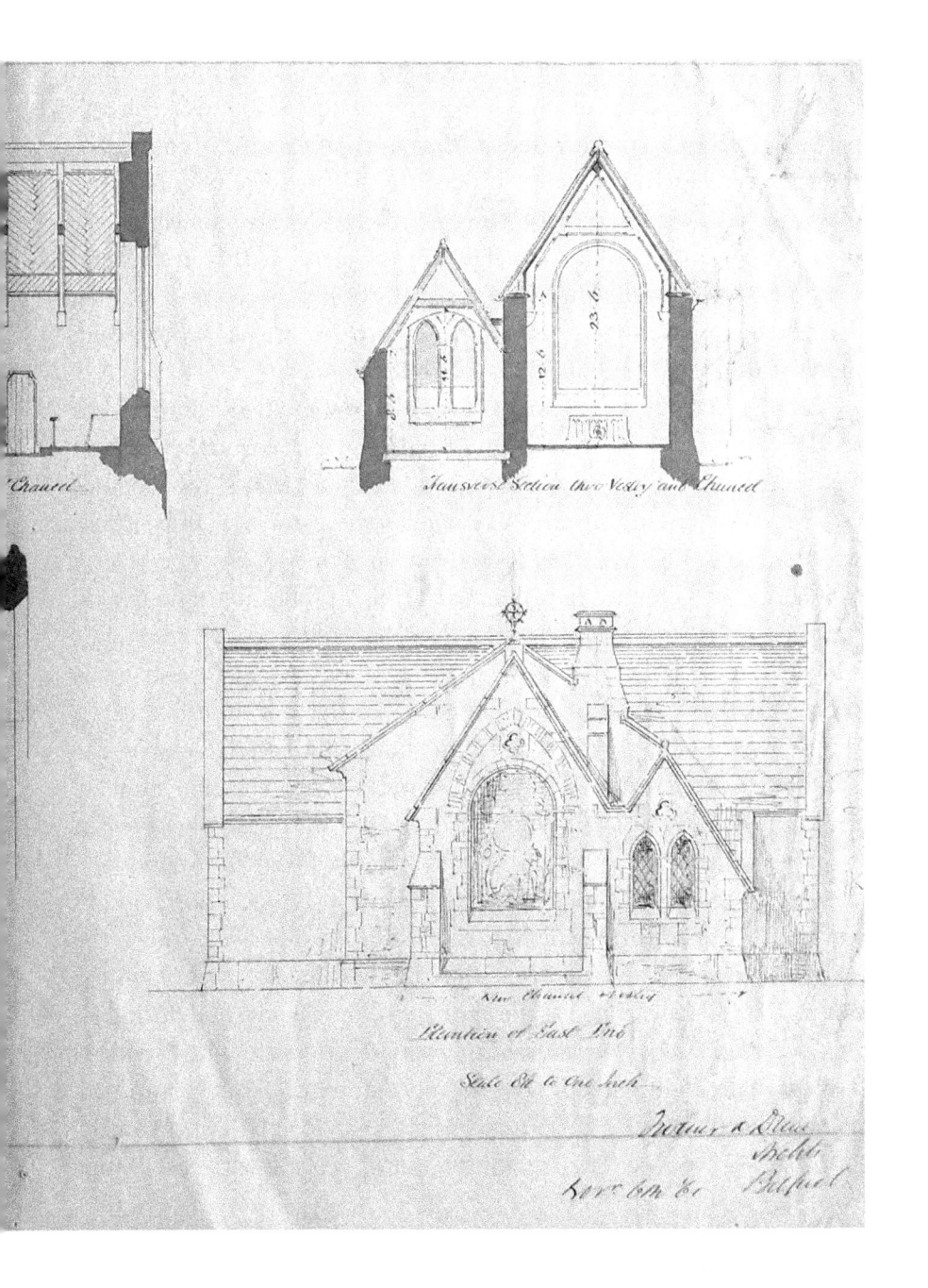

Elevation of East End

Scale 8ft to One Inch

Watson & Drew
Arch'ts
Lower 6th St Belfast

onstage, celebrating the fact that so many Protestant gentlemen had joined with his Orange brethren to stand against Romanism. Drew's particular critique was directed at Maynooth, which, he argued, continued to send forth graduates burdened with "false teachings and theology." These were men who were not likely, Drew reasoned, to use their influence "to reduce the shedding of blood at this moment in the South of Ireland." He ended his speech on a more positive note, celebrating his twenty-six years in Sandy Row, where he had baptized, married, and taught so many of those in the audience.[21]

The episode also underlines how Irish nationalists continued to see Drew as a vital symbol of the fundamental irrationality of Belfast Orangeism. The *Freeman's Journal* mocked Drew's performance in Ulster Hall, saying that he was a worthy successor to Hanna, a man who "descanted on the coming hour when 'Popery' and 'the hole of Maynooth' will cease to have a place in Ireland." The newspaper went on to argue that it was high time that the "enlightened" merchants who had built Belfast challenged these "mountebanks" who made such a "ribald mockery of their religion."[22] After rioting broke out in the aftermath of another Protestant demonstration in September, the *Freeman's Journal* returned its attention to Drew (who had not attended the event): "But what will Orange Ulster say in its indignation when it learns that the Rev. Thomas Drew, the Rev. W. McIlwaine, and the Rev. Theophilus Campbell were absent on the occasion without leave. . . . These three worthies for the last sixteen years were the clerical watchmen who were stationed by their lay brethren upon the towers to sound the alarm at the approach of an enemy; and during all that period the most faithful sentinel was Dr. Drew."[23] The *Freeman's Journal* again highlighted Drew's Orange harangues, which, it argued, had produced "so much animosity and party strife in Belfast," but worried that his "back-sliding" might get him in trouble with his Orange

21. *Belfast News-Letter*, August 13, 1862.
22. *Freeman's Journal*, August 14, 1862.
23. *Freeman's Journal*, September 19, 1862.

brethren.[24] It would not be the last time that the *Freeman's Journal* used Drew in this way.

The *Freeman's Journal* need not have worried, for Drew remained one of the most popular speakers on the Orange circuit throughout the 1860s, mobilizing the faithful and galvanizing his enemies with special sermons on the 12th of July and the 5th of November. Drew's remarkable popularity as an Orange speaker is perhaps best emblemized by the fact that his speeches occasionally were performed by others in advertised sessions. In October 1864, Stewart Blacker, a prominent landlord and Orange leader in north Armagh, recited a lecture that Drew had given at a recent Protestant Association meeting in Ballymena to supporters who had gathered at a school on the outskirts of Portadown.[25] One of Drew's final public lectures was a 12th of July sermon delivered at St. Thomas Church in Dublin on July 10, 1870, where the elderly minister celebrated the deliverance of the Irish Protestant people and admonished his audience to fulfill their Protestant responsibilities and duties.[26] For friend and foe alike, he was the epitome of the Orange political minister. Drew remained steadfast in the belief that the clergy had to play a more active political role if Britain was to recapture its status as a godly nation. He made this case forcefully in a public letter in July 1867, arguing that the continued exclusion of Anglican clergy from the House of Commons was "unnatural and injurous [sic] to the state."[27] Drew never lost his political focus.

We have already seen that Drew's use of Down Cathedral in Downpatrick to give special sermons to Orangemen generated public

---

24. *Freeman's Journal*, September 19, 1862. Mark Doyle has argued that the September 1862 riots in Belfast illustrate the ways that Dublin Castle's approach to sectarian riots fostered ultra-Protestant alienation and resentment. See Doyle, *Fighting like the Devil for the Sake of God*, 148–54.

25. *Belfast News-Letter*, October 18, 1864.

26. *Belfast News-Letter*, July 14, 1870.

27. *Downpatrick Recorder*, July 13, 1867.

controversy, drawing opposition from a range of commentators who found such partisan performances inappropriate in what was, after all, a venue of the established church. The issue came to a head in the summer of 1860, when Thomas Woodward, dean of Down, allowed the Reverend Samuel Potter, deputy grand chaplain of the Grand Orange Lodge of Ireland, to preach a 12th of July sermon in the cathedral. Potter was subsequently invited to preach in Belfast despite the public opposition of Knox, whose efforts to prevent the Orange sermon triggered predictable outrage from the *Downshire Protestant*, which argued that Knox was now returning to his true colors, showing that it was clear that Drew's promotion had been more about getting him out of Belfast than recognizing his considerable merits. Opposing a good evangelical service was, Johnston argued, a strange way to promote Protestantism in Ireland.[28]

When Johnston wrote to Woodward to ask if Drew could provide a special 5th of November service for the Lecale Orangemen, Woodward demurred, saying that it had never been the custom to celebrate that day with divine service in the cathedral and that he would have to say no in this case. Both the *Belfast News-Letter* and the *Downshire Protestant* critiqued Woodward and Dublin Castle for their lack of support for what they termed *true Protestantism*, with the latter arguing that Woodward's refusal showed how "ardent zeal in maintaining the Protestant religion was now incompatible" with Liberal government in Ireland.[29] When the state refused to accept the partisan demands of Orange loyalty, ultra-Protestant cries of betrayal were rarely far behind. The defeat was temporary; Drew gave Orange sermons on the 12th of July and the 5th of November at parish churches across the diocese throughout the decade, commemorating the Gunpowder Plot

28. *Downshire Protestant*, August 17, 1860.

29. *Downshire Protestant*, October 19, 1860; *Belfast News-Letter*, October 20, 1860. Frustrated by the Church of Ireland, the Orangemen settled for a sermon by the Reverend Hugh Hanna in a local Presbyterian church instead. See Rankin, *Down Cathedral*, 137–38. Drew continued to give 12th of July sermons to the Lecale Orangemen in Downpatrick throughout the decade.

in Down Cathedral in November 1866 in front of a large and enthusiastic audience.[30]

Drew's response to the Belfast riots of 1864 sounded a similar theme. The riots themselves originated in a heated controversy over the right to march, always a touchstone issue for working-class Orangemen. On August 8 Irish nationalists celebrated the erection of a monument to Daniel O'Connell with a massive procession through central Dublin, a festival that attracted an estimated thirty thousand people from outside the capital. Sponsored by the Catholic hierarchy and associated with various strands of Irish nationalism, the procession was deemed to be legal by Dublin Castle, a general reflection of the state's tendency to allow partisan marches to occur in areas where they were not controversial. However logical, this was a decision that enraged Orangemen and their supporters already aggrieved by the regular arrests of Orange marchers under the terms of the Party Processions Act. When a group of Belfast Catholics who had attended the Dublin festivities returned to Belfast that evening via excursion train, they were greeted by several thousand people at the Boyne Bridge in Sandy Row, an unruly crowd that featured men firing shots in the air and a burning effigy of O'Connell. While the Sandy Row loyalists seemed to be content to have sent a clear partisan message that night, the ritualized provocation initiated a cycle of rumor and suspicion that quickly escalated into deadly city-wide riots that left at least three people dead, and 325 men, women, and children wounded. In addition to Belfast's own municipal police force, over 1,000 members of the Royal Irish Constabulary and 1,300 troops were deployed in the northern capital to quell the violence, generating accusations of police partisanship and provocation that dominated public discussion in the aftermath of the 1864 riots.[31]

---

30. *Downpatrick Recorder*, November 10, 1866.

31. For policing and the 1864 riots, see Doyle, *Fighting like the Devil for the Sake of God*, 160–91; Hirst, *Religion, Politics and Violence in 19th Century Belfast*, 165–70; Griffin, *Bulkies*, 116–39. For new work on the 1864 riots, see Miller and Mac Suibhne, "Frank Roney and the Fenians," 23–54.

9. Attack on St. Malachy's Church, Belfast riots, 1864. *Illustrated Times*, September 10, 1864. Newspaper image © The British Library Board. All rights reserved. With thanks to the British Newspaper Archive: www.britishnewspaperarchive.co.uk.

Drew's response was predictable. In a letter first published in the *Cork Constitution*, he made it clear that he believed Irish nationalists and Dublin Castle were responsible for the Belfast riots of 1864. Claiming to know Belfast politics quite well after his twenty-five years at Christ Church, Drew argued that "Northern Protestants" had been aroused to fury by the illegal and disloyal celebration in Dublin, a feeling made all the worse by the government's allegedly one-sided application of the Party Processions Act:

> The people of the North felt judgment to see Protestants withering in every county jail in Ulster because of some infinitesimal breaches of the Anti-Processions Act, while the Mayors and other corporate folk from the South, with the Romish Lord Mayor of Dublin, exhibited their crimson trappings associated, with green banners, harps without crowns, pikes, and party tunes. There could be no mistake

as to the ulterior objects to which all this demonstration tended. Sir, the contentious, heart-burnings of Belfast, nay, the blood which has been spilled, must all be traced to rebel manifestations and uninterrupted illegality in the chief city in the land.[32]

Drew argued that Roman Catholics might be a minority in the united nation of Britain and Ireland, but they were an increasingly aggressive one. In this case, a British government dependent on Catholic support had refused to enforce the law of the land, and now "the wind had been sown, and the whirlwind has been reaped." Thankfully, he argued, there were still Irish Protestants who were watchful and vigilant in protecting hard-won Protestant freedoms.[33] It was a familiar argument; one that mobilized faithful supporters and offended nearly everyone else.

A similar dynamic can be seen in the Drew chaplaincy scandal of 1866, a controversy produced by Lord Derby government's less than artful handling of political patronage. Drew initially had been left off the list of nominees for the new government's viceregal chaplaincies (a position he had held under previous Conservative ministries), a decision that generated angry responses from a noisy array of Orange and Conservative elites and their supporters. The Earl of Enniskillen, Hugh Cairns, and other Conservative political leaders used their influence at Dublin Castle to get Drew back on the nomination list, which created a predictable backlash in the liberal and nationalist press. The *Northern Whig* and the *Dublin Evening Post* were particularly caustic, with the latter describing the appointment as "a gratuitous insult and wanton defiance of the opinion of the country" and calling Drew "the chief clerical representative of Orangeism in Ulster," a man who is often "made responsible for sectarian feeling by both

---

32. *Belfast News-Letter*, September 5, 1864.

33. *Belfast News-Letter*, September 5, 1864. In particular, Drew celebrated the work of the *Cork Constitution* and other local advocates for Protestantism, who saved this "remote outpost from disgrace."

friends and enemies."[34] Concerned about the nature of the selection process and doubtless weary of the bother, both the Lord Lieutenant, the second Marquess of Abercorn, and Lord Derby had Drew's name removed from consideration. It was now the Orange party's time to be aggrieved. Johnston took up Drew's cause with a characteristic fervor. Speaking at a dinner in Ballymoney, he blamed the Liberals and their newspapers for treating "the Orangeman as if he were a mad dog."[35] Drew also played an energetic role in keeping the controversy firmly in public view, mobilizing support for his nomination and attacking his opponents long after his name had been withdrawn.[36] It made no difference, and the matter was soon replaced by more weighty discussions of Fenianism, land reform, and disestablishment.

Drew soon returned to public view to support his former son-in-law, providing energetic backing for Johnston's campaign against the Party Processions Act in 1867–68.[37] This was a particularly important issue for the Orange rank and file, whose attachment to the marching tradition often generated tension with Orange leaders who wanted to avoid the resultant party clashes that undermined the order's relationship with government officials. While there was a great deal of regional variation in enforcement, over five hundred participants were arrested and imprisoned under the terms of the Party Processions Act between 1850 and 1867, generating a powerful sense of grievance among plebeian Orangemen who believed the law should be on their side.[38] Drew had been involved in the first serious challenges

34. *Dublin Evening Post*, September 22, 1866; *Northern Whig*, September 10, 1866.

35. *Dublin Evening Mail*, October 29, 1866.

36. For a detailed (if partisan) history of the Drew chaplaincy scandal, see *Dublin Evening Post*, September 19, 1866. Thomas Larcom, undersecretary to the Lord Lieutenant from 1853 to 1866, kept a cutting file of newspaper stories on the Drew controversy from the *Daily Express*, the *Dublin Evening Mail*, the *Dublin Evening Post*, and the *Northern Whig*, amongst others. See PRONI, MIC 417/2.

37. Farrell, "Recapturing the Flag," 52–78.

38. Summary of convictions on the northeast and northwest circuits for violations of the Party Processions Act, 1850–67, Mayo Papers, NLI, MS 11,202/2.

to British legislation regulating party processions in December 1860 when, with Johnston, he spoke to a gathering of the Apprentice Boys in St. Columb's Cathedral after a procession through the walled city of Derry. The issue gained more public prominence in the aftermath of the 1864 riots and Johnston and others began to mobilize support amongst Orange lodges in 1865 and 1866, when the Lecale district master hosted a large 12th of July celebration on his Ballykilbeg estate near Downpatrick, a gathering that passed off without incident despite the anxieties of Dublin Castle officials.[39] Attempting to capitalize on this momentum and the favorable political climate in the aftermath of the 1867 rising, Johnston organized a massive protest meeting against the Party Processions Act in Bangor on July 12, 1867, leading a large procession from Newtownards to Bangor. The marching issue had been particularly fraught in County Down, where at least 134 people had been charged with violating the terms of the Party Processions Act.[40] Crowd estimates for the Bangor demonstration varied widely, with the *Northern Whig* reporting that fourteen thousand people (117 Orange lodges) were in attendance, many conveyed by special trains hired to take them from Belfast and other towns and villages across the county.[41]

Johnston did not disappoint that day. He challenged the British government directly, saying that "[Orangemen and Protestants] had been trampled upon and trodden upon long enough, but they would hide their light under a bushel no longer."[42] Two months later, the government reluctantly moved to prosecute the Orange leader and twenty-three others for violating the terms of the Party Processions Act. Johnston refused to admit that he had done anything wrong, and after a period of rather awkward negotiations, he was brought to trial, found guilty, and sentenced to a brief term in jail. Prison only strengthened

39. *Correspondence between the Lord Lieutenant and William Johnston.*
40. Cases to be prosecuted for violations of the Party Processions Act at spring assizes, 1868, Mayo Papers, NLI, MS 11,202/6.
41. *Northern Whig*, July 13, 1867.
42. *Belfast News-Letter*, July 13, 1867.

Johnston's political appeal—proof that martyrdom crossed political affinities on the island. While he languished in jail, a large crowd of supporters met in Ulster Hall on March 4 to declare their sympathy and support for the Orange martyr. This was all part of a broader campaign that featured the formation of Protestant Working Men's Association, one of a host of popular loyalist organizations formed to mobilize support for Johnston's candidacy for a parliamentary seat in Belfast in the upcoming general election.[43]

Thomas Drew was one of his leading advocates, support that was both political and personal, since his late daughter Arminella had been married to Johnston before dying in childbirth in 1862. The families remained quite close, ties reflected in both the press and William Johnston's personal diaries. In March 1868 Drew appeared with Georgiana Johnston (Johnston's third wife) at a meeting in Downpatrick, where he underlined the imprisoned Johnston's qualities as a "tender husband and loving father," a man who would defend Protestant rights against an unconstitutional law. Two weeks later, Drew greeted a deputation of Lisburn Orangemen at Ballykilbeg House, while his daughter cared for the ailing Mrs. Johnston.[44] When William Johnston was freed from jail in late April, Drew appeared at his side at yet another meeting in Downpatrick, celebrating his release and calling upon the crowd to study the true history of Irish Protestantism.[45]

Johnston moved immediately to capitalize on his newfound fame, campaigning for one of Belfast's open parliamentary seats. Speaking to largely working-class audiences (many newly enfranchised by the Irish Reform Act of 1868), Johnston portrayed himself as the champion of the independent Protestant working men of Belfast, denouncing the Party Processions Act and supporting land reform. He argued that Belfast Orangemen and working-class men should have the right to nominate their own candidates rather than depend on conservative

---

43. *Belfast News-Letter*, March 5, 1868; Walker, *Ulster Politics*, 60.
44. *Belfast News-Letter*, March 20, 1868; *Downpatrick Recorder*, March 21, 1868; *Belfast News-Letter*, April 6, 1868.
45. *Belfast News-Letter*, April 28, 1868.

elites who too often ignored plebeian interests. This reflected longer running tensions within Belfast conservatism, where populists like Johnston and Drew resented the executive control held by the leaders of the conservative establishment.[46] Many Belfast Protestant workers clearly agreed in 1868, electing Johnston and Thomas McClure (a liberal Presbyterian merchant who had worked with Drew on famine relief in 1847) over the two Conservative candidates (Sir Charles Lanyon and Thomas Mulholland, owner of the prominent linen firm). Johnston's stances on the Party Processions Act, land reform, and political independence proved to have a powerful appeal in Protestant working-class districts such as Sandy Row and the Shankill Road, where the Orange hero far outdistanced his rival candidates.[47] While it was clearly a secondary factor, Drew's enthusiastic support for Johnston doubtless helped with his former congregants and Orange brethren in Belfast.

Drew's most prominent intervention in the election came on a rather surprising issue: land reform. As we have seen, Drew had always expressed concerns about the social impact caused by the excessive pursuit of profit. His critique of capitalism, however, typically was constrained and ephemeral, with Drew swiftly returning to more conventionally conservative support for business and landlord interests. In September 1868 Drew created something of a sensation when he penned a public letter to Isaac Butt critiquing the landlord-tenant system in Ireland. The letter was a direct response to a well-advertised lecture Butt had given in Limerick on tenant right, a talk that closed with an impassioned call for freedom for the "serfs of Ireland."[48] Drew's letter made clear that he agreed with the longtime Irish Tory about the need for land reform. There were good landlords, he insisted,

---

46. Bew, *Glory of Being Britons*, 193–222.

47. Wright, "Protestant Ideology and Politics in Ulster," 254–55; Walker, *Ulster Politics*, 62.

48. *Freeman's Journal*, September 5, 1868. For Butt, see Jackson, *Home Rule*, 20–37; Spence, "Isaac Butt, Irish Nationality, and the Conditional Defence of the Union," 65–89.

naming the late Lord Downshire and Lord Roden in particular, but too often landlords became petty tyrants whose financial and political demands all but eliminated the independence of their impoverished tenants.[49] The timing of Drew's call for greater political independence dovetailed nicely with Johnston's candidacy in 1868, but it also echoed his long-standing populist frustration with conservative politicians, candidates who too often were "persons born never to rise above a billiard room or a dog kennel."[50]

Drew's letter was a more coherent and tightly argued version of a lecture he had given in Belfast in March 1868, where he had identified the tenant right issue as one of the primary causes of Protestant rural depopulation.[51] Drew developed a more searching critique of the Irish land system in his response to Butt, and went even further in a remarkable public letter to Johnston published in early October, where the elderly minister wrote that Johnston's arrest and incarceration had "opened his eyes to the audacity and the selfishness of the Irish gentry." While he knew that many of his longtime friends would be offended, Drew made clear that he needed to defend a Protestant tenantry in Ireland driven into despair and poverty by an inequitable land system that denied them "the freedom, justice, and comfort . . . enjoyed by the owners of the soil."[52] When a correspondent for the *Cork Examiner* argued that it was a pity that Drew's evident humanity did not extend beyond the Protestant tenantry, Drew responded that this simply reflected his own experience with the rural Protestant population, and that the North and the South had to deal with this issue fairly if there was to be any hope of changing the unhappy state of rural Ireland.[53] Drew's critique of landlord-tenant relations took a number of liberal and nationalist commentators by surprise. The *Dublin Evening Post*, long one of Drew's fiercest critics, jokingly

49. *Northern Whig*, September 14, 1868.
50. *Dublin Evening Mail*, October 1, 1868.
51. *Belfast News-Letter*, March 12, 1868.
52. *Dublin Evening Mail*, October 1, 1868.
53. *Northern Whig*, October 13, 1868.

admitted that they might had been wrong about this most Orange of Orangemen, that perhaps the minister was "the worst understood man of his times."[54]

Drew's letter continued to have a public purchase long after the 1868 election was over, a product of his power as a Conservative and Orange symbol in the public mind. Nearly a year later, in September 1869, John Gray, an Irish Liberal MP and the owner of the *Freeman's Journal*, invoked Drew's letter repeatedly in a public letter to Johnston asking the Orange leader to advocate more forcefully for land reform. Drew had understood, Gray argued, that tenant farmers needed greater protections against evictions and increased rents.[55] Johnston went on to support Prime Minister William Gladstone's Irish Land Act of 1870. Drew's career as a land reformer, however, was over, a product of his own populist tendencies and support for Johnston's campaign for Orange democracy.

Drew's determined advocacy for Johnston only confirmed his status as a Protestant champion in the minds of his former parishioners in Sandy Row, where he and Johnston attended a ceremony laying the first stone of a new Orange Hall in July 1868.[56] When a new Orange and Protestant Hall was proposed for Agnes Street in August 1869, Drew was asked to be patron. He agreed to the honor, saying that "we cannot have too many Protestant fortresses erected now."[57] A month later, when the new Sandy Row Orange Hall was opened, several speakers celebrated "dear old Dr. Drew," hoping that "his name would be embalmed in the hearts and minds of the men and women of that district, where he had so faithfully labored as a Protestant minister, and a noble champion of their common Protestantism."[58]

If Drew's Orangeism dominated his public reputation, he remained active in a variety of other causes. He continued to be an

54. *Dublin Evening Post*, September 14, 1868.
55. *Dublin Evening Mail*, September 7, 1869.
56. Diary of William Johnston, July 4, 1868, PRONI, D.880/2/20.
57. *Belfast News-Letter*, August 5, 1869.
58. *Belfast News-Letter*, September 27, 1869.

energetic advocate for children's religious education, participating in the Church Education Society, the Church of Ireland Young Men's Society, the Protestant Orphan Society, and a variety of associations connected to Sunday school education. This was clearly a personal matter for Drew. For nearly twenty years, the minister had presided over the children's examinations at Lady Forde's schools in Hollymount, combining sermons with "rapid-fire" questions for the young students. An 1860 article on the Hollymount examinations in the *Belfast News-Letter* reported that the children's answers—particularly those of the girls—produced "great delight and animation" in Drew.[59] But this was not simply a matter of Drew currying favor in exchange for aristocratic patronage. In 1862 and 1863, for example, Drew presided over parochial school celebrations in neighboring Inch Parish, and in Downpatrick, where he helped to host an elaborate ceremony for young students of the Down Parish Church schools. The day closed with a children's party in the Grove, where John Wesley had preached during his visit to the area in June 1778, an association that doubtless pleased the historically minded Drew.[60]

Drew also remained active in regional and national Sunday school organizations, regularly traveling to Belfast and Dublin for meetings. At an April 1864 gathering of the Sunday School Society for Ireland at the Rotunda in Dublin, Drew surveyed his own involvement in religious education in Limerick, Dublin, and Belfast. In a long speech, he celebrated the Sunday school movement's transformative impact on the nation, using military metaphors to argue that it had fostered tens of thousands of supporters for the British Empire: "But here is a sight for approving angels—the young and old—warriors of God—warriors male and warriors female; for here women can work battle for God, as well as man; here we are a real militant church, and for the sake of our celestial occupation, one grown old in the work beseeches you to hear him patiently. . . . It is a grand thought—300,000 teachers in Great

---

59. *Belfast News-Letter*, August 13, 1860. For another example, see *Downpatrick Recorder*, August 13, 1864; *Belfast News-Letter*, August 15, 1864.

60. *Belfast News-Letter*, September 23, 1862, July 31, 1863.

Britain and Ireland, and 3,000,000 of Sunday-School scholars. What an army of the empire's best defenders!"[61] For all of the hyperbole, Drew's commitment to children's religious education was lifelong and substantial. Two months before his death in late August 1870, Drew chaired a meeting on Sunday schools in Clarence Place Hall in Belfast, where he pushed for Sunday school expansion in the fast-growing Victorian city.[62] After his death, the Christ Church congregation had a memorial window placed in the church with the Sunday school's motto: "Feed My Lambs."

The final years of Drew's life saw yet another political disappointment: the disestablishment of the Church of Ireland.[63] Like many of his fellow Irish Protestant conservatives, Drew believed that while church reform might be necessary, Gladstone's proposal to disestablish the church was a national betrayal, an argument he made with particular force at a public meeting in March 1869: "We are here to interfere with national sin of the blackest dye ever attempted at the Church of Christ. We are here to rescue her Gracious Majesty from evil counsellors and crafty lawyers who would twist and turn and tell her that a solemn oath is no oath at all. We are here to rescue our country from certain calamities that must come upon it if the Truth of God be banished, and the clergy be dispossessed and extirpated."[64] Ill health that summer prevented Drew from taking an active part in various ultra-Protestant efforts to halt the offending legislation. Predictably enough, these initiatives had little to no political traction, and the measure was passed in July 1869. While clearly disappointed, Drew's eventual response to the fact of disestablishment proved to be more measured than his crusading rhetoric might have suggested, perhaps

---

61. *Belfast News-Letter*, April 9, 1864, April 6, 1867.

62. *Belfast News-Letter*, August 25, 1870.

63. Donald Harman Akenson's detailed examination of disestablishment remains the best starting point; see Akenson, *Church of Ireland*, 226–74. For brief overviews, see Acheson, *History of the Church of Ireland*, 200–212; McDowell, *Church of Ireland*, 26–50.

64. *Belfast News-Letter*, March 17, 1869.

reflecting Knox's careful diocesan leadership on a matter that he long had viewed as inevitable.

After his health recovered in the fall of 1869, Drew was an active participant in the ensuing discussions of how to refashion the Church of Ireland. To this end, he wrote a series of thoughtful public letters to Thomas Hincks, his old Belfast friend and ally, now archdeacon of Connor, reflecting on the current state of the Church of Ireland as well as some of the primary challenges it faced moving forward.[65] Drew argued that Anglicans needed to take pride in their own Church: "Be charitable and kind to all your Christian fellows; but never forget this as regards yourselves you are Episcopalians."[66] He repeatedly celebrated lay involvement in the church, arguing that one of Knox's great virtues was that he had long championed the inclusion of the laity in church discussions that were too often held in secret. While admitting that nothing was perfect, he stoutly defended the Church of Ireland's institutions, practices, and theology, supporting its prelates, chapters, deans, and liturgy against hasty excision and reform. Each of these distinctive Anglican features had their own histories and purposes, he argued, too often forgotten by the ineffective men who led the modern church. Given Drew's prominent involvement in earlier controversies over Anglican rituals, it is worth noting here that he supported the wearing of the clerical surplice, a controversial practice for many Victorian evangelicals: "I never could understand this antipathy of many good people, who like an unsavoury hermit, have an abhorrence of clean linen." He was open to the possibility that disestablishment might even bring some advantages, enabling better relations between various Protestant denominations as well as between the Church of Ireland's own clergy and laity. Responding to a Presbyterian critic from Ballymena, Drew insisted that the Episcopalian laity loved their

---

65. Drew's correspondence with Hincks seems to have originated in his failed effort to get the archdeacon to discuss the idea of a Church of Ireland Convocation in public, something that Drew opposed for fear that it would alienate the Irish Church from its English brethren. See *Downpatrick Recorder*, September 12, 1869.

66. *Belfast News-Letter*, December 17, 1869.

church, celebrating the area's virtues in particular, its excellent ministers, and active lay support.[67] Other aspects of his defense were more characteristic of Irish Conservatives, including his celebration of Saint Patrick, whose reputed grave in Downpatrick should be marked, he insisted, with a memorial pillar.[68]

If Drew sounded a rather uncharacteristically optimistic note about the general state of the Church of Ireland, he made it clear that he feared for many of the island's rural parishes, which were in desperate need of revitalization and would be hit particularly hard by disestablishment. He drew a stark contrast between "noble Belfast," where there were lively conversations about the church and its needs, and rural parishes, where a lack of leadership and relative social isolation prevented these important discussions from occurring. Citing his own experience as a preacher for the Church Education Society, Drew argued that new initiatives were desperately needed, particularly zealous men to spread the news in rural pulpits. He closed the letter by celebrating the quality of a number of Belfast ministers, arguing that the city alone could provide much of the talent needed to arouse the prosperous farmers of the rural districts.[69] Despite a career spent working in Belfast, in some ways Drew remained a populist rural Tory, celebrating a nostalgic vision of an idealized countryside where pastors and their churches were supported by godly Protestant noblemen, gentry, and yeoman farmers.

In his final years, Drew published a number of poems that featured a different type of sentimentality, exhibiting a personal warmth often celebrated by his congregants and friends but rarely seen in his contentious public life. Six were printed in an 1869 volume that featured the essays and poetry of the Reverend Robert Hannay, Drew's eventual successor at Christ Church. Most of the poems featured an aging but

---

67. *Belfast News-Letter*, January 6, 1870.
68. *Belfast News-Letter*, February 5, 1870. For a clear overview of the arguments made by Irish Conservative political leaders against disestablishment, see Shields, "Irish Conservative Perspective on the Defence of the Church of Ireland," 106–14.
69. *Belfast News-Letter*, December 28, 1869.

emotional voice focused on the consolation and joy of the hereafter. In "When I'm Gone," Drew described his own funeral service in evocative detail, celebrating the community of those who loved him, who could take solace in the promise "that Heaven longs to welcome them, Into the New Jerusalem!"[70] In "Life's Last Hour," Drew reflected on the uncertainty of life, underlining the fact that a person never knew when they were going to die. In this situation, all one could do was know that God would be present at the end and that "faith and love and hope and prayer" would "then bless my soul with glad surprise, And, gift with heaven, my longing eyes."[71] The contrast with Drew's public persona could not have been starker. Drew's politics were never completely absent, however, even in the homely rhymes of this more conventionally evangelical religious poetry, a point made all too clear in "The Rebel and the King," which featured an aging rebel begging for God's forgiveness. Even rebels, Drew made clear, were welcomed in heaven if they were truly contrite and sought God's favor.[72]

Thomas Drew died at his son's house at 60 Upper Sackville Street in Dublin on Saturday, October 22, 1870. He had recently moved to the capital, renting a house in Blackrock so that he could live in close proximity to his son. Drew never lived in his new home, falling ill shortly after arriving in Dublin. Contemporary depictions of his final hours avoided the political controversies that had marked so much of his public life, painting the minister in an uncharacteristically frail if warm light. Surrounded by his surviving son and daughters, as well as close friends such as Blacker, Hannay, and the Reverend Edward Hartrick, Drew reportedly talked mostly about his life at Christ Church, singing a verse from one of his favorite hymns before lapsing into fevered unconsciousness and passing away in the early morning.[73]

---

70. Drew, "When I'm Gone," in Hannay, *Selected Writings*, 24. For a rich treatment of Irish attitudes toward death and public history, see O'Brien, *Darkness Echoing*.

71. Drew, "Life's Last Hour," in Hannay, *Selected Writings*, 20.

72. Drew, "The Rebel and the King," in Hannay, *Selected Writings*.

73. *Belfast News-Letter*, October 25, 1870, October 26, 1870; *Belfast Morning News*, October 24, 1870.

Matters did not remain private for long. Drew's remains were conveyed to Belfast via train two days later. A crowd gathered at the platform at the station in Great Victoria Street to accompany the body to Christ Church, where a service was held that evening. The pallbearers who carried Drew's body into the church were evenly split between members of the Christ Church congregation and the Orange Order, a fair reflection of Drew's public life. Speaking from Romans 14:7, Hannay celebrated what he termed the two different but interconnected aspects of Drew's public career: his work as a pastor and as a political leader. Calling him the most loved minister in Ireland, Hannay celebrated Drew's ability to sympathize with the suffering of his congregants, highlighting the warmth of his dedication to children's religious education and church extension. Hannay also emphasized Drew's support for Conservative politics, arguing that his political commitments stemmed from his steadfast and principled belief in the truth of Irish Protestantism rather than party motivations themselves. In Hannay's view, Drew was a Conservative because that was the party that best defended God's truth. His outspoken politics may have generated critique and opposition, he argued, but even his opponents loved the outspoken minister for his earnest and genial manner.[74]

The funeral service took place at Christ Church the following day, presided over by Hartrick. The funeral sermon was preached by the Reverend Charles Seaver, who celebrated Drew's work in Belfast, emphasizing both the social improvement that Christ Church had brought to the area under Drew's tutelage and his dedication to children's religious education. After the service, Thomas Drew Jr. and Stewart Blacker led a public procession through central Belfast, a massive march that featured many leading clergymen and gentry, the Christ Church congregation, and representatives of seventy Orange lodges. Thousands of onlookers lined the streets of Belfast to watch the spectacle. As the procession wound its way from College Square toward the Lagan, it passed the office of the US Consulate, where the

---

74. *Belfast Morning News*, October 25, 1870.

American flag was flown at half-staff as a sign of respect. Crossing over the river, the procession made its way to Newtownards, before heading south to Ballynahinch, and, eventually, to Seaforde village. Along the way the procession was joined by members of the congregation as well as prominent regional elites such as Johnston, Lord Roden, Colonel Forde, and William Keown, amongst others. After a service that celebrated the life of this "great and good man," as the *Belfast News-Letter* put it, Thomas Drew was buried alongside his wife Isabella in the graveyard of Loughinisland Parish Church.[75]

---

75. *Belfast Morning News*, October 26, 1870.

Conclusion

Thomas Drew and the Making of Victorian Belfast

Thomas Drew played a critical role in the making of Victorian Belfast. It is vital to note that the argument here is not about indispensability. Even if we focus on sectarian politics, the aspect of public life most often associated with Drew, the historical forces involved in the creation and evolution of the increasingly powerful communal identities on display in mid- to late nineteenth-century Belfast were far deeper and more complicated than any one man. This should be no surprise. After all, the confessional identities and often binary politics that Drew celebrated and strengthened were hardly new to Belfast and the north of Ireland. They were never exhaustive. What Drew's career does illustrate, however, is the hybridity of even the most extreme anti-Catholic politics. It is essential to acknowledge the complexity of a figure like Drew, not simply because to do otherwise is to risk caricature of the populist Orange minister, but because it is the only way to make sense of his relationships with a variety of communities in a complex and fast-changing place like Victorian Belfast. This was not a simple, monochrome story.

The physical markers of Drew's legacy in Belfast are the easiest to assess. Leaders in both the Church of Ireland and the Orange Order lost little time in dedicating a number of Belfast sites to Drew, a process that began while he was still alive. In April 1870 Robert Hannay and other church leaders laid the foundation stone for the Drew Memorial School on Grosvenor Road. Drew attended the ceremony, celebrating his clerical friends, Sandy Row, and the Orange Order in a short speech. Within a year the site was reconfigured to add a church to accommodate the area's rapidly growing population. Drew Memorial Church (St. Phillip's) housed a lively and successful congregation until 1994, when the church was closed because of the area's changing religious demography. The building itself was purchased by Dwyer's Gaelic Athletic Club, which eventually demolished the church to make way for a more purpose-built structure. Directly across Grosvenor Road from the church was Drew Street (1880), a relatively short residential street just east of the Royal Victoria Hospital.[1]

The Orange Order honored Drew in a similar fashion. In August 1869 Drew was asked to become a patron to a new "company" that was being put together to build a new Orange and Protestant Hall on Agnes Street off the Shankill Road. He agreed, and the Orangemen "hailed with great delight" Drew's willingness to become their patron. It seems particularly fitting that the meeting occurred in Huss School House, which Drew had helped found in the 1830s.[2] Belfast Lodge no. 684 became Drew LOL 684, cementing his status as one of the clerical heroes of the modern Orange Order, itself reflected in the lodge banner, which featured a stolid portrait of the minister encircled by a wreath of holly against a backdrop of orange and purple.

Thomas Drew was an anti-Catholic demagogue whose violent public harangues had a toxic impact on communal relations in Victorian Belfast, setting up confrontations that strengthened sectarian divisions in the fast-growing northern capital, a role vividly on display in July 1857. He was a populist political pastor; a man who derived much of his notoriety for his status as an ultra-Protestant champion, a figure whose consistent—if often difficult—support for the Conservative Party and the Orange Order created warm friends and foes alike. Very few people were ambivalent about Thomas Drew. For all the seeming simplicity of Drew's Orange demagoguery, his public career

1. *Belfast News-Letter*, April 11, 1870, November 12, 1870, April 12, 1871, March 8, 1872; *Irish Builder*, February 15, 1886; Royle, *Belfast Part II*, 17, 41.
2. *Belfast News-Letter*, August 5, 1869.

highlights the complex and interwoven nature of Victorian Belfast's religious politics. He was an energetic and largely effective Church of Ireland minister, whose outreach initiatives and pastoral care helped to create and sustain a sizable and diverse congregation at Christ Church. Recent scholarship rightly has emphasized the centrality of evangelicalism in the making of Victorian Belfast. Drew played a critical role in fostering the extension of vital religion to working-class Anglicans.

This book underlines the necessity of understanding the contingencies and hybridity involved in Drew's largely successful operation within the complex mosaics of mid-nineteenth-century Belfast politics. At various points in his career, his energetic advocacy for church extension and religious education strengthened ties to a more moderate conservative establishment often exasperated by his furious sectarian rhetoric, while his intermittent Orange populist challenges to political and religious elites delighted his plebeian supporters. Drew's status and success were closely tied to his ability to maintain a balance between these two poles.

Thomas Drew helped to create the paradigm for a modern populist political minister, a figure that has cast a long shadow over modern Belfast. He was not alone. The obvious contemporary parallel is the Reverend Henry Cooke, whom R. Finlay Holmes described as the "archetypal Ulster protestant political parson" in his excellent biography of the powerful Presbyterian minister.[3] Cooke was a far more sophisticated and influential figure than Drew, but they certainly shared a penchant for mobilizing popular support for conservative political and religious causes. A more direct legacy figure is Richard Rutledge Kane, rector of Christ Church (1882–98), and grand master of the Orange Order in Belfast, one of the primary leaders of opposition to Irish Home Rule and a dominant figure in Belfast politics in the 1880s and 1890s. Others might think of Ian Paisley, who shared Drew's fiery populist politics, staunch aversion to Roman Catholicism, and evangelicalism, although it must be stressed that, like Cooke, he

---

3. Holmes, *Henry Cooke*, 208.

worked within a Presbyterian religious tradition that differed from Drew's Anglicanism in significant ways. The comparison to Paisley is particularly fraught, since the head of the Free Presbyterian Church and Democratic Unionist Party leader operated in a political environment where he could run for office, and use the modern media to mobilize his supporters, all of whom could vote.[4]

These comparisons also serve to highlight another of Drew's attributes: his relative ineffectiveness as a political leader. Like these other political pastors, Drew lost most of the political battles of his life, particularly those on a national stage. When he died in 1870, Irish Catholics were more influential in British and Irish political life that ever before, the Church of Ireland had been disestablished, and voluntary religious education was shrinking before the advance of a more secular vision of state-funded schools.

But Drew's political legacy was by no means one of failure. After all, his former son-in-law and ally, William Johnston, remained a member of Parliament for the rest of his life (1868–78; 1886–1902), championing the same type of loud and idiosyncratic Orange populist politics that Drew had advocated throughout his career. And, of course, politics cannot be measured by legislative accomplishments alone. When Drew started the Christ Church Protestant Association in 1854, the organization's primary goals were to educate Irish Protestants about the nature of the Catholic threat and to mobilize them to act in defense of Protestant interests and principles. If his efforts had little impact on legislation or policy in London or Dublin, they certainly seem to have worked on the streets of Belfast. Sandy Row, the industrial suburb and neighborhood that Drew had done so much to shape, remained a bastion of working-class Orangeism throughout the nineteenth and twentieth centuries. While by no means all-encompassing, sectarian division was, if anything, a more potent force

---

4. Henry Cooke, Richard Rutledge Kane, and Ian Paisley have been written about quite extensively. For Cooke, see Holmes, *Henry Cooke*. For Kane, see Beiner, *Forgetful Remembrance*, 387–89, and Jenkins, "Two Irelands beyond the Sea," 36–54. The best study of Paisley's career remains Bruce, *Paisley*.

in late Victorian Belfast political life than it had been when Drew began at Christ Church in 1833.

Drew's legacies were not confined to politics, however broadly conceived. While his success at Christ Church was aided significantly by the church's favorable location in the heart of a fast-growing part of Belfast, Drew's ambitious energy and prodigious work ethic helped to place Christ Church at the center of life in Sandy Row. His pastoral activism and efforts in church extension were particularly important, bringing the language of vital religion to men, women, and children across Belfast, messages that were strengthened for his congregation by his everyday sermons. Drew's commitment to religious education was also critical to his success in Belfast, symbolized by Christ Church's extensive network of day and Sunday schools. Many of Drew's contemporaries were critical of the quality and content of the church's programs, but Drew was certainly successful in helping to make evangelicalism the ideal against which other forms of Protestant religious practice were judged.

One of the keys to Drew's success in these various endeavors was his reputation as a Protestant champion, a man always willing to stand up in defense of Protestant principles and the Orange Order, a trait celebrated repeatedly by his hard-line supporters. But Orangeism was not the only thing Drew championed. By the late 1830s, Drew was seen by many as a kind of tribune for the Protestant working class in Belfast, a reputation forged by his energetic advocacy for the town's poor. In ideological terms, these efforts were those of a conservative and evangelical Church of Ireland minister, designed to uphold the existing social order and promote emergent Victorian codes of civility and respectability. He abhorred collective action, working from a model of hierarchically based societal consensus that emphasized plebeian forbearance and the importance of the next life rather than this one. His support often seemed more rhetorical than real, and despite his populist tendencies, Drew rarely moved too far away from his conservative aristocratic supporters. But if his policy prescriptions seem hesitant, limited, and condescending, his advocacy was no less real. At the very least, Drew consistently raised the issues faced by the poor in public venues throughout the twenty-five years of his ministry at Christ Church. If his speeches were often bombastic and self-serving, they also served to fashion his reputation. His influence with his working-class constituents was not simply a matter of sectarian politics.

If Thomas Drew helped to make Victorian Belfast, the converse was also true: Drew's beliefs and talents were well suited to the chaotic and formative years of this city in the making. Christ Church's extensive outreach initiatives—particularly its day school and Sunday schools but also its community centers and Dorcas Depot—effectively placed the church at the center of Sandy Row life. This was particularly important in the turbulent 1830s and 1840s, when migrants from Belfast's rural hinterlands came to a town with a relatively undeveloped social infrastructure. Drew's paternalist rhetoric and, above all, his muscular anti-Catholicism, provided a reassuring sense of continuity for plebeian Protestants finding their feet in early Victorian Belfast. Drew's Orangeism and the ties and support provided by the Orange Order clearly served much the same function.

Drew's public performances had significant costs, both to his career within the Church of Ireland and to the city and region. His confrontational anti-Catholicism was too extreme, a step too far for most members of the Belfast political and religious establishment, who may have been well versed in the anti-Catholic language that Drew so often wielded, but viewed his performances as provocative and counterproductive. When Belfast newspapers feigned surprise that Drew had not been rewarded by the party he had served so well, they knew exactly why Drew had not been promoted. And, of course, Drew's rabid anti-Catholicism served to alienate another important constituency in Belfast and across the island: Irish Catholics. After 1850, Drew was viewed as the epitome of the aggressively anti-Catholic minister, a man whose combative partisan speeches both mobilized communal sentiment and legitimated sectarian violence. This view was hardly confined to Irish Catholics. For many British and Irish contemporaries, the Belfast riots of 1857 confirmed Drew's status as Ireland's leading Orange cleric, a symbol of Belfast's supposedly foundational and irrational sectarianism. It was here that Thomas Drew played a vital role in the making of Victorian Belfast. The Christ Church minister may have succeeded in his efforts to build the house of God on Durham Street, but the costs of the way that he achieved that success were very high indeed.

Bibliography

Index

Bibliography

MANUSCRIPT SOURCES

Belfast, Northern Ireland

Down and Connor Diocesan Archives
    Denvir Papers
    Dorrian Papers

Gamble Library, Union Theological College
    Reports of the Belfast Town Mission, 1828, 1830, 1833–1838

Museum of Orange Heritage
    County Antrim Grand Lodge of Ireland Reports, 1847, 1852–1859
    Eldon Orange Lodge, LOL 7, Minute Book
    Loyal Orange Order, Belfast County Minute Book, 1851–1859
    Registry of the Loyal Orange Institution of Ireland, 1823, 1828–1829, 1856 (Grand Orange Lodge of Ireland, Belfast)

Public Record Office of Northern Ireland (PRONI)
    Aiken McClelland Papers, D.3815
    "The Annals of Christ Church, Belfast" (unpublished manuscript by Abraham Dawson, 1858), T.2159/1
    Baptism, Marriage, and Death Registers for Christ Church, Belfast, 1835–1860, MIC/583/23/3
    Belfast Poll Book, 1832–1837, D.2472/1
    Belfast Police Committee, Minute Books, LA/7–8
    Belfast Poor Law Union Board of Guardians, Minutes, 1842–1860 BG/7/1–12

Belfast Street Directories (1840–1866), http://streetdirectories.proni.gov.uk/
Belfast Town Council Records, LA/7/1–5
Blacker Correspondence, T.1638/10/8
Christ Church Religious Census, 1852, CR1/13D/1
Church of Ireland Diocesan Papers
Church of Ireland Young Men's Society, D.3936
Diary of Anthony McIntyre, D.1558/2/3
Diary of James MacAdam (1836–1842), D.2930/7/4
Downshire Papers, D.671
Drennan-Duffin Papers, T.1252
Emerson Tennent Papers, D.2922
McIlwaine Papers, D.2877/5/1
Records of the Young Family, D.2930/3/8/5
Reeves Manuscripts, DIO1/24/12
Roden Papers, MIC.147/5–6
Tennent Papers, D.1748
William Johnston of Ballykilbeg Papers, D.880

St. Aidan's Church
  Baptism, Marriage, and Death Records for Christ Church, Belfast

St. George's Church
  Parish Records
    Preacher's Book, 1823–1840
    Subscribers List
    Vestry Minutes

Dublin, Republic of Ireland

National Archives of Ireland
  Chief Secretary's Office Registered Papers
  Outrage Papers
  Protestant Orphan Society Papers

National Library of Ireland
  Larcom Papers, MS 7624–27

Mant Correspondence, MS 15,361 (1)
Mayo Papers, MS 11,202

Representative Church Body Library
Mant-St. John Smyth Correspondence, MS 772/3/26

London, England, United Kingdom

British Library
Peel Papers, General Correspondence, vol. CCC LVII (ff. 433–ff. 23)

PARLIAMENTARY PAPERS

Correspondence between the Lord Lieutenant and William Johnston, Esq. Relative to a Proposed Meeting of Orangemen in Ballykilbeg on 12th July 1866. HC 1866 (461), lx.
First Report of the Commissioners Appointed to Inquire into the Municipal Corporations of Ireland. HC 1835 (23–28), xxvii.
First Report of the Commissioners of Public Instruction, Ireland. HC 1835 (45), xxxiii.
Report from the Select Committee to Inquire into the Nature, Character, Extent, and Tendency of Orange Lodges, Associations, or Societies in Ireland, with Minutes of Evidence and Appendix. HC 1835 (377), xv.
Report of the Commissioners of Inquiry into the Origin and Character of the Riots in Belfast in July and September 1857; Together with Minutes of Evidence and Appendix. HC 1857–8 (2309) xxvi.
Report to the Lord Lieutenant by Messrs. Fitzmaurice and Goold, with the Minutes of Evidence Taken by Them at the Inquiry into the Conduct of the Constabulary during the Disturbances at Belfast in July and September 1857. HC 1857–8 (333), xlvii.
Royal Commission on the Condition of the Poorer Classes in Ireland, Appendix C, Part I, State of the Poor and Charitable Institutions in Principal Towns in Ireland. HC 1835 (35), xxx.
Royal Commission on Hand Loom Weavers. HC 1840 (43), xxiii.
Select Committee on Hand-Loom Weavers' Petitions; With the Minutes of Evidence, and Index. HC 1835 (341), xiii.
Third Report of the Commissioners for Inquiring into the Condition of the Poorer Classes in Ireland, Appendix (C.)—Part 1. HC 1836 (43), xxx.

Third Report of the Select Committee to Inquire into the Nature, Character, Extent, and Tendency of Orange Lodges, Associations, or Societies in Ireland, with Minutes of Evidence and Appendix. HC 1835 (476), xvi.

NEWSPAPERS AND PERIODICALS

Banner of Ulster
Belfast Commercial Chronicle
Belfast Daily Mercury
Belfast Morning News
Belfast News-Letter
Belfast Protestant Journal
Christian Examiner and Church of Ireland Magazine
Downpatrick Recorder
Downshire Protestant
Dublin Evening Mail
Dublin Evening Post
Dublin Mercantile Advertiser
Dublin University Magazine
Enniskillen Chronicle and Erne Packet
Illustrated Times
Irish Ecclesiastical Gazette
Irish Ecclesiastical Journal
Irish Presbyterian
Limerick Reporter
Northern Whig
Protestant Orphan Society Record
Ulster Times
Ulsterman
Vindicator

CONTEMPORARY PUBLICATIONS

Account of the Proceedings of the Down and Connor Clergy Aid Society, for the Year Ending September 11, 1838. Belfast: *Ulster Times* Office, 1838.
Association for the Relief of Distressed Protestants. Dublin: W. Espy, 1842–1863.

Authenticated Report of the Discussion between the Rev'd T. D. Gregg and the Rev'd Thomas Maguire. Dublin: William Carson, 1839.

Barrow, John. *A Tour around Ireland, through the Sea-Coast Counties, in the Autumn of 1835*. London: John Murray, 1836.

Batt, Narcissus. "Belfast Sixty Years Ago: Recollections of a Septuagenarian." *Ulster Journal of Archaeology* 2, no. 2 (January 1896).

Belfast and Ulster Street Directories, 1835–1870. http://streetdirectories.proni.gov.uk.

Benn, George. *A History of the Town of Belfast from 1799 till 1810, Together with Incidental Notices on Local Topics and Biographies of Many Well-Known Families*. Belfast: Alexander Mackay, 1823.

Berens, Edward. *A Memoir of the Life of Bishop Mant*. London: Francis and John Rivington, 1849.

Birmingham, George A. *Pleasant Places*. London: William Heinemann, 1934.

Catalogue of the Christ-Church Library, Belfast, Established 1836. Belfast: *Ulster Times* Office, 1837.

Christ Church Belfast: Details Respecting the Church and Various Institutions Connected Therewith; and Appeals to the Christian Public on Behalf of Those Institutions. Belfast, 1838.

Church Architecture Considered, in Relation to the Mind of the Church since and before the Reformation: In Two Addresses, Delivered on 7 February and 7 March to the Down and Connor and Dromore Church Architecture Society. Belfast: George Phillips, 1843.

Church Education Society. *First Annual Report of the Church Education Society for Ireland*. Dublin: George Folds, 1840.

———. *Second Annual Report of the Church Education Society for Ireland*. Dublin: James Charles, 1841.

———. *Third Annual Report of the Church Education Society for Ireland*. Dublin: James Charles, 1842.

———. *Fourth Annual Report of the Church Education Society for Ireland*. Dublin: James Charles, 1843.

———. *Fifth Annual Report of the Church Education Society for Ireland*. Dublin: James Charles, 1844.

———. *Sixth Annual Report of the Church Education Society for Ireland*. Dublin: James Charles, 1845.

———. *Seventh Annual Report of the Church Education Society for Ireland*. Dublin: James Charles, 1846.

———. *Eighth Annual Meeting of the Church Education Society for Ireland Being for the Years 1846 and 1847.* Dublin: James Charles, 1848.

———. *Ninth Annual Meeting of the Church Education Society for Ireland.* Dublin: Edward Bull, 1849.

———. *Tenth Annual Meeting of the Church Education Society for Ireland.* Dublin: Edward Bull, 1850.

———. *Eleventh Annual Meeting of the Church Education Society for Ireland.* Dublin: Edward Bull, 1851.

———. *Thirteenth Annual Meeting of the Church Education Society for Ireland.* Dublin: George Drought, 1853.

———. *Sixteenth Annual Meeting of the Church Education Society for Ireland.* Dublin: James Charles, 1856.

———. *Occasional Intelligence, Being Extracts from Correspondence, Reports of Inspectors, and Other Documents Connected with the Operations of the Society.* Dublin: Church Education Society, 1848–1850.

Cottage Sermons: Consisting of Twelve Short and Plain Discourses Adapted for General Circulation, and Also for Reading in Families. 2 vols. London: Religious Tract Society, 1820–1830.

Dawson, Abraham. "The Annals of Christ Church, Belfast." Unpublished manuscript, 1858.

———. "Biographical Notice of George Walker, Governor of Derry during the Siege of 1688 and 1689—Part I and II." *Ulster Journal of Archaeology* 2, series 1 (1854): 129–35, 261–77.

———. "Clog Ban, the Name Given to a Handbell Anciently used at Funerals, and on Solemn Religious Occasions." *Journal of the Historical and Archaeological Association of Ireland* 4, no. 6, (1883): 126–60.

———. "Notes Relating to the Re-Afforesting of Ireland, thru the Parish Records of Seagoe." *Journal of the Historical and Archaeological Association of Ireland* 4, no. 6, pt. 2 (1884): 351–53.

———. "St. Patrick's View of the Braid Valley, and the Burning of Milchu's Homestead." *Ulster Journal of Archaeology* 3, no. 2 (January 1897): 113–19.

———. "Terrier of the Parish of Seagoe, Diocese of Dromore, 1742: A Fragment." *Ulster Journal of Archaeology* 3, no. 4 (July 1897): 224–26.

Douglass, Frederick. *Narrative of the Life of Frederick Douglass, an American Slave.* Dublin: Webb and Chapman, 1846.

Doyle, J. B. *Tours in Ulster: A Handbook to the Antiquities and Scenery of the North of Ireland*. Dublin: Hodges and Smith, 1854.
Drew, Thomas. "Annals of Loughinisland." Unpublished manuscript.
———. *The Church in Belfast: A Few Facts and A Few Hints, Respectfully Offered to All Whom It May Concern*. Belfast: *Ulster Times* Office, 1838.
———. "The Church in Belfast." *Ulster Times*, September 8, 1838.
———. *National Education: Letter from the Rev. Thomas Drew, Minister of Christ Church, Belfast, to the Rev. Hugh McNeile, Minister of St. Jude's, Liverpool*. Belfast: *Belfast Commercial Chronicle* Office, 1840.
———. *Protestant Anniversaries, Originally Published in the* Downshire Protestant *Newspaper*. Dublin: Curry and Co.; Belfast: G. Phillips and Sons, 1858.
———. "Recommendatory Preface." In *The Young Instructed in the Gospel Narrative*. Dublin: John Robertson, 1846.
———. "The Rich and the Poor." In *The Irish Pulpit: A Collection of Original Sermons by the Clergyman of the Established Church of Ireland*. Series 3. Dublin: William Curry, Jr. and Co., 1839.
———. "Sabbath Blessings: A Sermon Delivered in Christ Church, Belfast, on Sunday, December 25, 1842." In *The Irish Pulpit*, January 5, 1843. Dublin: John Robertson, 1843.
———. *Selection of Psalms, Adapted to the Services of the United Church of England and Ireland, throughout the Year, Together with a Number of Hymns, Selected for the Use of Schools and Families of Christ Church, Belfast*. Belfast: William Ferguson, 1838.
———. *Sermon (on Eccl. 9:13–16), Preached in Christ Church, Belfast, on Sunday Evening, February 21, 1858*. No publication data.
———. *A Sermon, Preached at St Peter's Church, Dublin on Sunday, 5th of April 1840, on Behalf of the Orphans Connected with the Protestant Orphan Society*. Dublin: Curry and Co., 1840.
———. *A Sermon Preached at the Request of the Committee of the Protestant Orphan Society on the Death of Rev. John T. Whitestone, A.M., at St. Mary's Church, Dublin on the Evening of the 12th of April 1853*. Dublin: William Curry, Jr. and Co., 1853.
———. *A Sermon Preached in Christ Church, Belfast, on Sunday Evening, Feb. 21, 1856*. Downpatrick: *Downshire Protestant* Office, 1856.
———. *A Sermon Preached in Christ Church, Belfast, on the Evening of November 5, 1856, Being the Anniversary of Deliverance from the Popish Gunpowder*

Plot and Also the Arrival of William III, Prince of Orange, before the Assembled Orangemen of Belfast. Belfast: A. Welsh, 1856.

———. *A Sermon Preached in Christ Church, Belfast, on Sunday Evening, February 21, 1858*. No publication data.

———. *A Sermon, Preached on Behalf on the Protestant Orphan Society, in Trinity Church, Dublin, on Thursday, April 2, 1840*. No publication data.

———. *Sermons on Various Subjects, Preached in Christ Church, Belfast, and Now Published for the Use of the Families of the Congregation*. 2 vols. Belfast: William Ferguson, 1839.

———. *State Education Considered: A Sermon, Not Preached. The Church, the State, the Parent, the Child*. Belfast: George Philips and Sons, 1862.

———. "Sunday School Teaching: A Sermon Preached in St. George's Church, Dublin, on Wednesday Evening, 10 April 1839, at the Request of the Committee of the Sunday School Society for Ireland." In *The New Irish Pulpit, or Gospel Preacher*, vol. 4, 155–64. Dublin: John Robertson, 1840.

———. *Thoughtful Protestantism: A Sermon Preached Before the Congregation of Christ Church, Belfast, on Sunday, September 1856*. Downpatrick: *Downshire Protestant* Office, 1856.

———. *Two Sermons Preached before the University of Dublin in January 1842, by Thomas Drew, D.D., Perpetual Curate of Christ-Church, Belfast and Chaplain to His Excellency the Lord Lieutenant of Ireland*. Dublin: Curry and Co.; Belfast: Phillips; Downpatrick: Pilson, 1843.

———. "The Vision of Holy Waters: A Sermon, Preached on the Day when the Church of Hollymount, Parish of Down, Diocese of Down, was First Opened for the Celebration of Divine Service, Sunday, March 1st, 1840." In *The New Irish Pulpit, or Gospel Preacher*, 87–94. Dublin: John Henderson, 1840.

Engels, Friedrich. *The Condition of the Working Class in England*. Edited by David McClellan. Oxford: Oxford Univ. Press, 1993.

First Annual Report for the Society for the Religious Improvement of the Poor in Belfast and its Vicinity; or Belfast Town Mission. Belfast: Alexander MacKay, 1828.

Flora Verner or the Sandy Row Convert: A Tale of the Belfast Revival. Belfast: George Phillips and Sons, 1861.

Fourth and Final Report of the Down and Connor Church Accommodation Society Adopted at a General Meeting, Held on the 19th January 1843. Belfast: Printed for the Society, 1843.

Gardiner, Grace, ed. *The Lectures, Essays and Letters of the Right Ho. Sir Joseph Napier*. Dublin: Hodges, Figgis and Co., 1888.
Great Meeting of the Diocese of Down and Connor for Church Extension. Belfast: Ulster Times, 1838.
Hannay, Robert. *Selected Writings*. Belfast: Ulster Tract, Book, and Bible Depository, 1869.
Hardy, Phillip D. *Twenty-One Views in Belfast and Its Neighbourhood*. Belfast: Ulster Architectural Heritage Society, 2005.
Heaney, Henry, ed. *A Scottish Whig in Ireland: The Irish Journals of Robert Graham of Redgorton*. Dublin: Four Courts Press, 1999.
Hints for Conducting Sunday Schools; Useful Also for Day Schools and Families, Compiled by the Committee of the Sunday School Society for Ireland. Dublin: M. Goodwin and Co., 1835.
Inglis, Henry D. *Ireland in 1834: A Journey throughout Ireland during the Spring, Summer and Autumn of 1834*. London: Whitaker and Company, 1835.
John Knox and the Reverend Thomas Drew Or, the Book of Common Order, No Liturgy. Belfast: William McComb, 1840.
Kerr, George. *Legislative Tyranny, and Defence of the Trades Union*. Belfast: J. Smyth, 1834. Reprinted as an appendix in Andrew Boyd, *The Rise of the Irish Trade Unions, 1729–1970*.
Killen, W. D. ed., *Memoir of John Edgar*. Belfast: C. Aitchison, 1867.
Knox, Alexander. *A History of the County Down, from the Most Remote Period to the Present Day*. Dublin: Hodges, Foster and Co., 1875.
Lewis, Samuel. *County Down: A Topographical Dictionary of the Parishes, Villages and Town of County Down in the 1830s*. London: Aldershot Press, 1837.
———. *A Topographical Dictionary of Ireland*. 2 vols. London: S. Lewis and Co., 1837.
Malcolm, Andrew. *The Sanitary State of Belfast, with Suggestions for Its Improvement*. Belfast: Henry Grier, 1852.
MacKnight, Thomas. *Ulster as It Is: Or, Twenty-Eight Years as an Irish Editor*. 2 vols. London: MacMillan and Co., 1896.
Mant, Richard. *Church Architecture Considered, in Relation to the Mind of the Church since and before the Reformation: In Two Addresses, Delivered on 7 February and 7 March 1843 to the Down, Connor and Dromore Church Architecture Society*. Belfast: George Phillips, 1843.

———. *A Churchman's Apology*. Belfast: George Phillips, 1844.
———. *History of the Church in Ireland*. 2 vols. London: John W. Parker, 1840.
———. *Sermons for Parochial and Domestic Use, Designed to Illustrate and Enforce, in a Connected View, the Most Important Articles of Christian Faith and Practice*. 3 vols. Oxford: John W. Parker, 1823.
Mant, Walter. *Memoirs of the Right Reverend Richard Mant*. Dublin: McGloushan and Gill, 1857.
McComb, William. *McComb's Guide to Belfast, the Giant's Causeway, and the Adjoining Districts of the Counties of Antrim and Down*. Belfast: William McComb, 1861.
———. *The Repealer Repulsed*. Edited by Patrick Maume. Dublin: Univ. College Dublin Press, 2003.
McIlwaine, William. *The Dressmaker: A Prize Essay*. London: Aylott and Jones, 1846.
———. *Ecclesiologism Exposed: Being the Letters of "Clericus Connorensis," as Originally Published in the* Belfast Commercial Chronicle. Belfast: George Phillips, 1843.
———. *Revivalism Revived*. Belfast: T. McIlroy, 1859.
McNeile, Hugh. *The Famine a Rod of God: Its Provoking Cause—Its Merciful Design*. London: Seeley, Burnside and Seeley; Arthur Newling, 1847.
Milner, Joseph. *Practical Sermons*. 4 vols. Edited by Isaac Milner, W. Richardson, John Fawcett, and Edward Bickersteth. London: J. and E. Hodson; L. Hansard and Sons, 1804–1830.
Monsall, John S. B. *The Church of Ramoan: A Lay*. Belfast: George Phillips, 1848.
Morgan, James. *Recollections of My Life and Times: An Autobiography*. Belfast: William Mullan, 1874.
———. *Reflections on the Death of Mr. William Cochrane, Being One of the Agents of the Belfast Town Mission*. Belfast: William McComb, 1837.
Napier, Joseph. *The Lectures, Essays, and Letters of the Right Hon. Sir Joseph Napier*. Dublin: Hodges, Figgis, and Co., 1888.
Norgate, Gerald le Grys. "Arthur Trevor-Hill." *Dictionary of National Biography 1885–1900*. Vol. 57. London: Smith, Elder and Co., 1899.
O'Connell, Maurice, ed. *The Correspondence of Daniel O'Connell*. 8 vols. Dublin: Blackwater Press, for the Irish Manuscripts Commission, 1972–1980.
O'Hanlon, William. *Walks among the Poor of Belfast*. Belfast: Henry Grier, 1853.

O'Sullivan, Mortimer. *Case of the Protestants of Ireland. Stated in Addresses Delivered at Dublin, Liverpool, Bristol, and Bath in 1834*. London: J. Hatchard and Son; Dublin: William Curry Jr., 1836.

———. *A Sermon Delivered in Christ-Church Belfast*. Belfast: William Matear and George Druit, 1837.

Pilson, James Adair. *History of the Rise and Progress of Belfast, and Annals of the County Antrim*. Belfast: John Mullan, 1846.

Presentation of a Testimonial to the Rev. Thomas Drew, A.M., Minister of Christ Church, Belfast by His Congregation, on Monday, 10th April 1837. Belfast: Ulster Times, 1837.

Reid, James Seaton, and W. D. Killen. *History of the Presbyterian Church in Ireland*. 3 vols. Belfast: William Mullen, 1867.

Report of the Belfast Town Mission. Belfast: William McComb, 1833.

Report of the First Meeting of the Down and Connor and Dromore Church Architecture Society, October 4, 1842. Belfast: George Phillips, 1842.

Report on the Irish Poor, Appendix C. London: His Majesty's Stationary Office, 1836.

Roney, Frank. *Irish Rebel and California Labor Leader: An Autobiography*. Edited by Ira B. Cross. Berkeley: Univ. of California Press, 1931.

Sadler, Michael Thomas. *Ireland, Its Evils and Remedies*. London: John Murray, 1828.

Scott, Michael, ed. *Hall's Ireland: Mr. and Mrs. Hall's Tour of 1840*. 2 vols. London: Sphere Books, 1984.

Seeley, Robert Benton. *Memoirs of the Life and Writings of Michael Thomas Sadler*. London: Seeley and Burnside, 1842.

Seventh Annual Report of the Association for the Distressed Protestants, 1843. Dublin: W. Espy, 1844.

Speeches of the Rev. Hugh Stowell, A.M. of Manchester and the Rev. Thomas Drew, D.D. of Belfast at the Annual Meeting of the Protestant Orphan Society, Held in the Rotunda, Dublin, on Friday, the 5th of April, 1850, the Right Honourable Earl of Roden in the Chair, the 370 Orphans being Present. Dublin: Goodwin, Son and Nethercott, 1850.

Statistical Report of the Injuries sustained during the Riots in Belfast, from 8th to 22nd August 1864. Belfast: W. G. Baird, 1864.

Statistics of Protestantism and Romanism in Belfast. Belfast: Johnston and McClure, 1857.

Testimonials to the Character and Labours of the Rev. Thomas Drew, D.D. Whitchurch: Atlas Press, 1842.
Thackeray, William Makepeace. *The Irish Sketch Book, 1842*. London: Chapman and Hall, 1843.
Trevelyan, Charles. *The Irish Crisis*. London: Longman, Brown, Green and Longmans, 1848.
The Voluntaries in Belfast: Report on the Discussion on the Civil Establishment of Religion. Belfast: William McComb, 1836.
Yorke, Charles I. *A Respectful Address to the Bishop of London, Concerning Some Prevailing Notions Apparently Countenanced by His Lordship's Late Charge*. London: Nisbet and Co., 1842.

SCHOLARLY PUBLICATIONS

Acheson, Alan. *A History of the Church of Ireland, 1691–2001*. Dublin: Columba Press, 1997.
———. *Bishop John Jebb and the Nineteenth-Century Anglican Renaissance*. Toronto: Clements Publishing, 2007.
Akenson, Donald Harman. *The Church of Ireland: Ecclesiastical Reform and Revolution, 1800–1885*. New Haven, CT: Yale Univ. Press, 1971.
———. *Discovering the End of Time: Irish Evangelicals in the Age of O'Connell*. Montreal: McGill-Queen's Univ. Press, 2016.
———. *God's Peoples: Covenant and Land in South Africa, Israel, and Ulster*. Montreal: McGill-Queen's Univ. Press, 1992.
———. *The Irish Education Experiment: The National System of Education in the Nineteenth Century*. London: Routledge, 1970.
Arnstein, Walter, L. *Protestant versus Catholic in Mid-Victorian England: Mr. Newdegate and the Nuns*. Columbia: Univ. of Missouri Press, 1982.
Atkins, Gareth. "Evangelical Anglican Theology, c.1820–1850—The Case of Edward Bickersteth." *Journal of Religious History* 38 (2014): 1–19.
Atkinson, E. D. *Dromore: An Ulster Diocese*. Dundalk: W. Tempest, 1925.
Baker, Sybil. "Orange and Green: Sectarian Riots in Victorian Belfast." In *The Victorian City: Images and Realities*, edited by H. J. Dyos and Michael Woolf, 787–815. 2 vols. London: Routledge, 1973.
Barnard, T. C. "The Uses of 23 October 1641 and Irish Protestant Celebrations." *English Historical Review* 106, no. 421 (October 1991): 899–920.

Barr, Colin. "Introduction: Religion and Greater Ireland." In *Religion and Greater Ireland: Christianity and Irish Global Networks, 1750–1950*, edited by Colin Barr and Hillary Carey, 3–29. Montreal: McGill-Queen's Univ. Press, 2015.

———. "The Re-Energising of Catholicism, 1798–1880." In *The Cambridge History of Ireland: Volume 3, 1730–1880*, edited by James Kelly, 280–304. Cambridge: Cambridge Univ. Press, 2017.

Baxter, Catherine. *The Drews of Drumlohan Townland, Kilcornan Parish, County Limerick, Ireland*. Self-published, 1996.

Bebbington, David W. *Evangelicalism in Modern Britain: A History from the 1790s to the 1980s*. London: Unwin Hyman, 1989.

Beckert, Sven. *Empire of Cotton: A Global History*. New York: Vintage Books, 2014.

Beiner, Guy. *Forgetful Remembrance: Social Forgetting and Vernacular Historiography of a Rebellion in Ulster*. Oxford: Oxford Univ. Press, 2018.

———. *Remembering the Year of the French*. Madison: Univ. of Wisconsin Press, 2007.

Belchem, John. *Irish, Catholic, and Scouse: The History of the Liverpool Irish*. Liverpool: Liverpool Univ. Press, 2007.

Belfast County Orange Lodge. *Centenary Official History, 1863–1963*. Newtownabbey: Universal Publishing Company, 1963.

Bender, Jill C. "Ireland and Empire." In *The Princeton History of Modern Ireland*, edited by Richard Bourke and Ian McBride, 343–60. Princeton, NJ: Princeton Univ. Press, 2016.

Benedict, Phillip, Nora Berend, Stephen Ellis, Jeffrey Kaplan, Ussama Makdisi, and Jack Miles. "AHA Conversation: Religious Identities and Violence." *American Historical Review* 112, no. 5 (November 2007): 1433–81.

Bew, John. *The Glory of Being Britons: Civic Unionism in Nineteenth-Century Belfast*. Dublin: Irish Academic Press, 2009.

Bew, Paul. *Ireland: The Politics of Enmity, 1789–2006*. Oxford: Oxford Univ. Press, 2007.

Bielenberg, Andy, James S. Donnelly Jr., and John Borgonovo. "'Something of the Nature of a Massacre': The Bandon Valley Killings Revisited." *Eire-Ireland* 49, no. 3–4 (Fall/Winter 2014): 7–59.

Blackstock, Allan. "Armed Citizens and Christian Soldiers: Crisis Sermons and Ulster Presbyterians, 1715–1803." *Eighteenth-Century Ireland* 22, no. 1 (January 2007): 81–105.

———. *An Ascendancy Army: The Irish Yeomanry, 1796–1834*. Dublin: Four Courts Press, 1998.

———. *Loyalism in Ireland, 1789–1829*. Woodbridge, UK: Boydell Press, 2007.

———. "Orange Songs in Green Books: Colonel William Blacker." In *Politics and Popular Culture in Britain and Ireland, 1750–1850*, edited by Allan Blackstock and Eoin Magennis, 65–90. Belfast: Ulster Historical Foundation, 2007.

———. "Tommy Downshire's Boys: Popular Protest, Social Change, and Political Manipulation in Mid-Ulster, 1829–47." *Past and Present* 196 (August 2007): 125–72.

Blackwood, Reginald. *Some Biographical Notices of the Rectors of Loughinisland*. Downpatrick: *Down Recorder*, 1911.

Bourke, Richard. *Empire and Revolution: A Political Life of Edmund Burke*. Princeton, NJ: Princeton Univ. Press, 2015.

Bourke, Richard, and Ian McBride, eds. *The Princeton History of Modern Ireland*. Princeton, NJ: Princeton Univ. Press, 2015.

Bowen, Desmond. *History and the Shaping of Irish Protestantism*. New York: Peter Lang, 1995.

———. *The Protestant Crusade in Ireland, 1800–70*. Dublin: Gill and MacMillan, 1978.

Boyce, D. George, and Alan O'Day, eds. *The Making of Modern Irish History: Revisionism and the Revisionist Controversy*. London: Routledge, 1996.

Boyd, Andrew. *Holy War in Belfast*. Tralee: Anvil Books, 1969.

———. *The Rise of the Irish Trade Unions, 1729–1970*. Tralee: Anvil Books, 1972.

Brady, Ciaran, ed. *Interpreting Irish History: The Debate of Historical Revisionism*. Dublin: Irish Academic Press, 1994.

Brewer, John D., and Gareth I. Higgins. *Anti-Catholicism in Northern Ireland, 1600–1998: The Mote and the Beam*. London: MacMillan, 1998.

Briggs, Asa. *Victorian Cities*. London: Odham Press, 1963.

Brown, Callum G. *The Death of Christian Britain: Understanding Secularisation, 1800–2000*. New York: Routledge, 2001.

———. *The Social History of Religion in Scotland since 1730*. Edinburgh: Methuen, 1987.

Brown, Ralph. "Victorian Anglican Evangelicalism: The Radical Legacy of Edward Irving." *Journal of Ecclesiastical History* 58 (2007): 675–704.

Brown, Stewart. "The New Reformation Movement in the Church of Ireland." In *Piety and Power in Ireland, 1760–1960: Essays in Honour of Emmet Larkin*, edited by Stewart Brown and David W. Miller, 180–208. Belfast: Institute of Irish Studies, 2000.
———. *Providence and Empire, 1815–1914*. Harlow, UK: Pearson Longman, 2008.
———. *Thomas Chalmers and the Godly Commonwealth*. Oxford: Oxford Univ. Press, 1982.
Bruce, Steve. *Paisley: Religion and Politics in Northern Ireland*. Oxford: Oxford Univ. Press, 2009.
de Brun, Fionntan. "Expressing the Nineteenth Century in Irish: The Poetry of Aodh Mac Domhnaill (1802–67)." *New Hibernia Review* 15, no. 1 (Spring 2011): 81–106.
Bryan, Dominic, Sean Connolly, and John Nagle. *Civic Identity and Public Space: Belfast since 1780*. Manchester: Manchester Univ. Press, 2019.
Brydon, Michael. *The Evolving Reputation of Richard Hooker: An Evaluation of Responses, 1600–1714*. Oxford: Oxford Univ. Press, 2007.
Budge, Ian, and Cornelius O'Leary. *Approach to Crisis: A Study of Belfast Politics, 1613–1970*. New York: St. Martin's Press, 1973.
Byrne, Ophelia. *The Stage in Ulster from the Eighteenth Century: Selected from the Theatre Archive of the Linen Hall Library*. Belfast: Linen Hall Library, 1997.
Cambridge Dictionary of Irish Biography. Cambridge: Cambridge Univ. Press, 2010.
Carey, Hilary M. *God's Empire: Religion and Colonialism in the British World, c. 1808–1908*. Cambridge: Cambridge Univ. Press, 2011.
Carter, Grayson. *Anglican Evangelicals: Protestant Secession from the Via Media, c. 1800–1850*. Oxford: Oxford Univ. Press, 2001.
Chadwick, Owen. *The Spirit of the Oxford Movement: Tractarian Essays*. Cambridge: Cambridge Univ. Press, 1992.
———. *The Victorian Church: Part 1*. Oxford: Adam and Charles Black, 1966.
Chaffin, Tom. *Giant's Causeway: Frederick Douglass' Irish Odyssey and the Making of an American Visionary*. Charlottesville: Univ. of Virginia Press, 2014.
Chase, Malcolm. *Chartism: A New History*. Manchester: Manchester Univ. Press, 2007.
Clark, Anna. *The Struggle for the Breeches: Gender and the Making of the British Working Classes*. Berkeley: Univ. of California Press, 1997.

Clark, J. C. D. *English Society, 1688–1832: Ideology, Social Structure, and Political Practice during the Ancien Régime.* Cambridge: Cambridge Univ. Press, 1985.

Clark, Michael. *Albion and Jerusalem: The Anglo-Jewish Community in the Post-Emancipation Era, 1858–1887.* Oxford: Oxford Univ. Press, 2009.

Clark, Peter. *British Clubs and Societies, 1580–1800: The Origins of an Associational World.* Oxford: Oxford Univ. Press, 2000.

Clark, Samuel, and James S. Donnelly Jr. *Irish Peasants: Violence and Political Unrest, 1780–1914.* Madison: Univ. of Wisconsin Press, 1983.

Clarke, R. S. J. *Gravestone Inscriptions: Belfast: Volume 1: Shankill Graveyard and Tablets in Christ Church and St. George's Church.* Belfast: Ulster Historical Foundation, 1982.

Cohen, Marilyn. ed. *The Warp of Ulster's Past: Interdisciplinary Perspectives on the Irish Linen Industry.* Dublin: Four Courts Press, 1997.

Colley, Linda. *Britons: Forging the Nation, 1707–1837.* New Haven, CT: Yale Univ. Press, 1994.

Comerford, R. V. *The Fenians in Context: Irish Politics and Society, 1848–82.* Dublin: Wolfhound Press, 1985.

Connolly, Sean J., ed. *Belfast 400: People, Place, and History.* Liverpool: Liverpool Univ. Press, 2013.

———. "Belfast: The Rise and Fall of a Civic Culture?" In *Belfast: The Emerging City, 1850–1914,* edited by Olwen Purdue, 25–48. Dublin: Irish Academic Press, 2013.

———. "The Church of Ireland: A Critical Bibliography: Part IV, 1690–1800." *Irish Historical Studies* 28, no. 112 (November 1993): 362–69.

———. "Like an Old Cathedral City: Belfast Welcomes Queen Victoria, August 1849." *Urban History* 39, no. 4 (November 2012): 571–89.

———. "Mass Politics and Sectarian Conflict, 1823–30." In *A New History of Ireland: Ireland under the Union, 1800–70,* edited by W. E. Vaughan, 74–107. Oxford: Oxford Univ. Press, 1989.

———. *Religion, Law, and Power.* Oxford: Oxford Univ. Press, 1992.

Connolly, Sean J., and Gillian McIntosh. "Imagining Belfast." In *Belfast 400: People, Place, and History,* edited by Sean J. Connolly, 13–62. Liverpool: Liverpool Univ. Press, 2013.

———. "Whose City? Belonging and Exclusion in the Nineteenth-Century Urban World." In *Belfast 400: People, Place, and History,* edited by Sean J. Connolly, 237–70. Liverpool: Liverpool Univ. Press, 2013.

Cooper, June E. *The Protestant Orphan Society and Its Social Significance in Ireland*. Manchester: Manchester Univ. Press, 2015.
Cordery, Simon. *British Friendly Societies, 1750–1914*. London: Palgrave MacMillan, 2003.
Corish, Patrick. *The Irish Catholic Experience: A Historical Survey*. Dublin: Gill and MacMillan, 1985.
Covington, Sarah. *The Devil from over the Sea: Remembering and Forgetting Oliver Cromwell in Ireland*. Oxford: Oxford Univ. Press, 2022.
Cox, Jeffery. *The English Churches in a Secular Society: Lambeth, 1870–1930*. Oxford: Oxford Univ. Press, 1982.
Crawford, John. "'An Overriding Providence': The Life and Ministry of Tresham Dames Gregg (1800–81)." In *The Clergy of the Church of Ireland, 1000–2000*, edited by T. C. Barnard and W. G. Neely, 157–68. Dublin: Four Courts Press, 2006.
Crossman, Virginia. "Attitudes and Responses to Vagrancy in Ireland in the Long Nineteenth Century." In *Crime, Violence, and the Irish in the Nineteenth Century*, edited by Kyle Hughes and Donald MacRaild, 264–79. Liverpool: Liverpool Univ. Press, 2017.
———. *Poverty and the Poor Law in Ireland, 1850–1914*. Liverpool: Liverpool Univ. Press, 2013.
Cronin, Maura, "Popular Politics, 1815–45." In *The Cambridge History of Ireland: Volume 3, 1730–1880*, edited by James Kelly, 128–49. Cambridge: Cambridge Univ. Press, 2017.
Cullen, Frank. "The Provision of Working and Lower-Middle Class Housing in Late Nineteenth-Century Urban Ireland." *Proceedings of the Royal Irish Academy* 111C (2011): 238–41.
Cullen, Louis M. *The Emergence of Modern Ireland*. New York: Holmes and Meier, 1981.
———. "Late Eighteenth-Century Politicisation in Ireland." In *Culture et Pratiques Politiques en France et en Irelande XVIe-XVIIIe Siecle*. Paris: Centre de Recherches Historiques, 1990.
Cunningham, John. "Popular Protest and a 'Moral Economy' in Provincial Ireland in the Early Nineteenth Century." In *Essays in Irish Labour History: A Festschrift for Elizabeth and John W. Boyle*, edited by Francis Devine, Fintan Lane, and Niamh Purséil, 26–48. Dublin: Irish Academic Press, 2008.

Curran, Darragh. *The Protestant Community in Ulster, 1825—45*. Dublin: Four Courts Press, 2014.

Das, Suranjan. *Communal Riots in Bengal, 1905–1947*. Oxford: Oxford Univ. Press, 1991.

Das, Veena. "Violence, Gender, and Subjectivity," *Annual Review of Anthropology* 37 (October 2008): 283–99.

Datta, P. K. *Carving Blocs: Communal Ideology in Early Twentieth-Century Bengal*. Oxford: Oxford Univ. Press, 1999.

Davis, Natalie Zemon. "The Rites of Violence." In *Society and Culture in Early Modern France*, chap. 6. Stanford, CA: Stanford Univ. Press, 1975.

———. "Writing the Rites of Violence and Afterward." *Past and Present*, supplement 7 (2012): 8–29.

Dickey, Brian. "'Going about and Doing Good': Evangelicals and Poverty c.1815–70." In *Evangelical Faith and Social Zeal*, edited by John Wolffe, 38–58. London: Society for the Promotion of Christian Knowledge, 1995.

Dickson, J. N. Ian. *Beyond Religious Discourse: Sermons, Preaching and Evangelical Protestants in Nineteenth-Century Irish Society*. Milton Keyes, UK: Paternoster Press, 2007.

———. "Evangelical Women and Victorian Women: the Belfast Female Mission, 1859–1903." *Journal of Ecclesiastical History* 55, no. 5 (October 2004): 700–725.

Donnelly, James S. Jr. *Captain Rock: The Irish Agrarian Rebellion of 1821–1824*. Madison: Univ. of Wisconsin Press, 2009.

———. *The Great Irish Potato Famine*. Stroud, Gloucestershire: Sutton Publishing, 2001.

———. *The Land and People of Nineteenth-Century Cork: Rural Economy and the Land Question*. New York: Routledge and Kegan Paul, 1975.

———. "Pastorini and Captain Rock: Millenarianism and Sectarianism in the Rockite Movement of 1821–4." In *Irish Peasants: Violence and Political Unrest, 1780–1914*, edited by Samuel Clark and James S. Donnelly, 102–39. Madison: Univ. of Wisconsin Press, 1983.

Donnelly, James S. Jr., and Kerby A. Miller, eds. *Irish Popular Culture, 1650–1850*. Dublin: Irish Academic Press, 1998.

Downer, David. "William Murphy and Orangeism in Mid-Victorian England." *History Ireland* 24 (2016): 26–29.

Doyle, David. *The Reverend Thomas Goff, 1772–1844. Property, Propinquity and Protestantism*. Dublin: Four Courts Press, 2015.
Doyle, Mark. *Communal Violence in the British Empire: Disturbing the Pax*. London: Bloomsbury Academic, 2016.
———. *Fighting like the Devil for the Sake of God: Protestants, Catholics and the Origins of Violence in Victorian Belfast*. Manchester: Manchester Univ. Press, 2009.
———. "Martyrs of Liberty: Open-Air Preaching and Popular Violence in Victorian Britain and Ireland." In *Faith, War, and Violence: Religion & Public Life*, vol. 39, edited by Gabriel Ricci, 149–64. New Brunswick, NJ: Transaction Publishers, 2014.
———. "The Sepoys of the Pound and Sandy Row: Empire and Identity in Mid-Victorian Belfast." *Journal of Urban History* 36, no. 6 (November 2010): 849–67.
"Drew, Thomas (Sir)." *Dictionary of Irish Architects, 1720–1940*. http://www.dia.ie/architects/view/1650/DREW-THOMAS%28SIR%29.
Elliott, Marianne. *The Catholics of Ulster*. New York: Basic Books, 2002.
———. *When God Took Sides: Religion and Identity in Ireland*. New York: Oxford Univ. Press, 2009.
Farrell, Nigel. "Cholera in Belfast in 1832 and 1848/49." *History of Medicine in Ireland* (blog), September 12, 2013. http://historyofmedicineinireland.blogspot.com/2013/09/cholera-in-belfast-1832-and-184849-by.html.
Farrell, Sean. "Building Connections: The Mant Controversy and the Church of Ireland in Early Victorian Belfast." *Irish Historical Studies* 154 (November 2014): 52–71.
———. "Challenging the Consensus of Complex Avoidance: Ulster Sectarianism and the Lessons of South Asian Historiography." *History Compass* 8, no. 9 (September 2010): 1023–35.
———. "Contested Histories? Richard Mant's *History of the Church in Ireland* and Religious Politics in Early Victorian Belfast." In *The Church of Ireland and Its Past*, edited by Mark Empey, Alan Ford, and Miriam Moffitt, 95–107. Dublin: Four Courts Press, 2017.
———. "Feed My Lambs: The Reverend Thomas Drew and Protestant Children in Early Victorian Belfast." *New Hibernia Review* 19, no. 2 (Summer 2015): 43–58.
———. "Going to Extremes: Anti-Catholicism and Anti-Slavery in Early Victorian Belfast." *European Romantic Review* 28, no. 4 (2017): 461–72.

———. "Providence, Progress and Silence: Writing the Irish Famine from Sandy Row." *Canadian Journal of Irish Studies* 36, no. 2 (Winter 2013): 101–13.

———. "Recapturing the Flag: The Campaign to Repeal the Party Processions Act, 1860–72." *Eire-Ireland* 32, no. 2–3 (Summer/Fall 1997): 52–78.

———. *Rituals and Riots: Sectarian Violence and Political Culture in Ulster, 1784–1886*. Lexington: Univ. Press of Kentucky, 2000.

———. "The Trillick Railway Outrage: The Politics of Atrocity in Post-Famine Ulster." In *Glaubenskämpfe: Katholiken und Gewalt im 19. Jahrhundert* [Battles over Belief: Catholics and Violence in the 19th Century], edited by E. G. Bouwers, 217–40. Berlin: Vandenhoeck and Ruprecht, 2019.

———. "Writing an Orange Dolly's Brae." In *Shadows of the Gunmen: Violence and Culture in Modern Ireland*, edited by Sean Farrell and Danine Farquharson, 90–106. Cork: Cork Univ. Press, 2007.

Faught, C. Brad. *The Oxford Movement*. University Park: Penn State Univ. Press, 2004.

Fegan, Jennifer. *Literature and the Irish Famine, 1845–1919*. Oxford: Clarendon Press, 2003.

Ferreira, Patricia. "Frederick Douglass and the 1846 Dublin Edition of His Narrative." *New Hibernia Review* 5, no. 1 (Spring 2001): 53–67.

Fitzgerald, Desmond. "The Trillick Derailment of 1854." *Clogher Record* 15, no. 1 (1994): 31–47.

Fitzpatrick, David. *Descendancy: Irish Protestant Histories since 1795*. Oxford: Oxford Univ. Press, 2015.

———. *Politics and Irish Life, 1913–21: Provincial Experiences of War and Revolution*. Dublin: Gill and MacMillan, 1977.

Ford, Alan. "High or Low? Writing the Irish Reformation in the Early Nineteenth Century." *Bulletin of the John Ryland's Library of Manchester* 90 (2014): 93–112.

———. "Living Together, Living Apart: Sectarianism in Early Modern Ireland." In *The Origins of Sectarianism in Early Modern Ireland*, edited by Alan Ford and John McCafferty, 1–23. Cambridge: Cambridge Univ. Press, 2005.

Ford, Alan, James McGuire, and Kenneth Milne, eds. *As by Law Established: The Church of Ireland since the Reformation*. Dublin: Lilliput Press, 1995.

Foster, John. *Class Struggle in the Industrial Revolution: Early Industrial Capitalism in Three English Towns*. London: Weidenfeld & Nicholson, 1974.

Foster, R. F. *Modern Ireland, 1600–1972*. London: Penguin Books, 1990.
Francis, Keith A. "Sermons: Themes and Developments." In *The Oxford Handbook of the British Sermon, 1689–1901*, edited by Keith A. Francis and William Gibson, 31–46. Oxford: Oxford Univ. Press, 2012.
Francis, Keith A., and William Gibson, eds. *The Oxford Handbook of the British Sermon, 1689–1901*. Oxford: Oxford Univ. Press, 2012.
Frogatt, Richard. "Rev. John Edgar (1798–1866)." *Dictionary of Ulster Biography*. http://www.newulsterbiography.co.uk.
Fudge, Thomas A. *Jan Hus: Religious Reform and Social Revolution in Bohemia*. London: Bloomsbury, 2017.
Furse-Roberts, David. *The Making of a Tory Evangelical: Lord Shaftesbury and the Evolving Character of Victorian Evangelicalism*. Eugene, OR: Pickwick Publications, 2019.
Gaffikin, Thomas. *Belfast Fifty Years Ago: A Lecture Delivered in the Working Men's Institute, Belfast*. 2nd ed. Belfast: *News-Letter* Printing Press, 1885.
Geoghegan, Vincent. "Robert Owen, Co-operation and Ulster in the 1830s." In *Politics and the Irish Working Class, 1830–1945*, edited by Fintan Lane and Donal Ó Drisceoil, 6–26. Basingstoke, UK: Palgrave, 2005.
Ghosh, Durba. "Another Set of Imperial Turns?" *American Historical Review* 117, no. 3 (2012): 789–93.
Gibbon, Peter. *The Origins of Ulster Unionism*. Manchester: Manchester Univ. Press, 1975.
Gibson, William. "The British Sermon, 1689–1901: Quantities, Performance, and Culture." In *Oxford History of the British Sermon*, edited by Keith A. Francis and Gibson, 3–30. Oxford: Oxford Univ. Press, 2012.
Gill, Conrad. *The Rise of the Irish Linen Industry*. Oxford: Oxford Univ. Press, 1925.
Gillespie, Raymond. *Devoted People: Belief and Religion in Early Modern Ireland*. Manchester: Manchester Univ. Press, 1997.
———. "Temple's Fate: Reading *The Irish Rebellion* in Late Seventeenth-Century Ireland." In *British Interventions in Early Modern Ireland*, edited by Ciaran Brady and Jane Ohlmeyer, 315–33. Cambridge: Cambridge Univ. Press, 2005.
Gillespie, Raymond, and W. G. Neely, eds. *The Laity and the Church of Ireland, 1000–2000: All Sorts and Conditions*. Dublin: Four Courts Press, 2002.
Gillespie, Raymond, and Roibeard Ó Gallachóir. *Preaching in Belfast, 1747–72: A Selection of the Sermons of James Saurin*. Dublin: Four Courts Press, 2015.

Gillespie, Raymond, and Stephen Royle. *Irish Historic Towns Atlas No. 12: Belfast, Part I, to 1840.* Dublin: Royal Irish Academy, 2003.

Goldie, Mark. "The Unacknowledged Republic: Officeholding in Early Modern England." In *The Politics of the Excluded, c.1500–1850*, edited by Tim Harris, 153–94. London: Palgrave MacMillan, 2001.

Gould, William. *Religion and Conflict in Modern South Asia.* Cambridge: Cambridge Univ. Press, 2012.

Gray, Jane. *Spinning the Threads of Uneven Development: Gender and Industrialization in Ireland during the Long Eighteenth Century.* Oxford: Lexington Books, 2005.

Gray, Peter. "Accounting for Catastrophe: William Wilde, the 1851 Census and the Great Famine." In *Power and Popular Culture in Modern Ireland: Essays in Honour of James S. Donnelly, Jr.*, edited by Michael de Nie and Sean Farrell, 50–66. Dublin: Irish Academic Press, 2010.

———. *Famine, Land and Politics: British Government and Irish Society, 1843–50.* Dublin: Irish Academic Press, 1999.

———. *The Making of the Irish Poor Law.* Manchester: Manchester Univ. Press, 2009.

———. "Potatoes and Providence: British Government's Responses to the Great Famine." *Bullán: An Irish Studies Journal* 1 (1994): 75–90.

———. "Thomas Chalmers and Irish Poverty." In *Ireland and Scotland in the Nineteenth Century*, edited by Frank Ferguson and James McConnel, 93–107. Dublin: Four Courts Press, 2009.

Grant, James. "The Great Famine and the Poor Law in Ulster: The Rate-in-Aid Issue of 1849." *Irish Historical Studies* 27, no. 105 (May 1990): 30–47.

———. "The Great Famine in County Down." In *Down: History and Society*, edited by Lindsay Proudfoot, 353–82. Dublin: Geography Publications, 2007.

Green, S. J. D. *Religion in the Age of Decline: Organization and Experience in Industrial Yorkshire, 1870–1920.* Cambridge: Cambridge Univ. Press, 1996.

Gribben, Crawford, and Andrew R. Holmes, eds. *Protestant Millennialism, Evangelicalism, and Irish Society, 1790–2005.* London: Palgrave Macmillan, 2005.

Griffin, Brian. *The Bulkies: Police and Crime in Belfast, 1800–1865.* Dublin: Irish Academic Press, 1997.

Griffin, Emma. *Liberty's Dawn: A People's History of the Industrial Revolution.* New Haven, CT: Yale Univ. Press, 2014.

Griffin, Patrick. *The People with No Name: Ireland's Ulster Scots, America's Scots Irish, and the Creation of a British Atlantic World, 1689–1764*. Princeton, NJ: Princeton Univ. Press, 2001.

Gunn, Simon. *The Public Culture of the Victorian Middle Class: Ritual and Authority in the English Industrial City, 1840–1914*. Manchester: Manchester Univ. Press, 2007.

Hall, Gerald. *Ulster Liberalism, 1778–1876: The Middle Path*. Dublin: Four Courts Press, 2011.

Hamilton, Susan. "'Her Usual Daring Style': Feminist New Journalism, Pioneering New Women and Traces of Frances Power Cobbe." In *Women in Journalism at the Fin de Siècle: Making a Name for Herself*, edited by F. Elizabeth Gray, 39–42. London: Palgrave MacMillan, 2012.

Hammond, B. B., and J. L. Hammond. *The Skilled Labourer*. London: Longmans, Green and Co., 1919.

———. *The Town Labourer*. London: Longmans, Green and Co., 1917.

———. *The Village Labourer*. London: Longmans, Green and Co., 1911.

Hempton, David. "Belfast: The Unique City?" In *European Religion in the Age of Great Cities*, edited by Hugh McLeod, 145–64. London: Routledge, 1995.

Hempton, David, and Myrtle Hill. *Evangelical Protestantism in Ulster Society, 1740–1890*. London: Routledge, 1992.

Herbert, Christopher. *War of No Pity: The Indian Mutiny and Victorian Trauma*. Princeton, NJ: Princeton Univ. Press, 2008.

Herringer, Carol Englehardt. *Victorians and the Virgin Mary: Religion and Gender in England, 1830–85*. Manchester: Manchester Univ. Press, 2008.

Hill, Jacqueline, R. *From Patriots to Unionists: Dublin Civic Politics and Irish Protestant Patriotism, 1660–1840*. Oxford: Clarendon Press, 1997.

———. "National Festivals, the State, and 'Protestant Ascendancy' in Ireland, 1790–1829." *Irish Historical Studies* 24, no. 93 (May 1984): 30–51.

Hilton, Boyd. *Age of Atonement: The Influence of Evangelicalism on Social and Economic Thought*. Oxford: Oxford Univ. Press, 1988.

———. "Evangelical Social Attitudes: A Reply to Ralph Brown." *Journal of Ecclesiastical History* 60, no. 1 (January 2009): 119–25.

———. *A Mad, Bad, and Dangerous People? England, 1783–1846*. Oxford: Clarendon Press, 2006.

Himmelfarb, Gertrude. *The Idea of Poverty: England and the Early Industrial Age*. New York: Knopf, 1983.

Hirst, Catherine. *Religion, Politics and Violence in 19th Century Belfast: The Pound and Sandy Row, 1820–1886.* Dublin: Four Courts Press, 2001.

Hobsbawm, E. J. "The British Standard of Living, 1790–1850." *Economic History Review* 10, no. 1 (1957): 46–68.

———. "Labour Traditions." In *Labouring Men: Studies in the History of Labour*, by E. J. Hobsbawm, 371–85. New York: Basic Books, 1964.

———. "Methodism and the Threat of Revolution in Britain." In *Labouring Men: Studies in the History of Labour*, by E. J. Hobsbawm, 23–33. New York: Basic Books, 1964.

Holmes, Andrew, R. *The Irish Presbyterian Mind: Conservative Theology, Evangelical Experience, and Modern Criticism, 1830–1930.* Oxford: Oxford Univ. Press, 2018.

———. "Protestantism in the Nineteenth Century: Revival and Crisis." In *The Cambridge History of Ireland: Volume 3, 1730–1880*, edited by James Kelly, 331–49. Cambridge: Cambridge Univ. Press, 2017.

———. "Religion, Anti-Slavery and Identity: Irish Presbyterians, the United States, and Transatlantic Evangelicalism, 1820–1914." *Irish Historical Studies* 39, no. 155 (2015): 378–98.

———. *The Shaping of Ulster Presbyterian Belief and Practice.* Oxford: Oxford Univ. Press, 2006.

———. "The Ulster Revival of 1859: Causes, Controversies, and Consequences." *Journal of Ecclesiastical History* 63, no. 3 (2012): 488–515.

Holmes, Janice. "Irish Evangelicals and the British Evangelical Community, 1820s–1870s." In *Evangelicals and Catholics in Nineteenth-Century Ireland*, edited by James H. Murphy, 209–22. Dublin: Four Courts Press, 2005.

———. "The Role of Open-Air Preaching in the Belfast Riots of 1857." *Proceedings of the Royal Irish Academy* 102C (2002): 47–66.

Holmes, R. Finlay. *Henry Cooke.* Belfast: Christian Journals, 1981.

Huddie, Paul. *The Crimean War and Irish Society.* Oxford: Oxford Univ. Press, 2015.

Hughes, A. J. *Robert Shipboy MacAdam (1808–95): His Life and Gaelic Proverb Collection.* Belfast: Institute of Irish Studies, 1998.

Hughes, Kyle. *Scots in Victorian and Edwardian Belfast: A Study in Elite Migration.* Edinburgh: Edinburgh Univ. Press, 2013.

Humphries, Jane. *Childhood and Child Labour in the British Industrial Revolution.* Cambridge: Cambridge Univ. Press, 2011.

Hunt, Tristram. *Building Jerusalem: The Rise and Fall of the Victorian City*. London: Penguin Books, 2019.
Huzzey, Richard, and Henry J. Miller. "The Politics of Petitioning: Parliament, Government, and Subscriptional Cultures in the United Kingdom, 1780–1918." *History* 106, no. 370 (April 2021): 221–43. https://doi.org/10.1111/1468-229X.13103.
Jackson, Alvin. *Home Rule: An Irish History, 1800–2000*. Oxford: Oxford Univ. Press, 2003.
James, Kevin J. *Handloom Weavers in Ulster's Linen Industry, 1815–1914*. Dublin: Four Courts Press, 2007.
Jenkins, Mick. *The General Strike of 1842*. London: Lawrence and Wishart, 1980.
Jenkins, William. "Two Irelands beyond the Sea: Exploring Loyalist Networks in the 1880s." In *Migrations: Ireland in a Global World*, edited by Mary Gilmartin and Allen White, 36–54. Manchester: Manchester Univ. Press, 2013.
Johnson, Alice. *Middle-Class Life in Victorian Belfast*. Liverpool: Liverpool Univ. Press, 2020.
Jones, Emyrs. *A Social Geography of Belfast*. Oxford: Oxford Univ. Press, 1960.
Jordan, Allison. *Who Cared? Charity in Victorian and Edwardian Belfast*. Belfast: Institute of Irish Studies, 1992.
Joyce, Patrick. *Work, Society and Politics: The Culture of the Factory in Later Victorian England*. New Brunswick, NJ: Rutgers Univ. Press, 1980.
Kadel, Bradley. *Drink and Culture in Nineteenth-Century Ireland: The Alcohol Trade and the Politics of the Irish Public House*. London: I. B. Tauris, 2014.
Kennedy, Liam. *Colonialism, Religion and Nationalism in Ireland*. Belfast: Institute of Irish Studies, 1996.
———. "The Rural Economy." In *An Economic History of Ulster, 1820–1945*, edited by Liam Kennedy and Phillip Ollerenshaw, 1–61. Manchester: Manchester Univ. Press, 1985.
Kenny, Kevin. *Making Sense of the Molly Maguires*. Oxford: Oxford Univ. Press, 1998.
Kidd, Colin. "North Britishness and the Nature of Eighteenth-Century British Patriotisms." *Historical Journal* 39, no. 2 (1996): 364–81.
Kinealy, Christine, and Gerard Mac Atasney. *The Hidden Famine: Hunger, Poverty and Sectarianism in Belfast*. Dublin: Pluto Books, 2000.

Kinealy, Christine, and Trevor Parkhill. *The Famine in Ulster*. Belfast: Ulster Historical Foundation, 1997.

Koditschek, Theodore. *Class Formation and Urban Industrial Society: Bradford, 1750–1850*. Cambridge: Cambridge Univ. Press, 1990.

Larkin, Emmet. *The Making of the Roman Catholic Church in Ireland, 1850–1860*. Chapel Hill: Univ. of North Carolina Press, 1980.

Larmour, Paul. *Belfast: An Illustrated Architectural Guide*. Belfast: Friar's Bush Press, 1989.

Laqueur, Thomas. *Religion and Respectability: Sunday Schools and Working Class Culture, 1780–1850*. New Haven, CT: Yale Univ. Press, 1976.

Lawrence, Jon. "Paternalism, Class, and the British Path to Modernity." In *The Peculiarities of Liberal Modernity in Imperial Britain*, edited by Simon Gunn and James Vernon, 147–64. Berkeley: Univ. of California Press, 2011.

Leslie, J. B. *Clergy of Connor, from Patrician Times to the Present Day*. Belfast: Ulster Historical Association, 1993.

Lewis, Matthew, and Shaun McDaid. "Bosnia on the Border? Republican Violence in Northern Ireland during the 1920s and 1970s." *Terrorism and Political Violence* 29 (2017): 635–55.

Liechty, Joseph. "The Problem of Sectarianism and the Church of Ireland." In *As by Law Established*, edited by Alan Ford, Martin McGuire, and Kenneth Milne, 204–22. Dublin: Lilliput Press, 1995.

Liechty, Joseph, and Cecelia Clegg. *Moving beyond Sectarianism: Religion, Conflict, and Reconciliation in Northern Ireland*. Dublin: Columba Press, 2001.

Luddy, Maria. *Prostitution and Irish Society, 1800–1940*. Cambridge: Cambridge Univ. Press, 2007.

———. *Women and Philanthropy in Nineteenth-Century Ireland*. Cambridge: Cambridge Univ. Press, 1995.

Lunney, Linde. "Singer, Joseph Henderson." *Dictionary of Irish Biography*, October 2009. https://www.dib.ie/biography/singer-joseph-henderson-a8093.

Macauley, Ambrose. *Patrick Dorrian: Bishop of Down and Connor, 1865–85*. Dublin: Irish Academic Press, 1987.

Mac Domhnaill, Aodh. *Dánta*. Edited by Colm Beckett. Dublin: An Clóchomhar Tta, 1987.

MacNeice, John Frederick. *The Church of Ireland in Belfast*. Belfast: *Belfast News-Letter*, 1931.

MacRaild, Donald. *Faith, Fraternity and Fighting: The Orange Order and Irish Migrants in Northern England, c. 1850–1920*. Liverpool: Liverpool Univ. Press, 2005.

———. "Transnationalising 'Anti-Popery': Militant Protestant Preachers in the Nineteenth-Century Anglo World." *Journal of Religious History* 39, no. 2 (June 2015): 224–43.

MacSuibhne, Breandán, ed., *Hugh Dorian: The Outer Edge of Ulster: A Social Memoir of Nineteenth-Century Donegal*. Dublin: Lilliput Press, 2001.

Madden, Kyla. *Forkhill Protestants and Forkhill Catholics, 1787–1858*. Montreal: McGill-Queen's Univ. Press, 2005.

Maguire, Martin. "The Church of Ireland and the Problem of the Protestant Working-Class of Dublin, 1870s–1930s." In *As by Law Established: The Church of Ireland since the Reformation*, edited by Alan Ford, Martin McGuire, and Kenneth Milne, 195–203. Dublin: Lilliput Press, 1995.

Maguire, W. A. *Belfast*. Keele, UK: Ryburn Publishing, 1993.

———. *The Downshire Estates in Ireland, 1801–1845*. Oxford: Oxford Univ. Press, 1972.

———. *Living like a Lord: The Second Marquis of Donegall, 1769–1844*. Belfast: Appletree Press, 1984.

———. "Lord Donegall and the Sale of Belfast: A Case History from the Encumbered Estates Court." *Economic History Review* 29, no. 4 (1976): 570–84.

Malik, Salahuddin. *1857: War of Independence or Clash of Civilisations? British Public Reactions*. Oxford: Oxford Univ. Press, 2008.

Markovits, Stefanie. *The Crimean War in the British Imagination*. Cambridge: Cambridge Univ. Press, 2009.

Maume, Patrick. "Repelling the Repealer: William McComb's Caricatures of Daniel O'Connell." *History Ireland* 13, no. 2 (March-April 2005): 43–47.

Maxwell, Constantia. *A History of Trinity College, Dublin, 1591–1892*. Dublin: Univ. Press of Trinity College, 1946.

McBride, Ian. "Religion." In *The Princeton History of Modern Ireland*, edited by Richard Bourke and Ian McBride, 292–319. Princeton, NJ: Princeton Univ. Press, 2014.

———. *Scripture Politics: Ulster Presbyterians and Irish Radicalism in the Late Eighteenth Century*. Oxford: Oxford Univ. Press, 1998.

———. "The Shadow of the Gunmen: Irish Historians and the I.R.A." *Journal of Contemporary History* 46, no. 3 (July 2011): 686–710.

———. *The Siege of Derry in Ulster Protestant Mythology.* Dublin: Four Courts Press, 1997.

McCabe, Ciarán. *Begging, Charity, and Religion in Pre-Famine Ireland.* Liverpool: Liverpool Univ. Press, 2018.

McCabe, Desmond, and Cormac O'Grada. "'Better off Thrown behind a Ditch': Enniskillen Workhouse during the Great Famine." In *Power and Popular Culture in Modern Ireland: Essays in Honour of James S. Donnelly, Jr.*, edited by Michael de Nie and Sean Farrell, 8–30. Cork: Cork Univ. Press, 2010.

McCann, Donna. *The Row You Know: Memories of Old Sandy Row.* Belfast: Sandy Row Community Centre, 1997.

McClelland, Aiken. "The Early History of the Brown Street Primary School." *Ulster Folklife* 17 (1971): 52–60.

———. *William Johnston of Ballykilbeg.* Lurgan: Ulster Society Publications, 1990.

McConnel, James. "Remembering the Gunpowder Plot in Ireland, 1605–1920." *Journal of British Studies* 50 (October 2011): 863–91.

McDowell, R. B. *The Church of Ireland, 1869–1969.* London and Boston: Routledge and Kegan Paul, 1975.

McDowell, R. B., and D. A. Webb. *Trinity College Dublin, 1592–1992.* Cambridge: Cambridge Univ. Press, 1982.

McGee, Thomas D'Arcy. *A Life of the Reverend Edward Maginn.* New York: Patrick O'Shea, 1857.

McGuire, James, and James Quinn, eds. *Dictionary of Irish Biography: From Earliest Times to the Year 2002.* 9 vols. Cambridge: Cambridge Univ. Press, 2009.

McLeod, Hugh. "New Perspectives on Victorian Working-Class Religion: The Oral Evidence." *Oral History Journal* 14, no. 1 (1986): 31–49.

———. *Religion and the Working Class in Nineteenth-Century Britain.* London: MacMillan, 1984.

McMahon, Cian T. *The Coffin Ship: Life and Death at Sea during the Great Irish Famine.* New York: New York Univ. Press, 2021.

McNeilly, Norman, *The First Hundred Years: A History of the Development of the Church of Ireland's Young Men's Society.* PRONI, D.3936/H/5/6.

Miller, David W. "The Armagh Troubles." In *Irish Peasants: Violence and Political Unrest, 1780–1914*, edited by Samuel Clark and James S. Donnelly, 155–91. Madison: Univ. of Wisconsin Press, 1983.

———. "Irish Christianity and Revolution." In *Revolution, Counter Revolution and Union: Ireland in the 1790s*, edited by Jim Smyth, 195–210. Cambridge: Cambridge Univ. Press, 2000.

———. "John MacHale, Henry Cooke and the Demise of the Confessional State in Ireland." In *Power and Popular Culture in Modern Ireland: Essays in Honour of James S. Donnelly, Jr.*, edited by Michael de Nie and Sean Farrell, 109–24. Dublin: Irish Academic Press, 2010.

———. *Peep O'Day Boys and Defenders: Selected Documents on the County Armagh Disturbances, 1784–1796*. Belfast: Public Record Office of Northern Ireland, 1990.

———. "Presbyterianism and 'Modernisation' in Modern Ulster." *Past and Present* 80 (August 1978): 68–90.

———. *Queens Rebels: Ulster Loyalism in Historical Perspective*. Dublin: Gill and MacMillan, 1978.

Miller, Kerby A. "Belfast's First Bomb, 28 February 1816: Class Conflict and the Origins of Unionist Hegemony." *Eire-Ireland* 39 (Spring-Summer 2004): 262–80.

———. *Emigrants and Exiles: Ireland and the Irish Exodus to North America*. Oxford: Oxford Univ. Press, 1985.

———. "'Scotch-Irish Myths' and 'Irish' Identities in Eighteenth- and Nineteenth-Century America." In *New Perspectives on the Irish Diaspora*, edited by Charles Fanning, 75–92. Carbondale: Southern Illinois Univ. Press, 2000.

Miller, Kerby A., Arnold Schrier, Bruce D. Boling, and David N. Doyle, eds. *Irish Immigrants in the Land of Canaan: Letters and Memoirs from Colonial and Revolutionary America, 1685–1815*. Oxford: Oxford Univ. Press, 2003.

Miller, Kerby A., and Breandán Mac Suibhne. "Frank Roney and the Fenians: A Reappraisal of Irish Republicanism in 1860s Belfast and Ulster." *Eire-Ireland*, no. 3–4 (Fall/Winter 2016): 23–54.

Miller, Kerby A., Bruce D. Boling, and Liam Kennedy. "The Famine's Scars: William Murphy's Ulster and American Odyssey. In *New Directions in Irish American History*, edited by Kevin Kenny, 36–60. Madison: Univ. of Wisconsin Press, 2003.

Miller, Kerby A., Liam Kennedy, and Brian Gurrin. "The Great Famine and Religious Demography in Mid-Nineteenth-Century Ulster." In *Atlas of the Great Famine*, edited by John Crowley, William J. Smyth, and Mike Murphy, 426–34. New York: New York Univ. Press, 2012.

Moffitt, Miriam. *The Society for Irish Church Missions to the Roman Catholics, 1849–1950*. Manchester: Manchester Univ. Press, 2010.

———. *Soupers and Jumpers: The Protestant Missions in Connemara, 1848–1937*. London: History Press, 2008.

Morash, Christopher. *Writing the Irish Famine*. Oxford: Clarendon Press, 1995.

Morris, R. J. "Reading the Riot Commission: Belfast, 1857." *Irish Historical Studies* 43, no. 164 (2019): 194–219.

Murdock, Lydia. *Imagined Orphans: Poor Families, Child Welfare, and Contested Citizenship in London*. New Brunswick, NJ: Rutgers Univ. Press, 2006.

Murphy, Willa. "A Germ in the Blood." *Irish Literary Supplement* (Spring 2003): 10–11.

Nally, David. *Human Encumbrances: Political Violence and the Great Irish Famine*. Notre Dame, IN: Univ. of Notre Dame Press, 2011.

Navickas, Katrina. *Protest and the Politics of Space and Place, 1789–1848*. Manchester: Manchester Univ. Press, 2016.

Neal, Frank. *Sectarian Violence: The Liverpool Experience*. Manchester: Manchester Univ. Press, 1988.

Newman, Gerald. "Nationalism Revisited." *Journal of British Studies* 35, no. 1 (1996): 118–27.

Nockles, Peter. "Church of Protestant Sect? The Church of Ireland, High Churchmanship, and the Oxford Movement, 1822–69." *Historical Journal* 41, no. 2 (January 1998): 457–93.

———. *The Oxford Movement in Context: High Anglican Churchmanship, 1780–1857*. Cambridge: Cambridge Univ. Press, 1994.

Norman, E. R. *Anti-Catholicism in Victorian England*. London: Allen & Unwin, 1968.

O'Brien, Gillian, *The Darkness Echoing: Exploring Ireland's Places of Famine, Death, and Rebellion*. London: Random House, 2020.

O'Connor, Emmet. *A Labour History of Ireland, 1824–2000*. Dublin: Gill and MacMillan, 1992.

O'Ferrall, Fergus. "The Church of Ireland: A Critical Bibliography: Part V: 1800–1870." *Irish Historical Studies* 28 (May 1992): 369–76.

O'Hearn, Dennis. "Irish Linen: A Peripheral Industry." In *The Warp of Ulster's Past: Interdisciplinary Perspectives on the Irish Linen Industry*, edited by Marilyn Cohen, 161–90. Dublin: Four Courts Press, 1997.

O'Luain, Kerron. "Young and Old Ireland: Repeal Politics in Belfast, 1846–8." *New Hibernia Review* 22, no. 2 (Summer 2018): 38–53.
Owen, D. J. *History of Belfast.* Belfast: W. & G. Baird, 1921.
Pandey, Gyanendra. *The Construction of Communalism in Colonial North India.* Delhi: Oxford Univ. Press, 1990.
Patterson, David. *The Provincialisms of Belfast and the Surrounding Districts Pointed Out and Corrected.* Belfast: Alex Mayne, 1860.
Patterson, Henry. *Class Conflict and Sectarianism: The Protestant Working Class and the Belfast Labour Movement, 1868–1920.* Belfast: Blackstaff Press, 1980.
———. "Industrial Labour and the Labour Movement, 1829–1914." In *An Economic History of Ulster, 1820–1939,* edited by Liam Kennedy and Phillip Ollerenshaw, 158–83. Manchester: Manchester Univ. Press, 1985.
Patton, Marcus. *Central Belfast: A Historical Gazetteer.* Belfast: Ulster Archaeological Heritage Society, 1993.
Paz, D. G. *Popular Anti-Catholicism in Victorian England.* Stanford, CA: Stanford Univ. Press, 1992.
Pennington, Brian K. *Was Hinduism Invented? Britons, Indians, and the Colonial Construction of Religion.* Oxford: Oxford Univ. Press, 2005.
Pincus, Steven. "Review of Linda Colley's *Britons.*" *Journal of Modern History* 67, no. 1 (1995): 132–36.
Plotz, Judith. *Romanticism and the Vocation of Childhood.* London: Palgrave MacMillan, 2001.
Proudfoot, Lindsay, ed. *Down: History and Society.* Dublin: Geography Publications, 2007.
Purdue, Olwen, ed. *Belfast: The Emerging City, 1850–1914.* Dublin: Irish Academic Press, 2013.
Rafferty, Oliver. *Catholicism in Ulster, 1603–1983: An Interpretive Essay.* Dublin: Gill and MacMillan, 1994.
Rankin, J. Frederick. *Down Cathedral: The Church of Saint Patrick of Down.* Belfast: Ulster Historical Foundation, 1997.
Regan, John M. "Irish Public Histories as an Historiographical Problem." *Irish Historical Studies* 37, no. 146 (November 2010): 265–92.
Ritchie, Daniel. "Abolitionism and Evangelicalism: Isaac Nelson, the Evangelical Alliance, and the Transatlantic Debate over Christian Fellowship with Slaveholders." *Historical Journal* 57, no. 2 (June 2014): 421–46.
———. "Antislavery Orthodoxy: Isaac Nelson and the Free Church of Scotland, c. 1843–65." *Scottish Historical Review* 94, no. 1 (April 2015): 74–99.

———. "William McIlwaine and the 1859 Revival in Ulster: A Study of Anglican and Evangelical Identities." *Journal of Ecclesiastical History* 65, no. 4 (October 2014): 803–26.

Roberts, M. J. D. *Making English Morals: Voluntary Association and Moral Reform in England, 1787–1886*. Cambridge: Cambridge Univ. Press, 1998.

Roddy, Sarah. *Population, Providence, and Empire: The Churches and Emigration from Nineteenth-Century Ireland*. Manchester: Manchester Univ. Press, 2014.

Rodgers, Nini. *Belfast Slavery and Anti-Slavery*. London: Palgrave MacMillan, 2007.

Royle, Stephen A. *Belfast Part II, 1840 to 1900: Irish Historic Towns Atlas, No. 17*. Dublin: Royal Irish Academy, 2007.

———. *Portrait of an Industrial City: "Clanging Belfast", 1750–1914*. Belfast: Ulster Historical Foundation, 2011.

———. "The Socio-Spatial Structure of Belfast in 1837: Evidence from the First Valuation." *Irish Geography* 24, no. 1 (1991): 1–9.

———. "Workshop of the Empire, 1820–1914." In *Belfast 400: People, Place, and History*, edited by Sean Connolly, 199–236. Liverpool: Liverpool Univ. Press, 2013.

Royle, Stephen A., and T. J. Campbell. "East Belfast and the Suburbanization of Northwest County Down in the Nineteenth Century." In *Down: History and Society*, edited by Lindsay Proudfoot, 629–52. Dublin: Irish Geography Publications, 1997.

Rubinstein, W. D. *A History of the Jews in the English-Speaking World: Great Britain*. London: Palgrave MacMillan, 1996.

Sawyer, Roger. *"We Are But Women": Women in Irish History*. London: Routledge, 1993.

Scranton, Phillip. "Varieties of Paternalism: Industrial Structures and the Social Relations of Production in American Textiles." *American Quarterly* 36, no. 2 (Summer 1984): 235–57.

Searle, G. R. *Morality and the Market in Victorian Britain*. Oxford: Clarendon Press, 1998.

Seeley, R. B. *Memoirs of the Life and Writings of Michael Thomas Sadler*. London: Seeley and Burnside, 1842.

Senior, Hereward. *Orangeism in Ireland and Britain, 1794–1836*. London: Routledge, 1966.

Shields, Andrew. "An Irish Conservative's Perspective of the Defence of the Church of Ireland, 1865–1868." *Journal of Religious History* 31, no. 1 (March 2007): 103–14.

———. *The Irish Conservative Party, 1852–1868: Land, Politics and Religion.* Dublin: Irish Academic Press, 2007.

Sibbett, R. R. *For Christ and Crown: The Story of a Mission.* Belfast: Witness, 1926.

Simut, Corneliu C. *Richard Hooker and His Early Doctrine of Justification.* London: Routledge, 2005.

Skinner, S. A. *Tractarians and the "Condition of England": The Social and Political Thought of the Oxford Movement.* Oxford: Clarendon Press, 2004.

Smith, James. *The Magdalene Laundries and the Nation's Architecture of Containment.* Notre Dame, IN: Univ. of Notre Dame Press, 2007.

Smith, Mark. *Religion in an Industrial Society: Oldham and Saddleworth, 1740–1865.* Oxford: Clarendon Press, 1994.

Smyth, James. *The Men of No Property.* New York: St. Martin's Press, 1992.

Snell, K. D. M. "The Sunday-School Movement in England and Wales: Child Labour, Denominational Control and Working-Class Culture." *Past and Present*, no. 164 (August 1999): 122–33.

Spence, Joseph. "Isaac Butt, Irish Nationality, and the Conditional Defence of the Union, 1833–70." In *Defenders of the Union: A Survey of British and Irish Unionism since 1801*, edited by D. G. Boyce and Alan O'Day, 65–89. London: Routledge, 2001.

Stedman-Jones, Gareth. *Languages of Class: Studies in English Working-Class History, 1833–1982.* Cambridge: Cambridge Univ. Press, 1983.

Stewart, A. T. Q. *The Narrow Ground: Aspects of Ulster, 1609–1969.* London: Faber and Faber, 1977.

Sunderland, Willard. *The Baron's Cloak: A History of the Russian Empire in War and Revolution.* Ithaca, NY: Cornell Univ. Press, 2014.

Sweeney, Fionnaghula. *Frederick Douglass and the Atlantic World.* Liverpool: Liverpool Univ. Press, 2007.

Tanner, Marcus. *Ireland's Holy Wars: The Struggle for a Nation's Soul.* New Haven, CT: Yale Univ. Press, 2001.

Thompson, Dorothy. *The Chartists: Popular Politics in the Industrial Revolution.* London: Pantheon Books, 1984.

Thompson, E. P. *The Making of the English Working Class.* New York: New Press, 1963.

———. "Time, Work Discipline and Industrial Capitalism." *Past and Present* 38 (December 1967): 56–97.

Tosh, John. *A Man's Place: Masculinity and the Middle-Class Home in Victorian England*. New Haven, CT: Yale Univ. Press, 1999.

van der Veer, Peter. *Imperial Encounters: Religion and Modernity in India and Britain*. Princeton, NJ: Princeton Univ. Press, 2001.

Vaughan, W. E., and A. J. Fitzpatrick. *Irish Historical Statistics: Population 1821–1971*. Dublin: Royal Irish Academy, 1978.

Vernon, James. *Politics and the People: A Study in English Political Culture, 1815–67*. Cambridge: Cambridge Univ. Press, 1993.

Wagner, Kim. *The Skull of Alum Bheg: The Life and Death of a Rebel of 1857*. Oxford: Oxford Univ. Press, 2018.

Walker, Brian M. "1641, 1689, 1690 and All That: The Unionist Sense of History." *Irish Review* 12 (1992): 56–64.

———. *Dancing to History's Tune: History, Myth and Politics in Ireland*. Belfast: Institute of Irish Studies, 1996.

———. *A History of St. George's Church Belfast: Two Centuries of Faith, Worship and Music*. Belfast: Ulster Historical Foundation, 2016.

———. "Landowners and Parliamentary Elections in County Down, 1801–1921." In *Down: History and Society*, edited by Lindsay Proudfoot, 297–325. Dublin: Geography Publications, 2007.

———, ed. *Parliamentary Election Results in Ireland, 1801–1922*. Dublin: Royal Irish Academy, 1978.

———. *Ulster Politics: The Formative Years, 1868–86*. Belfast: Ulster Historical Foundation and the Institute of Irish Studies, 1989.

Wallis, Frank. *Popular Anti-Catholicism in Victorian Britain*. Lewiston, NY: Edwin Mellen Press, 1993.

———. "The Revival of the Anti-Maynooth Campaign in Britain, 1850–52." *Albion* 19, no. 4 (Winter 1987): 527–47.

Wallis, John. "Recent Studies on Religion and Violence." *Novo Religion: The Journal of Alternative and Emergent Religions* 11 (August 2007): 97–104.

Walsh, David. *Making Angels in Marble: The Conservatives, the Early Industrial Working Class, and Attempts at Political Incorporation*. London: Breviary Stuff Publications, 2012.

Weaver, Stewart. *John Fielden and the Politics of Popular Radicalism, 1830–1847*. Oxford: Clarendon Press, 1987.

Whelan, Irene. "The Bible Gentry: Evangelical Religion, Aristocracy and the New Moral Order in the Early Nineteenth Century." In *Protestant Millenialism, Evangelicalism and Irish Society, 1790–2005*, edited by Crawford Gribben and Andrew R. Holmes, 52–82. London: Palgrave MacMillan, 2006.

———. *The Bible War in Ireland: The Second Reformation and the Polarization of Protestant-Catholic Relations in Ireland, 1800–40*. Madison: Univ. of Wisconsin Press, 2005.

———. "The Stigma of Souperism." In *The Great Irish Famine, 1845–52*, edited by Cathal Porteir, 135–54. Cork: RTE/Mercier Press, 1995.

Whelan, Kevin. "Politicisation in County Wexford and the Origins of the 1798 Rebellion." In *Ireland and the French Revolution*, edited by Hugh Gough and David Dickson, 156–78. Dublin: Irish Academic Press, 1990.

White, James. F. *The Cambridge Movement*. Cambridge: Cambridge Univ. Press, 1962.

Williams, Sarah. *Religious Belief and Popular Culture in Southwark, c. 1880–1939*. Oxford: Oxford Univ. Press, 1999.

Wolffe, John, ed. *Evangelical Faith and Public Zeal: Evangelicals and Society in Britain, 1780–1980*. London: Society for the Promotion of Christian Knowledge, 1995.

———. *The Expansion of Evangelicalism: The Age of Wilberforce, More, Chalmers, and Finney*. Downers Grove, IL: InterVarsity Press, 2007.

———. "Exploring the History of Catholic-Protestant Conflict." In *Protestant-Catholic Conflict from the Reformation to the 21st Century*, edited by John Wolffe, 1–21. London: Palgrave MacMillan, 2013.

———. *God and Greater Britain: Religion and National Life in Britain and Ireland, 1843–1945*. London: Routledge, 1994.

———. *The Protestant Crusade in Great Britain, 1829–60*. Oxford: Oxford Univ. Press, 1991.

Woodham Smith, Cecil. *The Great Hunger: Ireland, 1845–49*. London: H. Hamilton, 1962.

Worboys, Michael. *Spreading Germs: Disease Theories and Medical Practice in Britain, 1865–1900*. Cambridge: Cambridge Univ. Press, 2000.

Wright, Frank. *Northern Ireland: A Comparative Analysis*. Dublin: Gill and MacMillan, 1987.

———. "Protestant Ideology and Politics in Ulster." *European Journal of Sociology* 14, no. 2 (1973): 213–80.

———. "Reconciling the Histories: Protestant and Catholic in Northern Ireland." In *Reconciling Memories*, edited by Alan Falconer and Joseph Liechty, 68–83. Dublin: Columba Press, 1998.

———. *Two Lands on One Soil: Ulster Politics before Home Rule*. Dublin: Gill and MacMillan, 1996.

Wright, Jonathan Jeffrey. *Crime and Punishment in Nineteenth-Century Belfast: The Story of John Linn*. Dublin: Four Courts Press, 2020.

———. *The "Natural Leaders" and Their World: Politics, Culture and Society in Belfast, c.1801–1832*. Liverpool: Liverpool Univ. Press, 2012.

———. "'The Perverted Graduates of Oxford': Priestcraft, 'Political Popery' and the Transnational Anti-Catholicism of Sir James Emerson Tennent." In *Transnational Perspectives on Modern Irish History*, edited by Niall Whelehan, 127–48. London: Routledge, 2014.

Yates, Nigel. *The Religious Condition of Ireland, 1770–1850*. Oxford: Oxford Univ. Press, 2006.

Zimmerman, Georges-Denis. *Songs of Irish Rebellion: Irish Political Street Ballads and Rebel Songs, 1780–1900*. Dublin: Allen Figges, 1967.

UNPUBLISHED DISSERTATIONS

Farrell, Nigel. "Asiatic Cholera and the Development of Public Health in Belfast, 1832–78." PhD diss., Univ. of Ulster, 2014.

Jeffrey, Linda. "Women in the Churches of Nineteenth-Century Stirling." Master's thesis, Univ. of Stirling, 1996.

Kerr, S. P. "The Church of Ireland in Belfast, 1800–70." Master's thesis, Univ. of Edinburgh, 1978.

McBride, Stephen. "Bishop Mant and the Down and Connor and Dromore Church Architecture Society, 1837–1878." PhD diss., Queen's Univ. Belfast, 1996.

Slater, Gerald James. "Belfast Politics, 1798–1868." PhD diss., Univ. of Ulster, 1982).

Sutherland, Philomena. "The Role of Evangelicalism in the Formation of Nineteenth-Century Ulster Protestant Identity." PhD diss., Open Univ., 2010.

Index

Italic page numbers denote illustrations.

Act of Union, 53, 176, 237
Agar, Richard Arthur, 129
Akenson, Donald, 60
Alderdice, David, 177
"Annals of Christ Church, Belfast, The" (Drew), 14, 129, 180, 194
"Annals of Loughinisland," 193
anti-Catholicism: characteristics of, 9; criticism of, 201; of Thomas Drew, 1, 6, 7, 8, 9, 15, 46–47, 81–82, 147, 200–205, 231, 302; effects of, 18; evangelicalism and, 146; hybrid politics and, 7; ministers and, 16; moderate, 201; sectarianism and, 8–9, 266. *See also* Catholicism/Catholic Church
antisemitism, 223
Apprentice Boys, 285
Armstrong, George, 252
Association for the Relief of Distressed Protestants, 92
Austria, 248

"Ballad of Roaring Hanna, The" (*Punch*), 260
Ballymacarrett: committee, 180–82; Emigration Society, 182; overview of, 168–69, 180–81; weavers, 19, 33–34, 70, 83, 165–79, 181
Ballymena Brunswick Constitutional Club, 39, 54, 104–5
Banner of Ulster, 187, 192, 239, 249
baptismal regeneration, 121
Bates, John, 54–55, 105
Battle of Aughrim, 87, 107
Battle of the Boyne, 87, 107
Bebbington, David, 43–44
Beers, Francis, 233
Beers, William, 233
Beiner, Guy, 12
Belfast: Catholic-Protestant division within, 3; cemeteries within, 190; characteristics of, 3, 22; civic culture of, 23; contrasts within, 30; demographics of, 26, 28; geography of, 32; growth of, 2, 14–15, 22, 26, 214; housing within, 31–32; industrialization within, 79–80; interdenominational tensions within, 137; leadership within, 4; map of, *xv*, 24, *25*, *27*; migration to, 23–24; organizations within, 30; overview of, 23–35, 297–303; politics of, 29–30, 55; religious landscape of, 26, 28, 32; religious politics of, 299;

Belfast (*cont.*)
    riots in, 29; societal conditions of, 32–33; sociopolitical conflict within, 33; women's societal roles within, 161
Belfast Charitable Society, 35
Belfast Commercial Chronicle, 52, 125, 127, 132, 133–34, 193
Belfast Conservative Society, 52
Belfast Daily Mercury, 249–50, 272
Belfast General Relief Fund, 19, 180, 182, 183, 185–86, 188–89, 190–91, 192
Belfast Ladies Association for Connacht, 183, 187
Belfast municipal police, riots of 1857 and, 253
Belfast News-Letter, 48, 57, 125n17, 138, 141, 171–72, 208, 210, 245, 249, 272, 274, 296
Belfast Parochial Mission, 202, 255
Belfast Police Committee, 258–59
Belfast Poor Law Board of Guardians, 189
Belfast (Ulster) Protestant Association, 211
Belfast Protestant Journal, 185, 196
Belfast Repeal Association (BRA), 176
Belfast riots of 1843, 178, 197
Belfast riots of 1857: anti-Catholicism and, 199; blame for, 259–60; Christ Church and, 250, 252, 258–59; at Corporation Square, 258; Thomas Drew's response to, 265, 281; effects of, 243–45, 302–3; government investigation of, 204, 259–66; influences to, 244; map regarding, 246; military presence regarding, 265–66; open-air preaching and, 254–58; overview of, 243–44, 259–60; phases of, 116, 227, 245, 252, 256, 258; process of, 247–48, 251; reporting of, 6; resurgence of, 264–65; sermon regarding, 86, 202, 245–46, 248–51, 264, 267
Belfast riots of 1864, 281, 282–83
Belfast Soup Kitchen, 186, 189
Belfast Town Mission, 60, 73, 74, 75, 121–22
Beresford, Archbishop, 63
Bethesda Orphanage, 81
Bew, John, 53–54
biblicism, 44
Bindon, Harris, 247–48
Blacker, Stewart, 279, 294, 295
Blackstaff River, 31–32
Bland, Robert W., 76, 122
Board of First Fruits, 35, 36n28
Boyd, John, 168
Boyne Bridge, 264, 281
Brown, John, 48
Brown Street School controversy, 51–52
Bryan, Dominic, 66–67
Bryce, R. J., 74
Burke, Biddy, 252
Butt, Isaac, 287

Cairns, Hugh, 105, 224, 283
Cambridge Camden Society, 123–24, 128, 131, 133, 140
Campbell, Theophilus, 217, 278
Campbell, T. J., 166
Carlyle, Thomas, 111
Case of the Protestants of Ireland, The, 50
Catholic Gun Club, 245
Catholicism/Catholic Church: critiques of, 201, 210; fears and anxieties regarding, 212; number inflation

by, 52–53; offenses to, 207–8; politics and, 53–54; population of, 28; power of, 222; Protestantism vs., 3, 9, 10; threat from, 219–20, 269–70. *See also* anti-Catholicism

Catholic Relief Act of 1829, 229

Cawnpore massacre, 229n75

cemeteries, 190

Chalmers, Thomas, 59–60, 73

chaplaincy scandal, of Thomas Drew, 283

Charles I (King), 131

Chichester, George Augustus, 24

Christ Church: Belfast riots of 1857 and, 250, 252, 258–59; capacity of, 38; census data of, 77–81; centrality of, 5–6; conflict and, 57; congregational nature within, 13; construction of, 15; deaths in, 69–70; demographics of, 77–78, 79; design of, 36–37; district of, 59; donations for, 37; Thomas Drew's impact on, 272; extension and outreach of, 69–85; features of, 38; Great Irish Famine and, 193; growth of, 6, 15, 18; illustration of, 37; importance of, 13–14; influence of, 13–14; libraries of, 69; location of, 15, 36, 250; map of, 27; municipal police and, 253; occupations within, 78; opening of, 48; Orange Order and, 15–16, 53, 56, 57–58, 106, 234–35; overview of, 23, 35–49; politics and, 49–58; Protestant politics and, 205–31; purpose of, 22, 29, 36; records of, 14; restoration of, 38; riots and, 178–79; schools of, 58–69, 290–91; support for, 48; vision of, 72; women within, 79. *See also* sermons/lectures, of Thomas Drew

Christ Church Cathedral, 40

Christ Church Protestant Association (CCPA): Crimean War and, 226–27; Thomas Drew's leadership within, 105, 217–18, 267; event sponsorship by, 216; goals of, 229, 300; Indian Rebellion of 1857 and, 227–28; leadership within, 217; meetings of, 199, 217–18, 223–24, 230; membership within, 215–16; origin of, 19–20, 214–15; petition of, 216–17, 221–22; purpose of, 47, 214–15, 218; quote of, 217; war viewpoint of, 225; writings regarding, 216

"Church, the Guide of Her Ministers' Conduct and Teaching, The" (Mant), 122

Church Accommodation Society of Down and Connor, 72, 76, 128–29, 141, 163

Church Architecture Society, 118, 124, 125, 128–29, 130–31, 132–35, 139, 145, 146–47

Church Education Society, 61, 62–63, 67, 76

Church Home Mission Society, 76, 121–22

Church of Ireland: construction project of, 120; decline of, 7; disestablishment of, 275, 291–92; domestic mission of, 76; evangelicalism within, 18; Richard Mant's interest in, 123; national school system of, 62–63; population of, 28; pride in, 292–93; refashioning of, 292–93; relationship with Presbyterians by, 118, 122n11, 136; societal position of, 120; struggle with, 18

Church of Ireland Young Men's Society, 127

Clark, Anna, 160
Clark, J. C. D., 130
Clergy Aid Society, 76
Coates, Francis, 217
Coates, William, 168, 174, 217
Cole, William, 220
Colley, Linda, 130
Commission of Public Instruction, 52
Connolly, Sean, 23, 55, 66–67, 197
conservatism, 54, 55n74
Conservative Party, 46, 55, 56, 105, 206
conversionism, 44
Cooke, Henry: characteristics of, 207, 256; description of, 299; Thomas Drew and, 62; emigration viewpoint of, 170–71; as minister, 4, 21, 117, 136; national school system campaign of, 51–52; public opinion use of, 141; in *Weekly Vindicator*, 230
Cork Examiner, 288
Corporation Square, 258
Courtenay, Charles, 181
Covington, Sarah, 111
Cranmer, Thomas, 110
Crawford, William, 39, 169
Crimean War, 224–27, 229
Crolly, William, 70
Cromwell, Oliver, 111
Cronin, Maura, 110n60
cross-class movements, 144
crucicentrism, 44
Cry for Connacht, A (Edgar), 182
Custom House, 2, 40, 204, 257–58

Dalton Drew, Isabella, 40
Davison, Richard: Belfast Parochial Mission and, 254; Christ Church Protestant Association (CCPA) and, 217, 224; Church Architecture Society and, 139, 143; as congregant, 48; description of, 206; Orangeism and, 213–14; public letter of, 172–73
Dawson, Abraham, 14, 32, 110–11, 129, 163–64, 180, 194, 217, 222
Deaf and Dumb Institution, 240
Denvir, Cornelius, 183, 210
depression of 1842–43, 19
Derby, Lord, 223, 283
Destitute and Sick Society, 190
Diocesan, Home Mission, 76
Discourse on Justification (Hooker), 130
Disraeli, Benjamin, 223
Dixon Hardy, Phillip, 36
Dolly's Brae, 221, 233
domestic mission, 121–22
Donegall, Lord, 24, 36, 72
Donegall (Chichester) family, 24, 26
Dorcas Depot, 69, 302
Down and Connor and Dromore Church Architecture Society, 18, 118, 140
Down Cathedral, 269–70, 279–80
Down Hunt, 184–85
Downpatrick Recorder, 275
Downshire, Lord, 138, 139–40, 143, 144, 174, 288
Downshire Protestant (Johnston), 108, 264, 271, 280
Doyle, Mark, 116, 243, 244, 258, 268
Drew, Arminella Frances, 42
Drew, Catharine, 40, 42, 161–62
Drew, George and Sarah, 38
Drew, Isabella Dalton, 40
Drew, Thomas: activism of, 301; "The Annals of Christ Church, Belfast," 14, 129, 180, 194; anti-Catholicism

of, 1, 6, 8, 9, 15, 46–47, 81–82, 147, 200–205, 231, 302; as chaplain, 46, 283; characteristics of, 1, 5, 7, 8, 22, 45, 201, 301; civic engagement of, 19; as clerical elite, 4–5; confrontationalism of, 152; controversies regarding, 253–54, 283; core religious beliefs of, 42, 44, 45; criticism of, 48, 57, 113, 139, 201–2, 249–50, 251, 272–73, 278, 288; death of, 20, 294; departure from Belfast of, 270–71; as Doctor Drew, 45; donations from, 164; early ministry experience of, 39–40; education of, 39, 44–45; emergence of, 209–10; emigration viewpoint of, 172–73; evangelicalism of, 43–44; extremism of, 268, 302; family of, 40, 42, 238; funeral of, 295–96; gender norms viewpoint of, 161–63; income of, 122n12; inconsistency of, 139; influence of, 7, 29–30, 202, 230, 266–68; interdenominationalism of, 137; investigation regarding, 261–66; leadership of, 23, 300; lectures of, 48, 81; legacy of, 297–98, 300, 301; "Life's Last Hour," 294; "The Light, Protection and Bounty of God," 93–94; as Low Church evangelical, 43; middle-class respectability values and, 157; mission of, 73, 103, 202; networks of, 271–72; overview of, 2, 4–5, 6, 38–39, 298–303; pastoral challenges of, 271; paternalism of, 19, 99, 151–65, 302; philanthropy of, 158; photo/illustration of, *xvii*, *41*, *203*; political economy viewpoint of, 155; political influence of, 202–3; political involvement of, 46–48, 51–52, 54, 90, 104–5, 200, 212; political legacy of, 300; popularity of, 209–10, 279; population viewpoint of, 154–55; *Protestant Anniversaries*, 12, 112, 113, 152, 229; Protestant paternalism of, 83; quotes of, 43, 45–47, 86, 94, 95, 128, 148, 155, 159, 173, 186, 205, 210, 216, 218, 223–24, 249, 273–74; "The Rebel and the King," 294; religious demography and, 52–53; reputation of, 152, 199, 230, 242, 256n31, 267; "The Rich and the Poor," 156; *Sermons on Various Subjects*, 159; social activism of, 275, 289–90; societies of, 39, 44–45; success template of, 20–21, 48–49; support for, 70–71; testimonials regarding, 272–74; viewpoint of, 13; violent rhetoric of, 206; vision of, 72, 83–84; "When I'm Gone," 294; work attitude of, 156; working class and, 18–19; worldview of, 109, 206; writings of, 293–94; writings regarding, 1
Drew, Thomas, Jr., 40, 274, 295
Drew Memorial Church, 298
Drew Memorial School, 297–98
Dublin Castle, 107, 216–17, 221–22, 265–66, 280
Dublin Evening Post, 1, 283–84, 288–89
Duke of Cumberland, 106
Dunseath, James, 142

Ecclesiological Society, 123
Edgar, John, 4, 117, 137, 155, 158, 182–83, 185
education: Christ Church schools for, 58–69; Thomas Drew's viewpoint regarding, 63–65, 100, 223, 301;

education (*cont.*)
  elementary, 60; importance of, 58; national school system for, 60–63; Sunday schools, 58–60, 64–69, 290–91, 301
1848 rebellion, 210, 211, 220
Eldon Lodge, 106–7
elections, in Belfast, 29, 55–56, 286–89
Elizabeth I (Queen), 110
Emerson Tennent, James, 53, 72, 105, 123, 169, 201
emigration, 172–73, 174–75, 189
Enniskillen, Lord, 232, 232–33n83, 283
Evangelical Alliance, 105
evangelicalism: activism and, 44; in Belfast/Victorian Belfast, 32; biblicism and, 44; campaign of, 146–47; characteristics of, 44; conversionism and, 44; crucicentrism and, 44; evangelical Protestantism, 16, 94, 117, 118, 141, 146, 151; pastoral success and, 142–43; rise of, 18; of Thomas Drew, 43–44; working class and, 77, 146
Evans, Samuel, 38
Ewart, Lavens, 38
"Existence of God, The" (Drew), 97

Farrell, William, 37
Fenian Rising of 1867, 275
Ferguson, John Francis, 185, 186–87
Ferguson, William, 93
Fitzpatrick, David, 82
Ford, Alan, 20, 43
Forde, Colonel, 296
Forde, Harriet, 163, 271, 272
Forde, William Brownlow, 274
Four Courts, 40
Francke, August, 81

Freeman's Journal, 262, 278–79
Friendly Societies Act, 237
Fund for the Temporal Relief of the Suffering Poor of Ireland, 192

Gaskin, Eliza, 79
Geoghegan, Vincent, 156
"George Walker and His Times" (Dawson), 110–11
Gillespie, Raymond, 29, 91
Gladstone, William, 289, 291
grace, 97
Gray, John, 289
Great Irish Famine, 19, 179–96, 210
Great Protestant Demonstration, 275, 278
Gregg, Tresham, 62, 114, 144, 176, 207–8, 209, 216, 217, 230
Griffin, Brian, 253
Griffin, Emma, 65
Gunn, Simon, 4
Gunpowder Plot, 87, 104, 107, 220, 245, 280–81
Gurrin, Brian, 29n8
Gwynne, William J., 217

Hacket, John, 261, 264
Hall, Samuel and Anna, 30–31
Hanna, Hugh "Roaring," 202, 204, 244, 255–56, 258n36, 260, 275, 280n29
Hanna, Samuel, 53
Hannay, James Owen, 2n2, 294, 295
Hannay, Robert, 1, 1–2n2, 5, 293, 297
Harrison, John, 184
Hartrick, Edward, 294
Hempton, David, 16, 91, 145, 146
Henderson, Joseph, 253

Herbert, Christopher, 229n75
High Church, 43, 143, 147
Hill, Adam, 107
Hill, Myrtle, 16, 91, 145, 146
Hilton, Boyd, 42, 94, 151
Hincks, Thomas, 40, 292
Hirst, Catherine, 31, 178, 209, 244
History of the Church of Ireland (Mant), 119
Holden, John, 191
Hollymount Church, 92, 96n25, 271, 290
Holmes, Andrew, 102
Holmes, Janice, 74
Holmes, R. Finlay, 299
home missions, 73–74
Home Rule Crisis, 235
Hooker, Richard, 130
Hope, Alexander, 123
housing, in Belfast, 31–32, 33
Hughes, Bernard, 264
Hull, Francis, 236
Humphries, Jane, 65
Hus, Jan, 110
Huss School House, 59, 67–68, 298

Indian Rebellion of 1857, 224, 227–28, 229
industrialization, 33–34, 77–80, 184
Inglis, Henry, 30
Irish Land Act of 1870, 289
Irish nationalist politics, 212
Irish Poor Law Act of 1838, 154, 157, 186, 195, 196
Irish Pulpit, The, 92, 156
Irish Rebellion of 1641, 227
Irwin, Sarah, 252
"Is Popery Christianity?" (McIlwaine), 255

James II (King), 248
Jocelyn, Robert, 233
Johnson, Alice, 159
Johnston, Georgiana, 286
Johnston, William: activism of, 286–87; Christ Church Protestant Association (CCPA) and, 217; criticism of, 201; *Downshire Protestant*, 108, 264, 271, 280; Thomas Drew and, 42, 47, 108, 115–16, 221, 286, 288–89, 296; election of, 287; Great Protestant Demonstration and, 275; legacy of, 300; letter to, 288; Orange democracy of, 18; prosecution of, 285–86; Protestant Orphan Society and, 270; writings of, 96n25, 223
Johnston, W. J., 213, 285
Jordan, Allison, 176
justification, 130

Kane, John, 181
Kane, Richard Rutledge, 299
Kennedy, Liam, 29n8, 166n51
Keogh, William, 220
Keown, William, 296
Knox, Edmund, 270
Knox, Robert, 51n66, 270–71

laity, impulses of, 131–32
land reform, 287–89
Lanyon, Charles, 40, 48, 254, 273, 287
Larcom, Thomas, 262
Laud, William, 131
Laverty, Hugh, 236, 239, 240
"Life's Last Hour" (Drew), 294
"Light, Protection and Bounty of God, The" (Drew), 93–94

Limerick, 186, 187–88
Linn, John, 34–35
Locke, Thomas, 39
Loughinisland Parish Church, 20, 96n25, 270–71, 274–75, 276–77, 296
Loughran, John, 251
Low Church, 43
Luther, Martin, 110
Luther Daily School, 68
Luther House of Prayer and School House, 59
Lynch, David, 259, 262–63

MacAdam, James, 34
Macartney, Arthur, 40, 68
Mac Domhnaill, Aodh, 34
MacGowan, John, 237
MacKnight, Thomas, 9–10
MacRaild, Donald, 237
Madden, Kyla, 10–11
Maginn, Edward, 260
Maguire, Thomas, 208
Makepeace Thackeray, William, 35
Mallin, Christopher, 217, 220, 222–23, 226
Malthus, Thomas Robert, 154
Mant, Richard: agreement of, 140; arguments against, 118–19; "The Church, the Guide of Her Ministers' Conduct and Teaching," 122; Church of Ireland and, 120, 121; criticism of, 138; fury of, 138; *History of the Church of Ireland*, 119; home missions viewpoint of, 76; leadership of, 72, 73; overview of, 118–20; petition response of, 134–36; proposal by, 35–36; sermon of, 48, 91–92. *See also* Mant controversy

Mant, Robert, 142
Mant, Walter B., 142
Mant controversy, 17–18, 117–18, 123–45
Mathew, Theobald, 178
Matthews, George, 241
Maxwell, Henry, 271
Maynooth Grant, 19, 212–13, 218–19, 229, 278
McClenaghan, George, 237
McClure, Thomas, 182, 287
McConnel, James, 107–8
McCullogh, Thomas, 240
McCusker, Catherine, 79
McGee, Thomas D'Arcy, 260
McGhee, Robert, 114, 219
McIlwaine, William: argument of, 125; Belfast riots and, 278; conflicts of, 255; Thomas Drew and, 4, 261; illustration of, *126*; as minister, 117, 118, 142–43, 256; overview of, 126–28; Puseyism viewpoint of, 130; sermon of, 255; support from, 72; viewpoint of, 162; in *Weekly Vindicator*, 230; writings of, 127
McIntosh, Gillian, 197
McIntyre, Anthony, 68–69, 77
McKneight, James, 53
McLaughlin, John, 261
McNeile, Hugh, 114
McNeill, Mary Harriet, 224
middle class, 4, 157, 159–60, 235
Miller, Kerby A., 29n8
Miller, Thomas F., 213
missions, 73–74, 76, 121–22
Molly Maguires, 106, 232
Molyneux Asylum, 92
Moncrieffe, Alexander, 168
Montgomery, Henry, 36
Moore, Anne, 57

More, Hannah, 17, 64–65
Morgan, James, 4, 32, 72, 75, 117, 137
Morris, R. J., 245
Muggeridge, Richard, 169
Mulholland, Thomas, 287
mutual aid societies, 237–38

Nagle, John, 67
Napier, Joseph, 105, 224, 265
national school system, 60–63, 163n42, 223. *See also* education
Neale, John Mason, 123
New Irish Pulpit, The, 63
Newman, John Henry, 123–24, 128
Nicholson, William, 21
Night Asylum for the Homeless Poor in Belfast, 158
Noble, James, 193
Northern Whig, 29, 48, 57, 125n17, 185, 187, 192, 228, 255, 283–84

Oastler, Richard, 153
O'Brien, James, 39
O'Brien, William Smith, 211
O'Connell, Daniel: Act of Union campaign of, 53, 54, 176; attacks on, 177, 178, 281; Ballymacarrett Weavers Committee and, 169; Catholic emancipation viewpoint of, 49, 104–5; criticism by, 230; Irish Catholic politics and, 15; monument to, 281; threat of, 208
O'Hanlon, William, 33, 64, 153
O'Hara, Charles, 142, 144
open-air preaching, 254–58. *See also* sermons/lectures, of Thomas Drew
Orange Order: Belfast riots of 1857 and, 248–51; Belfast riots of 1864 and, 285; benevolent fund proposal within, 237–38; books of, 14; celebration of, 56–57, 247; Christ Church and, 15–16, 53, 56, 57–58, 234–35; Church of Ireland orientation of, 233–34; community within, 238–39; conflicts of, 56–57; criticism of, 210–11; defined, 232; discussion of issues within, 239; Thomas Drew and, 5, 7, 17, 46, 49–50, 57, 84, 87, 103, 104–5, 204, 205, 231–42, 267, 275–76, 289–90, 298; fundraising within, 240–41; growth of, 233–34; influence of, 145, 213; leadership of, 232, 235–36; meetings of, 237; membership of, 233, 235; Orange Hall of, 241, 289; overview of, 49; parades of, 221; Party Processions Act and, 247; plebeian orientation of, 236–37; political influence of, 213–14; as public force, 106–7; public reappearance of, 232–33; ritual calendar of, 87; sermons for, 105–6, 107–11, 113, 115–16, 147, 280–81; social composition of, 235; suspensions within, 237; violence and, 233; working-class orientation of, 237, 241–42
O'Rorke, Alexander, 253, 261
orphans, 81–82, 83
O'Sullivan, Mortimer, 50–51, 92, 114
Oxford Movement, 124, 128

Paisley, Ian, 21, 299–300
Papal Aggression, 212
Party Processions Act, 232, 247, 281, 282–83, 284–85, 287
paternalism, 19, 99, 151–65, 302

pawn shops, 70
"Peter Galligan's Welcome" (Fáilte Pheadair Ui Ghealacáin) (Mac Domhnaill), 34
petitions: of Christ Church Protestant Association (CCPA), 216–17, 221–22; against Church Architecture Society, 132–36; for emigration, 174–75; for handloom weavers, 168; Richard Mant's response to, 134–36; against national school system, 163n42
Plug Plot Riots, 170
politics: anti-Catholicism and, 7; of Belfast/Victorian Belfast, 29–30, 55; Catholicism/Catholic Church and, 53–54; changes in, 17; Christ Church and, 49–58, 205–31; Thomas Drew's participation in, 46–48, 51–52, 54, 90, 104–5, 200, 212; Irish Catholic, 15; Irish nationalist, 212; Protestant, 205–31; religion and, 145, 299; rivalries within, 56; within Sandy Row, 55–56
Poor House, 35
Poor Law, 174–75
Poor Law Amendment Act of 1847, 174–75, 191
poor/poverty: Thomas Drew's dedication to, 68, 70, 99–100, 101–2, 148–51, 152–53, 157–58, 179, 196–98, 301; missions for, 73–74; Protestant obligation to, 84
Posnett, George, 241
Posnett, Hutcheson, 106–7, 236, 238–39
Potter, Samuel, 280
Potts, J. H., 166, 167

Pound, 3, 28, 29, 31, 178, 243, 251, 258, 267
"Power, the Priesthood, and the Glory of the Lord, The" (Drew), 97–98
prayer, 115–16, 159–60
Presbyterian Church, 28, 118, 122n11, 136, 137–38, 207–8, 234
Protestant Anniversaries (Drew), 12, 112, 113, 152, 229
Protestant Association, 215n30, 220
Protestantism/Protestants: Catholicism vs., 3, 9, 10; Thomas Drew and, 2, 4, 6, 7, 82, 104, 108, 179, 201; evangelical, 16, 94, 117, 118, 141, 146, 151; grievances of, 50; heroes of, 12–13; historical narrative of, 130; masculinity within, 17; political associations of, 47, 147; politics of, 144, 200, 205–31; population of, 28; purpose of, 84; as sermon theme, 12–13, 17, 87–88, 97, 110–16, 146; theological views of, 43, 130; values of, 212–13, 215, 249; vigilance within, 221. *See also* Christ Church; Christ Church Protestant Association (CCPA)
Protestant Operative Society, 105, 176–77, 207, 208–9
Protestant Orphan Society, 81, 82, 83, 84, 247, 270, 275
Protestant Working Men's Association, 286
Puritanism, 122
Puseyism, 128, 129–30, 131

railroad, 220
rate-in-aid controversy, 194–96
Rathmines Town Hall, 40

Rea, John, 253, 261
"Rebel and the King, The" (Drew), 294
Rebellion of 1798, 12
Rebellion of 1848, 19
Reform Act of 1832, 29, 53, 54
"Rich and the Poor, The" (Drew), 98–99, 156
riots: Christ Church and, 178–79; Thomas Drew and, 199, 202; effects of, 177–78; of 1835, 56, 57; of 1843, 178, 197; of 1864, 186, 189; election, 55–56; Plug Plot Riots, 170; of working class, 177–78. *See also* Belfast riots of 1857
Roden, Lord, 232, 288, 296
Roe, Thomas, 255
Royal Belfast Academical Institution, 37
Royal Hibernian Academy, 40
Royal Institute of the Architects of Ireland, 40
Royal Society of Antiquaries of Ireland, 40
Royal Society of Ulster Architects, 40
Royle, Stephen, 29, 29n9, 166
Russell, John, 194–95
Rutledge Kane, Richard, 21

Sabbatarianism, 102
Sadler, Michael, 112, 153–54
Sahib, Nana, 229n75
salvation, 94
Sandy Row: Belfast riots of 1857 in, 247, 251, 264; Belfast riots of 1864 in, 281; conflict within, 57; Thomas Drew's contribution to, 103; housing in, 31; living conditions of, 33, 68–69; location of, 28; Orangemen, 29; overview of, 300–301; politics within, 55–56
Saurin, James, 94, 124–25
Scullabogue in County Wexford, 12
Seaver, Charles, 295
sectarianism: anti-Catholicism into, 266; complexity of, 11, 20; conflict of, 19; of Thomas Drew, 83, 244; evangelicalism and, 145; force of, 11–12; historicizing, 3–4, 11; impact of, 20; influence of, 146; overview of, 8–9; problem of, 3; whitewashing with, 12; writings regarding, 9–10
sermons/lectures, of Thomas Drew: anniversary, 88–89, 107–8, 246–47; as anti-Catholic, 86, 87–88, 90, 113–14, 147; Belfast riots of 1857 and, 86, 202, 245–46, 248–51, 264, 267; as biographies, 112–13; charity, 92–93; as cultural experience, 89; at Down Cathedral, 269–70; education theme of, 63–64; everyday, 16–17, 87–88, 91–103; "The Existence of God," 97; extremism of, 90, 114–15; faith/reason themes of, 100–101; family theme of, 159; Gunpowder Plot and, 104, 245, 280–81; on India, 228–29; Indian Rebellion of 1857 and, 228; "The Light, Protection and Bounty of God," 93–94; marriage theme of, 161; national school system theme of, 60–61; occasional, 88–89; open-air preaching of, 254–58; for Orange Order, 105–6, 107–11, 113, 115–16, 147; overview of, 86–91; political themes of, 86–87, 103–16;

Index

sermons/lectures, of Thomas Drew (*cont.*)
poor/poverty themes of, 99–100, 101–2; "The Power, the Priesthood, and the Glory of the Lord," 97–98; Protestant theme of, 12–13, 17, 87–88, 97, 110–16, 146; purpose of, 89; religious education themes of, 100; "The Rich and the Poor," 98–99; Scripture choices within, 94–95; *Sermons on Various Subjects*, 93, 159; state education theme of, 223; structure of, 93–94; support and opposition to, 48; tone of, 94–95; violence of, 114–15, 206; weaver theme of, 83; working-class audience of, 93–94, 98, 102
Sermons on Various Subjects (Drew), 93, 159
Shankill Parish, 214
Sibbett, R. R., 137
Siege of Derry, 110
Simms, James, 251
Singer, Joseph Henderson, 39
Smith, Mark, 71, 80–81
Smith, William/Smith family, 79
Smyth, William St. John, 142
Society for the Amelioration of the Working Classes, 197
Society for the Relative Improvement of the Poor of the Town of Belfast, 73–74
Soho Iron Foundry, 34
soup kitchen, 173, 174, 186, 189
Spooner, Richard, 219, 224
St. Anne's Cathedral, 40, 94, 122
St. Catherine's Church, 92
St. Malachy's Church, 259, 282
St. Mark's Church, 92
St. Patrick's Cathedral, 40
St. Patrick's Church, 36n29
St. Patrick's College and Seminary at Maynooth, 212
St. Thomas Church, 279
Stevenson, James, 237
Stowell, Hugh, 114
strikes, 174
Sunday schools, 58–60, 64–69, 290–91, 301
Sunday School Society for Ireland, 290–91
Swatara, 189

Tea Lane, 31
Temple, John, 227
Tennent, Dr. Robert, 176
Tennent, Robert J., 70, 175, 185
textile industry, 77–79, 165–79
Thomson, S. S., 186–87
Tombe, George, 163
Tories, 54
Tory paternalism, 151–65
Tractarian movement, 123–24
Tract Number Ninety (Newman), 128
Tracy, William, 261, 264, 266
Trevor-Hill, Arthur, 236
Trillick, 220
Trinity College Dublin, 39
Troubles in Northern Ireland, 3
Troup, Charles, 181
Twenty Reasons for Being an Orangeman (Drew), 231
Tynan, Mary Ann, 248

Ulster Hall, 2, 278
Ulster Magdalene Asylum, 69, 163
Ulsterman, 202, 230, 249, 256
Ulster Protestant Association, 105, 107

Ulster Times, 71, 125, 140, 158
Ussher, James, 110

vagrancy, 158
Vagrancy (Ireland) Act of 1847, 158
Verner, William, 275
Victorian Belfast. *See* Belfast
Victoria Street, 55
visitation, 74–75, 76–77

Walker, George, 110, 110n60, 194
Wardlaw, Hamilton, 134
Waring, Robert, 237–38, 240
Watson, William, 251–52
weavers, 19, 33–34, 70, 83, 165–79, 181
Webb, Benjamin, 123
Weekly Vindicator, 113, 188, 192, 230
Wesley, John, 290
"When I'm Gone" (Drew), 294
Whitefield, George, 81
Wickliffe School House, 59

Wilberforce, William, 220
Wilde, William, 194
William III (King), 110, 111
William IV (King), 106
Williamite War, 12, 87
William of Orange, 178, 248
Willis, Henry de la, 51n66
Wilson, James, 239, 240
Wolffe, John, 9, 225, 266
Woodroffe, J. N., 223
Woodward, Thomas, 280
working class: Thomas Drew and, 2, 4–6, 18–19, 70–73, 83, 93–95, 98–103, 149–53, 169–74, 175–77, 179, 191–97, 216–17, 229–30, 250, 267, 299–302; and 1857 riots, 243–44; housing for, 31; Orangeism and, 57, 213–14, 232, 235–42; religion and, 18, 32, 61, 65, 73–77, 93–95, 146, 159–60; sectarianism and, 145; vulnerability of, 34–35, 70, 83–84, 160
Wright, Jonathan Jeffrey, 30, 34–35, 60, 201

Printed in the USA
CPSIA information can be obtained
at www.ICGtesting.com
LVHW070820011023
759794LV00002B/114

9 780815 638148